Enabling Healthcare 4.0 for Pandemics

Scrivener Publishing
100 Cummings Center, Suite 541J
Beverly, MA 01915-6106

Publishers at Scrivener
Martin Scrivener (martin@scrivenerpublishing.com)
Phillip Carmical (pcarmical@scrivenerpublishing.com)

Enabling Healthcare 4.0 for Pandemics

A Roadmap Using AI, Machine Learning, IoT and Cognitive Technologies

Edited by
Abhinav Juneja,
Vikram Bali,
Sapna Juneja,
Vishal Jain
and
Prashant Tyagi

Scrivener Publishing

WILEY

This edition first published 2021 by John Wiley & Sons, Inc., 111 River Street, Hoboken, NJ 07030, USA and Scrivener Publishing LLC, 100 Cummings Center, Suite 541J, Beverly, MA 01915, USA

For more information about Scrivener publications please visit www.scrivenerpublishing.com.

Wiley Global Headquarters
111 River Street, Hoboken, NJ 07030, USA

For details of our global editorial offices, customer services, and more information about Wiley products visit us at www.wiley.com.

Library of Congress Cataloging-in-Publication Data

ISBN 978-1-119-76879-1

Cover image: Russell Richardson
Cover design by Pixabay.Com

Set in size of 11pt and Minion Pro by Manila Typesetting Company, Makati, Philippines

Printed in the USA

Contents

Preface

The history of the universe has seen remarkable milestones in human evolution. We have evolved over the ages and witnessed a lot of disruption in this journey. However, human beings have matured and are now capable of harnessing the environment to make their lives easier. This ability of humans to adapt and make the best of natural resources has been a spectacular achievement. Today, we continue to explore existing technology and newer emerging technologies are also being rendered for making human lives more comfortable and reliable. However, there still are certain aspects of nature which remain unexplored by us. Several decades ago, epidemics were a common phenomenon which affected human civilizations economically as well as socially. Millions of lives were lost, but the spread of epidemics was limited to some particular geographical boundaries, and the demographics were confined. Currently, society has witnessed a newer phenomenon known as a "pandemic," which is even a more critical situation compared to an epidemic as its geographical boundaries are not fixed and it spreads very quickly even before it can be sensed. COVID-19 is such a pandemic, as it originated in late 2019 in China and within a span of just three months affected every country across the globe.

The technological developments in the fields of artificial intelligence (AI) and machine learning (ML) are very exciting and encouraging. Using these techniques, we are able to make remarkable predictions and decisions. But our experiences during the current outbreak show that our technological arsenal was incapable of predicting the outbreak well in advance. Though there have been tremendous efforts by researchers to make such predictions and explore AI and allied technologies to tackle such problems and minimize their impact, this current pandemic has exposed many open issues. Apart from socioeconomic issues, such incidents have a long-term impact on civilizations. Due to COVID-19 the world came to a halt—there were no flights, trains, buses, cars and machines running anywhere. Industries and organizations across the globe were not prepared for such a big disruption in their daily operations and changes in the market supply and demand equilibrium. Though some countries have been able to control the outbreak in masses, by and large all the processes were trial and error approaches; and it has been observed that when restrictions on movements and recommended gathering size limitations are removed, the pandemic starts to spread its wings again.

In this book, we will explore the current state of practice using Healthcare 4.0 as a roadmap for harnessing AI, ML, the internet of things (IoT) and other modern cognitive technologies to help deal with various aspects of a pandemic outbreak. There is a need to improvise our healthcare system with the increasing intervention of modern computing and data management platforms to increase the reliability of human processes and life expectancy. There is also an urgent need to come up with smart IoT-based systems which can aid in detection, prevention and cure of these pandemics with precision. There are lots of challenges associated with all the open issues. The objective of this book is to provide a new approach for preparing for and organizing technological warfare against future pandemics with advances in Healthcare 4.0.

The significant contributions made by various authors have contributed to making this book a ready reference for developing an understanding of the technological resolutions sought in order to devise tools for addressing pandemic situations like those we are currently facing. The chapters of this book are related to processes and technologies that may be helpful for dealing with pandemics of the modern era and other such related unforeseen natural disasters. A brief chapter-by-chapter description of the book follows:

Chapter 1, "COVID-19 and Machine Learning Approaches to Deal with the Pandemic," gives an overview of the efforts and strategies used by organizations across the globe during the COVID-19 pandemic using AI and ML techniques in various fields ranging from manufacturing, resource management, remote monitoring, etc. In addition, an ML approach being used by researchers for supporting healthcare-related issues raised by COVID-19 is discussed.

Chapter 2, "Healthcare System 4.0 Perspectives on the COVID-19 Pandemic," explores the leading HCS 4.0 techniques that could address this pandemic, highlighting real-world applications, opportunities, challenges and future insights.

Chapter 3, "Analysis and Prediction of COVID-19 Using Machine Learning," makes use of various Python libraries, namely, scikit-learn, matplotlib for data visualization, NumPy and pandas for data manipulation.

Chapter 4, "Rapid Forecasting of a Pandemic Outbreak Using Machine Learning," proposes a strategy for the preliminary estimation of how

COVID-19 spreads across the globe, its possible treatments, and the prevention of outbreaks by making use of technologies like ML, which may prove beneficial in saving the human race from pandemics like COVID-19 in the future.

Chapter 5, "Rapid Forecasting of Pandemic Outbreak Using Machine Learning: The Case of COVID-19," assesses different models and proposes an early warning system that uses AI to make conjectures on the likelihood of potential flare-ups of ailments.

Chapter 6, "Emerging Technologies for Handling Pandemic Challenges," focuses on computational strategies and factors wherein AI and big data can help in dealing with the gigantic, unprecedented number of records obtained from open health surveillance.

Chapter 7, "Unfolding the Potential of Impactful Emerging Technologies Amid COVID-19," reviews the technologies used in combating previous epidemics such as Ebola and SARS, and provides significant insights into emerging technologies used to combat COVID-19. It classifies the technology into five major groups and then discusses its use in the least developed, developing, and developed countries.

Chapter 8, "Advances in Technology: Preparedness for Handling Pandemic Challenges," outlines the role of technological advancements during the time of the pandemic. As digital technology intervenes to control the disastrous effect on humankind, it simultaneously introduces several challenges that are highlighted in the chapter.

Chapter 9, "Emerging Technologies for COVID-19," presents several innovative emerging technologies for handling the pandemic challenges discussed. The new technologies that can tackle these key challenges include blockchain, drone facilities, Mobile APK, wearable sensing, internet of healthcare things, AI, 5G and virtual reality. Soon these technologies will be used in managing pandemic challenges.

Chapter 10, "Emerging Techniques for Handling Pandemic Challenges," proposes the latest technologies used in making predictions that are more accurate than ever in dealing with crisis situations such as a pandemic. It covers all major factors and emerging technologies that will help to efficiently manage, handle and control such pandemic situations now and in the future.

Chapter 11, "A Hybrid Metaheuristic Algorithm for Intelligent Nurse Scheduling," addresses issues such as staff scheduling problems in hospitals. The challenge is to assign nurses to various shifts over a certain planning period to meet a number of constraints such as the contractual working time, maximum working time per day and so on. Also proposed is a method that groups nurses into clusters, where each cluster is served by a schedule optimized by a hybrid metaheuristic which is a combination of particle swarm optimization (PSO) and grey wolf optimizer (GWO).

Chapter 12, "Multipurpose Robotic Sensing Device for Healthcare Services," focuses on the fabrication of a robot that has multiple uses and is employed in different areas required by the user.

Chapter 13, "Prevalence of the Internet of Things in a Pandemic," presents an overview of IoT-driven systems in the healthcare sector for monitoring patients. Implementation of such technology will help to decrease healthcare expenses and enhance treatment of infected patients.

Chapter 14, "Mathematical Insights into COVID-19 Infection: A Modeling Approach," discusses the increasing use of mathematics in epidemic disease research. The complexity of disease is appropriate for quantitative methodologies as it allows for in-depth probing of issues and the probability of a new turn of events. Computational models can supplement exploratory and clinical investigations, and can also challenge flow standards, reclassify our comprehension of systems driving epidemiology and shape future research.

Chapter 15, "Machine Learning: A Tool to Combat COVID-19," proposes a model that uses ML approaches based on the analysis of data of two Indian states—Delhi and Maharashtra—where the maximum number of infected cases are found. This study is an attempt to help improve decision-makers planning and actions. In this study, neural network (NN) and M5P model trees are applied to forecast the number of infected cases with each progressive day.

In conclusion, the editors believe that readers will find that the efforts of all the contributing authors will enhance their research needs in various disciplines. It will also open up new opportunities and avenues by exploring different ways of dealing with unforeseen sudden changes in our environment. Overall, every effort has been made to present a book that acts as an encyclopedia of the current state of practice in the domain and also furnish investigative knowledge on future technologies which will promote human evolution and provide a framework for innovative resolutions to real-world problems. Happy learning!

Vishal Kumar
July 2021

Part 1

MACHINE LEARNING FOR HANDLING COVID-19

1

COVID-19 and Machine Learning Approaches to Deal With the Pandemic

Sapna Juneja[1]*, Abhinav Juneja[2], Vikram Bali[3] and Vishal Jain[4]

[1]*IMS Engineering College, Ghaziabad, India*
[2]*KIET Group of Institutions, Ghaziabad, India*
[3]*JSS Academy of Technical Education, Noida, India*
[4]*Sharda University, Greater Noida, India*

Abstract
The whole world is struggling to live with COVID-19 and even a single step of technology revolution can help in dealing with this pandemic. Artificial Intelligence and Machine Learning approaches are being used by the researchers around the globe to completely understand and address this situation. In this Corona crisis, companies are trying to implement this AI and ML techniques in various fields ranging from manufacturing, resource management, remote monitoring etc. On the other hand, ML approach is being used by the researchers for supporting healthcare related issues arisen due to COVID-19.

Keywords: COVID-19, support vector machine, convolutional neural network, drones

1.1 Introduction

Pandemics are a serious issue for human community. In general COVID-19 is not the first pandemic ever in the history and it will not be the last also. Many researchers across the globe are working towards the same in order to deal with it. The aim of this research is to shed a light on their efforts in order to identify that how machine learning approach can be

**Corresponding author*: sapnajuneja1983@gmail.com; ORCID ID: 0000-0003-4601-7679

Abhinav Juneja, Vikram Bali, Sapna Juneja, Vishal Jain and Prashant Tyagi (eds.) Enabling Healthcare 4.0 for Pandemics: A Roadmap Using AI, Machine Learning, IoT and Cognitive Technologies, (3–20)

useful in such situation. Machine Learning techniques can help out the researchers in determining the people who are more prone to risk of COVID-19, diagnosing such patients, help in the speedup of drug development, analyze the existing medicines which can be useful in this disease, prediction of escalation of the disease, help out in recognizing the virus in a more better way, and forecast the upcoming or next pandemic if any using the deep learning and machine learning approaches. Corona virus is a part of virus family and it is very hazardous for human body [1]. Many viruses of this family spread globally few years back, one of which is SARS in year [2] 2003 and another one was MERS in year 2012 [3]. The first case of Corona virus or Novel Corona virus appeared in Dec. 2019 so the World Health Organization named it as COVID-19 which stands for Corona virus Disease 2019. In March, 2020 the WHO announced Corona virus as a pandemic because of its huge spread among several countries which caused many persons critical ill and many got dead. It originated from a city of China named Wuhan where the first case of COVID appeared. The whole world is fighting against this deadly disease as no solution or vaccine till now has been developed against this disease that has the capability of generating antibodies in human being towards this corona virus. By July 24, the confirmed COVID cases in the whole world are 15,519,580 out of which 8,824,408 patients has been recovered and 633,605 deaths [4].

1.1.1 COVID-19 and its Various Transmission Stages Depending Upon the Severity of the Problem

COVID-19 is a contagious disease and can transmit through touch, contact or droplets of infected person. This transmission of COVID-19 is divided into 4 stages as:

1st Stage: During 1st stage infection spread across the countries. People with travel history of foreign countries are being tested for this virus. There is no local transmission at this stage so the possibility of number of patients suffering from disease remains quite low.

2nd Stage: At this stage the infection occurs locally and transmits through the infected patients of stage 1. In this stage along with the testing of the suspected patient, the source of the infection has also been identified to get him separate out from the entire community. The number of patients increases at this stage, though is not very difficult to manage. Social distancing is the best option to remain in stage 2 for avoiding further spread of the infection.

3rd Stage: In this stage, group transmission occurs and the number of cases increases rapidly. It becomes very difficult to find and isolate the

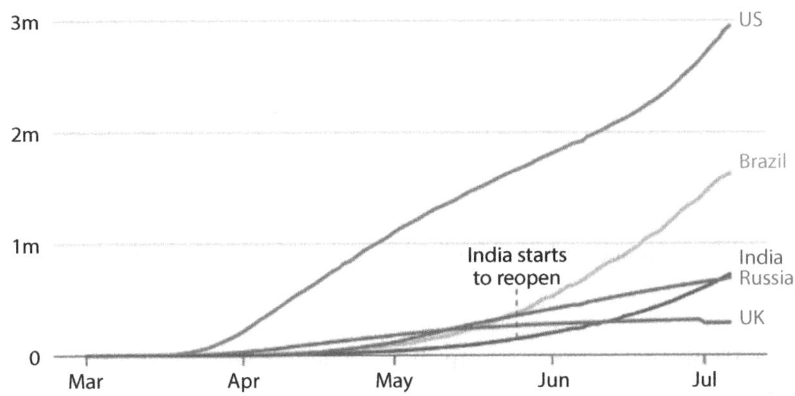

Figure 1.1 Confirmed cases in top 3 countries in the number of cases (Cumulative).

source of transmission. It becomes difficult to deal with the situation in this stage because of substantial growth of number of patients [5].

4th Stage: This stage is the most risky and deadly stage of this pandemic because infection transmits in the form of batches in the entire city or country. A large number of population gets infected during this stage irrespective of their age and immunity. The death cases also get increased during this stage and old age people and people with low immunity become the most affected patients from this disease. It becomes very difficult or almost impossible to control the spread the virus at this stage.

Figure 1.1 above shows the confirmed cases in the top three countries in number of cases across the world, starting from March, 2020 till mid July 2020. The US has the highest number of cases, followed by Brazil and then India on number three in the number of confirmed COVID-19 cases [6].

1.2 COVID-19 Diagnosis in Patients Using Machine Learning

This pandemic is spreading in the whole world and crossed almost 15 million cases till now. As there is no vaccine or proper treatment available, early diagnosis of the disease is quite important to control the further spread and for serving better patients as well [7]. The infection of COVID-19 can cause pneumonia and this can be detected early by using CT scan of the chest. This test can detect the COVID-19 at an early stage even if the patient is asymptomatic. As the COVID test kits are limited, Chest CT scan can be a useful source to identify whether the person is suffering from

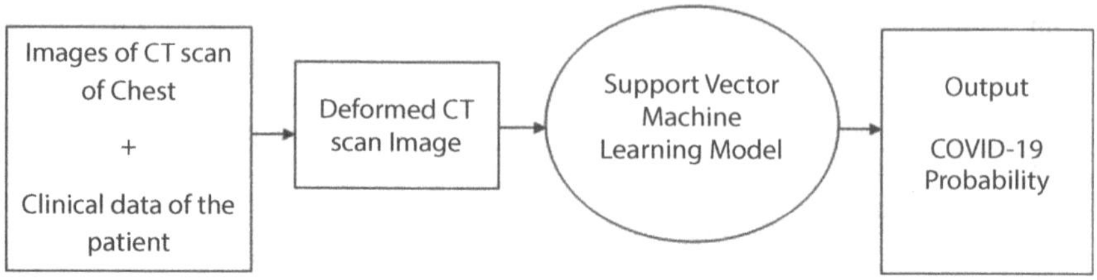

Figure 1.2 Diagnosis of COVID-19 using support vector based machine learning approach.

COVID-19 or not. Using CT scan, if there seems any deformity or divergence in the Lung or Chest, the person becomes more suspected to suffer from Corona Virus [8].

Machine Learning may present a solution for detecting COVID Infection at an early stage. A proposed machine learning model has been defined here, which can diagnose if patient is having SARS Cov 2 contagion using the CT scan images of Chest and Lungs [5].

Figure 1.2 above shows how a suspected person can be tested against corona virus infection using ML approach. First CT scan of the chest of the patient can be done by the physicians. Along with the CT scan, the preliminary data of the patient has been collected like symptoms appeared, age of patient and exposure of the patient if any. Using these images, the deformed images have been identified and that images have been processed using Support vector machine learning model. The output result obtained from SVM shows information that has been compared with the expected result to verify whether there is any probability of COVID infection to the patient or not [4].

1.2.1 Machine Learning to Identify the People who are at More Risk of COVID-19

Apart from the COVID-19 diagnosis, Machine Learning can also be used to identify which community of people is at more risk of COVID-19 and what are the chances of getting recovery at the same. This approach can be modeled by gathering the information of the patient about the type of symptoms that appeared in the body of the person, results of blood test and other body functioning test like kidney, lungs, liver etc. and from this collected information, detect the severity of the problem for the patient [9]. This information needs to be collected from all types of patients having different types of symptoms like mild, severe and critical. The information to be collected can be classified into various categories using classification algorithm and then data set of patients is to be used to train the machine learning algorithm. The algorithm thus obtained can be used to determine the probability of recovery of any patient from COVID-19 [9].

1.2.2 Machine Learning to Speed Up Drug Development

In the current scenario, a number of research organizations are trying to develop Artificial Intelligence and Machine Learning-enabled tool for the process of speed up of the development of drug of COVID-19. Many developers are trying to use their AI software to recognize possible therapy for COVID-19. We are learning more and more about the Corona Virus after its breakout. So AI along with ML can use this information to identify which combination of chemicals will be more efficient towards a particular target [10]. But in order to find this, more and more amount of data is a must. This drug development process using ML approach can easily be represented using Figure 1.3.

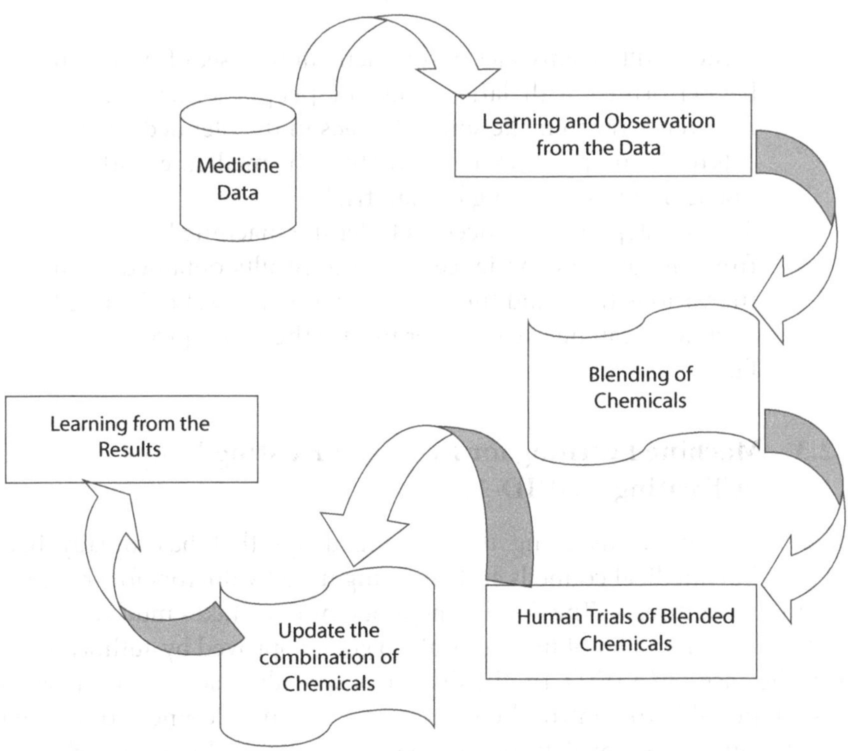

Figure 1.3 Machine learning process for drug development.

The process of drug development can be divided into various steps as

1. First researchers gather the data collected from various resources about COVID-19, its associated symptoms, categories of patients, available secondary treatments given by the doctors etc.
2. After data collection, learning from that collected data can be done and compared with the diseases with similar symptoms and severity to determine the medications given in similar set of diseases.
3. After learning and observation, a blended mixture of chemicals can be prepared as a testing medicine to check whether this mixture is useful in the treatment or cure from the illness.
4. This blended mixture is now tested to a limited set of people and this process is known as human trial to observe the effectiveness of the medicine in order to decide whether this drug is safe and successful for people fighting with Corona Virus.
5. If the results seems successful, then another set of trials can be performed with large group of people, otherwise the researcher try to make some changes in the blended chemicals or its composition to see whether the medicine works or not again by conducting human trials.
6. The last step of this process is to let the machine learn itself from the above experiences and the results obtained from the various trials and then decide that which set of blended chemicals can be used further in case the above process gets fail.

1.2.3 Machine Learning for Re-Use of Existing Drugs in Treating COVID-19

Reuse of drug means using the existing drugs that has already been approved by medical councils and are being used by doctors for treatment of some other disease. The development of new drug takes much effort and time and requires a lot of human trials to get it approved by authorities. So as in the case of COVID-19, the disease is spreading so fast and it seems quite impossible to control the disease with the development of the new drug because it might develop very late [11]. So at this stage, when no permanent possible solution of treating the disease is there, doctors are looking for reuse of the existing medicines like Hydroxychloroquine and Remdesivir etc. But the main problem in the reusage of the existing drug is that how to identify which drug can be reused in which symptoms and situations. So a variety of techniques have been developed by the researchers in order to find out this solution and AI with ML is one of them [12]. Figure 1.4 below defines Machine Learning process that can be used for reusage of drug from existing chemical.

The process starts with taking database of probable drugs that can be used in treating COVID-19 [13]. This can be taken by considering the database of all the drugs that has been used for treatment of diseases having symptoms similar to the symptoms of COVID-19. Next in the queue is to use database of all possible chemicals that can be helpful in the development of the new drug, and lastly is to take database of all the available drugs that are available in the market for usage [14]. A machine learning based Convolutional Neural Network Model can be applied upon all

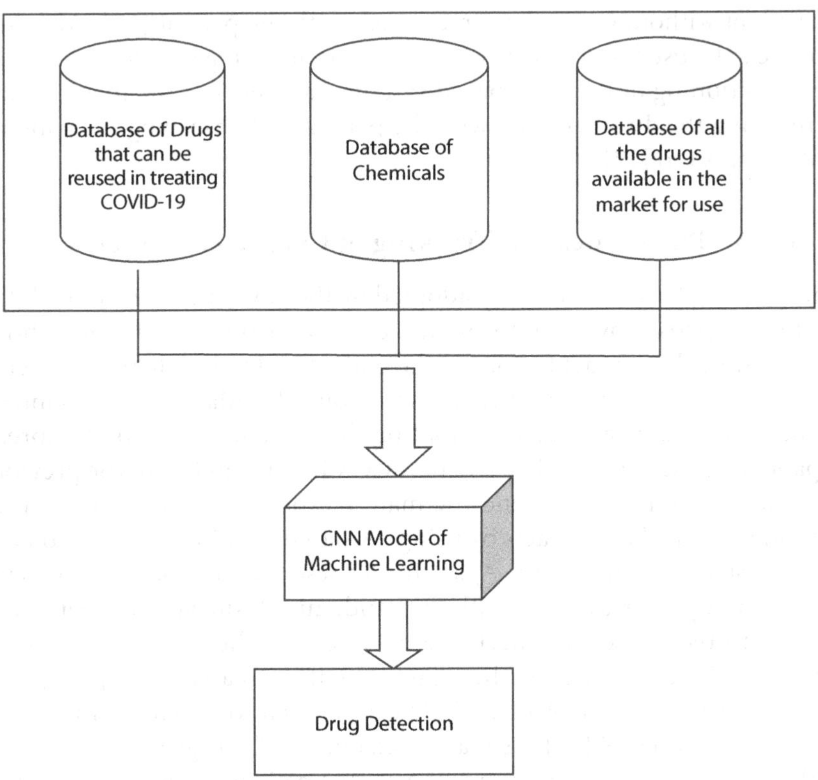

Figure 1.4 Machine learning approach for reuse of drug in COVID-19.

these kinds of databases by taking the dataset of the patients suffering from COVID-19 as input and the possible drug will be suggested by the system as the output [2].

1.3 AI and Machine Learning as a Support System for Robotic System and Drones

Although the life is quite difficult during these pandemic times, still the AI is enabling to make it somehow easy by providing assistance. All of us know well that in order to avoid the spread of the virus, the easies and the best solution is the avoidance of social gathering [15]. AI-based drones are being used by the government to perform this task without any need of manpower. Government is using these drones and robots in the public areas to keep an eye on people and to check whether the people are actually following social distancing or not. Drones are also used in hospitals and COVID centers to transfer food, medicines and other utility items to the patient without getting in direct touch with the patient [16]. AI-based robots can be used in the areas where patients are being kept to sanitize the area. Positioning of these AI-based systems can help out the medical staff by reducing the direct contact with the patient and observing the patient's health status too [17].

1.3.1 AI-Based Location Tracking of COVID-19 Patients

One more AI-based technology adopted by the government is to track the location of person by the information obtained from their mobile phone to determine the contact history of the patient and to isolate the contacted people for further avoiding the transmission [18]. Many of the countries including China, Spain etc. are adopting this system to control the spread of pandemic. New Zealand has no new COVID case and all of the previous cases have been recovered, and the main reason behind this was to track the patient and all its contacts by using AI-based location tracker and keep them in strict isolation [19]. Apart from these AI technologies has been used in multiple ways to fight with the pandemic. Artificial Intelligence can be used to recognize and check the outspread of the virus transmission. Different AI technologies are being used by the researchers, experts, doctors etc. Various AI-enabled chatbots can be used to provide information about the COVID-19 [19]. Its real life example is "Aarogyasetu" App used by the Indian government to track the corona patient and to provide information about COVID-19 to all the registered users.

1.3.2 Increased Number of Screenings Using AI Approach

It is concluded that the nations having large number of COVID tests are somehow working better in controlling the spread of COVID-19. More the number of tests more is the information received about how to control the transmission of the pandemic. So in that case, government can plan better strategies for controlling the transmission. Precise screening at various places must be considered on high priority [19]. So manual screening in such a large amount on everyday basis is not possible. Hence, AI-based approach for conducting large number of tests can be used in such scenario. This AI-based approach for screening of people can work by monitoring the temperature of the population even when they are on the move [20]. If any variation in the temperature is to be found, the system notify the same to the authorities for taking any further action and the person is kept in isolation for further controlling the transmission. Many countries have already started this technology to control the situation caused by pandemic including China, Israel etc.

1.3.3 Artificial Intelligence in Management of Resources During COVID-19

This pandemic is spreading more by each passing day and till the time of development of vaccine; the resources like PPE kit, COVID testing kit etc. which are limited and related to the pandemic l are needed to be managed. So with the help of machine learning approach, it can be easily identified which person is more susceptible towards the disease and needed to be tested first, in order to decide the healthcare professionals that the person should be tested or not leading to the better management of the resources [21].

1.3.4 Influence of AI on Manufacturing Industry During COVID-19

COVID-19 pandemic impacted a lot on the manufacturing market because of lockdown on the whole country. A report stated that around seventy five percent of the business got declined in the manufacturing industry in the month of March. So in general it can be said that COVID-19 affected overall manufacturing process ranging from purchasing, repository, shipping, handling, dispatching, distribution and customer market [21]. However, Artificial Intelligence can somehow control the negative impacts of pandemic on manufacturing industry. The key areas where the machine learning and artificial intelligence approach can be used in manufacturing industry are as:

1. *Pre-prediction of the upcoming demand of the product for the management and planning of stock manufacturing and distribution:* Stock pre planning is an important task needed to be done before the start of manufacturing because the demand of customer is varying in the market due to lockdown. The situation even gets worse because in order to plan, there is no previous data available of any pandemic. Thus there may be the possibility that due to this variation in the demand, there will be overbuying or under buying of the product [22]. With the help of pre prediction of product demand, the stock manufacturing and distribution can be managed in a better way, leading to the increasing profit and more customer satisfaction. The available prediction approaches are capable of predicting market needs only on the basis of previously available data. As there is no previous data available of inventory in pandemic, Artificial Intelligence can easily plan the upcoming demand of the product even in the tough circumstances like COVID-19. Usage of social media content, analytical data of market demographics including stocks and earnings to the predictive model, complementing the previous traces of inventory inputs is one of the best indicators of demand pattern of the product. Through this arrangement, it is feasible to have a customer centric manufacturing mechanism exhibiting better efficiency for inventory control in order to maintain optimum inventory costs [23].
2. *Remote maintenance of the products:* At the time of this pandemic, producers want to control their instruments and manage their employees from home or any other remote location, as a fault in the any of the component or unit can lead to the failure of the entire production system. This can lead to the non availability of the product in the market and thus cause loss in the business. Machine Learning based prognostic maintenance approach can be used in such an area for the purpose of monitoring the data, observing the records of staff, accounts, finances, expenditure, revenue etc. using real time data. Machine learning methodology has the ability to uncover even the slight patterns in the records or

any document. It can also reveal that which areas are needed to be focused as they are at high risk. It actively diverts the supplies, material and staff towards that area before a threat matures into a real time disaster. This results into the cost cutting, optimal use of manpower, improvisation of management process and above all contentment of the client thus upgrading the overall manufacturing process [18].

3. *Social Distance Monitoring in the repositories:* The best possible solution to deal with this pandemic is to main social distancing so Artificial Intelligence based tool to manage and monitor the social distancing between the employees can be used. Such tools work by first monitoring the location of the employee and then apply some AI-based protocol to keep them away if they are in contact with each other either by sending signal or the message to the employee [24].
4. *Automatic Checking/Evaluation for maintaining the quality of the product in the organization:* Automatic checking for maintaining the product's quality can be done in the industries visually using Artificial Intelligence based approach. Various processes can be evaluated ranging from packing, transportation etc. in the stockroom. It has been discovered that evaluation that can be done visually, can find out more faults in manufacturing and packaging [25]. Automatic evaluation is fruitful in areas such as:

    a) Finding of any fault in the auto industry.
    b) Finding of fault in very large scale integration IC foundry
    c) Finding of any leaking in the packaging
    d) Finding of any incorrect point during the manufacturing of drugs.

5. *Increased Use of Robots for manufacturing using AI:* Organizations must try to implement a robotic environment for manufacturing as well management. Due to this pandemic, isolation is much needed and if any employee get sick, all other employees will also go to self quarantine and hence the total manufacturing process of the organization will get shut down. AI enabled robots can continue the pending operations in such a case and help out the organization to continue its manufacturing. These robots can even work out by following complete guidelines about the budget,

time limit and functionality. These robots can also be used to sanitize the organizational area [26].

1.3.5 Artificial Intelligence and Mental Health in COVID-19

This pandemic has introduced a lot of changes in our routine life and the impact it has made on us are long lasting. The major change it put on the lives is to maintain social distancing. Due to social distancing people are not able to meet, to share their feelings and thus facing stress, depression and other problems related to their mental health. People are facing many issues like fear of death, getting ill, loss of savings, joss of jobs, isolation, tension and poverty [27]. Some initiative to deal with this problem is much needed in the current circumstances otherwise this will cause long term effects on the mental status of the whole community. Artificial Intelligence technology can help out people in improving their mental health or keeping it stabilized [28]. The most appropriate solution provided by AI in this situation is usage of Chatbot. Many Chatbot services are available in the market without any cost and they are serving the people without any difficulty and even there is no risk leakage of user's privacy. It has been found that users are much interested in taking online therapy or counseling sessions through these chatbots instead of visiting to some counselor or therapist because of either fear from corona or due to privacy issues [29]. Various types of data, probable mental problems associated with the person and their possible solutions etc. can be taken from various counselors and that data is fed into these chatbots as input. Although these types of chatbots are new for people now days, still these are beneficial for people in this COVID times. Researchers have concluded that these chatbots will be very fruitful for the patients dealing with mental issues [30]. Usage of smartphones and availability of internet makes these chatbots easy to use for the user [31].

1.3.6 Can AI Replace the Human Brain Intelligence in COVID-19 Crisis?

Artificial intelligence has the power in supporting us to deal with the crucial matter upraised by the corona virus. AI has not developed the human being; instead the human has developed AI. In this pandemic, apart from the benefits [32], some shortcomings of AI has also been evolved. Machine Learning theory of AI system works by understanding patterns of data. More accurate the data more are the chances of getting precise results but in order to obtain the perfect results, first ML needs a huge amount of training data which is difficult to collect and second it also works on the assumption that the data collected in the previous time will work perfectly even in the upcoming times as well which leads to imperfection in the results [33]. Human beings can learn from previous experiences and implement those experiences in the new situation by using that information in order to decide what can be done in any specific situation while artificial intelligence based systems takes the decision based upon the information fed to them. Their learning process begins from the initial level even when there is a minor change of the process. So AI is basically a mechanism and which value is to be put in which situation has been defined by the person who has defined and further using that mechanism [34]. In the current pandemic environment, the whole decision making of AI system is totally dependent upon steps taken by the human. In order to solve this problem, the person who is designing AI system must collect more and more training data that relates to every possible situation. More will be the training data; it will become easy for the AI system to reach to the goal [35]. In general, it can be easily concluded that although AI and ML both are better than human in appropriate decision making, still it is driven by human being and its decision making capacity is totally dependent upon the thought process of the human's brain [34].

1.3.7 Advantages and Disadvantages of AI in Post COVID Era

Artificial Intelligence is getting more and more popularity in the various organizations now days. This technology has performed an evolution among various companies.

Here are some advantages of AI that can be functional in post COVID times.

1. More focus on automation of the system—Artificial Intelligence is automating the system day by day. Machines are overtaking the human beings in various tasks. Robots can perform better in the analysis, decision making and solving the problems. So as the AI is decreasing the burden of the work on the human beings, People are spending more time in enhancing their skill set [36]. Now personnel can focus on the technical aspects of their work to increase the growth of their organization. Humans and machines altogether will be capable of performing well and providing more accurate results and outcomes after COVID-19 [37].
2. Reduced possibilities of Failures—Artificial Intelligence can replace the manpower from the area where the chances

of risk are maximum like boilers, fires etc. The system can be managed and controlled with the help of drones. These AI-based devices can't abolish the hazards completely, but help in dealing with the crisis [15].
3. No slow down/deceleration—The main advantage of AI enabled devices is that they don't require any break from their work like human being. They can work anytime without any interruption or without being exhausted. Further they can work with more productivity and efficiency. Physiological factors, tension, sentiments etc. can impact the working capacity of the people but AI machines are far away from these factors. They just require appropriate programming and maintenance [38].
4. Negligible errors in the job done-Tasks performed by AI robots and devices are free from errors and can provide precise solutions leading to the more revenue to the organization apart from the task performed by the human being [39].
5. Lessen Household tasks—Many AI-based systems are available in the market that assist people in doing their household works and managing their homes even if they are at remote location. These devices can be aligned with Smartphone, Smart televisions, Cars and many other household gadgets to perform the task. So people can control these devices anytime, anywhere. These systems also help in saving electricity and other resources and thus reducing the overall budget required to manage these resources [40].
6. Better Prediction Technology—These systems can predict any upcoming disaster like flood etc. with the help of Machine Learning and Deep Learning approach. This feature helps the governments to timely make a plan for the calamity and save the millions of lives and money [41].

Here are some drawbacks of using AI systems:

1. Restrict the manpower—AI will replace the manpower and degrade the job market leading to the huge unemployability in various sectors like production, farming and other industries where manual work can be replaced by the robots.
2. Lack of thinking power—AI driven systems are unable to decide by themselves if no data is being provided to them. They are only machines that are being run by the thinking

process of human being. So if immediate decision is to be made in crucial situation without feeding the system with proper data set, the system won't be able to reach to conclusion.

1.4 Conclusion

It is expected that the usage of artificial intelligence will shoot up in the post COVID world. AI has the capability of solving the problems and can perform decision making better than human beings. Various kinds of Artificial Intelligence enabled tools are also available in the market which perform analysis on a huge amount of data in order to understand the pattern about that data, for accurate decision making and for analyzing voice and image. Artificial Intelligent systems can also grasp new things continually. These features will be much useful as organizations will face and adjust with the new system developed due to this current crisis.

References

1. Allam, Z., Dey, G., Jones, D.S., Artificial Intelligence (AI) Provided Early Detection of the Coronavirus (COVID-19) in China and Will Influence Future Urban Health Policy Internationally. *AI*, 1, 2, 156–165, 2020.
2. Mohanty, S., Harun Ai Rashid, M., Mridul, M., Mohanty, C., Swayamsiddha, S., Application of Artificial Intelligence in COVID-19 drug repurposing. *Diabetes Metab. Syndr.*, 14, 5, 1027–1031, 2020.
3. Alimadadi, A., Aryal, S., Manandhar, I., Munroe, P.B., Joe, B., Cheng, X., Artificial intelligence and machine learning to fight COVID-19. *Physiol. Genomics*, 52, 4, 200–202, 2020..
4. Binti Hamzah, F.A. *et al.*, CoronaTracker: World-wide COVID-19 outbreak data analysis and prediction. *Bull. World Health Organ.*, Submitted, March 2020.
5. Mei, X. *et al.*, Artificial intelligence-enabled rapid diagnosis of patients with COVID-19. *Nat. Med.*, 2020, https://pubmed.ncbi.nlm.nih.gov/32427924.
6. Shinde, G.R., Kalamkar, A.B., Mahalle, P.N., Dey, N., Chaki, J., Hassanien, A.E., Forecasting Models for Coronavirus Disease (COVID-19): A Survey of the State-of-the-Art. *SN Comput. Sci.*, 1, 4, 1–15, 2020.
7. Ashraf Uddin, M., Shafiur Rahman, M., Anwar Hussen Wadud, M., Akhter, A., Akter, O., I. Commerce Security Lab, *A Study on Epidemiological Characteristics and ML-Based Detection of novel COVID-19 Efficient Data Mining Approach View project Ensure Patient Privacy Given Internet of*

Things Data Transmitted from Wearable Sensors View project A Study on Epidemiological, March, 2020.

8. Elaziz, M.A., Hosny, K.M., Salah, A., Darwish, M.M., Lu, S., Sahlol, A.T., New machine learning method for image-based diagnosis of COVID-19. *PLoS One*, 15, 6, e0235187, 2020.
9. Luengo-Oroz, M. *et al.*, Artificial intelligence cooperation to support the global response to COVID-19. *Nat. Mach. Intell.*, 2, 6, 295–297, 2020.
10. Abaker, I. *et al.*, A Machine Learning Solution Framework for Combatting COVID-19 in Smart Cities from Multiple Dimensions. *Medrxiv*, 2020, https://doi.org/10.1101/2020.05.18.20105577.
11. Scott, I.A., The Medical Journal of Australia—Pre-print—19 June 2020 Can AI help in the fight against COVID-19? *Med. J. Aust.—Pre-print*, June, 19 2020.
12. Iwendi, C., Bashir, A.K., Peshkar, A., Sujatha, R., COVID-19 Patient Health Prediction Using Boosted Random Forest Algorithm. 8, July, 1–9, 2020.
13. Alom, Z., Rahman, M.M.S., Nasrin, M.S., Taha, T.M., Asari, V.K., 2020.
14. Naudé, W., *Artificial Intelligence against COVID-19: An Early Review*, pp. 2019–2020, Towar. Data Sci., March 2020, [Online]. Available: https://towardsdatascience.com/artificial-intelligence-against-covid-19-an-early-review-92a8360edaba.
15. Whitelaw, S., Mamas, M.A., Topol, E., Van Spall, H.G.C., Applications of digital technology in COVID-19 pandemic planning and response. *Lancet Digit. Health*, 2, 8, e435–e440, 2020.
16. Ahmed, S. and Khan, R.H., Blockchain and Industry 4.0. *Blockchain Data Anal.*, 28, January, 1–22, 2020.
17. Kumar, A., Gupta, P.K., Srivastava, A., A review of modern technologies for tackling COVID-19 pandemic. *Diabetes Metab. Syndr. Clin. Res. Rev.*, 14, 4, 569–573, 2020.
18. Javaid, M., Haleem, A., Vaishya, R., Bahl, S., Suman, R., Vaish, A., Industry 4.0 technologies and their applications in fighting COVID-19 pandemic. *Diabetes Metab. Syndr. Clin. Res. Rev.*, 14, 4, 419–422, 2020.
19. Zuo, S., Khosa, K., Ahmad, Z., Almaspoor, Z., Comparison of COVID-19 Pandemic Dynamics in Asian Countries with Statistical Modeling. *Comput. Math. Methods Med.*, 2020, 4296806, 2020.
20. Zhu, G. *et al.*, Learning from Large-Scale Wearable Device Data for Predicting Epidemics Trend of COVID-19. *Discrete Dyn. Nat. Soc*, 2020, Cdc, 2020.
21. Dahiwade, D., Patle, G., Meshram, E., Designing disease prediction model using machine learning approach. *Proc. 3rd Int. Conf. Comput. Methodol. Commun. ICCMC 2019*, Iccmc, pp. 1211–1215, 2019.
22. Vaishya, R., Javaid, M., Khan, I.H., Haleem, A., Artificial Intelligence (AI) applications for COVID-19 pandemic. *Diabetes Metab. Syndr. Clin. Res. Rev.*, 14, 4, 337–339, 2020.
23. Donthu, N. and Gustafsson, A., Effects of COVID-19 on business and research. *J. Bus. Res.*, 117, June, 284–289, 2020.

24. Punn, N.S., Sonbhadra, S.K., Agarwal, S., *Monitoring COVID-19 social distancing with person detection and tracking via fine-tuned YOLO v3 and Deepsort techniques*, pp. 1–10, 1927.
25. Shirai, Y., Artificial Intelligence for Industrial Application in Japan. *IFAC Proc. Vol.*, 16, 20, 15–24, 1983.
26. Uchmeister, B., Alcic, P., Jstersek, O., Artificial Intelligence in Manufacturing Companies and Broader: An Overview. 81–98, 2019.
27. Ćosić, K., Popović, S., Šarlija, M., Kesedžić, I., Impact of human disasters and COVID-19 pandemic on mental health: Potential of digital psychiatry. *Psychiatr. Danub.*, 32, 1, 25–31, 2020.
28. Rajkumar, R.P., COVID-19 and mental health: A review of the existing literature. *Asian J. Psychiatr.*, 52, 102066, March 2020.
29. Mahase, E., COVID-19: Mental health consequences of pandemic need urgent research, paper advises. *BMJ*, 369, April, m1515, 2020.
30. Hamouche, S., COVID-19 and employees' mental health: Stressors, moderators and agenda for organizational actions. *Emerald Open Res.*, 2, 15, 2020.
31. McCall, B., COVID-19 and artificial intelligence: Protecting healthcare workers and curbing the spread. *Lancet Digit. Health*, 2, 4, e166–e167, 2020.
32. Bøgehøj, L., *Artificial Intelligence vs. Human Intelligence Man vs. Machine Lucas Kromann Bøgehøj Nielsen*, pp. 1–20, December 2016.
33. Signorelli, C.M., Can computers become conscious and overcome humans? *Front. Robot. AI*, 5, OCT, 2018.
34. Chawla, P., Juneja, A., Juneja, S., Anand, R., Artificial intelligent systems in smart medical healthcare: Current trends. *Int. J. Adv. Sci. Technol.*, 29, 10 Special Issue, 1476–1484, 2020.
35. Juneja, S., Juneja, A., Anand, R., Role of big data as a tool for improving sustainability for the betterment of quality of life in metro cities. *Int. J. Control Autom.*, 12, 5, 553–557, 2019.
36. Peng, Y. and Nagata, M.H., An empirical overview of nonlinearity and overfitting in machine learning using COVID-19 data. *Chaos Solitons Fractals*, 139, 2020.
37. Mortimer, E.F., Construtivismo, mudança conceitual e ensino de Ciências: para onde vamos? *Invest. Ensino Ciênc.*, 1, 1, 20–39, 1996.
38. Rigby, M.J., Ethical dimensions of using artificial intelligence in healthcare. *AMA J. Ethics*, 21, 2, 121–124, 2019.
39. Leslie, D., Tackling COVID-19 through responsible AI innovation: Five steps in the right direction. *SSRN Electron. J.*, 2020, http://dx.doi.org/10.2139/ssrn.3652970.
40. Wisskirchen, G. *et al.*, *Artificial Intelligence and Robotics and Their Impact on the Workplace*, p. 120, IBA Glob. Employ. Inst., April 2017.
41. Li, L. *et al.*, Using Artificial Intelligence to Detect COVID-19 and Community-acquired Pneumonia Based on Pulmonary CT: Evaluation of the Diagnostic Accuracy. *Radiology*, 296, 2, E65–E71, 2020.

2

Healthcare System 4.0 Perspectives on COVID-19 Pandemic

Rehab A. Rayan[1]*, **Imran Zafar**[2] **and Iryna B. Romash**[3]

[1]*Department of Epidemiology, High Institute of Public Health, Alexandria University, Alexandria, Egypt*
[2]*Department of Bioinformatics and Computational Biology, Virtual University Pakistan, Lahore, Pakistan*
[3]*Department Propaedeutics of Internal Medicine, Ivano-Frankivsk National Medical University, Ivano-Frankivsk, Ukraine*

Abstract

COVID-19 has generated needs for health tools, medications, and applications in information technology. Industry 4.0 is about techniques like artificial intelligence (AI) or robots as tools that are designed to carry improvement in responding to the changing world. According to scientific data, industry 4.0 offers novel insights and solutions to national and international health agencies. Healthcare system 4.0 (HCS 4.0), a part of the fourth industrial transformation, could meet demands in the disaster of COVID-19. There are valuable HCS 4.0 techniques that could assist in controlling and managing the pandemic via detecting and diagnosing COVID-19 and other associated issues. For instance, HCS 4.0 could meet the demands for face masks, gloves, and gather information for health sectors to adequately address the infected cases with COVID-19. It is also important to deliver daily updates about infected cases, including demographics via surveillance systems. Applying such techniques adequately could improve public health communication and education. Ultimately, the techniques for HCS 4.0 could offer many novel interventions for addressing local and universal catastrophes in health. This chapter explores the leading HCS 4.0 techniques that could address this pandemic, highlighting real-world applications, opportunities, challenges, and future insights.

**Corresponding author*: rayanr@alexu.edu.eg

Abhinav Juneja, Vikram Bali, Sapna Juneja, Vishal Jain and Prashant Tyagi (eds.) Enabling Healthcare 4.0 for Pandemics: A Roadmap Using AI, Machine Learning, IoT and Cognitive Technologies, (21–38) © 2021 Scrivener Publishing LLC

***Keywords*:** Healthcare System 4.0, information technology, COVID-19, coronavirus, public health

2.1 Introduction

Coronavirus pandemic, so-called COVID-19, has significantly affected almost the entire universe, particularly the healthcare systems, hence the need for innovative techniques to address the growing burden related to such a viral pandemic. The fourth industrial revolution (Industry 4.0) includes novel information and production technologies, to timely fulfill human needs such as wireless connectivity in the production and service industries. Under the revolutionary Healthcare System 4.0 (HCS 4.0), all technologies get connected, and health stakeholders could interact together for producing and using medications, vaccines, medical equipment, logistics, surveillance, and implementing the required steps with the least real human engagement [1].

In the era of advanced technology, computer learning, storing, managing and manipulating processes are possible to solve daily life challenges of the world population using the most powerful technology including artificial intelligence (AI), machine learning (ML), deep learning (DL), Internet of Things (IoT), big data analysis, data mining and other complex tasks and technologies in healthcare systems. The complex structure of the advanced technology based on sensors and wireless connectivity in the contexts of healthcare, known as HCS 4.0, is responsible for large pathways to make its own decisions, interpretation, or communication among physical, digital and large biological datasets. HCS 4.0 provides the opportunity for a resource chain of biological disposables and equipment with responsible phenomena to handle the pandemic situation of COVID-19 outbreak via smooth developed methods. This digital system is also important to handle COVID-19 crisis and deliver medical items on time for patients [2, 3].

HCS 4.0 is an advanced system for smart productivity of wide-ranging production processes based on applied technologies. In a medical field like management of COVID-19 outbreak, HCS 4.0 can design and develop medical instruments for patients based on advanced tools and technologies like 3D printing, automatic medical robotics, and multitasking system, etc. for manufacturing required material [4, 5]. In this domain, HCS 4.0 give significant benefits on COVID-19 outbreak via providing the best digital solutions such as planning and explanations of the COVID-19 risk factors with goal-based, experience, and rational systems, virtual reality and model system, robotic based treatment, supply chain processes in medical terms, manufacturing of safety item regarding current virus related issues, among others for promoting many other flexible environments. This informational Technogym of HCS 4.0 helps healthcare individuals to perform retune wise activities for the international open well-being crisis of this virus with several recent innovations [6]. For availability of telemedicine in the domain of COVID-19, it is possible based on advanced digital systems for suitable prevention and control and also provides feedback about additional challenges regarding patients or aware the medical staff during the serious situation on an instant basis. Therefore, the ability of a remote control system for healthcare is important to handle problems and challenges of this virus based on HCS 4.0 technologies [7, 8]. Many high-throughput technologies and techniques provide wide-ranging applications like sensors etc. to manage the physiological data of patients by doctors and achieve innovative solutions for the current outbreak of COVID-19. During the lockdown, digital systems and technologies also provide smart access and remote control strategy to handle distance education resources about COVID-19 documentation, relevant information, and guidance [9, p. 19].

HCS 4.0, with the help of other advanced emerging techniques, provide the facility to determine COVID-19 outbreak's mode of transmission and symptoms and handle any confusing outcomes regarding this disease, like potential health challenges or probabilities of recovery. AI, ML, and DL-based video reconnaissance have a great proficiency for healthcare professionals to reduce the overload of hospital teams and activities of patients during the COVID-19 crisis. HCS 4.0 is a highly dependent system in medical science to handle biological data or provide future insights to store, manipulate sensitive data that will be applicable for upcoming similar pandemics from doctors, staff, and other professionals. HCS 4.0 can manage all centralized medical tools and technologies, virtual hospital consultations including unique treatment processes that are rapidly involving COVID-19 or related diseases. This squared phenomenon offers a disruptive revolution to diminish the effect of COVID-19 outbreak-related viruses in public domains.

This chapter discusses applying HCS 4.0 techniques in managing the COVID-19 pandemic. It starts by highlighting the key techniques, then reviews real world applications. It also describes opportunities, challenges and the future of HCS 4.0 in addressing similar pandemics.

2.2 Key Techniques of HCS 4.0 for COVID-19

HCS 4.0 techniques could predict the risk and detect COVID-19 symptoms to confirm cases. It enables monitoring of likely health issues and recovery [5]. Telemedicine services could monitor health remotely, enabling adequate prevention and control of such a virus via detecting abnormalities in patients and rapidly communicating healthcare providers, especially in emergencies [8]. Sensors for physiological monitoring could offer useful data for both the patients and the healthcare providers. Through the lockdown out of the COVID-19 pandemic emergency, digital techniques enabled online and distant learning through sharing updated information, guidance, documentation, and open educational resources for teaching in remote areas [10].

AI-based surveillance has the potential to minimize the burden over healthcare staff during this crisis where it could observe COVID-19 patients' activities. HCS 4.0 techniques could offer better alternatives and enhance the performance of healthcare providers to learn more about COVID-19 [11]. There was a wide communication of false information about COVID-19 to the public via different media channels. HCS 4.0 technologies could help to detect such false information and provide accurate one [12, p. 19]. This work discusses the potentials of different HCS 4.0 techniques in managing the pandemic of COVID-19. This review would help the health stakeholders and investigators in fighting this pandemic, applying such technologies efficiently now and for the future. Here we deliberate the important tools of HCS 4.0, which may provide further help in COVID-19 epidemics.

2.2.1 Artificial Intelligence (AI)

AI (man-made brainpower) is an amazing asset that can be helpful against the COVID-19 pandemic in evaluating the dangers of contamination and screening the populace. It is an application like AI, PC vision, and normal language preparation that can teach PCs to use models dependent on huge information to perceive, clarify, and expect the example. Today, the utilization of this innovation is constrained because of an absence of information. Accessible information is boisterous and degenerate. Artificial intelligence can expect the flare-up and can likewise limit or even break point the spread of the infection. Bogus data on social stages identified with COVID-19 could later be recognized and expelled by the help of AI. Clinical preliminaries of medications and immunizations against this infection could be streamlined using AI. It may be utilized to create robots for sanitization work and clinical exploration on the web. This procedure can perform CT filters expected to recognize pneumonia brought about by an infection. Using this innovation is helpful in creating the hardware required for the well-being framework.

2.2.2 The Internet of Things (IoT)

The IoT is a mechanized arrangement that has brought about gigantic development in robotized producing, resource the executives, and so forth. It comprises gathering, moving, examining, and putting away information. Information assortment is finished using sensors incorporated with cell phones, robots, and so on. The gathered information is then transferred for examination and dynamic to the focal cloud server [13]. The IoT is ending up being of incredible help in the battle against COVID-19. For example, drones are utilized in observation for guaranteeing the usage of isolation transport. This method can be utilized to follow the source of a scourge. It is helpful for disease transmission specialists to look for and furthermore recognize individuals who interact with patients. Persistence consistent with isolation can be ensured. Patients who break isolation can be followed. Also, this strategy might be helpful in mitigating clinical staff through far off checking of residential patients [14].

2.2.3 Big Data

COVID-19 is portrayed by a lengthy hatching period, high infectivity and hard to distinguish, which prompted an abrupt flare-up and the quick improvement of a scourge. This circumstance requires GIS and large information innovation to empower fast reactions and examinations, quick access to data on scourge elements, and a comprehension of the principles of pandemic improvement to offer quick help for preventive choices and activities and also, control [15]. Big Data is an expository method appropriate to recognizing and controlling the overall spread of the COVID-19 infection. This procedure makes it conceivable to store an enormous number of patients tainted with this infection. This innovation frames the reason for quicker, close to constant evaluation of dynamic. It assists spare with people's lives and rapidly distinguishes powerful treatments. Enormous information can be exceptionally valuable in dissecting and expecting the size and effect of the coronavirus on people [16]. COVID-19 trackers can gather close to constant information from sources far and wide, at that point give analysts, specialists, disease transmission experts, and policymakers the most recent data that can be useful in settling on better choices to battle the infection.

2.2.4 Virtual Reality (VR)

VR is rapidly getting progressively available, increasingly open, or more all reasonable. Computer generated reality is an advanced innovation that gives a recreated experience nearly equivalent to or not quite the same as the universe of work. The two innovations are utilized in many territories of the medical clinic segment, including the analytic area: the symptomatic imaging procedures as of now used extensively in class and permit to have an enormous and away images of the patient, without the need of the patient and work to find out additional; improvements around there incorporating the development opportunity offered by new gadgets which take static pictures, yet additionally move them to give the doctor a 10,000-foot perspective on organ work, not one minute in a period span [17]. The applications incorporate computer games, 3D games, instructive preparing, clinical preparing, military preparing, and so forth. The earth given by this innovation offers the upsides of incredible solace, imagination, and profitability [18]. Natural whiteboards permit individuals to team up progressively, visit reproductions, and catch content. During the COVID-19 flare-up, augmented reality innovation offers an incredible option in contrast to video calling. The principle preferred position of this medium is that it gives individuals the sentiment of being in a similar space together without moving. An additional advantage is that individuals can completely focus on the errand without interference. VR improves proficiency, improves bunch work, lessens travel costs, decreases non-attendance, and diminishes ecological effect. So during this season of COVID-19 infection, VR was an extraordinary instrument for correspondence and joint effort.

2.2.5 Holography

Holography is 3D-photography technique. It shows 3D with growing points of view. It is as opposed to photography; it keeps both the stage and the mind-boggling adequacy of the wave originating from the item. The picture is known as the visualization. It resembles a window with memory. The 3D image could remake a precise 3D picture of the first item. It offers organizations an option to virtualize their occasions without webcasting. This permits organizations to dispatch items, include recent clients, and develop their brands. Advanced holographic innovation has opened up another method of holding gatherings and live occasions. It lessens the presentation of responders, representatives, and clients to COVID-19 [7]. It looks like speakers are for all intents and purposes living from their home or office on a genuine occasion scene identified with COVID-19. A huge number of individuals can watch this live communicate simultaneously. Holography can give ultra-authenticity. In this season of the COVID-19 episode, when representatives need to remain at home, this holographic occasion spilling innovation is getting adequate.

2.2.6 Cloud Computing

Distributed computing or Cloud computing is a computerized innovation where PC assets are offered over the Internet, for example, servers, stockpiling, databases, systems, knowledge, and so forth. This innovation empowers quicker advancement and adaptable assets in lower working expenses and expanded productivity in working. In the current social disconnection amid the COVID-19 crisis, subjects could continue with their computerized lives with applications, for example, Slack collaboration, Zoom video-conferencing, and Netflix; via administrations, for example, Google Cloud, Microsoft Azure, or Amazon Web Services. Distributed computing might be valuable in a few distinct ways to battle COVID-19 [19]. For instance, presents a Salesforce Care arrangement structured especially for medicinal services providers who get an enormous number of COVID-19 solicitations.

2.2.7 Autonomous Robots

Autonomous robots are utilized to play out the assignments without the impact of an outer body. It may be utilized to accumulate data about the earth. It tends to be utilized without assistance for quite a while. It is viewed as a sub-innovation for mechanical technology and computerized reasoning. Robotics can disregard circumstances that can be perilous to individuals. The fundamental points of interest of careful robots are their accuracy and the capacity to perform negligibly intrusive medical procedures just as their capacity to get to every anatomical region of the patient, which gives a serious extent of adaptability in the careful setting. The Da Vinci careful framework, for instance, is a newcomer to apply autonomy. This framework is the subject of much examination and is applied in many medical procedures such as, heart medical procedure, urology, and gynecology. Its fundamental application is the technique for prostate expelling or the heart valve replacement, yet it could likewise be utilized for other neighborhood medical process. While the several benefits of the machine, the detriments can't be considered the significant expenses [20]. The other territory of use for mechanical technology is the recovery area.

Robot recovery today can possibly guarantee an arrival to practically rehabilitations much after extreme injury and major inactivating pathological cases. A case of this application is the utilization of exoskeletons that empower restoration of appendages, stance, and development. For this situation, the significant expenses are likewise the greatest disservices. During the current lock times in the COVID-19 epidemic, an independent robot can be conveyed to watch territories to affirm that individuals are following lockdown orders. Self-ruling robots can likewise be utilized in clinics to assist clinical staff to play out their assignments without interference. Improving the presentation of clinical staff and thus constraining the spread of COVID-19 can be extremely useful [21].

2.2.8 3D Scanning

3D scanning technology is utilized for changing over the physical component to advanced CAD information. Such an innovation is powerful in figuring out procedures. In medication, this innovation is utilized to filter the human body and its part as indicated by the specific measurement. The 3D check yield is utilized for the investigation of genuine articles to gather morphology information. Next, the 3D framework would be able to be worked with gathered information. This data can be utilized for some applications. 3D scanners are additionally valuable for creating computer games and motion pictures. 3D filtering is a contactless innovation that permits chest checking for COVID-19 [22]. Also, some unique applications for such an innovation are a great instrument in detecting and evaluating COVID-19 infections, computer generated reality, movement catch, robot planning and modern structure.

2.2.9 3D Printing Technology

3D printing is, as of now in the clinical area, to create custom parts from the import of CAD records. This could rapidly overhaul the past form of the item in short period and cash. It could structure and improve ventilation components for the vital holes. Along these lines, the need of the worldwide flexible chain is met by assembling the essential prudent components. 3D printing innovation could be applied to restrict the COVID-19 ailment transmission [23]. A face cover made with this innovation is as of now being developed. Such a face cover could test enormous quantities of individuals in 30 min for COVID-19. The utilization of careful covers and N95 respirators isn't appropriate for the earth and might be destructive to the environment. Then again, it is asserted that the new Nano Hack 3D printed veil is reusable via recycling [24].

2.2.10 Biosensors

Biosensors are utilized to change over the organic sign into an electrical sign. A portion of the fundamental sorts of biosensors are visual, warm, electrochemical, and piezoelectric biosensors. They are used in a wide scope of regions, for example, clinical science, the food business, the sea part, and so on. They are steady and touchy. On account of organic wars, biosensors can be utilized to help the military. This fresh out of the plastic new biosensor innovation, which is viably utilized as a remote gadget in a multi-quiet clinic condition, at the hour of the COVID-19 pandemic, biosensors can give gadgets that can be anything but difficult to utilize, touchy, efficient and high exactness. The glucose screen is an ideal case of the biosensor utilized in clinical examination and finding of sicknesses. A solitary utilize remote biosensor fix 1AX is a work in progress. This biosensor fix can be utilized for early location and checking of COVD-19 indications like continuous account of temperature, ECG waveform, respiratory rate, and so on [25].

2.3 Real World Applications of HCS 4.0 for COVID-19

In the first days of the WHO declaration about the pandemic of COVID-19, the Center for international governance innovation focused on 5 potential directions. These were tracking infected individuals and contacts, the potential of testing and response, early warning and monitoring compliance of quarantine, and social distancing, the treatment of patients [26]. In response to the query, in different countries of the world were massively running the development and implementation of new projects designed to help address these priorities. Despite the fact that in response to COVID-19 appears an extraordinary range of proposals and ideas based on modern digital information technologies, group projects focused on biomedical and social control have their own specifics and are under special control. So, moving along these lines, we follow what has already been achieved and what opportunities await us in the field of innovative electronic technologies to help in solving these global issues.

So, the first challenge is the tracking of infected individuals and their contacts. Since the coronavirus, COVID-19, can be transmitted from infected people to those who are close to them, health authorities called contact tracing, one of the most effective ways of containing the pandemic. The most popular product is the app to track the location of people in quarantine. One of the first developers of such innovations was China with its mobile application Yi Kuang, The Star, platforms Quant Urban, and We Chat, for them: Israel—Vocalis Health; UK—Covid Symptom Tracker; Singapore—Trace Together; South Korea—a special system based on GPS; Poland—Home quarantine. Germany is already in the beginning advanced in their development so far that it has even hooked up to the tracking of application data on the results of laboratory tests on COVID-19 [27]. France in April 2020 had successfully tested an app to track infected people. The project involved companies such as ANSSI, Capgemini, Dassault Systèmes, and others, as well as the public sector [28].

There are numerous examples of the use of certain kinds of trackers, which has generated a number of comments from organizations in the struggle for human rights. In particular, there were malicious products, such as the mobile application CovidLock, promising to provide users with information about the state of coronavirus infection in the world, the program blocked the phone and demanded a fee for maintaining confidential information. Therefore, the world' leading health services, universities and non-profit organizations around the world have set out to develop technology for voluntary contact tracking with the possibility of maximizing the confidentiality of users.

For the coordinated operation of applications and the creation of a joint system which will help track the spread of the coronavirus COVID-19, between operating systems Android and iOS, Google and Apple firstly developed the application programming interface (API), and then another, more modern platform which gives an opportunity to interact with a "wider ecosystem of applications and services health"; on the basis of Bluetooth technology. These technologies allow devices that use the operating systems iOS and Android to let clients take over their personal data with owned devices.

The possibilities of these technologies, one of the first in Europe began to use the Swiss citizens where the country released the app SwissCovid. This app should help to contain the spread of coronavirus emerging from quarantine. Only after the country's Parliament approved legislation that regulates the use of this program and data protection, did the app became available on App Store and Google Play for all residents. As noted by the head of the digital transformation of the Federal office of public health, such an app highly protect data and privacy, due to the decentralized information storage and has blocked geolocation. The approach uses encryption Bluetooth technique to connect two smartphones at a distance of not less than 1.5 m from each other during minimally 15 min, keeping both privacy and minimal power. Under these conditions, the smartphone users who install the app will share the anonymous signals "Ephemeral ID-s". On a centralized server, information will be transmitted only in the case where the user has tested positive for the COVID-19 and reported to the system—but also in anonymous form. The app will save the data on the smartphone of the user for maximum of a 14 day-period, during which the usual symptoms of coronavirus appear in a case of infection. Therefore, this new technology, in essence, from the beginning of its use, guarantees privacy for its user. Nothing like this has happened before. According to Carmella Troncoso, head of the laboratory of engineering of security and privacy at EPFL, who leads the project for decentralized tracking to ensure your privacy (DP-3T), such system is a critical change in the development of mass technologies. Soon Apple and Google want to implement this function directly into their operating systems [29, 30].

Quick was the reaction of the industry and developers in countries with a high level of robotics. They began to use robots effectively, reprogramming them to produce the tools needed to counter the pandemic: from the manufacture of personal protective equipment (PPE), ventilators, and the development of robots for automated testing. Thus, each technologically advanced country has shown a high ability to respond quickly to COVID-19 and launched in the relevant production. To speed up the testing process and respond to their result and to protect laboratory workers, the company Bright Machines has developed a robot to handle test samples of COVID-19 with the least human intervening. Process automation laboratory testing allows testing without interruption, which greatly increases the daily volume of tests [31].

About 600 American manufacturers were united in their intention to meet the needs of the country in the production of complex tools to deal with COVID-19 [32]. In France, the PSA group has teamed up with Valeo, Schneider Electric and Air Liquide for the production of the ventilators [33]. In Spain, cars manufacture SEAT in record time, just one week, reshaped for the fabrication of ventilators, and PPE. In the UK this practice in large companies, Airbus, Dyson, Ford and Rolls-Royce that are pooling their resources and reconfigure the production line for the production of 30 thousand of ventilators. Similar practices took over in industrialized countries of the world. Important is that business and government combine their efforts to maximize the use of national productive resources to combat COVID-19 and to stimulate economic activity of domestic manufacturers in conditions of economic crisis.

The reaction of the digital communities was quite similar—within 1–2 months we saw the flow of new products, projects and solutions to explore COVID-19 pandemic involving Big Data, neural networks, the possibility of AI [7]. In the framework of prevention, early diagnosis and monitoring COVID-19, coordinating scale and managing data necessary for implementing such strategies effectively in the highly successful countries dependent upon the integration of digital technologies in system health [34]. Thanks to the technology of AI, the IoT, augmented and virtual reality (AR/VR), capabilities of ML and Data Science, digital neural networks (DNN), and biotechnology, mankind has reached a new level of digital age with a new set of possibilities [35, 36].

Processing a large amount of information from the interconnected IoT devices has made possible the emergence of intelligent networks for proper health management systems, individually or collectively. This network monitors and prevents any types of diseases to improve patient safety. Without requiring human intervention, in language of facts it records data and information about the patient and starts the process of making solutions. Since in a pandemic, there is a great need to use appropriate and organized medical events, using the concept of IoT makes medical care more accessible to patients. Thanks to the technology of IoT, the patient can monitor glucometer data, blood pressure, heart rate, or online consulting with a doctor. An important application of this technology in the field of health is tracking sites for medical instruments and devices timely for robust management. This would enhance effectively the workflow of patient management and also useful for making decision in difficult conditions [37].

Efficiently working through big data, AI helped to simplify tracking people infected with COVID-19. Detecting the level of infection of this virus requires not only finding the accumulation "hot spots", but also predicting the spread of infection and the risk of complications associated with COVID-19 for people of different ages, and with different comorbid pathology. Using such algorithms, all countries have taken necessary measures to halt COVID-19 transmission, especially among vulnerable societal groups. Such tools as maps of migration that use mobile phones, applications for social media and mobile payments to gather data timely on the whereabouts of individuals helped to build a novel system for the detecting and treating cases of COVID-19, providing faster decision-making, which is economically advantageous. Special technology based on AI is able to recognize and remove false information about COVID-19 in the Internet and social platforms.

Thanks to the technology of AI, scientists have learned more about the nature of the virus, its characteristics and use it to develop vaccines and drugs to combat this disease. Scientists have turned to AI technology and IoT to optimize the procedure of the study drugs for managing COVID-19 patients. These technologies, together with DNN and ML capabilities can quickly and efficiently process the huge data to speed-up the process of testing vaccines and medicines developed by the samples in real-time.

2.4 Opportunities and Limitations

HCS 4.0 techniques would offer innovative digital interventions during everyday living in the crisis [38]. For example, evaluating risk worldwide, planning public health emergency actions against COVID-19, producing the protective equipment and delivering timely medical supplies via the intelligent supply chain, using robots in caring for infected patients and reducing the risk of exposure to infection among healthcare providers, training staff using virtual reality, supporting more adaptable healthcare setting, performing everyday living activities in the lockdown, and detecting misinformation in the different media channels [6].

The speed and scale of the COVID-19 pandemic is more or less ahead of the health systems of all countries. Diagnosing, maintaining, treating, and tracking people with suspected infections has become physically difficult because existing healthcare systems based on a historically necessary model of interaction between patients and their physicians have facilitated viral transmission. Globally, several governments have realized the need of an immediate digital revolution to counter this. Therefore, countries around the world have had to take steps to transform healthcare and expand it through the power of digital technology. Unfortunately, even in the developed world, where telemedicine has existed for decades, it has had a weak penetration of the services market, due to rigid, unresolved regulatory mechanisms. With the advent of the pandemic of COVID-19, several countries, including the US, repealed all provisions restricting remote and telemedicine services and began to actively implement it in healthcare.

In turn, prolonged and improper use of various trackers and mobile applications for smartphones can cause users side effects such as neck pain, elbows, upper back, shoulder girdle, and numbness in both fingers and hands. It is worth noting that long-term use of smartphones contributes to the development of a specific syndrome of "Text neck", which is accompanied by pain and curvature in the cervical spine. In addition, long-term use of smartphones and tablets contributes to the appearance of such unpleasant phenomena as: "smartphone", "selfie-wrist", "self-elbow", "computer hump". "Click finger", "Cell phone-elbow".

The development of tools for prevention, early diagnosis and forecasting based on the use of DL and ML with the involvement of IoT technologies and AI requires a huge amount of quality data. The key word—Quality! In order for these technologies to be able to generate qualitative conclusions, they must learn from qualitative and sufficient examples. After all, bad results would be obtained while training models on non-representative data. Unfortunately, data sets of medical images and textual analysis are limited in comparison to the needs of in-depth training. Many of them are not digitized in real time, or contain errors. The key cause of the shortage of collected data is their usual incompatibility in different geographical regions, poor accessibility of the population to medical facilities in developing countries.

2.5 Future Perspectives

HCS 4.0 techniques could offer disruptive innovations, mitigating the COVID-19 crisis. They are expected to grow, storing health-related data on COVID-19 to be used for similar pandemics. Such technologies could rapidly be applied by healthcare providers in managing COVID-19 or similar pandemics, hence making a smarter health system. However, upgrading the current software infrastructure and devices is required. Of course, the industry of trackers and smartphones with the latest applications can help in part. But in developing them, manufacturers must take into account elements like minimal expanses, constrained consumer resources, access for illiterate or disabled subject, and support for several languages to be effectively adopted in different areas. To overcome these limitations, we must apply analytical approach and critical thinking.

Thanks to the active use of AI-based robotics, contactless drug delivery and remote treatment of patients has been made possible, reducing the need for medical personnel to contact infected people. AI can also predict the risk of serious COVID-19-related illnesses for people of all ages and take proactive measures to halt the virus transmitting to vulnerable groups. Thus, the analysis of the literature showed how AI, advanced mathematical modeling, ML, and cloud computing could expect the epidemic growth, and how the future state of global health depends on their coordinated and high-quality work.

2.6 Conclusion

HCS 4.0 applies sensors that are connected wirelessly with a system to display and monitor the entire intelligent manufacturing processes, for example, designing and producing the needed medical disposables and equipment to meet the gap caused by the COVID-19 crisis through an intelligent supply chain for timely and effective patient care. HCS 4.0 includes intelligent, adaptable systems that operate timely with data provided by AI, IoT, and other automatic techniques. HCS 4.0 provides digital solutions for unique areas, for example, different production and automatic information techniques for gathering, sharing, storing, exploring, and adequately monitoring health-related data. Such innovative techniques could properly isolate infected patients, decreasing death rates, speeding up developing drugs, managing procedures, and care. With the help of such techniques, individuals could work virtually from homes; identifying novel working environments. HCS 4.0 could function distantly via intelligent technologies for fighting the COVID-19 pandemic. Such a revolution speeds up the digital transformation with enhanced public safety through virtual clinics that apply remote monitoring and telemedicine consultations, hence, decreasing patients' physical crowding in healthcare facilities. This chapter discussed applying HCS 4.0 techniques in managing the COVID-19 pandemic.

References

1. Ienca, M. and Vayena, E., On the responsible use of digital data to tackle the COVID-19 pandemic. *Nat. Med.*, 26, 4, Art. no. 4, Apr. 2020.
2. Manogaran, G., Thota, C., Lopez, D., Sundarasekar, R., Big Data Security Intelligence for Healthcare Industry 4.0, in: *Cybersecurity for Industry 4.0: Analysis for Design and Manufacturing*, L. Thames, and D. Schaefer, (Eds.), pp. 103–126, Springer International Publishing, Cham, 2017.
3. Zeng, J., Huang, J., Pan, L., How to balance acute myocardial infarction and COVID-19: the protocols from Sichuan Provincial People's Hospital. *Intensive Care Med.*, 46, 6, 1111–1113, 2020.
4. Ruan, Q., Yang, K., Wang, W., Jiang, L., Song, J., Clinical predictors of mortality due to COVID-19 based on an analysis of data of 150 patients from Wuhan, China. *Intensive Care Med.*, 46, 5, 846–848, 2020.
5. Haleem, A., Javaid, M., Vaishya, R., Industry 4.0 and its applications in orthopaedics. *J. Clin. Orthop. Trauma*, 10, 3, 615–616, Jun. 2019.
6. Haleem, A. and Javaid, M., Additive Manufacturing Applications in Industry 4.0: A Review. *J. Ind. Integr. Manage.*, 04, 04, 1930001, Aug. 2019.
7. Javaid, M., Haleem, A., Vaishya, R., Bahl, S., Suman, R., Vaish, A., Industry 4.0 technologies and their applications in fighting COVID-19 pandemic. *Diabetes Metab. Syndr.*, 14, 4, 419–422, 2020.

8. Alloghani, M., Al-Jumeily, D., Hussain, A., Aljaaf, A.J., Mustafina, J., Petrov, E., Healthcare Services Innovations Based on the State of the Art Technology Trend Industry 4.0, in: *2018 11th International Conference on Developments in eSystems Engineering (DeSE)*, Sep. 2018, pp. 64–70.
9. Fisher, D. and Wilder-Smith, A., The global community needs to swiftly ramp up the response to contain COVID-19. *Lancet Lond. Engl.*, 395, 10230, 1109–1110, 04 2020.
10. Li, Q., Feng, W., Quan, Y.-H., Trend and forecasting of the COVID-19 outbreak in China. *J. Infect.*, 469–496, 2020. Accessed: Jul. 10, 2020. [Online]. Available: https://dx.doi.org/10.1016/j.jinf.2020.02.014.
11. Morris, A., *Monitoring COVID-19 from hospital to home: First wearable device continuously tracks key symptoms*, May 04, 2020, https://news.northwestern.edu/stories/2020/04/monitoring-covid-19-from-hospital-to-home-first-wearable-device-continuously-tracks-key-symptoms/(accessed Jul. 13, 2020).
12. Haleem, A., Javaid, M., Vaishya, R., Deshmukh, S.G., Areas of academic research with the impact of COVID-19. *Am. J. Emerg. Med.*, 38, 7, 1524–1526, Jul. 2020.
13. Farahani, B., Firouzi, F., Chang, V., Badaroglu, M., Constant, N., Mankodiya, K., Towards fog-driven IoT eHealth: Promises and challenges of IoT in medicine and healthcare. *Future Gener. Comput. Syst.*, 78, 659–676, Jan. 2018.
14. Qi, J., Yang, P., Min, G., Amft, O., Dong, F., Xu, L., Advanced internet of things for personalised healthcare systems: A survey. *Pervasive Mob. Comput.*, 41, 132–149, Oct. 2017.
15. Zhou, C. *et al.*, COVID-19: Challenges to GIS with Big Data. *Geogr. Sustain.*, 1, 1, 77–87, Mar. 2020.
16. Bragazzi, N.L., Dai, H., Damiani, G., Behzadifar, M., Martini, M., Wu, J., How Big Data and Artificial Intelligence Can Help Better Manage the COVID-19 Pandemic. *Int. J. Environ. Res. Public Health*, 17, 9, 02 2020.
17. Liu, S., Xie, M., Ye, Z., Combating COVID-19—How Can AR Telemedicine Help Doctors More Effectively Implement Clinical Work. *J. Med. Syst.*, 44, 9, 141, Jul. 2020.
18. Singh, R.P., Javaid, M., Kataria, R., Tyagi, M., Haleem, A., Suman, R., Significant applications of virtual reality for COVID-19 pandemic. *Diabetes Metab. Syndr. Clin. Res. Rev.*, 14, 4, 661–664, Jul. 2020.
19. Tuli, S., Tuli, S., Tuli, R., Gill, S.S., Predicting the growth and trend of COVID-19 pandemic using machine learning and cloud computing. *Internet Things*, 11, 100222, Sep. 2020.
20. Fiani, B. *et al.*, Impact of robot-assisted spine surgery on healthcare quality and neurosurgical economics: A systemic review. *Neurosurg. Rev.*, 43, 1, 17–25, Feb. 2020.
21. Yang, G.-Z. *et al.*, Combating COVID-19—The role of robotics in managing public health and infectious diseases. *Sci. Robot.*, 5, 40, Mar. 2020.

22. Shi, F. *et al.*, Review of Artificial Intelligence Techniques in Imaging Data Acquisition, Segmentation and Diagnosis for COVID-19. *IEEE Rev. Biomed. Eng.*, 1–1, 2020.
23. Tino, R. *et al.*, COVID-19 and the role of 3D printing in medicine. *3D Print. Med.*, 6, 1, 11, Apr. 2020.
24. Cavallo, L., Marcianò, A., Cicciù, M., Oteri, G., 3D Printing beyond Dentistry during COVID-19 Epidemic: A Technical Note for Producing Connectors to Breathing Devices. *Prosthesis*, 2, 2, Art. no. 2, Jun. 2020.
25. Seo, G. *et al.*, Rapid Detection of COVID-19 Causative Virus (SARS-CoV-2) in Human Nasopharyngeal Swab Specimens Using Field-Effect Transistor-Based Biosensor. *ACS Nano*, 14, 4, 5135–5142, Apr. 2020.
26. McDonald, S., *The Digital Response to the Outbreak of COVID-19*, Mar. 2020, Accessed: Jul. 27, 2020. [Online]. Available: https://www.cigionline.org/articles/digital-response-outbreak-covid-19.
27. Lomas, N., *Germany's COVID-19 contacts tracing app to link to labs for test result notification*, TechCrunch, Apr. 23, 2020, https://social.techcrunch.com/2020/04/23/germanys-covid-19-contacts-tracing-app-to-link-to-labs-for-test-result-notification/ (accessed Jul. 27, 2020).
28. Orange: Reuters, *BRIEF-Orange, Dassault Systemes, CapGemini among top firms involved in French StopCovid app project*, Apr. 26, 2020.
29. MacNamee Terence, S.I., *Switzerland launches SwissCovid tracing app for residents*, SWI swissinfo.ch, Jun. 25, 2020, https://www.swissinfo.ch/eng/switzerland-launches-swisscovid-contact-tracing-app-for-residents/45859778 (accessed Jul. 27, 2020).
30. Kelion, L., *First Google/Apple-based virus-trace app launched*, BBC News, May 26, 2020.
31. Rayome, A.D., *This robot could make COVID-19 testing faster and safer*, CNET, Apr. 21, 2020, https://www.cnet.com/news/this-robot-could-make-covid-19-testing-faster-and-safer/ (accessed Jul. 27, 2020).
32. IW Staff, *600 US Manufacturers Ready to Assist with Pandemic Relief Effort*, IndustryWeek, Apr. 10, 2020, https://www.industryweek.com/covid19/article/21128586/600-us-manufacturers-ready-to-assist-with-pandemic-relief-effort (accessed Jul. 27, 2020).
33. *Air Liquid, Air Liquide, Groupe PSA, Schneider Electric, Valeo rise to the challenge of producing 10,000 Air Liquide Medical Systems respirators in response to the French government request*, Air Liquide, Apr. 01, 2020, https://www.airliquide.com/mainland-china/air-liquide-groupe-psa-schneider-electric-valeo-rise-challenge-producing-10000-air (accessed Jul. 27, 2020).
34. Whitelaw, S., Mamas, M.A., Topol, E., Spall, H.G.C.V., Applications of digital technology in COVID-19 pandemic planning and response. *Lancet Digit. Health*, Jun. 2020.
35. Vaishya, R., Javaid, M., Khan, I.H., Haleem, A., Artificial Intelligence (AI) applications for COVID-19 pandemic. *Diabetes Metab. Syndr. Clin. Res. Rev.*, 14, 4, 337–339, Jul. 2020.

36. Iyengar, K., Upadhyaya, G.K., Vaishya, R., Jain, V., COVID-19 and applications of smartphone technology in the current pandemic. *Diabetes Metab. Syndr.*, 14, 5, 733–737, 2020.
37. Singh, R.P., Javaid, M., Haleem, A., Suman, R., Internet of things (IoT) applications to fight against COVID-19 pandemic. *Diabetes Metab. Syndr. Clin. Res. Rev.*, 14, 4, 521–524, Jul. 2020.
38. Zhong, R.Y., Xu, X., Klotz, E., Newman, S.T., Intelligent Manufacturing in the Context of Industry 4.0: A Review. *Engineering*, 3, 5, 616–630, Oct. 2017.

3

Analysis and Prediction on COVID-19 Using Machine Learning Techniques

Supriya Raheja* **and Shaswata Datta**

Department of CSE, Amity University, Noida, India

Abstract
This paper presents an analysis and prediction of COVID-19 data using machine learning techniques. The present work discusses different machine learning techniques namely linear regression, logistic regression, random forest, and decision tree. The outbreak COVID-19 has attracted the attention of all researchers only on the corona virus. To focus on COVID-19, the present study attempts to analyze COVID-19 data using all machine learning techniques. The work also introduced a decision-making process for further prediction. The techniques are compared with respect to accuracy of prediction.

Keywords: COVID-19, data analysis, linear regression, logistic regression, random forest, decision tree, prediction

3.1 Introduction

These days, lots of data are generated due to tremendous use of internet worldwide which is useless without finding the hidden insights of the data. These findings can be used by organizations for their various future decisions making. As reviewed from literature, web has all the documents present in it and its volume is increasing in gargantuan rate of about 80% per year [1]. Moreover, almost all the data are stored in text format in websites in unstructured form. With a very powerful tool like machine learning, it becomes very easy to operate these enormous amounts of data and find

**Corresponding author*: supriya.raheja@gmail.com

Abhinav Juneja, Vikram Bali, Sapna Juneja, Vishal Jain and Prashant Tyagi (eds.) Enabling Healthcare 4.0 for Pandemics: A Roadmap Using AI, Machine Learning, IoT and Cognitive Technologies, (39–58) © 2021 Scrivener Publishing LLC

data prediction for better decision-making process in any field. Machine learning is the future of computer science. It makes the understanding and working process of the human brain more clearly. Machine learning has the capability to find insights from structured data and unstructured data and according to the report [1] there are approximately 90% data of all the data in the internet, which are unstructured. Here, machine learning can also find various insights of their data using the process of un-supervised learning and it is one of the most optimized ways for data driven decision making for various businesses. Machine Learning has been extensively used by various top IT companies, as they create a huge amount of customer data that they use for various important business decision-making and improve their services to get potential loyal customers. Machine learning has heavily impacted the decision-making process of various fields like IT fields, security fields and medical field.

Numerous [2] studies revealed machine learning as an emerging approach for prediction of diseases, just like the way Physicians do by understanding the symptoms of the patients. According to Ref. [3] COVID-19 is one of the major problems that the world is facing and World Health Organization (WHO) declared it as Public Health Emergency of International Concern (PHEIC). The virus first appeared in Wuhan, China and spread exponentially, infecting millions of people across the world. It is also called "severe acute respiratory syndrome coronavirus 2" or (SARS-CoV-2). The infection has similar symptoms of cold. It spreads through respiratory droplets in the air. The current work makes use of various libraries of python namely scikit learn, matplotlib for data visualization, NumPy and pandas for data manipulation.

In the future machine can be trained using small data set also [4]. Needless to say, a promising learnware industry will be opened.

3.2 Literature Review

Machine Learning is the technique of programming a computer in such a way that it can learn on its own. There are many people who tried to describe machine learning in a more generalized way. It is one of the most fantastic tools for getting things more simplified. According to authors, machine learning is used when the problem is very complex for traditional approaches or when there is no procedure to solve a problem. It is generally used to obtain insights from a large amount of data [5].

Machine learning has been used for predicting hypoxemia during surgery [6]. Thus helping doctors to take critical decision while doing surgeries. In the future it will impact our lives to a very great extent, making it easier. There are many more studies for more optimization of these algorithms. In this study authors has stated that the no. of iteration is inversely proportional to the training error until the least square is attained and it is best for optimizing Linear regression model. The incremental forward stagewise regression in Ref. [7] is another good option when it comes to optimization of Linear regression model.

There are many ways to optimize logistic regression model [8]. The study has shown the real life implementation of conjugate gradient and limiting memory BFGS techniques for optimization of logistic regression. The study of limiting memory BFGS is based on the technique of making posterior of cube and increasing it to its maximum level with each iteration. However, the study concluded that the iteration needs to be stopped when the required thing is 0, else it would blow up in the very next iteration [9].

In the last few years, numerous studies presented the efficiency of machine learning especially in medical fields. Research in the past concluded the successful prediction of diseases in both plants and humans. In this study [10] the authors used machine learning algorithms and deep learning algorithms for detection of diseases in plants using the images of healthy plants and infected plants. The author also claims that the best performance of the model was about 99.5%. In Ref. [11], the author created a model which detects dermatological diseases using machine learning algorithms. The model uses the images of the skin for prediction. The accuracy produced by the system is above 95%.

One of the studies [12] shows that machine learning can be used for drugs designing as well. The authors used Support Vector Mechanism (SVM) for the same.

According to study [12], the authors Bastian *et al.* created an early phase detection model of COVID-19. They used CT (Computed Tomography) images of viral activities for prediction of COVID-19 at an early phase. The accuracy of the algorithms they used was 99.6%. Machine learning can also be used to detect diseases in plants and humans. In the study the author used machine learning for the detection of rapidly designing nucleic acid. The experiment conducted by the authors was very comprehensive. Authors also claimed that the model is effective against variable targets. The model is most sensitive to full scope of targeted genomic diversity. The model has high specificity to those species and subspecies that are of known strains. This allows the model for better and accurate differentiation of related taxa. This was the way by which machine learning can be used to detect COVID-19 like viruses.

One of the best ways for preventing COVID-19 is by contact tracing. There are many studies in machine learning for contact tracing of infection.

In Ref. [13] a contact investigation model was made for tuberculosis disease using machine leaning model. The model used the skin test data for the contact tracing. The model created by the authors has the overall accuracy of 89% and positive predictive value of 36% and 26% (approx.). The authors claimed that the contact workload could be reduced up to 40% by this model.

According to a similar study [14] logistic regression is used for the making of contact tracing. The model consists of the analysis of age, gender, place of diagnosis, residence, place of birth, family history etc. According to the study about 900+ foreign TB positive cases were detected, and the accuracy of the model was of 81.6% approximately.

The study in Ref. [15] was conducted for better understanding and establishing of relation between the variable contact tracing and spreading of small pox virus. The author claims that, in the population equipped with 20% of immunization the outbreak can be controlled within a year using the strategy of contact tracing and self-isolation [16].

Other than contact tracing, there are many other strategies for the controlling of a pandemic like COVID-19 is by maintaining proper logistics and supply chain of medicines and healthcare equipment's. The study [17] was based on the prediction using machine learning tools and generic knowledge of logistic strategies. The study provides various insights about future planning strategies using machine learning algorithms. Authors suggested that the ability of the model was calculated by the process of KPIs for better accuracy of prediction.

According to study [18] machine learning can be used to tackle viruses like Ebola using the strategy of contact tracing. The study was obtained from the data set of Ebola infection of period 2014–2015. Information from the contact tracers and their supervisors and the review studies. The report states that the 3,838 positive cases and 32,000+ contacts were listed in the data set used for tracing. Author says that the main challenges linked to the effectiveness of the contact tracing are social trust, preventing the exposure of information, inadequately trained contact tracers, poor data set. The training strategies used in this study paper can be used in controlling the future community transmission. However, the accuracy of the model was about 70%.

3.3 Types of Machine Learning

Machine learning techniques [19] can be divided on the basis of king of supervision or guidance provided during training of the model. There are two major categories for machine learning techniques Supervised and Unsupervised learning. There are two more categories known as semi-supervised and re-enforcement learning.

Supervised learning [20]: these are well-organized learning of machine using properly labeled data set. Supervised learning involves modeling the relationship using properly arranged data set, it is just like spoon feeding to machine learning mode [21]. This type of learning is only possible when there is proper well defined data set available.

Unsupervised learning [22]: these are not a well-organized data set and so by observing the different patterns in the data set machine give predictions. This is often described as "letting the data set speak for itself" [21]. It means there is no specification given with the data and the machine has to find different patterns hidden inside the data and give the suitable output accordingly.

Semi-supervised learning [23]: these types of learning are used when there is a large amount of unlabeled and labeled data. According to Ref. [5], these types of learning are used in Google photos and many other photo hosting services.

Re-enforcement learning [24]: It is a very powerful learning technique. It calls a function, and according to environment selects and executes itself. It then learns by itself the best strategy for prediction.

As has been mentioned earlier in my review paper that on the internet approximately 90% of the data are not organized and labeled so unsupervised learning has an edge oversupervised learning.

Now it's time to jump into various machine learning algorithms.

3.4 Machine Learning Algorithms

There are different machine learning algorithms namely linear regression, logistic regression, random forest, decision tree etc. This section discusses these machine learning algorithms in detail.

3.4.1 Linear Regression

Linear regression [25] is one of the popular and easiest algorithms to understand among all other machine learning algorithms. It is used to find the inter dependence between a dependent variable and the independent variable on X-axis as illustrated through Figure 3.1. The data is forecasted with the help of an equation given as Equation (3.1).

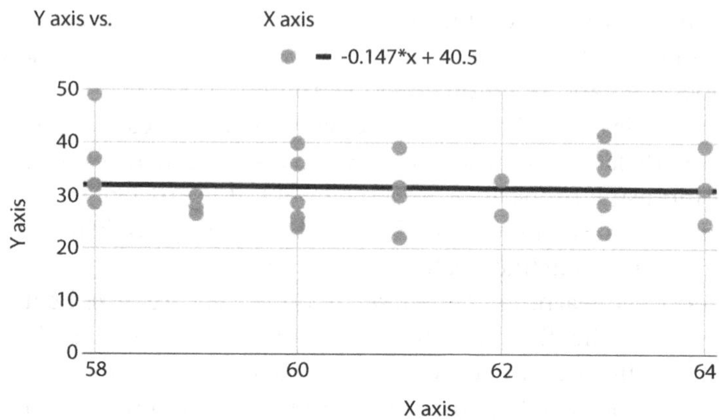

Figure 3.1 A typical linear regression graph.

$$y = mx + c \tag{3.1}$$

Here, '*m*' refers to the slope of the regression line. However, Linear regression [26] algorithm supports only the calculation of single dependent and single independent variables. For multi variable calculations [27], there exists a different method as shown in Figure 3.2. This is necessary because some predictions are not dependent on only one parameter such as rainfall. Rainfall is dependent on various factors like humidity,

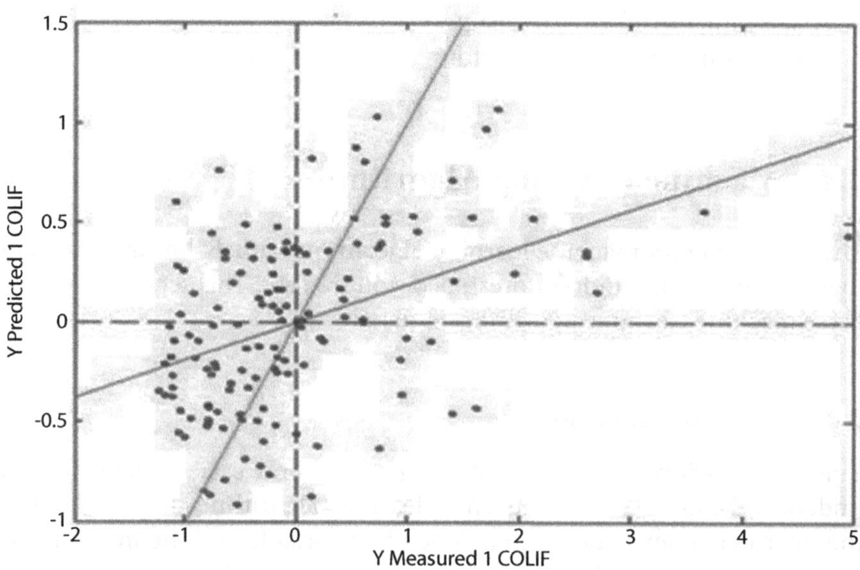

Figure 3.2 Multiple linear regression graph.

temperature, season, etc. Another example is stock price prediction, the stock price is dependent on various factors like the country's economic conditions, profit growth of the asset, etc.

$$y = m1 \times 1 + m2 \times 2 + m3 \times 3....... + c \tag{3.2}$$

Well, it depends on the quality of the dataset it is provided with and the training of the model but, to some extent only. Another way is by finding the distance between the point and the regression line along the Y-axis and finding the average value or the RMS value (Root mean square) of the distance as in Equation (3.2). Accuracy plays a crucial role in data forecasting. Statistical regression is used for both pre-occupancy and post-occupancy in industries. This type of model is used for the calculation of future profits for industries and for the calculation of future GDP growth of countries.

It is a basic and commonly used algorithm for predictive analysis. The accuracy of this model is quite appreciable in our work. The prediction accuracy given by this algorithm is 85%. Authors concluded that linear regression is one of the easiest algorithms to implement and given very accurate results too [11]. But at the same time, it proves to be very inefficient when it comes to nonlinear phenomena as it is not as easily trainable as other machine learning algorithms. Nowadays, the requirement for companies is to train the machine for different scenarios.

3.4.2 Logistic Regression

This regression [28] statistical model is based on sigmoid function which gives binary output like high or low, 0 or 1, true or false. The graph is shown in Figure 3.3.

From the graph, we can observe that the function representing 0 or 1 at the extremes. At 0.5 there is a threshold, which means above 0.5 the value is 1 and below 0.5 the value is 0. Well this is how the regression model works. Logistic regression unlike linear regression gives binary output and this type of algorithms is generally used for various classification of separation of data set. Linear Regression on the other hand is used for getting the future range of the data set, but logistic regression gives out discrete values. However, both the above machine learning algorithms are part of statistical regression and both are popular because of their easy to understand mathematical working, since it belongs to the category of statistical regression. There are the same limitations as mentioned in linear regression, as the requirement of a large amount of data set. But it is easy to implement in a practical scenario. And the accuracy is also pretty good.

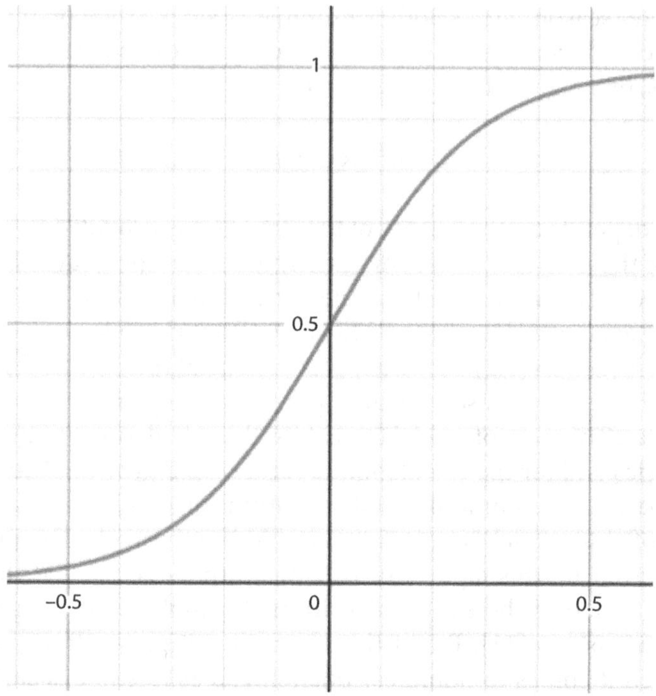

Figure 3.3 Logistic regression graph.

There are also various popular machine learning algorithms for classification like Decision Tree, K-NN. However, report [1] concluded that the feature selection plays an important role in the reprocessing of text data classification. According to this report good feature selection should be based on the algorithm requirements. Feature selection plays a crucial role in the accuracy of prediction. Many researchers concluded that the finding Z may increase the optimization to another level. The authors [12] explained parameter estimation and discussed the role of data analysis for the most accurate feature selection.

3.4.3 K-NN or K Nearest Neighbor

It is one of the most popular machine algorithms for cluster classification. This model is easy to implement on a given set of data, with so much of accuracy that, it has been used for short time forecasting in time series. According to the study, it plays a crucial role in data forecasting for the present scenario. Valgaev and Kupzog [29] developed a model on electricity forecasting of 24 h using this model and the prediction has an accuracy of ranged between [5.59%; 13.6%]/[5.23%; 17.6%] and [1.31%; 5.05%]/[0.83%; 3.68%], respectively [11].

This work presents a comparative analysis among all mentioned machine learning algorithms. In one of the study, authors have used all the KNN algorithms on the Titanic dataset to predict the names of survivors in the titanic disaster on the basis of various parameters like gender, age, class, health, room no, etc. and the model has given an accuracy of 86% on training dataset and 75% accuracy on testing data set.

3.4.4 Decision Tree

It is also one of the popular machine learning algorithms. It basically works on dividing the main dataset into sub data sets which is used for decision

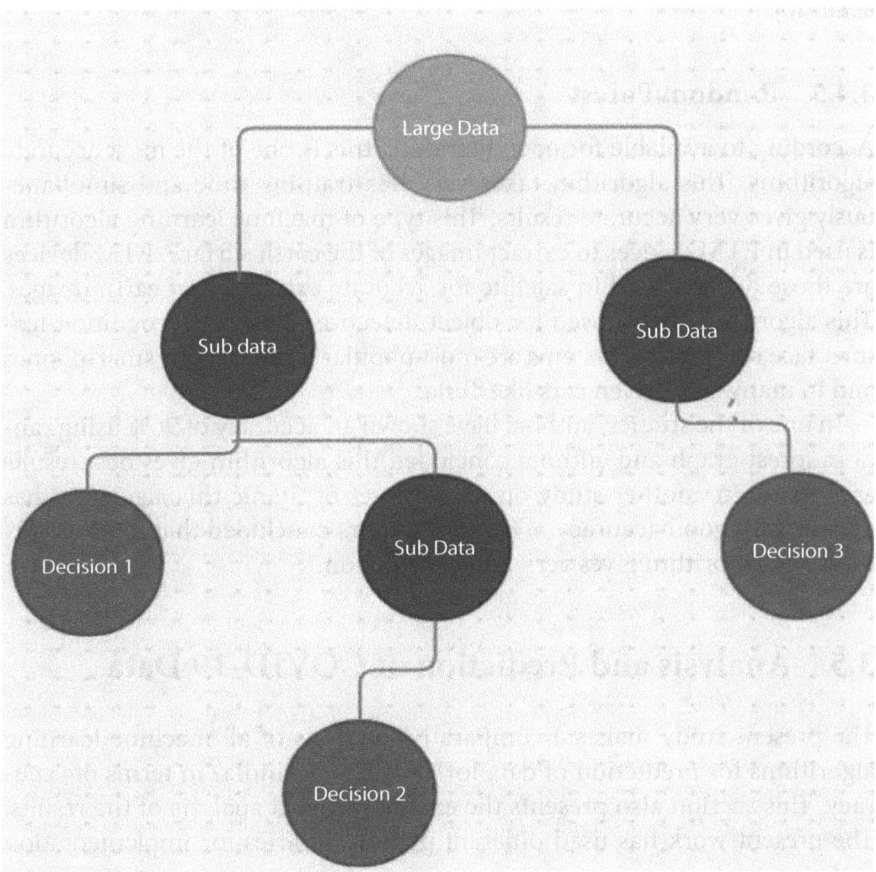

Figure 3.4 Decision tree graph.

making purposes. The primary challenge in the decision tree is to the find the suitable attribute for the root node and further for each level. This is known as attribute selection. From Figure 3.4, we can understand decision tree in a better way.

The data-set is divided into training data-set of order of K numbers which passes to decision tree.

Decision tree is one of the most flexible algorithms for data driven decision making technique. In the study, authors have stated that this algorithm have similar accuracy rate as compared to single support vector mechanism and Artificial neural networking [11]. They concluded an accuracy of 91.63% on training data set and 78.03% on testing dataset for decision tree. Decision tree algorithm is having an advantage of simple implementation over other data driven techniques like artificial neural networking system. Moreover, it is having approximately the same accuracy.

3.4.5 Random Forest

According to available for open literature, this is one of the most accurate algorithms. This algorithm takes very less training time and simultaneously gives very accurate results. This type of machine learning algorithm is used in ETM devices to extract images of the earth surface. ETM devices are those devices used in satellite for accurate extraction of earth images. This algorithm is also used for object detection like face recognition feature, face recognition systems are most popularly used in our smartphones and in many self-driven cars like Tesla.

In one of the studies, authors have shown an accuracy of 96% using random forest graph and authors concluded this algorithm gives best results among all. In another study on the data set of titanic this algorithm has given a very good accuracy of 81.9%. Authors concluded that random forest graph algorithm gives very good prediction.

3.5 Analysis and Prediction of COVID-19 Data

The present study makes a comparative analysis of all machine learning algorithms for prediction of data for COVID-19 (India) in terms of accuracy. This section also presents the extensive visual analysis of the results. The present work has used different python libraries for implementation and visualization.

3.5.1 Methodology Adopted

Dataset Used:
For present work, we have taken the dataset from the Kaggle for duration 30 Jan 20 to 30 March 20 [23]. The data set is having following features:

- age group of infected people.
- COVID-19 India details, which consist of state wise confirmed, not confirmed, recovered, details etc.
- Health infrastructure of all the states.
- Individual details who are infected by the virus.

Data Cleaning:
The second step is data cleaning as mentioned in Figure 3.5. It is important as there are a lot of missing data, irrelevant data types in the data set. It handles such kind of data in data set to normalize the data. All the unnecessary data are cleaned using pandas. Pandas make the data cleansing very easy and fast. Here in this present work, we replaced the missing place by 0 for attribute "number of hospital beds".

Understanding:
The third step includes three things that are:

- Transformation of data means there are various data which has wrong data type so, it will create a problem for a machine to understand that so, therefore data transformation becomes necessary.
- Data visualization: is necessary because that will provide us with proper analysis of the spreading of virus.
- Training the model (machine) to perform prediction most accurately.

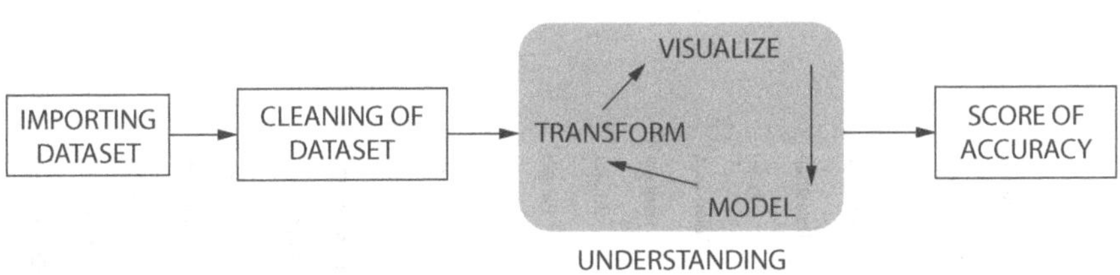

Figure 3.5 Workflow of the present study.

The present work performs the score calculation to evaluate the algorithms because of their score of accuracy.

Data visualization is the most important step for any type of data analysis. We have extracted some important information from the data set like states with confirmed cases, cases w.r.t. gender etc.

Figure 3.6 represents the state wise confirmed cases. Here, we have considered top 20 states for coronavirus infection. From this figure it can be observed that Kerala had the maximum no. of COVID-19 cases followed by Maharashtra, but at the same time it can be seen that the cured cases are more in Kerala than Maharashtra so there is a possibility that, in future can Maharashtra take the lead for COVID-19 cases. If we see the current scenario, then our observation is going in right way. Secondly, it can also be estimated that that the western states of India has more cases of infection than eastern states like West Bengal, Bihar and also to the northern states like Uttarakhand, Ladakh, Jammu and Kashmir.

Figure 3.7 illustrates who is more vulnerable to COVID-19 infection either Male or female. It can be observed that male are more prone to COVID-19 but, this doesn't mean that they are less immune to this. This may happen because males are more exposed to the outside than female in India or they may maintain less hygiene than female.

Figure 3.8 illustrates the number of observed cases w.r.t. dates and it shows a sudden increase in no. of confirmed cases and then sudden decrease which concludes that the government has taken all necessary steps to control the spread of virus. However, the recovery rate is very less

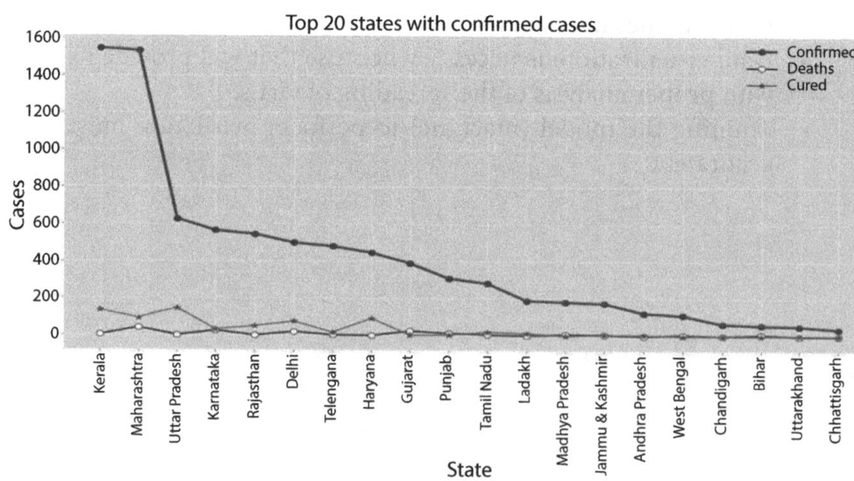

Figure 3.6 States with confirmed cases of COVID-19.

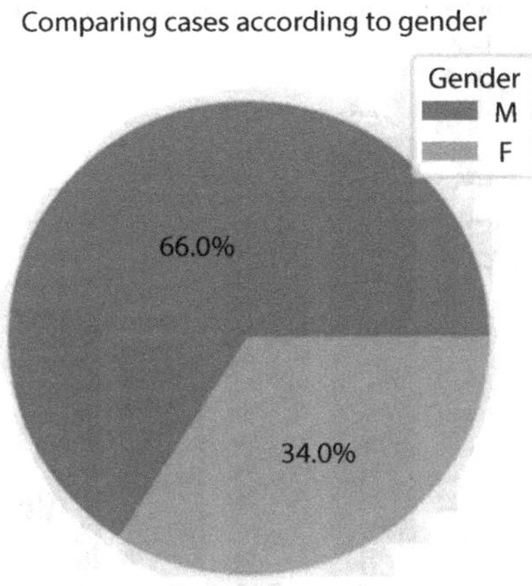

Figure 3.7 Comparing cases w.r.t. gender.

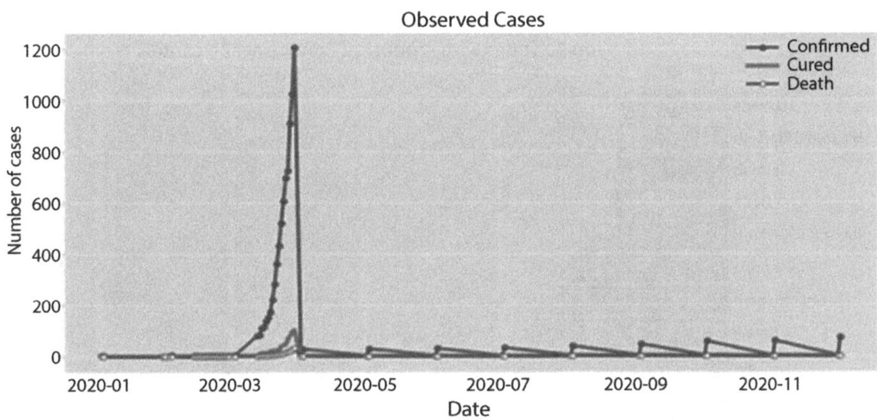

Figure 3.8 Observed cases vs dates.

as it can be compared to confirmed cases. The death rates are also very low which means that the mortality rate is very less by this virus.

From Figure 3.9, it can be seen that people with age group in between 20 and 49 have more confirmed cases than other age groups. Moreover, this is the same age group which belongs to the working population of the country. The age group in between 60 and 69 has also increased cases of COVID-19. However, this may be because of age factor and other chronic diseases, which affect the immune system of human beings.

From Figure 3.10, we have shown the state wise number of primary healthcare centers. Uttar Pradesh has the maximum primary healthcare

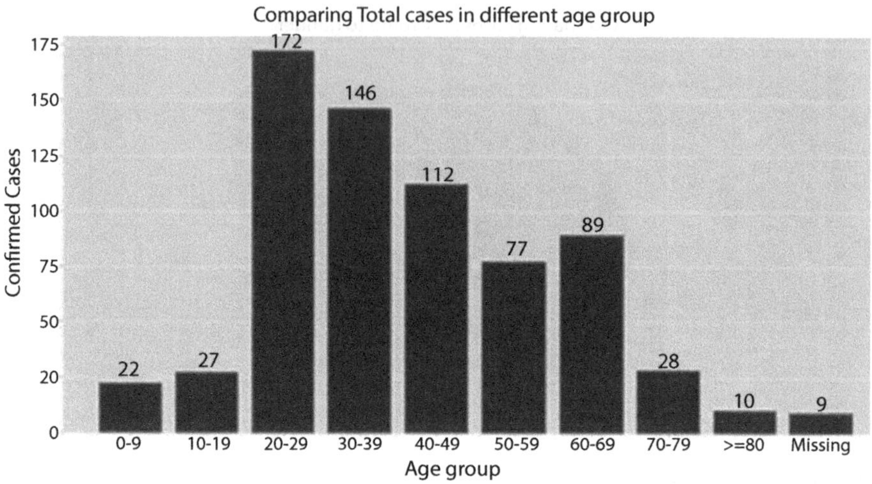

Figure 3.9 Age group vs COVID-19.

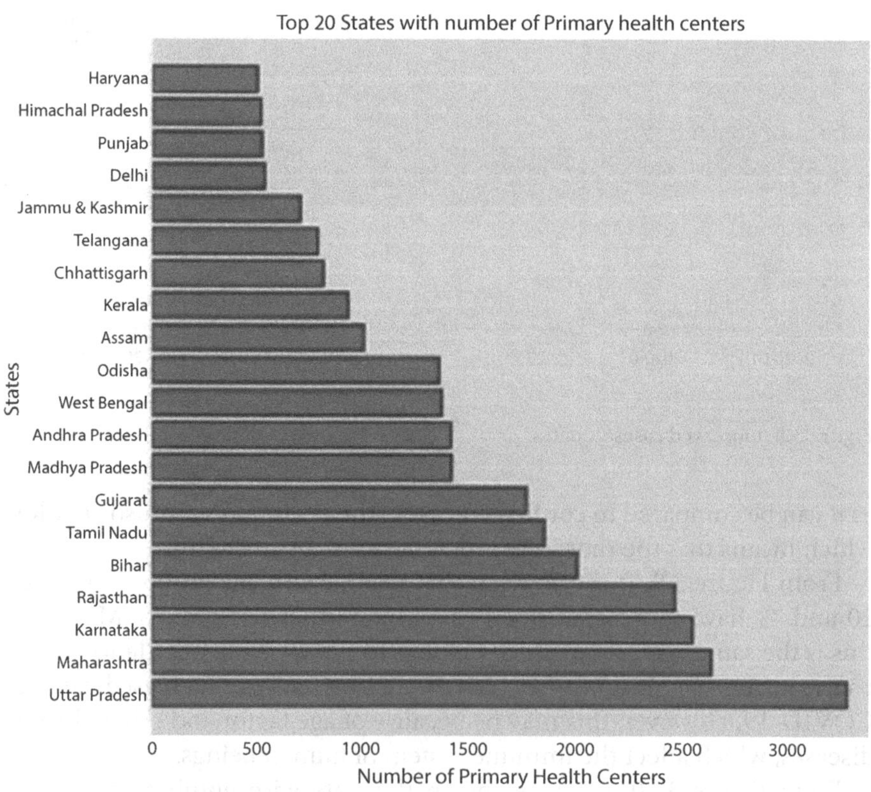

Figure 3.10 States with number of primary healthcare centers.

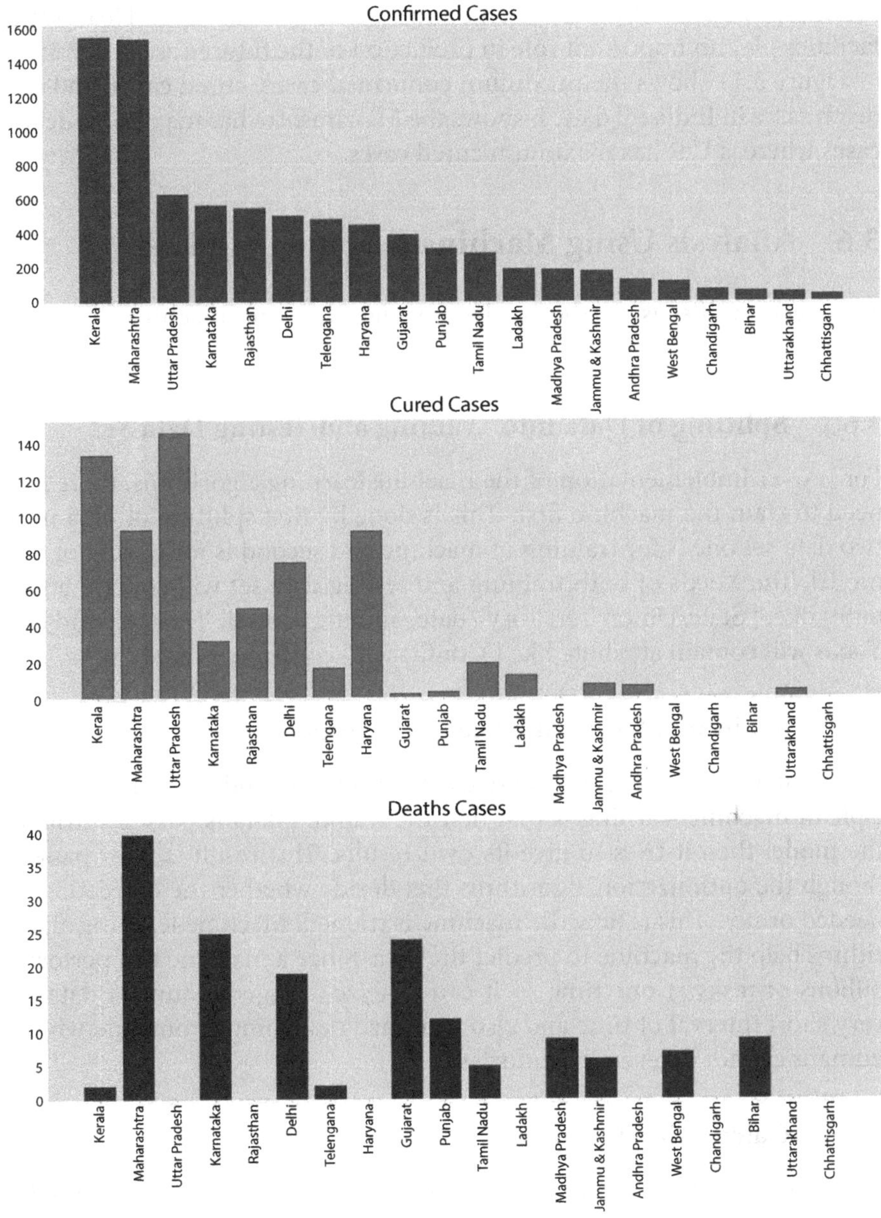

Figure 3.11 State wise confirmed/cured/death cases of COVID-19.

facilities; Maharashtra is at second and Karnataka is at third. Healthcare facilities play an important role in prediction of the future cases.

Figure 3.11 shows the maximum confirmed cases, cured cases, and the death cases in India till date. It shows the Maharashtra has maximum death cases whereas U.P. has maximum cured cases.

3.6 Analysis Using Machine Learning Models

This section discusses the analysis using different machine learning techniques.

3.6.1 Splitting of Data into Training and Testing Data Set

For proper implementation of the machine learning algorithms, there is a need to train the machine first. This is done by first splitting of data into two data set one is for training of machine and second is for testing of the model. The X axis of both training and testing data set will contain attributes like: ['State/Union Territory', 'date', 'month', 'Cured', 'Deaths'] and the Y axis will contain attribute like ['Confirmed'] confirmed cases.

3.6.2 Training of Machine Learning Models

In this, all the training data set are used to train the model. The basic principle of machine learning is that first the training data is passed through the model then it tries to give its own results. This result is then passed though the optimization algorithms that decide whether the correction is needed or not. This is how the machine is trained. Machine learning algorithms help the machine to predict the data. Since a machine can perform billions of tasks at one time so it can analyze a huge amount of data in very short interval of time and also can learn new things from data which humans cannot do even in centuries.

3.6.3 Calculating the Score

The main objective of the present work is to evaluate the algorithms in terms of accuracy, so, it becomes necessary to calculate the score of these algorithms. The score of accuracy is calculated by the sklearn matrices which contain r2score feature that makes calculation of score easy. The accuracy graph for all the algorithms are illustrated through Figure 3.12.

It can be observed from Figure 3.12 that the decision tree regression gives the best accuracy i.e. 96%, after that random forest gives 93% accuracy.

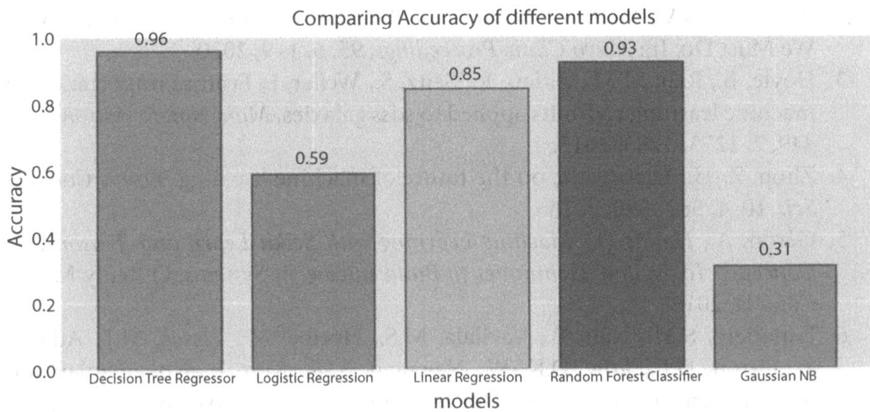

Figure 3.12 Comparison of accuracy of different models.

However, in our case, gaussian NB gives very less accuracy i.e. 31%. Both Logistics and Linear regression gives 59 and 85% of accuracy respectively. Since, the accuracy of linear regression and logistic regression are less than 90% there is a need for optimization of these algorithms.

3.7 Conclusion & Future Scope

The presented work discussed about the machine learning and different types of machine learning models exists like Linear regression, Logistic regression, K-NN, Decision tree, Random forest. This work also presented the analysis and predictions of India on different data for Covid-19 pandemic like number of confirmed, cured and death cases state wise, analysis on the basis of gender, number of primary health centers in a state and many more. This work also evaluated the accuracy of all mentioned algorithms for COVID-19 dataset. It is concluded that the Decision tree algorithm provides maximum accuracy i.e. 96% followed by Random forest algorithm which gives 93% accuracy. The work can be extended for new data set and with hybrid machine learning algorithms.

References

1. Khan, A., Baharudin, B., Lee, L.H., Khan, K., A review of machine learning algorithms for text-documents classification. *J. Adv. Inf. Technol.*, 1, 1, 4–20, 2010.

2. Rajkumar, S.V., Medication Shortages During the COVID-19 Crisis: What We Must Do. In: *Mayo Clinic Proceedings*, 95, 6, 1–9, 2020.
3. Hoyle, B., Rau, M.M., Zitlau, R., Seitz, S., Weller, J., Feature importance for machine learning redshifts applied to sdss galaxies. *Mon. Not. R. Astron. Soc.*, 449, 2, 1275–1283, 2015.
4. Zhou, Z.-H., Learnware: on the future of machine learning. *Front. Comput. Sci.*, 10, 4, 589–590, 2016.
5. Géron, A., *Hands-On Machine Learning with Scikit-Learn and TensorFlow: Concepts, Tools, and Techniques to Build Intelligent Systems*, O'Reilly Media, Canada, 2016.
6. Lundberg, S.M., Nair, B., Vavilala, M.S., Horibe, M., Eisses, M.J., Adams, T., Liston, D.E., Low, D.K.-W., Newman, S.-F., Kim, J. *et al.*, Explainable machine-learning predictions for the prevention of hypoxaemia during surgery. *Nat. Biomed. Eng.*, 2, 10, 749–760, 2018.
7. Freund, R.M., Grigas, P., Mazumder, R. *et al.*, A new perspective on boosting in linear regression via subgradient optimization and relatives. *Ann. Stat.*, 45, 6, 2328–2364, 2017.
8. Hosmer, D.W., Jr, Lemeshow, S., Sturdivant, R.X., *Applied Logistic Regression*, vol. 398, John Wiley & Sons, West Point, New York, 2013.
9. Daumé, H., III, Notes on CG and LM-BFGS optimization of logistic regression, *Paper available at http://pub. hal3. name# daume04cg-bfgs, implementation available at http://hal3. name/megam*, vol. 198, p. 282, 2004.
10. Barstugan, M., Ozkaya, U., Ozturk, S., Coronavirus (COVID-19) classification using CT images by machine learning methods. *arXivpreprintarXiv:2003.09424*, 2020.
11. Kumar, V.B., Kumar, S.S., Saboo, V., Dermatological disease detection using image processing and machine learning, in: *2016 Third International Conference on Artificial Intelligence and Pattern Recognition (AIPR)*, IEEE, pp. 1–6, 2016.
12. Burbidge, R., Trotter, M., Buxton, B., Holden, S., Drug design by machine learning: support vector machines for pharmaceutical data analysis. *Comput. Chem.*, 26, 1, 5–14, 2001.
13. Keskin, B.E., *Data science starter notebook with 3 ml algorithms*, 2020.
14. Ospina, J.E., Orcau, À, Millet, J.-P., Sánchez, F., Casals, M., Caylà, J.A., Community health workers improve contact tracing among immigrants with tuberculosis in Barcelona. *BMC Public Health*, 12, 1, 158, 2012.
15. Eichner, M., Case isolation and contact tracing can prevent the spread of smallpox. *Am. J. Epidemiol.*, 158, 2, 118–128, 2003.
16. Nickel, M., Murphy, K., Tresp, V., Gabrilovich, E., A review of relational machine learning for knowledge graphs. *Proc. IEEE*, 104, 1, 11–33, 2015.
17. Knoll, D., Prüglmeier, M., Reinhart, G., Predicting future inbound logistics processes using machine learning. *Proc. CIRP*, 52, 145–150, 2016.
18. Olu, O.O., Lamunu, M., Nanyunja, M., Dafae, F., Samba, T., Sempiira, N., Kuti-George, F., Abebe, F.Z., Sensasi, B., Chimbaru, A. *et al.*, Contact tracing

during an outbreak of ebola virus disease in the western area districts of Sierra Leone: Lessons for future ebola outbreak response. *Front. Public Health*, 4, 130, 2016.
19. Jiang, C., Zhang, H., Ren, Y., Han, Z., Chen, K.-C., Hanzo, L., Machine learning paradigms for next-generation wireless networks. *IEEE Wireless Commun.*, 24, 2, 98–105, 2016.
20. Zhu, X. and Goldberg, A.B., Introduction to semi-supervised learning. *Synth. Lect. Artif. Intell. Mach. Learn.*, 3, 1, 1–130, 2009.
21. VanderPlas, J., *Python Data Science Handbook*, O'Reilly Media, United States of America, 2016.
22. Barlow, H.B., Unsupervised learning. *Neural Comput.*, 1, 3, 295–311, 1989.
23. Chapelle, O., Scholkopf, B., Zien, A., Semi-supervised learning (Chapelle, O. *et al.*, eds.; 2006) [book reviews]. *IEEE Trans. Neural Networks*, 20, 3, 542–542, 2009.
24. Kaelbling, L.P., Littman, M.L., Moore, A.W., Reinforcement learning: A survey. *J. Artif. Intell. Res.*, 4, 237–285, 1996.
25. Ferrari, D. and Head, T., *Regression in R part I: Simple linear regression*, UCLA Department of Statistics-Statistical Consulting Center, Los Angles, California, 2010.
26. Sheather, S., *A modern approach to regression with R*. Springer Science & Business Media. Springer, TX, USA, 2009.
27. Tranmer, M. and Elliot, M., Multiple linear regression. The Cathie Marsh Centre for Census and Survey Research (CCSR), 5, 5, 1–5, 2008.
28. King, G. and Zeng, L., Logistic regression in rare events data. *Polit. Anal.*, 48, 1–27, 2001.
29. Valgaev, O., Kupzog, F., Schmeck, H., Low-voltage power demand forecasting using K-nearest neighbors approach. In *2016 IEEE Innovative Smart Grid Technologies-Asia (ISGT-Asia)*, IEEE, pp. 1019–1024, 2016.

4

Rapid Forecasting of Pandemic Outbreak Using Machine Learning

Sujata Chauhan[1*], Madan Singh[2†] and Puneet Garg[3‡]

[1]*Dronacharya Govt. College, Gurugram, India*
[2]*KIET Group of Institutions, Ghaziabad, India*
[3]*J.C. Bose University of Science and Technology, YMCA, Faridabad, India*

Abstract

Humans have faced a number of pandemics since the dawn of civilization, but today what we are facing is an invisible enemy novel COVID-19, causing the pandemic globally at an alarming rate, bringing a devastating effect on our lives and impacting our economy drastically. The infection in humans by COVID-19 was thought to be originally from bats perhaps as zoonotic agent (from animal to human) but the rapid increase in the figure of cases in Wuhan city and globally even after shutting the market off and quarantine whole city, indicated an alternative mode of transmission from human-to-human which is rarely observed in nature. The main objective of this chapter is to predict a rapid forecasting of pandemic outbreak using machine learning approaches. The chapter is based on a preliminary estimation about the disease, spread of disease across the globe, the possible ways of treatment, and prevention in its outbreak which makes use of technologies like machine learning which may prove beneficial to save the human race from pandemics like COVID19 in the future.

Keywords: COVID-19, India, rural areas, urban areas, machine learning

**Corresponding author*: sujatachauhan06@gmail.com
†*Corresponding author*: madan.singh@kiet.edu
‡*Corresponding author*: puneetgarg.er@gmail.com

Abhinav Juneja, Vikram Bali, Sapna Juneja, Vishal Jain and Prashant Tyagi (eds.) Enabling Healthcare 4.0 for Pandemics: A Roadmap Using AI, Machine Learning, IoT and Cognitive Technologies, (59–74) © 2021 Scrivener Publishing LLC

4.1 Introduction

Our civilization has faced a number of epidemic outbreaks like H1N1, SARS, MERS, EBOLA, Zika but of these, COVID-19 pandemic has affected the worldwide adversely in terms of loss of lives and irretrievable trauma it has caused to the society. COVID-19 was affirmed as a health crisis by World Health Organization (WHO) on February 2020 and soon it became greatest threat of the century to mankind. The zero case was detected in Wuhan, China in seafood whole sale market and quickly it became pandemic and spiraled all across the globe [1]. Sooner or later it exploded over all the continents except Antarctica. Subsequently WHO affirmed COVID-19 outburst as civic health emergency of international worry on 30 Jan 2020. This worldwide COVID-19 pandemic outbreak stirred a tragic wave of panic among the general masses owing to big numbers of fatalities, morbidities, and cost billions of dollars [2, 3].

SARS-CoV2 virus responsible for causing the COVID-19 belongs to Coronaviridae family, to which most of the viruses causing respiratory disorders belongs. SARS-CoV2 is the abbreviated form of Severe Acute Respiratory Syndrome-Corona Virus 2. SARS-CoV2 is thought to originate in the bat and transmitted to another animal probably Pangolin, which have infected humans [4]. Now it is being transmitted without animal intermediate i.e. Zoonotic transmission. The general symptoms of the virus include fever, sore throat, cough and breathlessness. SARS-CoV2 is a highly infectious virus and spread through respiratory and cough droplets [5]. Recently declared by World Health Organization, the virus may be airborne and it may persist in the air for a longer period of time accounting for the high rate of infection [6]. The pandemic has affected not only the lives of the masses but also the livelihood of the people. It has severed every section of the society. This remains the most adverse of the pandemic that has occurred in the history of mankind owing to the number of the lives it has claimed so far.

To combat the COVID-19 pandemic, many countries have adopted different kind of strategies like intermittent lockdowns, physical and social distancing, early detection, isolation and quarantine of COVID-19 patients, self quarantine of vulnerable sections of the society like children and old age people, people with medical illness, with compromised immune systems [7]. The razor-sharp rise in new-fangled infections and containment actions put in by governments has slowdown the transmission of the virus but nevertheless every nation is experiencing community transmission sooner or later. The development of an effective vaccine is the need of the hour. This article is divided into two halves. In the first half, we will try to summarize all the aspects of COVID-19 pandemic and how it has affected different sections of the society, then in the next half, we will discuss about the machine learning approaches which may be helpful in rapid forecasting of these kinds of pandemics in the future. Artificial Intelligence, machine learning and data science are some of the approaches which seem to be promising in dealing with pandemic situations like COVID-19.

4.2 Effect of COVID-19 on Different Sections of Society

4.2.1 Effect of COVID-19 on Mental Health of Elder People

Man is a social animal and depends on interaction with other people in the community for physical, social, mental and spiritual harmony [8]. As Corona virus pandemic quickly sweeps across the globe, it is revoking a considerable degree of anxiety, distress, and terror concern in the population at large particularly among older section of society with critical health conditions. Older people having weaker health and frail immune system are supposed to be more prone to infections. During these difficult times of COVID-19 when most of the countries are adopting certain preventive measures to save the lives of their people, people are going through tremendous levels of stress and apprehension. It has affected not only the physical health but their mental health as well. Due to implementation of social distancing and self quarantine strategies, people's usual routines and activities are disturbed. As the prolonged side effect of COVID-19 the levels of isolation and despair is expected to rise that may lead to alcohol and drug abuse. It may further lead to self-harm or suicidal tendencies. Their lives and livelihoods are affected adversely and their mental and spiritual harmony is at stake. The COVID-19 pandemic and economy downfall has negatively affected the people. Due to these unprecedented side effects of COVID-19 pandemic there is an alarming need to create awareness among people and psychological counseling of affected people.

4.2.2 Effect of COVID-19 on our Environment

Although COVID-19 has badly impacted our lives but still it has been proved bliss for our environment. The preventive measure adopted by many countries like lockdown has stopped smoke emission from the vehicles and industries has dropped down temporarily that has led to clean and improved environment. The levels of green house gases have decreased considerably. In India also, our honorable prime minister enforced lockdown twenty third March 2020 onwards. The lockdown forced people of India to sit inside their homes and allowed nature to flourish. Even birds and wild animals started to enjoy their freedom and they were captured roaming freely on the national highways by cameramen. Our holy river "Ganga" started to flow freely into the planes. Our nature is resurrecting well from the ill effects caused by the activities of human beings. Our air has become clean and purified. The quality of water has also improved. Rivers are also reviving and getting cleaned by their own. So surprisingly our nature has found a way to get back to its original form and shape. Although it is not a sustainable way to clean the environment, we need to look further for mitigating the ecosystem harmony.

4.2.3 Effect of COVID-19 on International Allies and Healthcare

Besides devastating effects of novel corona virus disease (COVID-19) on the human lives, it has also caused a major setback to the economy of many countries like China, USA, France, Germany, Italy, India. It is far more than a health crisis. At one end where many countries have joined their hands to fight against the pandemic by helping each other emotionally, financially and morally, the alliances between some nations are also at the brink during these times. China is facing boycott from USA and European Union. The economy is undergoing a slowdown phase worldwide. Countries like China have also tried to take illegal advantages of these situations by investing heavily into the economies of poor countries at these slowdown times. Due to these activities China is also facing public boycott by the international community. People are criticizing the country for two reasons. Firstly their country is birthplace of COVID-19 and secondly their country is taking illegal advantage of these hard times. COVID-19 has also put an extra burden on our healthcare infrastructure. Countries are bound to invest heavily on healthcare infrastructure and instruments. Deaths at mass level have caused healthcare systems to feel helpless, even in the developed countries like Italy, Spain, Denmark and many more. Semi-developed nations like India are also investing on healthcare at large level. Countries like India, Brazil who have leading population, are afraid of the situation and taking preventive measures at war-foot level.

4.2.4 Therapeutic Approaches Adopted by Different Countries to Combat COVID-19

Due to the highly contagious nature of virus spreading at an alarming rate among the communities and to contain the virus, a significant fraction of population needs to be immune to build the herd immunity. The herd immunity can be achieved either by vaccination as in most of the cases or a large section of people develop immunity by exposure to the virus. In the later case there are limitations like the death toll is high as compared to other common viral infections. It's higher still among vulnerable groups like the elderly, children and people with weakened immune systems. To achieve herd immunity in case of Sars-CoV2 at least 45–60% of population needs to be immune that is difficult to attain owing high mortality rate [9]. In absence of an effective vaccine or a drug and without clear knowledge of pathology of Sars-Cov2, it can prove fatal to achieve herd immunity by infection [10]. We need to take intermediate preventive measures to contain the virus like intermittent lockdowns, physical distancing at public places and quarantine of infected patients until a safe and effective vaccine is developed.

In the start of the pandemic, appropriate symptomatic treatment and supportive care was provided to the affected patients. Many of the patients were given oxygen therapy and plasma therapy including IgG (Immunoglobulin G) to some critical cases [12]. Chloroquine and hydroxychloroquine was found successful against COVID-19 [11, 12]. Drugs like remdesivir and chloroquine were very effective in the control SARS-CoV2 under *in vitro* conditions [13]. After the antibody serum is given, it remains effective in the recipient for at least three to four days. During this period, the sick person may recover. But transfusion plasma technique is a temporary solution of this problem and we need a safe and effective vaccine against this virus. Researchers and Scientists are working worldwide round the clock to develop a vaccine against SARS-CoV2. Normally the process of successful vaccine development takes about 12–18 months. Till date the first vaccine Sputnik-V developed by Russia got approval for human use was on 11 August 2020. The other three candidate vaccines for COVID-19 under trial phase 3 are being developed by USA in collaboration.

4.2.5 Effect of COVID-19 on Labor Migrants

Migrant workers during COVID-19 pandemic have undergone through a large no of hardships worldwide. Most of the daily wage laborers lost their livelihoods due to lockdown in response to COVID-19 [8]. Due to shut down of workplaces during lockdown in lieu of COVID-19 pandemic a large population lost their lives and livelihoods. It particularly affected the laborers who had to migrate to their hometown due to loss of their jobs, shortage of food and financial insecurities. They had to undergo the trauma of uncertainty about their future. Thousands of them were forced to walk back home on foot in absence of transport due to the initial lockdowns imposed by the government as a precautionary measure to contain the pandemic. On the other hand, due to the movement of labor towards their homes, industries are facing shortage of skilled labor in after-lockdown phase. Industries are forced to cope up with semi-skilled or fresher laborers only. The effect of this can be seen in the form of delayed product delivery. Even the migrant labor, who have gone to their homes are facing big challenges to their livelihood. They are not getting good jobs in proximity to their homes and the salaries are also not that good. In India state governments like Bihar, Bengal, and Uttar Pradesh have big challenges to provide good jobs to the migrants.

4.2.6 Impact of COVID-19 on our Economy

COVID-19 pandemic has swept our economy very rapidly. The spill of COVID-19 brought a downfall of global economy. A health crisis translated into economic crisis. It led to the complete or partial shutdown of corporate offices, financial markets and trade businesses. In India also we were moving towards five trillion economies in a shorter time span before the pandemic but it has been delayed due to COVID-19.

Due to COVID-19 pandemic that has gone up in 200+ countries, the economy all around the globe has been crippled badly. The COVID-19 pandemic has pushed the whole world on the brink of recession and loss of humankind. It is more than a mere financial crisis and a health crisis. The irreparable damage mounted by this pandemic is an eye opener that raises serious concerns about the condition of healthcare infrastructure of most advanced nations and its vigilance to combat such kinds of pandemic in future.

4.3 Definition and Types of Machine Learning

Machine learning [18], is a technique in which, a computer program learns some tasks and performs them with experience. In this process the performance of the program to perform that task is improved. It is well known that machine learning is an appliance of Artificial Intelligence (AI) which supports structure to perform robotically in order to become skilled at a task to improve on the basis of experience without taking any help of such explicit programming. It is an important aspect which deals with data sets and provides predictions under bounded environment.

4.3.1 Machine Learning & Its Types

There are three different types of machine learning as shown in Figure 4.1, which are as follows:

1. Supervised Machine Learning
2. Unsupervised Machine Learning
3. Reinforcement Machine Learning.

Supervised Learning: This type of learning consists of a set of variables i.e. dependent variables and independent variables. Aim of learning has been to predict the target variable from independent variable which also known as predictors [19]. With help of these variables, mapping of inputs to expected outputs is done through function. In order to perform mapping, function is generated. Until model is capable to attain expected accuracy on data which is undergoing training, the training process continues. There are a variety of examples of supervised learning like Decision trees, KNN, Regression, Logistic Regression and Random Forest etc. It's a course to predict target variables from independent variables. There are two algorithms for supervised learning which are as follows:

- Classification
- Regression.

Classification

The process of assigning new, previously unseen instances of a data set to a predefined class based on training provided from past data is called as

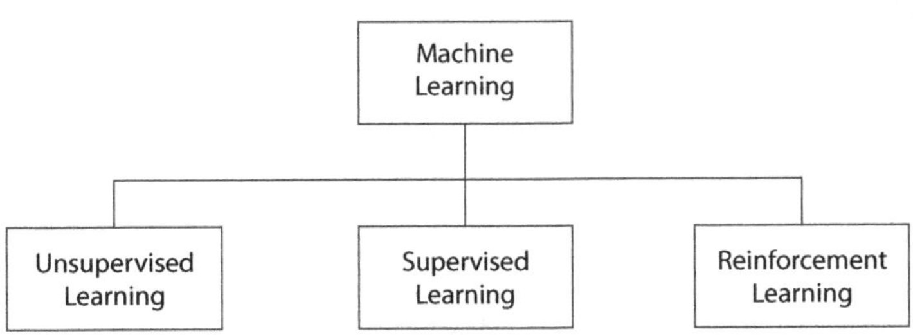

Figure 4.1 Machine Learning & its types.

classification. In general we use text classification, which can be further categorized into binary classification, multiclass classification etc.

Text classification or text categorization uses classification algorithm which is used to learn and predict best possible class for each and every document. In binary classification there exist only two classes. Any document belongs to either of these two classes. Examples of binary classification are—spam filtering, simple sentiments analysis, etc. in multiclass classification, more than two classes exist. Each document belongs to exactly one class. It can be further classified into ordinal and non-ordinal classification. Figures 4.2 and 4.3 represent binary and multi - class classification pictorially.

Text classification process follows a number of steps namely—data gathering, data cleaning, re-sampling, training and testing. In this process first of all, required data elements are collected and they are kept together. This phase is termed as data gathering. After this process irrelevant fields from the collected data sets are removed and data set is made to be optimized. This phase of the process persists of utmost importance because if we are not going to optimize the data then we need to perform the further processing along with the larger data set which increases the computational complexity. This computational complexity can be resolved with the help of data cleaning process. After data cleaning, re-sampling process takes place. In this process data set is properly organized into the chunks of information to be processed. This phase is further followed by training and

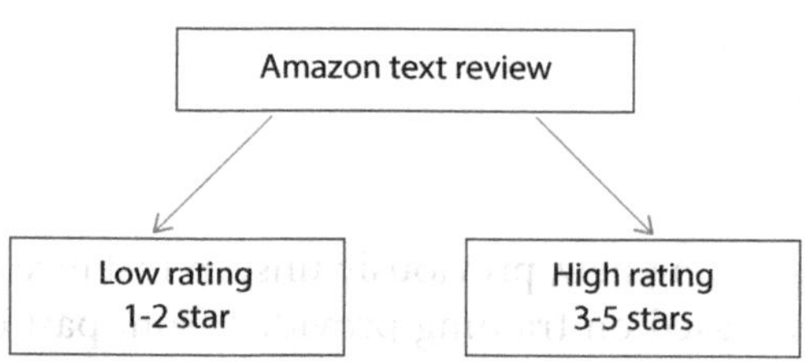

Figure 4.2 Binary classification.

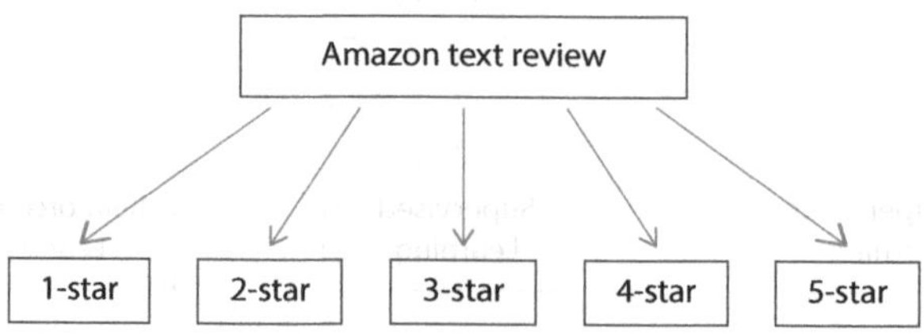

Figure 4.3 Multi-class classification.

Figure 4.4 Steps followed in text classification process.

testing phases which are used as a main step towards supervised learning. Figure 4.4 represents the steps followed in text classification process.

Regression

The relationship between dependent input variables to output variables is estimated by technique termed as regression. It provides a clear cut picture about variations in dependent variable in correspondence with the independent variable [21]. Output variable is of real or continuous value. Regression Analysis is a method to approximation the relations between the dependent variables and independent variables or predictors. It briefs about the changes in criterions in accordance to changes made in select predictors. The prime importance of regression analysis is in—figuring out the power of predictors, forecasting an effect and trend forecasting. Some of the types of Regression are—"Linear regression, Logistic regression, Polynomial regression, Stepwise regression, Ridge regression, Lasso regression and Elastic Net regression". The linear regression works on the conditional probability distribution of the responses. The logistic regression is applied to handle data with two possible criterions and the connection stuck between the criterions and the predictors. The polynomial regression is applied for curvilinear data. The stepwise regression is applied for apt regression models along with predictive models. It is performed by design. At every stride, the variable is amended from fixed bunch of explanatory variables. The ridge regression used for analyzing multiple regression data. The lasso regression is used for performing both variable selection and regularization. The elastic Net regression is used to linearly join the penalties of the lasso and ridge methods.

Unsupervised Learning: In unsupervised learning, machine is passed with inputs but it does not get any targets or rewards from the environment [24, 30]. It is one of the normal learning techniques. It is the preparation of machine by means of bunch of data elements without classifications and labels such as to allow the algorithm to take steps on that information without any particular guidance. Task assigned to machine is to unite unsorted information in accordance with matching similarities, patterns and differences without any prior training of data. Teacher is not available there due to which no training is provided to the machine. So, machine is restricted to locate the unknown composition in unlabeled data. Clustering works in same way of learning where similar instances of items are grouped all together into different clusters. In this algorithm, there is no target to estimate. Unsupervised learning can be classified as – Parametric Unsupervised learning and Non-Parametric Unsupervised learning. Some of the examples of unsupervised learning are K-Means and Apriori algorithms etc. [20, 22, 23, 26–29].

Reinforcement Learning: Reinforcement learning based machine interacts with its environment. It results in machine getting some rewards from the environment in the form of feedback of its performance [25, 31]. In this learning, training is provided to machine to take some particular decisions. Machine is making use of past experiences and tries to get best knowledge to improve decision capability. It is all about intriguing appropriate feat to make best use of recompense in a meticulous situation. It is engaged by software and machines to discover the finest probable path which is taken in a scrupulous situation. The reinforcement learning is not same as supervised learning. In supervised learning training data possess answer key with itself with the intention that the model can be trained with correct answer itself where as in the reinforcement learning, there exist no answer but instead the reinforcement agent decides the task to get specific results. In the absence of a training dataset, it requires to learn from its experience. Example: Markov Decision Process etc.

4.3.2 Applications of Machine Learning

Following are the application areas of Machine Learning:

- *Image Recognition:* The most common usage of machine algorithm is Image Recognition. For face detection and character detection, ML plays an important role in recognizing the images.
- *Speech Recognition:* It is process of translating spoken words into text. It is known by many names like ASR, CSR, and STT etc.
- *Medical Diagnosis:* In medical domains, ML found very useful in prognostic and diagnostic problems like as health map.
- *Prediction:* For prediction purpose, ML fulfills it nicely. Like—Prediction of weather, Probability of faults etc.
- *Video Surveillance:* Through AI, it becomes possible to detect crime before they take place.
- *Social Media Services:* Face book, Twitter etc. social sites making use of machine learning concepts.

4.4 Machine Learning Approaches for COVID-19

Machine learning mechanisms [17] have proven to be a vital tool in prediction and prevention of COVID-19. They are among the best approaches to deal with situations like this. At one end, they help in predictions whereas on the other hand they help to prepare in a better way. Some of the main helping mechanisms have been mentioned below.

4.4.1 Enabling Organizations to Regulate and Scale

In the era of COVID-19, public distancing has become need of the hour. It is one of the influential ways to break the chain of infection [13]. Wearing mask and washing hands time to time are some of the other measures. In the pandemic times, organizations and institutes have also found new ways to operate effectively. Machine Learning techniques are making the organizations comfortable in shifting by providing tools to support pandemic situations. Healthcare and government agencies are using machine learning in area wise predictions and providing solutions which are most convenient for contactless pandemics handling and to answer questions from the public.

4.4.2 Understanding About COVID-19 Infections

Machine learning [18] is serving the research community and practitioners to investigate huge data volumes to project the increase of COVID-19, to operate like a forewarning system for impending pandemics and to spot exposed populations. Quantity of COVID-19 infected people can be estimated with the help of sculpts, built by researchers. These are also helpful in analysis of various segments across the globe. People have developed and prepared new techniques to detect infections and analysis of virus life cycle. Researchers are able to identify how virus matures and spreads through the population with the help of machine learning based approaches.

4.4.3 Gearing Up Study and Finding Treatments

After the reporting of very first cases on COVID-19, the amount of information available is increasing day by day. The geared up study and exponentially growing data about the pandemic is proving to be helpful at a large level. With the help of machine learning it will be easier to find the medicines to treat COVID-19 [14]. Machine learning can find out the risk of an explicit person or group infected with COVID-19 referred as infectivity risk. It is also helpful in predicting the risk of severe pandemic symptoms requiring hospitalization or intensive care referred as sternness risk. It is also helpful in predicting death ratio of individual or group of people. It is referred as upshot risk. In this way machine learning is being helpful in predicting all three sorts of risks. This forecasting and prediction capabilities of machine learning are making it a game changer in the field of treatments for the pandemic situation.

4.4.4 Predicting Treatment and Healing Outcomes

Better predictions can result to better treatments. In the line of this thought machine learning has become one of the essential aspects of predictions of life and death. A patient survival from the pandemic can be predicted with the help of machine learning. If certain symbols are known at the early phase of patient's sickness then there exist more chances of survival of the patient. As we cannot treat all the patients in the same way, machine learning can be proven to be helpful in prediction of a separate treatment in accordance to the patient [15]. As cure options for COVID-19 are still sprouting, machine learning can easily be applied in predicting outcomes for specific treatments.

4.4.5 Testing Patients and Diagnosing COVID-19

Diagnosing any individual is a challenging task, when a new pandemic hits. Large scale testing is difficult and it is very expensive in the beginning due to lack of testing kits available. It remains very tough to even identify the symptoms because there is always lesser information about those symptoms and effects of the disease [16]. Machine learning based approaches are beneficial to collect data at a cheaper and effective rate. This data can be used for further predictions. As far as machine learning is concerned regarding help in diagnose of COVID-19, following are the promising research areas:

- Patient screening using face scans
- Applying wearable techniques to keep a watch on the patients
- Using chat bots for screening and diagnosis
- Fastening drug development
- Building biomedical knowledge graphs through research analysis
- Finding out how to attack the virus and finish it.

References

1. Huang, C., Wang, Y., Li, X., Ren, L., Zhao, J., Hu, Y. *et al.*, Clinical features of patientsinfected with 2019 novel coronavirus in Wuhan, China. *Lancet*, 395, 497–506, 2020, https://doi.org/10.1016/S0140-6736(20)30183-5.
2. Allocati, N., Petrucci, A.G., Di Giovanni, P. *et al.*, Bat-man disease transmission: Zoo-notic pathogens from wildlife reservoirs to human populations. *Cell Death Dis.*, 2, 16048, 2016.
3. Fan, Y., Zhao, K., Shi, Z.L. *et al.*, Bat coronaviruses in China. *Viruses*, 11, 210, 2019.
4. Gorbalenya, A.E., Baker, S.C., Baric, R.S., de Groot, R.J., Drosten, C., Gulyaeva, A.A., Severe acute respiratory syndrome related coronavirus: The species and its viruses—A statement of the Coronavirus Study Group. BioRxiv, 1, 1–20, 2020, https://doi.org/10.1038/s41564-020-0695-z.
5. Wang, C., Horby, P.W., Hayden, F.G., Gao, G.F., A novel coronavirus outbreak of global health concern. Lancet, 395, 470–473, 2020b.
6. Riou, J. and Althaus, C.L., Pattern of early human-to-human transmission of Wuhan 2019 novel coronavirus (2019-nCoV), December 2019 to January 2020. Eurosurveillance, 25, 4, 1–6, 2020.
7. Hong Kong protesters torch planned Wuhan virus quarantine building, CNA, Archived from the Reuters on 6 February 2020.
8. Chakraborty, I. and Maity, P., COVID-19 outbreak: Migration, effects on society, global environment and prevention. *Sci. Total Environ.*, 728, 1–7, 2020.
9. Kwok, *et al.*, Herd immunity—Estimating the level required to halt the COVID-19 epidemics in affected countries. *J. Infect.*, 80, e32–e33, 2020.
10. Hills, C., Hong Kong epidemiologist warns pandemic's end may not be straightforward: Public Radio International PRI, by world staff, 2020.
11. Rolain, J.M., Colson, P., Raoult, D., Recycling of chloroquine and its hydroxyl ana-logue to face bacterial, fungal and viral infections in the 21st century. *Int. J. Antimicrob. Agents*, 30, 297–308, 2007, https://doi.org/10.1016/j.ijantimicag.2007.05.015.
12. World Health Organization, Clinical Management of Severe Acute Respiratory Infection When Novel Coronavirus (2019-nCoV) Infection Is Suspected: Interim Guidance, pp. 1–10, WHO, 2020.
13. Wang, M., Cao, R., Zhang, L., Yang, X., Liu, J., Xu, M. *et al.*, Remdesivir and chloro-quine effectively inhibit the recently emerged novel coronavirus (2019-nCoV) *in vitro*. *Cell Res.*, 30, 3, 269–271, 2020a, https://doi.org/10.1038/s41422-020-0282-0.
14. Maaten, L.V.D. and Hinton, G., Visualizing data using t-SNE. *J. Mach. Learn. Res.*, 9, Nov, 2579–2605, 2008.

15. Jain, A.K., Data clustering: 50 years beyond K-means. *Pattern Recognit. Lett.*, 31, 8, 651–666, 2010.
16. Kotsiantis, S.B., Zaharakis, I., Pintelas, P., Supervised machine learning: A review of classification techniques, in: *Emerging Artificial Intelligence Applications in Computer Engineering*, vol. 160, pp. 3–24, 2007.
17. Zhang, Y., Jin, R., Zhou, Z.H., Understanding bag-of-words model: A statistical framework. *Int. J. Mach. Learn. Cybern.*, 1, 1–4, 43–52, 2010.
18. Singh, M., Chauhan, N., Popli, R., Machine Learning based Backlog Prioritization Techniques in Distributed Agile Software Development. *Int. J. Adv. Sci. Technol.*, 29, 06, 8699–8704, 2020.
19. Denton, E.L. and Birodkar, V., Unsupervised learning of disentangled representations from video, in: *Advances in Neural Information Processing Systems*, pp. 4414–4423, 2017.
20. Fraccaro, M., Kamronn, S., Paquet, U., Winther, O., A disentangled recognition and nonlinear dynamics model for unsupervised learning, in: *Advances in Neural Information Processing Systems*, pp. 3601–3610, 2017.
21. Goroshin, R., Mathieu, M.F., LeCun, Y., Learning to linearize under uncertainty, in: *Advances in Neural Information Processing Systems*, pp. 1234–1242, 2015.
22. Higgins, I., Sonnerat, N., Matthey, L., Pal, A., Burgess, C.P., Bošnjak, M., Shanahan, M., Botvinick, M., Hassabis, D., Lerchner, A., Scan: Learning hierarchical compositional visual concepts, in: *International Conference on Learning Representations*, 2018.
23. Hinton, G.E., Krizhevsky, A., Wang, S.D., Transforming auto-encoders, in: *International Conference on Artificial Neural Networks*, Springer, pp. 44–51, 2011.
24. Hyvarinen, A. and Morioka, H., Unsupervised feature extraction by time-contrastive learning and nonlinear ICA, in: *Advances in Neural Information Processing Systems*, pp. 3765–3773, 2016.
25. Jutten, C. and Karhunen, J., Advances in nonlinear blind source separation, in: *Proc. of the 4th Int. Symp. on Independent Component Analysis and Blind Signal Separation (ICA2003)*, pp. 245–256, 2003.
26. Karaletsos, T., Belongie, S., Rätsch, G., Bayesian representation learning with oracle constraints. arXiv preprint arXiv:1506.05011, 2015.
27. Kim, H. and Mnih, A., Disentangling by factorising, in: Proceedings of the 35th International Conference on Machine Learning, pp. 2649–2658, 2018.
28. Kingma, D.P. and Welling, M., Auto-encoding variational bayes, in: *International Conference on Learning Representations*, 2014.
29. Kulkarni, T.D., Whitney, W.F., Kohli, P., Tenenbaum, J., Deep convolutional inverse graphics network, in: *Advances in Neural Information Processing Systems*, pp. 2539–2547, 2015.
30. Kumar, A., Sattigeri, P., Balakrishnan, A., Variational inference of disentangled latent concepts from unlabeled observations, in: *International Conference on Learning Representations*, 2017.

31. Challenging Common Assumptions in the Unsupervised Learning of Disentangled Representations, Ridgeway, K., Mozer, M.C., Learning deep disentangled embeddings with the f-statistic loss, in: *Advances in Neural Information Processing Systems*, pp. 185–194, 2018.

5

Rapid Forecasting of Pandemic Outbreak Using Machine Learning: The Case of COVID-19

Nishant Jha and Deepak Prashar*

Computer Science & Engineering, Lovely Professional University, Phagwara (Punjab), India

Abstract

Some huge scope outside impact pandemics has risen in the course of the most recent two decades, including human, natural life, and plant plagues. Authorities face strategy issues that are reliant on deficient information and require sickness gauges. In this manner, there is an earnest need to create models that empower us to outline all accessible information to estimate and screen an advancing pandemic in an ideal way. This chapter targets assessing different models and proposing an early-cautioning AI approach that can conjecture potential flare-ups of ailments. For gauge COVID-19 episodes, the SEIR model, molecule channel calculation and an assortment of pandemic-related datasets are utilized to investigate different models and strategies. In this chapter, various intermediaries have been clarified for the pandemic season prompting comparative conduct of the powerful multiplication number. We found that a solid relationship exists among conferences and analyzed datasets, particularly when considering time based models. Singular parameters gave like distinctive episode seasons esteems, in this way offering an open door for future flare-ups to utilize such data.

Keywords: COVID-19, SEIR, particle filter, reproduction number, machine learning, epidemic

**Corresponding author*: deepak.prashar@lpu.co.in

Abhinav Juneja, Vikram Bali, Sapna Juneja, Vishal Jain and Prashant Tyagi (eds.) Enabling Healthcare 4.0 for Pandemics: A Roadmap Using AI, Machine Learning, IoT and Cognitive Technologies, (75–90) © 2021 Scrivener Publishing LLC

5.1 Introduction

Pandemic illnesses are irresistible infections that can be circulated the nation over if the computation of the virus has surpassed the purpose of a plague and will clear out the entire population [1–3]. There are a few noticeable episodes of pestilences that have happened everywhere throughout the world, for example, dengue, yellow fever, cholera, COVID-19, diphtheria, measles, fledgling influenza and numerous others. This irresistible disease has caused pivotal issues in open prosperity and was accepted to be one of the key causes that caused the overall loss of 43% of life. India has just observed a portion of the flare-ups of irresistible ailments like dengue, hepatitis, chikungunya and some more. The ongoing episode of COVID-19 is additionally a significant reason for stress. Illnesses like Diphtheria can make the host experience nerve irritation, loss of motion and draining problems [4]. The transmission typically happened by close contact and contaminated soil. All things considered, the anomaly of immunizations was additionally suspected to have caused this sickness. Pandemics represent a grave danger. COVID-19 isn't the first, or the last. Artificial Intelligence (AI) has demonstrated value in numerous zones of hazard to executives. AI is hypothetically significant in three primary zones, including direct clinical hazard. The threat of contamination: What is the opportunity of having COVID-19 for a particular individual or gathering? Force hazard: What is the probability of having genuine COVID-19 manifestations or confusions that would require hospitalization or serious consideration of a particular patient or gathering? Result hazard: What is the probability that a particular drug will be fruitless for a specific patient or gathering, and how likely they will bite the dust? AI may hypothetically help with anticipating every one of the three dangers [7]. While it is still too soon to have finished and distributed any COVID-19-explicit AI work, early outcomes are extremely encouraging. We can likewise take a gander at exactly how AI is utilized in related territories, and figure how this can help with COVID-19 early discovery. Beginning reports propose that huge hazard factors that choose the likelihood of an individual contracting COVID-19 incorporate age, prior conditions, general prepping practices, social conduct, measure of human contacts, the seriousness of contacts, spot and condition, financial status. Work on the dangers of the worldwide pandemic is likewise in its beginning periods. DeCapprio *et al.* [8] implemented Machine Learning (ML) to make an initial Vulnerability Index for COVID-19. Interference interventions such as sporting hats, laundry hands and social distancing are possible measure at this situation. As additional and higher knowledge is out there and findings square measure being generated by current trials, we are going to undoubtedly see additional realistic ML implementations for predicting the danger of infection. Once a private or cluster is contaminated we are going to foresee the probability that the person or cluster could experience symptoms or want emergency medical attention. Some patients have solely minor symptoms, and a few have serious respiratory organ failure, or Acute Metastasis Distress Syndrome (ARDS), that is probably fatal. It's unfeasible to diagnose and track anyone with moderate symptoms closely, however if additional serious symptoms are expected to occur, it's a lot easier to begin medical care early. Researchers additionally revealed a piece demonstrating that ML will on paper forecast the chance of a patient getting respiratory illness additionally because of the risk of death, just by gazing at the initial symptoms. The researchers acknowledge the constraints of this analysis "The scale of the sample could be a vital limitation of this review; fifty three patients with some missing knowledge additionally as a restricted severity vary." However, the study provides the precious groundwork for implementing ML as additional knowledge is out there. Associate growth of the estimation of seriousness is foretelling the results of the procedure and is additionally merely a matter of foretelling life and death. Clearly, with different signs, it would be useful to find out however possible a patient is to recover. However, in the prime of that, it is necessary to be connected in mind that not all patients get constant care.

If we are able to foresee the consequences of various kinds of treatment therefore physicians can treat patients a lot expeditiously. Victimization of ML to tailor care plans isn't distinctive to COVID-19, though traditionally, ML was accustomed to forecast clinical outcomes for patients with brain disorder, jointly example. Researchers have additionally used ML to model therapy reactions to cancer. Since treatment decisions for COVID-19 square measure are still rising, it's going to most likely be a challenging situation before we tend to see ML applied to predict effects for various treatments. Nevertheless, result estimation remains a vital facet of risk management, operational hand in hand with the forecasts of infection and seriousness we tend to mention higher than. Such variables could contribute through the classification of options to the popularity, diagnosis, prediction and management of the sickness and due to the convergence of the functions, the agglomeration of the apps. Agglomeration approach of those options can contribute to the less precise and preliminary identification and prediction of the communicable disease. Therefore, during this chapter work has been done on the optimum outcome of the mixing of clustered options is enforced with the tactic of back propagation which will classify and compare the factors influencing unfold of the infectious disease [5, 6].

5.2 Related Work

Growing numbers of researchers have applied empirical investigation studies on infectious diseases to enhance current structures and develop new models [9]. Studies on the detection of infectious diseases mistreatment massive knowledge like net search queries area units presently among these. Search knowledge on the net is often collected and processed at a speed that's on the brink of time period. Net search technology will turn out police investigation knowledge a lot simpler than ancient police investigation systems, in keeping with Towers *et al.* As such, additionally to forecasts in a very variety of different analysis fields, researchers have used Twitter proof to forecast infectious disease. One of the work by Shin *et al.*, especially, according to high correlations between infectious diseases and twitter knowledge. Future use of digital police investigation systems for observation infectious diseases is possible. Once considering these factors, the employment of search question knowledge and large knowledge from social media can have a helpful impact on forecasts of infectious diseases. Samples of communicable disease prediction are obtainable, supported environmental factors like weather. Past analysis has shown that weather knowledge may be a predictor that features an important impact on communicable disease activity. Liang and Wang have inferred that rainfall and temperature are risk factors for a renal condition hemorrhagic fever followed by the work done by Huang and Wang mentioning that dengue fever statistics show a strong correlation between temperature and humidity [10]. Sujatha *et al.* [15] presented a method for COVID-19 prevention using regression analysis. They have taken Multilayer Perceptron (MLP) and Vector autoregression model on COVID-19 using the Kaggle data. They used an AI model designed for past SARS dataset that reveals additional promise for potential scourge predictions. Sujath *et al.* [11] described COVID-19, named by the World Health Organization (WHO), as an early-stage destination through machine learning strategies. CT scans pictures updated on the stomach. Elmousalami and Hassanien [12] present on COVID-19 influenced cases of correlation of day level gauging models using time series models. Rizk-Allah and Hassanien [13] used another model for COVID-19 assessment. de Abajo *et al.* [14] introduced an approach to the situation of predicting assurances of medical clinics in Madrid every day due to respiratory and circulatory cases dependent on biometeorological markers. Cui and Singh [16] developed and applied the MRE hypothesis with spectral power as a random variable for the month to month stream flow prediction. Torky and Hassanien [17] introduced a block chain built-in structure that investigates the possibility of COVID-19 infections. Rates of involvement and response are very significant in epidemiological surveys. Accordingly, the right methodologies are required to ensure a sufficient response rate with minimal testing bias. Respondents also focus their decision on self-medical diagnoses on a variety of questions; this is considered a significant factor of epidemiological research because it promotes pandemic prevention measures through self-management activities and limited access to healthcare facilities, thereby helping to suppress viral spread [17]. Koo *et al.* [18] considered surveys to have valuable knowledge on key epidemiological influenza based parameters are of great interest by the use of surveys to recognize multiple differences that are absent from diverse viewpoints.

Nsoesie *et al.* [19] in light of observational investigations expected to anticipate flu flare-ups at a neighborhood, provincial, national or worldwide level in one of the ongoing complete examinations of the flu scourge elements gauging. The efficient examination tends to various models, including time arrangement models, non-parametric figures (utilized in meteorology), SIR and SEIR models. Any of these models utilize recorded proof, just as other ongoing flu related factors. Specialists utilized different procedures to break down the expectations exactness. To assess the normal qualities against the genuine qualities, a few specialists use relationship analysis. Certain devices utilized included rate errors, Root Mean Squared Error (RMSE), extent of precise predictions, and time periods. By utilizing different data sources, authentic records, models and procedures, one can try to create determining techniques. Analysts are endeavoring to utilize a blend of measurable, displaying, and streamlining techniques to anticipate a pandemic curve by utilizing past plague parameter esteems. The utilization of different methodologies can help flu conjectures and can end up being the route forward continuously estimating, furnishing the right speculations alongside solid datasets. So as to follow a valuable methodology and model with fitting methodologies, it is imperative to fuse the prescribed procedures to figure influenza. Through the above literature it is evident that many researchers are working in the direction for COVID-19 and we also try to provide some solution in the same direction.

5.3 Suggested Methodology

The proposed approach for the classification can be achieved through the back propagation concept. The method of propagation is the standard process and can be efficiently utilize for the same. The back propagation can be effectively

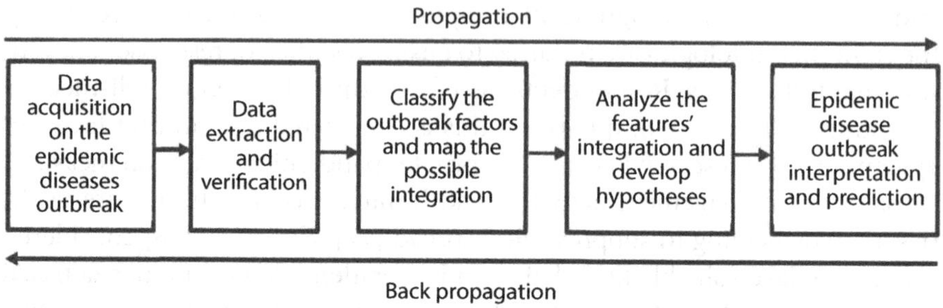

Figure 5.1 Illustration of Back propagation [20].

utilized for the classification purpose. ML methods are already used in disease prediction. Finding and spreading of disease by cross-validation can be done using training data of the infectious diseases using back propagation method. The method of back propagation would then classify multiple major factors which caused the infectious disease to spread. After that these factors will be considered in to account and then analyzed which classifier correlation is best one to operate [20]. The data collection used for this analysis is the Electronic Health History which is the clinical history of the patient and has also been adopted for monitoring, data management and clustering purposes by nearly all health institutions in the developing nations.

The proportion of the infected population in a particular region will be determined by creating the area as a matrix and specifying the target area as the grid cells with the number of days to be chosen and the area to be analyzed. From this contagious disease prediction, the infectious proportion of the disease can be analyzed and foreseen if the infectious disease outbreak percentage rating is unchanged or decreases over a surveillance period of more than 7 days. If the infections have some continuations, the particular area may be quarantined, and then desired actions pertaining to the government guidelines can be applied. Figure 5.1 shows the data that can be predicted with back propagation [20].

Computer Vision-based on Python and Deep Learning libraries can be used for software creation and testing. In this method, we are using software like Anaconda Python, and libraries like Tensorflow, and Keras for effective analysis.

5.4 Models in Epidemiology

The emergence of models to predict diseases have originated throughout the eighteenth century by Bernoulli to analyze the effectiveness of

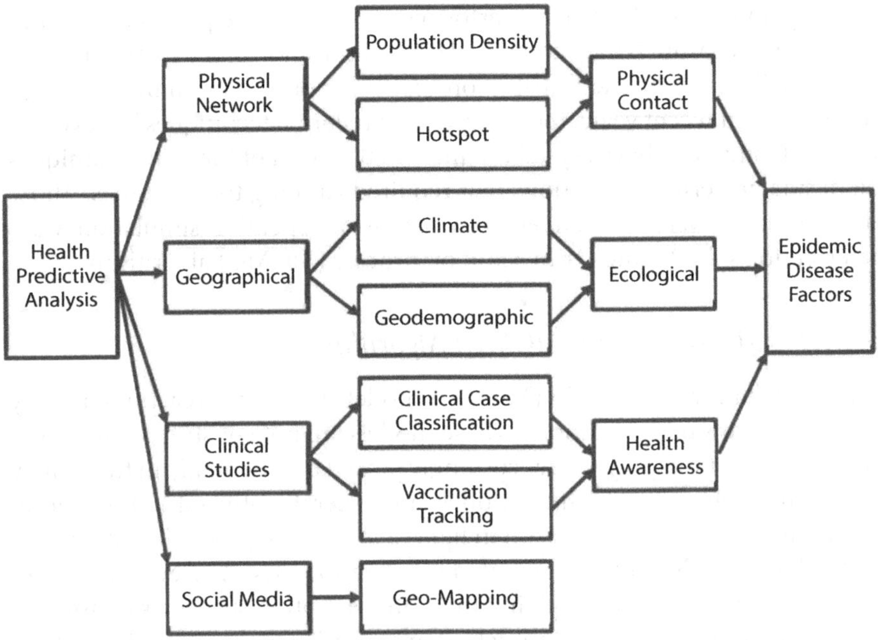

Figure 5.2 Correlation between health predictive analysis and epidemic disease factors [20].

England's mathematical methodologies against smallpox. Solely till the late nineteenth century did different researchers once more study mathematical medical specialty. Mathematical models exist to form the accessible proof a lot relevant by providing the calculation of malady parameters to think about the character and regulation of infectious diseases. Medical-based mathematical models provide the opportunity for predicting medical specialty dynamics, although there are large amount of uncertainties found in numerous medical specialty data; completely different ways exist for calculating the amount of individuals affected by numerous model compartments at various time spots (Figure 5.2).

5.4.1 Bayesian Inference Models

In the field of mathematical statistics, theorem illation or probability illation is of essential importance. This technique is currently utilized in a good type of mathematical areas and can be used extensively during this analysis. The theorem illation needs sampling models that, given the model's parameters, generate the chance to perform alongside a conditional distribution of the information. The theorem approach takes the previous distribution on model parameters. The chance performance and also the previous distribution square measure is then combined by the utilization of the mathematician theorem. This can be the distribution that every one theorem illation originates from. In recent years, the utilization of theorem techniques has evolved rapidly. Computers have crystal rectifiers to the event of theorem techniques alongside powerful applications that required running these models. Those developments were well added to a listing of repetitive simulation ways referred to as the Monte Carlo Mark off process (MCMC) algorithms.

5.4.1.1 Markov Chain (MCMC) Algorithm

Markov Chain Monte Carlo (MCMC) models have a far reaching activity and use in various applications. These models are not constrained to a little scope of executions and have accordingly picked up essentially in the money and gaming enterprises. These models are generally utilized in the field of the study of disease transmission in light of absence of proof. The utilization of MCMC models where fragmented information exists is viewed as a typical approach, in this way applying the right ascription strategies to 'top off' the missed openings. These models along with Bayesian worldview offer a capacity to handle the issue of missing information by including additional parameters into the model. Utilizing these MCMC models, the comprehension of epidemiological flare-ups has been extended as they offer more detail to explain the causes, pathogens and key parameters of an outbreak. Likewise, this data is exceptionally important for strategies for guideline, arrangement producers and activities in wellbeing. Parameter estimation for sickness conjectures by such MCMC models is of prime significance. Earlier disseminations in these scientific models may essentially impact the exactness of numerous Bayes variables and in these manner impact expectations for outbreaks. MCMC models are fundamentally significant for understanding appraisals of the transmission parameter between different phases of an outbreak. Obtaining right parameter esteems would likewise support the compartmental stochastic epidemiologic models. There have been numerous endeavors to streamline the MCMC calculations so that non-specialists can actualize them straightforwardly. That is to the drawback of having a diminished number of parameters.

5.5 Particle Filtering Algorithm

Particle filter algorithms are a unit unremarkably used for developing prediction processes and predictions of the parameters. Substantial studies use these algorithms that are a unit best-known to be the gold commonplace strategies of mathematical modeling. These algorithms provide a capability to recursively variables and also mention that how to use inferential techniques on parameters of the model. These strategies embrace easy Particle Filter (PF), most probability estimation through Markov particle chinatown (pMCMC), and several other mounted filter variants severally. Particle filters are unit town linear, particle-based methods. There are a unit varied sequent simulation strategies/algorithms for applying a particle filter. At the side of Kalman filters, these strategies use state-space models. Arulampalam *et al.* [21] projected totally different algorithms, all supported filtering the particles however with several variants. Substantial analysis comes are dispersed throughout these past twenty years to look at the appliance of those algorithms in medical specialty theory. Those areas unit basically the latest strategies for achieving correct calculations of parameters and precise predictions. These algorithms have the flexibility to alter varied actions and take a look at prospects for optimizing the performance. During this space, substantial analysis is afoot to boost the clarity and implementation of those algorithms. In recent years, Ionides *et al.* [22] recommended new findings in relevance to the preceding technique of Particle Filtration (PF). Substantial analysis comes are dispersed throughout these past twenty years to look at the appliance of those algorithms in medical specialty theory. Those area units are basically the latest strategies for achieving correct calculations of parameters and precise predictions. These algorithms have the flexibility to alter varied actions and take a look at prospects for optimizing the performance. During this space, substantial analysis is afoot to enhance the understanding and implementation of those algorithms. The easy particle filter algorithmic rule, on the opposite hand, changes the state parameter values supported each single time purpose, leading to one freelance spherical of particle filtration. Several combos occur, like derivatives of the ensemble filter that vary solely within the approach the discovered variables are unit updated. Those strategies embrace the Kalman Filter Ensemble (EnKF), the Kalman Filter Ensemble Adjustment (EAKF), and therefore the Rank bar chart Filter (RHF).

5.6 MCM Model Implementation

Recreations of the Markov Chain are generally utilized in epidemic based models, for example, SIR, SEIR, and SIRS. These epidemiological strategies are appropriate to different information types, and are frequently helpful where negligible information is accessible. There are different trials where the SEIR model are applied to occasions where just the compartment that was killed. Alongside the molecule sifting calculations, the above MCMC models are the most impressive strategies for the plan of typical SEIR models. Epidemiological models convey significant vulnerability and henceforth the obscure data and parameters of the epidemiological models can be assessed using Bayesian structure. These examinations intend to represent control measures identifying with the spread of the time of infection. Specialists utilized the SEIR model to break down the movement of contaminated people and the effectiveness of the disease's stochastic variation. Different analysts utilized the last way to deal with the steadiness of the SEIR scale harmony focuses from an increasingly expository perspective. Further hypothetical examination was directed by de Abajo *et al.* [14], in which productive computational methods and calculations were concentrated to investigate the stochastic SEIR model. What's more, the utilization of control components in these investigations is of exceptional importance. The SEIR model is broadly utilized as an antibody engineering the board strategy to shield helpless people from infection, and as a powerful technique for deciding the correct immunization procedures through illness spread. Others utilized the SEIR model to apply ongoing estimating, as characterized all through ensuing segments.

5.6.1 Reproduction Number

One of the parameters in epidemiological demonstration is the essential number of propagation (N), which determines whether an enormous pandemic flare-up may occur. Essentially positioned this worth mirrors the quantity of auxiliary cases in a totally helpless populace activated by an irresistible individual. At the point when the quantity of proliferations arrives at 1 the irresistible infection can spread, bringing about a major plague. The ailment would keep on spreading on the grounds that the number is short of what one. Subsequently, if N is more prominent than 1, there is a high likelihood that countless individuals will contract the malady, while if omnipresence turns out to be under 1, just a little measure of individuals will get polluted. This intrigue gives direction with regards to whether the populace is in danger from any new ailment. Scientific models attempt to anticipate that critical number to convey it as a decent social insurance pointer. Like where a continuous ailment is observed, straight programming procedures ought to be utilized to accomplish reasonable limits for the mean of N. Moreover, examining the elements of N is fascinating, therefore seeing how pathogens are spreading and transmitting inside their host populations. Most numerical models expect either that the pace of contact between has is directly identified with have (thickness subordinate) or that the pace of contact is free of thickness, accordingly considered as recurrence dependent. Bayesian Markov Chain Monte Carlo (BMCMC) techniques leads to settled calculations for demonstrating the generation number in some intricate pestilences dependent on spatial-worldly development (various models of transmission from one region to another) [23]. Such an investigation of the replication proportion permits to clarify certain attributes of different pestilences and to utilize this information for potential outbreaks. Epidemiological research and the replication proportion look to clarify the idea of irresistible infection in genuine time and subsequently foundation information may bolster such an objective.

5.7 Diagnosis of COVID-19

When a replacement pandemic strikes individuals it's tough to treat. Large-scale testing is difficult, and experiments are probably to be pricey, significantly at the starting time. Anyone with any COVID-19 signs ought to usually be terribly upset that they need to narrow the illness, though similar signs are characteristic of the many different, probably milder diseases yet. Rather than taking medical samples from every patient and waiting long, pricy testing tests to come back, a quicker, easier, and cheaper technique (even though it's less accurate) would be useful in gathering results on a wider scale. This knowledge can be used for more study, yet as for medical observation and sorting because it involves exploitation machine learning to assist diagnosing COVID-19, exciting work fields embody exploitation face scanners to observe symptoms, like whether or not or not the patient includes a fever, exploitation wearable technologies like good watches to seem for tell-tale changes in a very patient's resting pulse rate, exploitation machine learning-powered chat bots to trace patients supported self-reported indications.

It's important to come back up with an immunogen, a reliable diagnostic technique, and a treatment drug in response to a replacement pandemic-fast. Gift approaches need a great deal of long trial and error only 1 viable candidate for the immunogen can take months to isolate. Machine learning will dramatically speed up the cycle while not losing quality assurance. Once researchers tried to seek out tiny molecule inhibitors of the filovirus, they found that coaching theorem metric capacity unit models with a infectious agent pseudo type entry assay and knowledge from the filovirus replication assay helped speed up rating. (Scoring involves assigning a score to every molecule, looking on however probably it's to help). Similarly, researchers performing on H7N9 found that simulated screening and rating power-assisted by metric capacity unit results in major will increase within the exactitude of the tests. The most effective results with H7N9 were obtained by exploiting the random forest rule (a classification rule created of various call trees). In circumstances just like the COVID-19 pandemic, wherever an outbreak is quickly current, it's necessary to induce additional reliable scores faster to boost drug production. Firms are wasting longer and energy obtaining accredited new medications. They have to be as assured as they will that these medications don't have unmotivated, adverse facet effects. That cycle saves the United States of America, however throughout an outbreak; it still slows the United States of America down—even as we want a quicker response. One difference is to repurpose medicine already tested and used for different diseases. However there are thousands of drug candidates, and that we haven't any time to check all out—therefore can we realize the proper one? Through mechanically making data graphs and prognostication interactions between medicine and infectious agent proteins, machine learning can facilitate the United States of America establish drug candidates even quicker.

5.7.1 Predicting Outbreaks Through Social Media Analysis

In the illness of irruption, as we tend to square measure seeking to create ways to figure effectively against it, we want to be told wherever we tend to square measure 1st. queries like "How many of us square measure infected?" And "World Health Organization square measures these men?" Unfortunately, it's troublesome and dear to stay track of pandemics—notably those caused by viruses. Sometimes the government, beside the health system, answers those queries. The liable department, as an example, reports and advertises the quantity of latest patients diagnosed with the illness on a daily basis (or week). Fortuitously we tend to live in an exceedingly present time. A peasant World Health Organization continues to indicate symptoms could sleep in a tiny low city with no native hospitals capable of concluding the study. However, that very same farmer should be ready to access social networks and leave immediate hints concerning his health and illness unfold—hints that solely a model of machine learning will learn to method on a scale. A machine learning rule assesses the danger of novel viral infection by analyzing the standard of public communications on social media. The model might not be ready to establish individuals at a private level; however all of this information will be wont to predict the distribution of the pandemic in real time and to forecast distribution over the approaching weeks. In decision-making systems within the middle of a chop-chop rising pandemic, the importance of this intelligence cannot be overestimated. An extremely communicable disease irruption—just like the one we tend to square measure experiencing with the novel corona virus—may be a pandemic triggered by a contagion originating in another species (such as bats) and spreading to humans. Viruses like Ebola fever, HIV or COVID-19 will survive long unnoted within the wildlife, expecting the following mutation and also the next likelihood to infect the USA. They hide in species that don't seem to be infected by the disease-named reservoir hosts. Knowing World Health Organization these reservoir hosts square measure is significant to combating a pestilence—once we've found them, we are able to develop methods to regulate illness unfold and forestall additional outbreaks. The normal methodology of characteristic reservoir hosts can take years of study, and lots of orphan viruses square measure still not matched to associate in nursing animal hosts. Whole-Genome Sequencing (WGS, the strategy of deciding the complete polymer sequence of Associate in nursing organism) has become low-cost and straightforward, because of major technical advances. Analysis has shown that, beside professional data, machine learning models will use order sequencing information to spot the species that almost all seemingly served as hosts for the illness. By taking a glance at a tiny low proportion of species, the method of finding these pathogens within the wild will be dramatically speeded.

5.7.1.1 *Risk of New Pandemics*

Predicting exactly once Associate in nursing contagious disease virus will build an extremely infectious hop (jumping from one animal to another) can facilitate physicians and medical practitioners predict and arrange future pandemics consequently. Contagious disease A, as an example, primarily happens within the craniates community however it's the flexibility to maneuver to human hosts. Researchers engaged on contagious disease A isolated sixty seven, 940 sequences of proteins from the dataset. They sorted those sequences so solely those contagious disease strains with full sequencing of eleven influenza proteins were enclosed within the dataset. The researchers were then able to classify probably extremely infectious contagious disease strains with high accuracy rates mistreatment machine learning. A lot of analysis is needed to line up applied mathematics models for transmission mechanisms, however understanding that sickness strains are seemingly to form a leap may be an important initiative in designing for ensuring disease eruption.

5.8 Conclusion

The usage of mathematical models for study the outrage of infectious diseases is becoming increasingly prevalent worldwide, as they are a valuable tool for officials who especially wish to control epidemics. Machine learning is a major way of combating the current pandemic. When humans take this chance to incorporate evidence, enhance their knowledge and merge their skills, they can save many lives for the present population and for the future one also. The extension of the severity calculation forecasts the result of the treatment and is thus simply a function of predicting life and death. Clearly, learning how likely a patient is to recover would be helpful along with other signs. But in the prime of that, it is necessary to be connected in mind that not all patients get constant care. If we will predict the results of the particular strategies of treatment, then doctors will treat patients a lot more effectively. Mistreatment machine learning to individualize care schedules isn't distinctive to COVID-19, though recently, machine learning is accustomed to forecast clinical results for patients with brain disease. Researchers have conjointly used machine learning to predict therapy responses to cancer. Since treatment ways for COVID-19 square measure are still rising, it's likely to be a while before we have a tendency to see machine learning applied to predicting effects for various therapies. It offers a variety of options which can be leverage for predicting the disease in the early stages and thus saves the human life.

References

1. Alasaad, S., War diseases revealed by the social media: massive leishmaniasis outbreak in the Syrian Spring. *Parasites Vectors*, 6, 1, 94–94, 2013, https://dx.doi.org/10.1186/1756-3305-6-94.
2. Bishop, C.M., *Pattern recognition and machine learning*, vol. 4, Springer, New York, Inc., 2006.
3. Bradford, J.P. *et al.*, Pruning decision trees with misclassification costs, in: *dans Machine Learning: ECML-98*, pp. 131–136, 1998.
4. Brillman, J.C. *et al.*, Modeling emergency department visit patterns for infectious disease complaints: Results and application to disease surveillance. *BMC Med. Inf. Decis. Making*, 5, 1, 1–14, 2005, https://dx.doi.org/10.1186/1472-6947-5-4.
5. Buckee, C.O. *et al.*, Mobile phones and malaria: Modeling human and parasite travel. *Travel Med. Inf. Dis.*, 11, 1, 15–22, 2013, https://dx.doi.org/10.1016/j.tmaid.2012.12.003.

6. Buckeridge, D.L., Okhmatovskaia, A., Tu, S., O'Connor, M., Nyulas, C., Musen, M.A., Understanding detection performance in public health surveillance: Modeling aberrancy-detection algorithms. *J. Am. Med. Inform. Assoc.,* 15, 6, 760–769, 2008.
7. Predicting outbreak detection in public health surveillance: Quantitative analysis to enable evidence based method selection. *dans AMIA Annual Symposium Proceedings*, pp. 76–76, 2008.
8. DeCaprio, D., Gartner, J., Burgess, T., Garcia, K., Kothari, S., Sayed, S., McCall, C.J., Building a COVID-19 vulnerability index. arXiv preprint arXiv:2003.07347, 2020.
9. Chae, S., Kwon, S., Lee, D., Predicting Infectious Disease Using Deep Learning and Big Data. *Int. J. Environ. Res. Public Health*, 15, 8, 1596–1596, 2018, https://dx.doi.org/10.3390/ijerph15081596.
10. Huang, D.C. and Wang, J.F., Monitoring hand, foot and mouth disease by combining search engine query data and meteorological factors. *Sci. Total Environ.*, 612, 1293–1299, 2018.
11. Sujath, R., Chatterjee, J.M., Hassanien, A.E., A machine learning forecasting model for COVID-19 pandemic in India. *Stoch. Environ. Res. Risk Assess.*, 34, 959–972, 2020.
12. Elmousalami, H.H. and Hassanien, A.E., Day level forecasting for Coronavirus Disease (COVID-19) spread: Analysis, modeling and recommendations. *arXiv preprint arXiv:2003.07778*, 2020.
13. Rizk-Allah, R.M. and Hassanien, A.E., COVID-19 forecasting based on an improved interior search algorithm and multi-layer feed forward neural network. *arXiv preprint arXiv:2004.05960*, 2020.
14. de Abajo, F.J. *et al.*, Use of renin–angiotensin–aldosterone system inhibitors and risk of COVID-19 requiring admission to hospital: A case-population study. *Lancet*, 395, 10,238, 1705–1714, 2020.
15. Sujatha, R., Chatterjee, J., Hassanien, A., A machine learning methodology for forecasting of the COVID-19 cases in India. TechRxiv. Preprint. 2020. https://doi.org/10.36227/techrxiv.12143685.v1
16. Cui, H. and Singh, V.P., Application of minimum relative entropy theory for streamflow forecasting. *Stochastic Environ. Res. Risk Assess.*, 31, 3, 587–608, 2017, https://dx.doi.org/10.1007/s00477-016-1306-7.
17. Torky, M. and Hassanien, A.E., COVID-19 blockchain framework: Innovative approach. *arXiv preprint arXiv:2004.06081*, 2020.
18. Koo, K.O.T., Tan, D.M.K., Chong, A.K.S., Distal Radius Fractures: An Epidemiological Review. *Orthop. Surg.*, 5, 3, 209–213, 2013, https://dx.doi.org/10.1111/os.12045.
19. Nsoesie, E.O. *et al.*, A systematic review of studies on forecasting the dynamics of influenza outbreaks. *Influenza Other Respir. Viruses,* 8, 3, 309–316, 2014, https://dx.doi.org/10.1111/irv.12226.

20. Ibrahim, N., Akhir, N.S.M., Hassan, F.H., Predictive analysis effectiveness in determining the epidemic disease infected area. In *AIP Conference Proceedings, 1891,* 1, pp. 020064. AIP Publishing LLC, 2017.
21. Arulampalam, M.S. *et al.*, A tutorial on particle filters for online nonlinear/non-Gaussian Bayesian tracking. *IEEE Trans. Signal Process.*, 50, 2, 174–188, 2002, https://dx.doi.org/10.1109/78.978374.
22. Ionides, E.L. *et al.*, Iterated filtering. *Ann. Stat.*, 39, 3, 1776–1802, 2011, https://dx.doi.org/10.1214/11-aos886.
23. Li, M., Dushoff, J., Bolker, B.M., Fitting mechanistic epidemic models to data: A comparison of simple Markov chain Monte Carlo approaches. *Stat. Methods Med. Res.*, 27, 7, 1956–1967, 2018. https://dx.doi.org/10.1177/0962280217747054.

Part 2

EMERGING TECHNOLOGIES TO DEAL WITH COVID-19

6

Emerging Technologies for Handling Pandemic Challenges

D. Karthika* **and K. Kalaiselvi**

Department of Computer Science, School of Computing Sciences, Vels Institute of Science, Technology & Advanced Studies (Formerly Vels University), Chennai, India

Abstract

Most pandemic burdens, for instance, genuine extreme respiratory conditions, pandemic flu start in animals, are invited on utilizing contaminations and are pushed to ascend by strategies for ecological, direct, or budgetary changes. In this, how mechanical and self-proceeding with structures and quick wearable enhancement and help social protection transport and the restorative administrations gathering of workers for the term of the COVID-19 pandemic are presented. For instance, mechanized and telerobotic structures altogether limit the danger of powerful issue transmission to forefront human administrations people through creation it possible to triage, survey, screen, and treat casualties from a protected division great deal occurrences of the recognize the clinical, planning, and science systems get together to resource the restorative administration's structure, therapeutic administrations workers, and society all through the propelled disaster are presented. This section centers around computational strategies and real factors, artificial Intelligence (AI) and Big Data can help in dealing with the gigantic, unprecedented proportion of records got from open health surveillance, consistent plague flare-ups watching, vogue right now tossing/deciding, common condition briefing and invigorating from authoritative establishments and animals, and prosperity office utilization of information.

Keywords: Artificial Intelligence, bigdata, computational technologies, pandemic diseases, COVID-19

**Corresponding author*: d.karthi666@gmail.com

Abhinav Juneja, Vikram Bali, Sapna Juneja, Vishal Jain and Prashant Tyagi (eds.) Enabling Healthcare 4.0 for Pandemics: A Roadmap Using AI, Machine Learning, IoT and Cognitive Technologies, (93–116) © 2021 Scrivener Publishing LLC

6.1 Introduction

In December 2019, the Corona Virus (COVID-19) started in China where the first event appeared. It started spreading through China and, as a Global Health Problem of International Importance (PHEIC), the World Health Enterprise (WHO), which later turned into an unprecedented pandemic, transmitted COVID-19 scene on 30 January 2020. The WHO Condition Report-78 was written up on 7 April 2020. There are more significantly 2 million acceptance incidents and passes than an exhaustive 72,000. Infection is growing minimal through little and any infected citizen in the US, Italy, Spain, and in a variety of deprived countries in specific fights to tackle the social security system [1].

Given the reality who the characteristics of this new coronavirus are not excellent, it may derive its leadership from the bits of knowledge, e.g. fast spread, fate is greater in low immune, diabetes, and developing people. Mainly noteworthy for the recovery rate and other details that they have is that it spreads to humans through globules or by humans. It is astounding that neutralization of this new coronavirus is not feasible through medication for the settlement or by inoculation from 10 April 2020 [2]. Notwithstanding their monstrous effects on World general prosperity and creating vitality about the technique by using which they rise, no pandemic has been envisioned before tainting individuals, the pathogens that ascend, the hosts that they start in, and the segments that power their turn of events. A course of action of question and observation openings and dreams should assist with crushing these troubles and go the world pandemic strategy from the response to pre-exclusion.

Nations, however, often continued to using various appropriate medications without clear evidence and unmistakable care methods. The WHO's prevention steps consist of incremental handwashing, taking social emptying, and rehearsing of breathing order, with chemicals and water or through an alcoholic-based hand rub. The cover often plans research to shield persons from illness and it must know where and how to use the spread. Besides, the perfect solution to preserving a psychological distance from malaise is by staying at home and being away from the party, after social isolation and disengaging them from isolated individuals or entities that have been identified to be separate. Its expansion will therefore culminate in a firm commitment of all social institutions, the support system of the agency, legislation, and, above all, the society. They can also be superbly controlled to some extent [3]. The widespread application of planned passion, as well as convincing care of people and a large enterprise, would also complicate the defense of COVID-19. The COVID-19, which is a result of such efforts to support society through highly unconventional methodologies, has also made impressive progress.

In either case, the value of the history to social security is exemplary for management terms, as the system does not understand a lack of success for the purposeful, open-minded organization. It can be seriously affected or hurt by these advances in the war against new crown diseases [4]. The history shows that the management of pollutant production or the problems in the human organization is implemented. This included the progress of the Council and everyone in finding a solution to the problem. This study was designed to identify various growth strategies that help the world escape pandemics and related actions. The goal of the assessment is to help customers, experts and scientists recognize the difficulty of success in disease management and consider future developments.

6.2 Technological Strategies to Support Society During the Pandemic

Creative strategies that support the general public have any kind of influence and are sufficiently segregated after independent isolation to reduce the spread of the disease and therefore have any kind of effects on the management of the infinite. Healthnet firms began developing a technical solution to improve the research and patient outcomes even before the latest coronavirus spread. In addition to medical imaging techniques, the use of artificial intelligence (AI) improves diagnostic quality. Machine learning companies are developing systems that help decision-making on care. Innovations play a key role in addressing the challenges of the COVID-19 pandemic, from advanced robotics to remote patient monitoring [5].

During the COVID-19 pandemic, new healthcare models are expected. Because of the strong COVID-19 transmission rate, most countries have lock-downs, so it is difficult to contact and see the patient physicist. The emphasis on new models was transferred in the era of digital health technologies to telehealth (virtual appointments, visits), mobile apps (remote patient surveillance), and websites (risk assessment, screening, and triage). Figure 6.1 recognizes key stakeholders at the front of a COVID-19 crisis with significant examples of effective digital health approaches to date, applied on several levels (population, healthcare systems, research, and technology ecosystem in partnership with public health agencies or governments) [6].

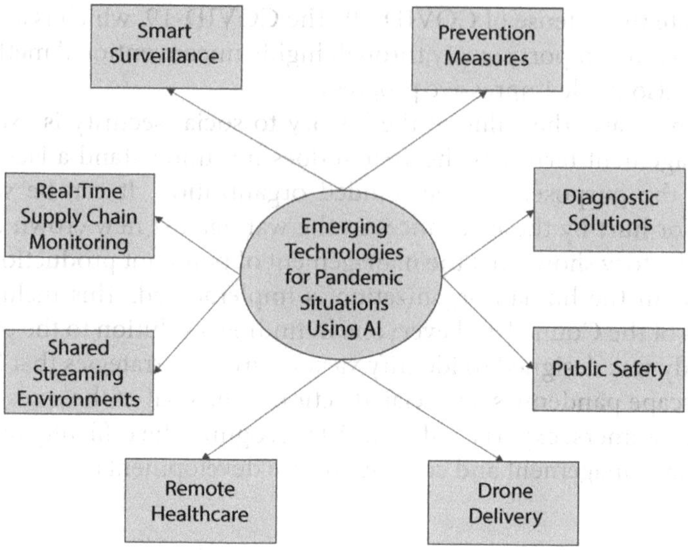

Figure 6.1 Emerging technologies for pandemic situations.

6.2.1 Online Shopping and Robot Deliveries

The SARS incident contributed to a gigantic growth in China at the end of 2002, both for the company and for business to buy online centers. Therefore, COVID-19 has transformed online shopping from enjoyable surfing to a worldwide absolute need. Several bars in Beijing have also served enjoyable online requests and transfers for many hours. A good collaboration structure will help web-based shopping. Personal transport is not indicative of disease. A variety of transport organizations and food stores in the US and China run contactless transportation systems, which gather and dispose of goods at a location rather than under the supervision of an individual [7]. The growth in robot transport by Chinese online business customers are also increasing. In either situation, transport organizations must set up to protect the sterile state of the transported goods before robot transport administrations become prevalent in every case.

6.2.2 Digital and Contactless Payments

Money spreads the infection, but national banks in China, the US, and South Korea have modified different banknote guarantees until they get underway [8]. At present, contactless device installations, such as cards or e-wallets, are the preferred deployment strategy to keep away from COVID-19 diffusion. Advanced installs enable people to make online purchases and install products, benefits, and even utility installations, just as support increases more quickly. However, as the World Bank has pointed out, more than 1.7 billion unbanked people may not have easy access to computerized installations. Advanced installations are also available on the grounds of web accessibility, gadgets, and a digital positioning system through money.

6.2.3 Remote Work

Several groups have pushed for the tele-commutation of members. Well-distance work is supported through innovations, including virtual private networks (VPN), voice-over-Internet protocols (VoIP), virtual meetings, online creativity, working joint efforts, and even facial recognition, which allow an individual to show up before a virtual base to defend his home. Given the avoidance of the spread of infections, practice in the distance often cuts travel time and makes it more adaptable [9]. However, far off research always forces companies and representatives to face difficulties. Data security, privacy, and perfect technical support can be enormous problems, as shown by ongoing Zoom class activities. Far off work can also involve complex work law problems, for instance, problems relating to having a safe workspace and personal expenses. Members may sense forlornness and lack of balance between work and life.

As far off jobs are increasingly essential after the COVID-19 contagion, bosses can settle for lower operating expenses and recruit people from premises at less expensive working costs. Rules and standards should be revised to allow faraway work and further psychiatric assessments should be carried out to understand the impact of far-reaching work on people. Therefore, not all work from home should be available, making them unique. According to the US Bureau of Labor Statistics, approximately 25% of job and pay workers telecommuted at any time between 2017 and 2018. In any event, workers with school orders are required to have work that enables them to telecommute connections and secondary school certificates. Other calls, for example, clinical administrators and assembly, could not be selected by any creativity. Arrangements on information streams and tax assessments should be matched if the computerized administrations around boundaries increase substantially [10].

6.2.4 Telehealth

Telehealth can be a viable method of limiting the spread of COVID-19 while remaining fundamental. Individual wearable IoT gadgets can follow essential signs. Chatbots can make initial conclusions dependent on patient-distinguished manifestations. Nonetheless, in countries where health expenses are high, it is critical to ensure protection for telehealth. Additionally, telehealth requires a certain degree of technical training as a decent web association. As an individual of the greatest intensively controlled clinical departments, experts can normally consider people working in a similar field. Guidelines could not have envisioned a world where telehealth is accessible at the time of their creation.

6.2.5 Online Entertainment

Although isolate measures have diminished face to face associations altogether, human inventiveness hosts united the get on the web. Cloud raves and internet spilling of shows have gained footing the world over. Chinese film creation organizations likewise discharged movies on the web. Exhibition halls and global legacy locales offer virtual visits. There has additionally been a flood of web-based gaming traffic since the episode.

6.2.6 Supply Chain 4.0

The global network has been gracefully disturbed by the COVID-19 pandemic. Several manufacturing plants are completely closed with demolition and insulation requests. Although interest in food and human defense equipment is on the rise, several nations have made different grades of fare prohibitions. Substantial reliance on paper records, lack of awareness of knowledge, and lack of variation and adaptability have made existing frameworks gracefully indefensible against any pandemic. Core developments in the industrial revolution 4.0, such as Big Data, Distributed Computing, IoT, and Blockchain, are creating a more robust and forward-looking chain to improve information quality and information sharing [8–11].

6.2.7 3D Printing

3D printing promises adaptability: a printer may generate different elements based on the framework documents and materials and can be easily made nearby without the need for a lengthy receiving phase and a substantial pause in shipping presence. 3D printing offers adaptability: Notwithstanding, gigantic creation utilizing 3D printing faces a couple of impediments. To begin with, there might be licensed innovation issues engaged with delivering parts that are secured by patent. Second, the creation of specific products, for example, careful covers, is dependent upon administrative endorsements, which can set aside a long effort to get. Other unsolved issues incorporate how configuration documents ought to be secured under patent systems, the spot of source, and the effect on exchange volumes and item risk related to 3D printed items [10].

6.2.8 Rapid Detection

A quick decision is an essential bit of human administration since it gives experiences concerning the clinical issue of a patient and lights up dynamic social protection decisions [9]. The expository methodology is a typical and complex activity that incorporates clinical assessment and offers information to choose the clinical issues of a patient. In continuous decades, flow methods have been made for the speedy diagnostics of different illnesses. The guideline focal points of snappy disclosure strategies are the opportunity of earlier intervention and snappier draws in the movement to likely issues, yet what's more improved throughput of assessment. Here we will discuss substantiating acknowledgment by qRT-PCR, preliminary screening through quick neutralizing operator test, in conclusion, AI-based picture planning methods using chest x-bar/CT/HRCT pictures.

6.2.9 QRT-PCR

The most extreme developing strategy for the subjective and quantitative recognition of nucleic corrosive from SARS-CoV-2 in higher and lower breath examples is quantitative real-time polymer chain response (qRT-PCR) and is generally quantifiable during the exceptional fragment of disease. QRT-PCR can understand as low as one infection molecule in swabs taken from the mouth or nose. Test aggregated from outline parts comprising the patient's nose or throat manages various compound answers that discard proteins and fats, leaving the best concentrates of RNA inside the example. The RNA separated is a total of a patient's own one of a kind hereditary fabric and, likewise crown infection RNA, if the viral disease is available [11].

6.2.10 Immunodiagnostic Test (Rapid Antibody Test)

The invulnerable symptomatic examinations play a vital work in the convenient area of COVID-19 as said earlier. This antigen area approach recognizes the proximity of viral proteins (antigens) conveyed by infers of the COVID-19 disease in a structure aggregated from the respiratory tract of a person [10, 11].

6.2.11 Work From Home

The COVID-19 often quickly spreads, and an infectious person does not know whether the person is infected so the organism may be removed with an infection lasting between 1 and 14 days before the side effects appear. In this way, any company, which does not even need to be close to its members at the office, is closed during an isolated term where the general population is not unexpectedly at the highest. Moreover, these companies may take care of business by upgrading the telecommunications process, which is commonly used worldwide. A registration gadget, network usability, and cam if appropriate are the main prerequisites for telecommuting [12]. Meetings and meetings may be held by video collection remotely. As the correspondence creativity and device functionality advanced, far away practice has performed very well. With protection in mind, calls can be filtered and the configuration of the firewall can be used.

6.2.12 Distance Learning

The rapid spread of COVID-19 also brought any instructive framework to an end. So, undergraduates at home must be dressed in a globule with some reaction to begin their study. E-learning is an apprenticeship that provides rich technical capabilities. E-learning is an online innovation through which a range of media may supply outlets. The nations that contribute to online instruction include the United States, the United Kingdom, India, China, and South Korea [13]. Many stages have been developed, such as Google Classroom, Coursera, Audacity, etc. for separation learning. During COVID, Cursers offered a wide variety of free courses to enhance their comprehension of home research. During the isolated time, numerous events encouraged e-learning to sustain instruction for undergraduate studies. In some situations, the online meeting was videoconference with a series of understudies by the educator.

6.2.13 Surveillance

Having an infected person and their history of activity under control will be powerful. Different administrations take to recognize this after different processes. A flexible application in Singapore, Follow Along [14] was expressly urged by the parliament. It uses Bluetooth mobile phone creation to detect potential transmission of coronary infection in close contact with others. When in Hong Kong, individuals were forced to wear a bracelet suited to the mobile phone application to warn the pros if they disabled alone.

6.3 Feasible Prospective Technologies in Controlling the Pandemic

The previous two areas deal with advancements that are routinely completed to fight against the novel crown infection ailment and are ordered as mechanical strategies that are used to control the across the board and support the general public. In this section, the sensible advances and creating propels that can help with encountering this far-reaching condition is discussed. These fast-approaching advances join Artificial Insights, Machine learning, Web of Things (IoT) [15].

6.3.1 Robotics and Drones

COVID-19 shows the world how much it depends on cooperation with humans to make things work. Serious work organizations are the worst affected, for example, grocery, health, assembly, and teamwork. COVID-19 provided a strong drive to introduce robotics and automation tests. Robotics was later used to sanitize the areas and distribute food to isolated individuals. Automatons went through the hounds and conveyed information. Strategies must be formed to ensure that the working force to recognize transition receives adequate planning and social government support [16].

6.3.2 5G and Information and Communications Technology (ICT)

All patterns of innovation depend on a stable, rapid, and logical network. While 5G has shown its value in remote control and social insurance events, its implementation in Europe remains postponed where progress may be most desired. For 5G coverage, the cost of perfect gadgets and information plans will be reduced. Taking these concerns into consideration, with the 5G system growing all-inclusive, will continue to be a check [15, 16].

6.3.3 Portable Applications

The improvement of Information Technology has made full-size applications in a lot of capacity and is quickly creating within the sight of the web. Further, the cell phones have cleared an approach to get admission to these applied sciences in a significantly less troublesome manner. In the current world, cell phones assume extraordinary jobs as they are implanted with intuitive dynamite shows, unnecessary choice cameras, enormous availability to the net, and support for different programming [16, 17]. Versatile application programming is imperative because of the reality they have the conceivable to get together with the world from only a hand-measured device and can work different assignments. In the pandemic circumstance, they can help in an assortment of approaches going from conferring cell wellbeing (M-wellbeing) office to supporting ranchers in coordination. M-wellbeing capacities can give clinical help whenever and any area subsequently, defeating the land limitations and it causes the social insurance individuals to allow perfect suppliers by utilizing cell innovation.

6.4 Coronavirus Pandemic: Emerging Technologies That Tackle Key Challenges

Innovation Analysts utilized information-driven, base up research way to distinguish 4,830 new companies and developing organizations attempting to moderate or stifle the spread and the impacts of the novel coronavirus [17].

A portion of the key difficulties that these developing advances address include:

- To avoid infection or transmission of the disease for the individual. Signs of Progress such as far-observation, self-management, and non-contact temperature weapons help avoid contamination from spreading.
- To provide additional aid for particularly defenseless social gatherings. The number of people required to visit an emergency clinic will be decreased with virtual specialists, chatbots, and online patient commitment machines alongside faraway demonstrative arrangements.
- In an episode to maintain open access and overall health. To stop uncontrol preventable coronavirus transmission network. Popular administrations, far from work, in addition to prescribing dejection, depression, and tension, enable residents and well-being workers to cope during a lockdown.

6.4.1 Remote Healthcare

Far-away patients can observe paces for temperature monitoring and record the potential bearers and identify them. The separation from wearables of psychological and biometrical data improves the accuracy of the detection of COVID-19 positives. The shortage of qualified professionals fills the vacuum with general health practitioners emphasizing the requirements for mutual isolation, telepsychology, and the medication. Related health changes allow professionals and patients to distantly use computerized professional support and electronic interfaces. 400 new companies and emerging organizations concerned with improvements to far-reaching medical services have been broken down and 7 of the most significant strategies have been carried out to make for a quicker and increasingly productive approach in the fields of COVID-19 [18]:

- Mobile
- Respiratory control
- Mental health chatbots-Respiratory tracking
- Wearable sensors
- Remote monitoring.

6.4.2 Prevention Measures

Doctors, nurses, and healthcare professionals use Realtime digital mobile apps to hold patients' diagnosis up-to-date. Face masks are crucial for ensuring that health workers are less likely to get polluted through the transmission. Sanitizers and antiviral soap producers are now under immense pressure to supply sufficiently and maintain quality control. The infected clusters must be provided with specific automated disinfectants and sanitizers. 121 entrepreneurs and innovative firms were studied to establish technology to prevent the virus from infection or diffusion. In a separate article of study, we identify five of the most important solutions for a more rapid and effective response to the outbreak of COVID-19, including [18]:

- Air Filtration Systems
- Disinfectants
- Spit Device
- Air Filtration Systems
- Disease surveillance.

6.4.3 Diagnostic Solutions

The WHO is advising all health authorities for coronavirus monitoring, identification, recording, and insulation. Home tests and diagnostic kits are important to slow the virus spread. When large scale quarantine measures are in place, the implemented metrics can be supplemented by virtual care, virtual medical visits, and interactive platforms. Mobile apps chatbots and symptom tests easily and interestingly provide details. Using weapons without contact make sure the frontline tasks are not at risk. To order to perform effective diagnosis in potential COVID-19 events, it studied 569 businesses and emerging companies. It discusses 5 of the most relevant solutions to react to the COVID-19 contagion faster and more efficiently, including [18, 19]:

- Mobile monitoring
- Telehealth
- Remote patient management
- Detection of Virus Kits
- Continuous Monitoring of Temperature.

6.4.4 Hospital Care

To achieve desired results, hospitals require concerted preparation and assistance. Artificial fans and bedside safety technology improve patient care dramatically. Sanitary caps, gowns, boots, masks, and surgical grades are vital to nurses and doctors on the front line. Blood test collections, respiratory rate monitoring devices, oxygen saturation tests, and stool samples are included. Indoor robotics carry essential tools and medications to provide nurses with free time to focus on their essential duties. This analyzes 125 startups and new companies that support healthcare institutions and policymakers during an outbreak. 5 of the most relevant solutions to react to the COVID-19 contagion quickly and efficiently include [19]:

- Medical Robotics
- 3D Printed Ventilator Pump
- Artificial Cough Unit
- AI Patient Monitoring Algorithms
- Anti-Pathogen Fabric.

6.4.5 Public Safety During Pandemic

AI-based and observational research, visual images, and simulations of any possible outbreak are powerful ways to inform the public regarding their defense against influenza. Mobility tracking technologies and robotic disinfection systems contribute to a reduction in the risk of virus transmission to front-line workers. When hospitals have achieved their maximum potential, specialist insulation facilities support public health systems. Doctors and nurses use handheld stress management tools and effective downtime. It analyzed 162 new companies and growing organizations that are supporting health institutions and policymakers to sustain public health and safety during an epidemic. Effective approaches that can react more accurately and thoroughly to the COVID-19 pandemic include [20]:

- Drone-based Distribution of Medical Supplies
- Advanced Insulation Devices
- Mobile Service Systems for Health Workers
- Simulation & Analysis of Disease Outbreaks
- Robotics for Monitoring & Disinfecting.

6.4.6 Industry Adapting to the Lockdown

Locking situations pose extreme challenges and lead to severe consequences for companies. The implementation of sensors to monitor the whole supply chain allows plants that set production objectives. Many citizens who must stay indoors will fill the gaps of the moving items around the floor with autonomous guidance vehicles and drones. In a plant, critical components and robots use expertly aided augmented reality (AR) to lessen the need for staff in a factory. In general, factories to digitize through their supply chains remain better prepared for unforeseen events, such as the coronaviral pandemic. 596 startups and emerging companies were examined that help industries and factories during a shutdown, particularly for critical production. It provides 8 of the most effective solutions to address the corvid-19 pandemic faster and productive. The core range of applications comprises [21]:

- Digital factory
- Human in loop technologies
- Real-time tracking supply chain
- Improved cooperation in practice
- Industrial sanitation
- Industrial safety.

6.4.7 Cities Adapting to the Lockdown

The pandemic and the resulting lock-down are important for cities to navigate and deal with imagery and video analysis. Some hospitals and administrations use geofencing techniques to ensure that infected individuals comply with the restrictions with millions of people living under forced quarantine. Mobile apps update citizens with interactive maps about outbreaks and discuss other policy questions with the public. With the prospect of an epidemic of self—checkout and cashier-free locations, food and other big rethink shops help people manage lockdowns in major cities. It analyzed 259 startups and emerging firms that assist individuals and desk workers during a lock-out situation to remain calm, refreshed, and informed. It offers 7 of the most relevant solutions to respond more quickly and efficiently to the pandemic of COVID-19, including [22]:

- Smart tracking
- Location-based systems
- Public online services
- Indoor farming
- Prebaby-made and mobile houses
- Sickness planning
- Automated shops
- Sickness mapping.

6.4.8 Individuals Adapting to the Lockdown

Web and mobile apps are used for interacting with the loved ones during these test times. Most schools now use e-learning platforms for this academic year or term. The office that is suddenly forced to close uses creative online tools to communicate and interact with employees. Smartphone cameras and entertainment apps were successful for some time before the outbreak. Technology makes it possible for people to stay as often as possible so that the cycle of distance and self-isolation is made easier. In the report, 521 firms and emerging enterprises were discussed, supporting individuals and employees in their quiet, updated, and secure education. It provides seven of the leading answers to the outbreak of COVID-19, including [23]:

- Remote work
- Management of soundness
- Reduction of stress & anxiety
- Online Learning
- An offering of online food and grocery
- Indoor workshops
- Shared streaming & entertainment.

6.5 The Golden Age of Drone Delivery

In the battle against both the grip-epidemic COVID-19, drones were valuable instruments to encourage the production of healthy supply chains and sustainable social services. The situations are as societies agree that drone use is beyond future hazards, due to the latest drone regulations. For cooperation and push, the complete integration of drones in supply chains is critical. The drones' mentality is changing. While baffled, there are drones, and now there are robots of COVID-19. Drones switch from super hyped-up production to a platform capable of adapting to real needs. It shifts helps one to concentrate on unique applications that are the real help. In some sectors, even though the markets surrounding these developments are evolving, capital spending is increasing. Different aviation technologies are required to play an important role in an atmosphere that seeks creative means to satisfy the needs of the crisis and strives to reset globally [24].

However, the integration of drones in supply chains is far more important than technology. For this, sponsors and audiences would pay. This needs perhaps suddenly a whole new approach to aviation. There are new working requirements. Fantasies. In this case, imagination is not science, it is personal. Although some contend that drone technology is not mature enough to sustain it on a widespread scale—and cultural safety, noise, and inconvenience hindered the extension of flights—a change in social and policy understanding of acceptable risks encourages more implementation. Although air traffic has decreased by nearly 90% and road cars by way of recommendations for shelters have been slightly smaller, air and land risks can be greatly minimized. Meanwhile, demand has increased to streamline drone use to provide essential goods, promote social divisions, and make it easier and safer for sensitive personnel to operate. Innovations are being called upon in times to connect the disconnected, escape risky supply chains and at last promote social distance. This can be an important role for drones, and this situation can lead to the Golden Age of drone production [20–23].

6.5.1 The Early Adopters are Winning

Early adopted citizens come willingly beside the drones. In Rwanda, its blood supply chain saved lives and avoided drone emissions and became the world's leading country for more than conventional drone flights. Switzerland welcomed drones in the years before other nations, which made a small-scale profit and became a European leader. Market items were supplied in Australia with mixed results and analyzed, but valuable lessons were gained. In Australia, JD.com began many ventures of growing use of COVID-19 in rural Chinese cities. The most beneficial airlines and countries in the last three years save lives and deliver the greatest drone outcomes. Because of how imaginative and familiar the original business aircraft was with World War I, the use of drones to transport merchandise has also been expanded by COVID-19 [24].

People worldwide rely on fruit, drugs, and other logistics items and drones are becoming helpful. The United Postal Service (UPS) and drone company Matter Net founded the first authorized drone delivery service in Germany on 27 April 2020. On 27 April 2020, on the drone packaging line with Wing Copter, the firm revealed its latest partnership. In the aftermath of the pandemic Alphabet's Arm now has expanded its delivery speeds, offering consumer connectivity and lifeline services to local firms. Wing partners stated 50% higher sales of those goods thanks to drone shipments during the crisis.

6.5.2 The Golden Age Will Require Collaboration and Drive

While it's exciting to incorporate drone operations in the US, it's not exactly a long-term change in thinking. COVID-19 is specifically stated in recent regulatory exceptions as an authorization trigger, which expires on 30 June and "where federal, State and local corvid-19 guides and conditions are expired." In the drone sector, a number of those who consider that this transition is done with cynicism by wide-ranged, well-connected firms collaborating with l-program authorities. The relationship as a business would be essential to demonstrate the advantages and how to deliver the best outcomes in the coming year and to develop internationally. For years it is understood that systemic approaches to drone licenses are required to compensate for social benefits danger. It needs the effective use of drones with detailed knowledge to help projects, resources, and other steps towards educating and encouraging regulators around the globe with businesses, charitable organizations, and civil society as well. The hardware is ready and the control systems eventually fail. When humanity wants them the most, the golden age of drones eventually falls [20, 21].

6.5.3 Standardization and Data Sharing Through the Smart City Network

In the last years, clusters of viruses have revealed that data from several sites in the metropolitan world, even patient data. The new proof of the outbreak of coronavirus (COVID-19) has been collected from airports by smart sensor scanning and tracking in airport installations and by employees of airports/seas. First, scans were conducted at 20 international airports in the U.S. to ensure that people remotely impacted were recognized at their quarantine point of entry. To provide patients with more scientific treatment, the evidence from Buckley and May has also been obtained from airports, bus stations, locations in Wuhan, underground, and health centers. These cases, especially in China and other Asian regions, have been detected and confirmed [22].

Although the key source of medical information comes from general practitioners or medical laboratories, as is often stated in the present case, its chapter explores how the data provided from an urban viewpoint will contribute to the medical study. The belief of urban life in the manuscript is based on whether the present epidemiology (COVID-19) is primarily expressed from humanity to humanity. In most instances, an urban area where large crowds, such as airports and underground stations, convene is the first point of touch where spreads in another country are registered. Monitoring devices have in most cases been implemented to make sure anyone with these signs, which are often present in urban environments, is detected and quarantined. However, in those cases, as illustrated by the present dissertation, medical details such as the security of the health and security of modern technology across different geographies must also be anonymized.

It will help to debate and organize infrastructure for data mining, new developments such as blockchain architectures, and quantum cryptography. This will boost communication services both from the medical profession and from expert urban planners while ensuring confidentiality and protection. Therefore, it may benefit from providing appropriate knowledge for educated decisions. However, given the undeniable function of the equipment installed in providing adequate medical information, it is important to investigate their data communication element [23]. First, contact is assumed to be geographically constrained (confined to someplace) so that it does not extend or interfere with anyone in its specific region. Second, the systems are typically assembled and installed by individual businesses, which have specific and specifications for data processing and storage, and therefore only associate cities with their goods.

The techniques are used to optimize economic gains for firms because of the competition and the possibility of the new media industry evolving and expanding. The standardization of the protocols established in this handbook should be continued to ensure the seamless sharing of information and data for its current implementation. This is intended to reduce or remove issues like demands for the processing of data, continuation, and other issues (when networks are fragmented). Standardization is done, for example, by ensuring that all equipment and facilities are associated in a single network, as was the case in the USA, where all health surveillance has been included in the NHSH network. The reality that cities are moving more and more to the idea of a smart city and the enhanced usage rates of linked technical devices enables current monitoring networks to re-calibrate these new databases [24].

6.5.4 The Procedure of AI and Non-AI-Based Applications

In this global health epidemic, the medical sector is looking for new ways of monitoring and controlling the transmission of the COVID-19 (Coronavirus) pandemic [25].

AI is a tool that can easily monitor the growth of the disease, classify high-risk patients, and is useful for treating the disease in real-time. Previous evidence may also estimate the death risk by patient monitoring. AI will support us in the battle against this epidemic by community surveillance, medical support, communication, and infection management advice. This method is a validated biomedical technique that can enhance

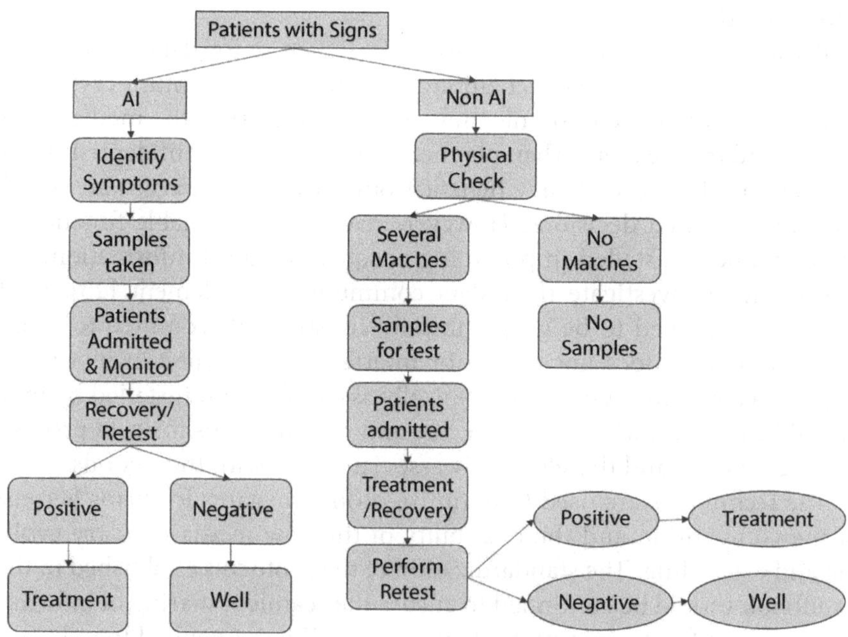

Figure 6.2 The general procedure of AI and non-AI based applications.

the preparation, rebuilding, and monitoring of patient COVID-19. Figure 6.2 indicates combined AI and non-AI therapies that enable the overall diagnosis of the COVID-19 symptoms by general physicians. The flow map highlights the difference between diminished non-AI treatment and AI treatment. The flow chart above shows the engagement of AI in high-precision procedures, minimizing the difficulty and time needed. The doctor not only stresses the patient's care, but also the care of AI diseases. AI with the best specificity is used for significant indications and tracking. It indicates also that the average number and availability of steps in the whole process are greater.

6.6 Technology Helps Pandemic Management

Epidemics often actively infect people with pandemics. SARS, H1N1, and Zika have already shown their names, but every epidemic offers new ways to fight and track these lethal viruses which kill millions of people. Technologies cannot eliminate a pandemic, but they can help prevent the dissemination, planning, notification, and knowledge to people on the ground and reduce the effect significantly. Converging technology has now become possible to explore numerous creative solutions to pandemics such as the Internet, the Cloud, Autonomous, robotics, AI/ML, 4G/5G, and High-Speed Mobile. It has identified eight areas of technology: splitting the number of deaths into misinformation individuals, medical and therapeutic options, vaccines, medical drugs, and environmental policies. It can lead to mass chaos, hysteria, stockpiling, rising inflation, street crime, bigotry, theories of conspiracy, etc. Companies such as Google, Twitter, and YouTube have worked hard to provide right-wing, verifiable statistics, such as WHO statistics, townships, and city councils. Delete the wrong information. Eliminate the wrong information. It might be a straightforward case because people know exactly how to approach both. Facebook and Google are partnered in the fight against bogus Coronavirus data to support GSP.

6.6.1 Tracking People With Facial Recognition and Big Data

Big data processing can help easily locate, interact with, log who they have met, and so on in the event of a pandemic. Recognition of facial and data technology, particularly when masked, may identify people with accuracy. This technology can help regulate and document the behavior of quarantined people. It will also help to trace people to see if they are in touch with an infectious person. In the quarantine time, contaminated people who violate the laws and travel out of them can be detected with CCTV cameras and facial recognition technology [26].

6.6.2 Contactless Movement and Deliveries Through Autonomous Vehicles, Drones, and Robots

Planes, helicopters, robotics, vehicles will all help avoid interaction with humans. Autonomous cars can be used safely, to and from health centers without endangering the lives of safe people. Robots can be used to cook, heat, sterilize hospitals, and traffic control. Helicopters may be used to provide fuel, track communities, carry research kits and medication to quarantine areas, thermal imaging, scrubbing with disinfectants, and more. There are some modern fields in which drones, robots, and self-sufficient vehicles are used. In the rivalry in contrast to coronavirus in China, drones and autonomous robots are used [27].

6.6.3 Technology Supported Temperature Monitoring

The most critical medical instruments used in businesses, airports, hospitals, train stations, and stores are the Digital Thermometer weapons and other related infrared temperature monitoring equipment. This technology tests the temperature of the body from a distance and is useful in recognizing individuals that may need more study. With automated thermal processing and facial recognition, the procedure is accelerated and effective [28].

6.6.4 Remote Working Technologies to Support Social Distancing and Maintain Business Continuity

When pandemics or other events threaten to endanger the corporate community, domestic practice ensures corporate stability and assists individuals in distress. The leading players in this field are technologies that provide secure access to information, company apps, virtual meetings, cloud conferences, and enhanced/mixed/increased reality to ensure that the deliverables have not been breached. A remote job is a strategic advantage and one of the easiest ways to discriminate between culture and society. While focusing on communication, the flow of data to individuals is considerably more important to handle the mass that the media and web-based social networking carry. The cultural response to the pandemic may at that time be affected by risk awareness by individuals [29]. To raise their patient intake cap and further boost TV companies to reduce their heap in emergency departments, the drug management offices have been easily updated. To evaluate numerous experiments in this pandemic scenario, research methods and departments are innovatively strengthened.

6.7 Conclusion

The incidence of Coronavirus 2019 (COVID-19) affected people globally and dramatically altered the usual aspects of society. The chapter presents mechanical improvements witnessed by the general population and nature from different viewpoints. The revolutionary systems that govern pandemic control function around data communication, AI, ML, and developments in the adaptive chain that specifically affect spreading relief. Consequently, this chapter notes the innovations that are useful in pandemic scenarios rely primarily on Artificial Intelligence and Computer. These developments include AI, ML, and IoT, intense creativity, and robot creativity. COVID-19's production has forced the improvement constraints, and various solutions have been suggested for the pandemic. This had intensified advancements happening in virtually every sector. During this time, the online experience of individuals can have a long-term impact onthe internet shopping, e-learning, computerized increments, telehealth offices, and scalable diversion. Increased and computer-generated fact, ramble creativity, add autonomy, cloud, and diversion technologies include artificial intuition, AI, Stuff Internet, field, and path inventions.

References

1. Sharma, H.B., Vanapalli, K.R., Cheela, V.S., Ranjan, V.P., Jaglan, A.K., Dubey, B., Goel, S., Bhattacharya, J., Challenges, opportunities, and innovations for effective solid waste management during and post COVID-19 pandemic. *Resour. Conserv. Recycl.*, 162, 105052, 2020 Jul 15.
2. Garg, S.K., Rodbard, D., Hirsch, I.B., Forlenza, G.P., Managing new-onset type 1 diabetes during the COVID-19 pandemic: Challenges and opportunities. *Diabetes Technol. Ther.*, 22, 431–439, 2020 Apr 17.
3. Rowan, N.J. and Laffey, J.G., Challenges, and solutions for addressing the critical shortage of supply chain for personal and protective equipment (PPE) arising from Coronavirus disease (COVID-19) pandemic—Case study from the Republic of Ireland. *Sci. Total Environ.*, 752, 138532, 2020 Apr 6.
4. Gradoń, K., Crime in The Time of The Plague: Fake News Pandemic and The Challenges to Law-Enforcement and Intelligence Community. *Soc. Regist.*, 4, 2, 133–48, 2020 Apr 7.

5. Elavarasan, R.M. and Pugazhendhi, R., Restructured society and environment: A review on potential technological strategies to control the COVID-19 pandemic. *Sci. Total Environ.*, 725, 138858, 2020 Apr 23.
6. Pandian, K.S. and Saxena, P., Unleashing the power of disruptive and emerging technologies amid COVID-19: A detailed review. *arXiv preprint arXiv*: 2005.11507, 1, 1–60, 2020 May.
7. Shaker, M.S., Oppenheimer, J., Grayson, M., Stukus, D., Hartog, N., Hsieh, E.W., Rider, N., Dutmer, C.M., Vander Leek, T.K., Kim, H., Chan, E.S., COVID-19: Pandemic contingency planning for the allergy and immunology clinic. *J. Allergy Clin. Immunol.: Pract.*, 8, 1477–1488, 2020 Mar 26.
8. Singh, R.P., Javaid, M., Kataria, R., Tyagi, M., Haleem, A., Suman, R., Significant applications of virtual reality for COVID-19 pandemic. *Diabetes Metab. Syndr.: Clin. Res. Rev.*, 14, 661–664, 2020 May 12.
9. Kulachinskaya, A., Akhmetova, I.G., Kulkova, V.Y., Ilyashenko, S.B., The Challenge of the Energy Sector of Russia during the 2020 COVID-19 Pandemic through the Example of the Republic of Tatarstan: Discussion on the Change of Open Innovation in the Energy Sector. *J. Open Innov.: Technol. Mark. Complex.*, 6, 3, 60, 2020 Sep.
10. Gasser, U., Ienca, M., Scheibner, J., Sleigh, J., Vayena, E., Digital tools against COVID-19: Taxonomy, ethical challenges, and navigation aid. *Lancet Digit. Health*, 2, 425–434, 2020 Jun 29.
11. Papagiannidis, S., Harris, J., Morton, D., WHO led the digital transformation of your company? A reflection of IT related challenges during the pandemic. *Int. J. Inf. Manage.*, 55, 102166, 2020 Jun 6.
12. Ramanathan, K., Antognini, D., Combes, A., Paden, M., Zakhary, B., Ogino, M., MacLaren, G., Brodie, D., Shekar, K., Planning, and provision of ECMO services for severe ARDS during the COVID-19 pandemic and other outbreaks of emerging infectious diseases. *Lancet Respir. Med.*, 23, 849–854, 2020 Mar 20.
13. Udgata, S.K. and Suryadevara, N.K., COVID-19: Challenges and Advisory, in: *Internet of Things and Sensor Network for COVID-19*, pp. 1–17, Springer, Singapore, 2021.
14. Fukuyama, F., The Pandemic and Political Order. *Foreign Aff.*, 99, 26, 2020.
15. Goel, S., Hawi, S., Goel, G., Thakur, V.K., Pearce, O., Hoskins, C., Hussain, T., Agrawal, A., Upadhyaya, H.M., Cross, G., Barber, A.H., Resilient and agile engineering solutions to address societal challenges such as coronavirus pandemic. *Mater. Today Chem.*, 100300, 2020 May 28.
16. Echedom, A.U. and Anyira, I.E., Challenges about Integration of Open Access to Libraries Collection Development Workflows in Nigeria. *IJRLS*, 6, 1, 190–199, 2020.
17. Malik, Y.S., Kumar, N., Sircar, S., Kaushik, R., Bhat, S., Dhama, K., Gupta, P., Goyal, K., Singh, M.P., Ghoshal, U., Zowalaty, M.E., Coronavirus Disease Pandemic (COVID-19): Challenges and a Global Perspective. *Pathogens*, 9, 7, 519, 2020 Jul.

18. Shrivastava, S., Trung, T.Q., Lee, N.E., Recent progress, challenges, and prospects of fully integrated mobile and wearable point-of-care testing systems for self-testing. *Chem. Soc. Rev.*, 49, 6, 1812–66, 2020.
19. Holmes, E.A., O'Connor, R.C., Perry, V.H., Tracey, I., Wessely, S., Arseneault, L., Ballard, C., Christensen, H., Silver, R.C., Everall, I., Ford, T., Multidisciplinary research priorities for the COVID-19 pandemic: A call for action for mental health science. *Lancet Psychiatry*, 7, 547–560, 2020 Apr 15.
20. Tapper, E.B. and Asrani, S.K., COVID-19 pandemic will have a long-lasting impact on the quality of cirrhosis care. *J. Hepatol.*, 73, 441–445, 2020 Apr 13.
21. Younes, N., Al-Sadeq, D.W., Al-Jighefee, H., Younes, S., Al-Jamal, O., Daas, H.I., Yassine, H., Nasrallah, G.K., Challenges in Laboratory Diagnosis of the Novel Coronavirus SARS-CoV-2. *Viruses*, 12, 6, 582, 2020 Jun.
22. Izuogu, C.U., Onyeneke, R.U., Njoku, L.C., Azuamairo, G.C., Atasie, M.C., Munonye, J.O., Review of Opportunities and Challenges of Agricultural Extension and Advisory Services among Rural Farm Households in Nigeria during Pandemics. *Asian J. Agric. Hortic. Res.*, 6, 1–2, 2020 Jul 31.
23. Kawamorita, H., Salamzadeh, A., Demiryurek, K., Ghajarzadeh, M., Entrepreneurial Universities in Times of Crisis: Case of COVID-19 Pandemic. *J. Entrepreneurship, Bus. Econ.*, 8, 1, 77–88, 2020 Jun 10.
24. Galanakis, C.M., The Food Systems in the Era of the Coronavirus (COVID-19) Pandemic Crisis. *Foods*, 9, 4, 523, 2020 Apr.
25. Ghernaout, D. and Elboughdiri, N., Environmental Engineering for Stopping Viruses Pandemics. *Open Access Lib. J.*, 7, 4, 1–7, 2020 Apr 7.
26. Aven, T. and Bouder, F., The COVID-19 pandemic: How can risk science help. *J. Risk Res.*, 23, 1–6, 2020 Jun 2.
27. Rhodes, T., Lancaster, K., Lees, S., Parker, M., Modelling the pandemic: Attuning models to their contexts. *BMJ Glob. Health*, 5, 6, e002914, 2020 Jun 1.
28. Klemeš, J.J., Van Fan, Y., Tan, R.R., Jiang, P., Minimising the present and future plastic waste, energy and environmental footprints related to COVID-19. *Renewable Sustain. Energy Rev.*, 127, 109883, 2020 Jul 1.
29. Malik, Y.S., Kumar, N., Sircar, S., Kaushik, R., Bhatt, S., Dhama, K., Gupta, P., Goyal, K., Singh, M.P., Ghoshal, U., El Zowalaty, M.E.M., Vinodh Kumar, O., Yatoo, M.I., Tiwari, R., Pathak, M., Patel, S.K., Sah, R., Rodriguez-Morales, A.J., Ganesh, B., Kumar, P., Singh, R.K., *Pandemic Coronavirus Disease (COVID-19): Challenges and A Global Perspective.* Preprints, 2020040469, 2020.

7

Unfolding the Potential of Impactful Emerging Technologies Amid COVID-19

Nusrat Rouf[1]*, Aatif Kaisar Khan[2†], Majid Bashir Malik[3], Akib Mohi Ud Din Khanday[1] and Nadia Gul[4]

[1]*Research Lab, Department of Computer Sciences, Baba Ghulam Shah Badshah University, Rajouri, India*
[2]*Department of Metallurgy & Materials Engineering, National Institute of Technology, Srinagar, India*
[3]*Department of Computer Sciences, Baba Ghulam Shah Badshah University, Rajouri, India*
[4]*School of Biosciences, Baba Ghulam Shah Badshah University, Rajouri, India*

Abstract

The unusual outbreak of Corona virus disease 2019 or COVID-19 (the disease caused by Severe Acute Respiratory Syndrome coronavirus 2) in December 2019 in the Wuhan city of China terrifically affected the people all over the world. People find it difficult to combat with COVID-19 due to insufficient availability of resources and expertise. Technologies are advancing with an exponential rate and are providing solutions to explore capabilities and mitigate the devastating impact of COVID-19. Emerging technologies are playing a major role in managing the current situation. People from all most all sectors are trying their best to delve into technological solutions to the problems caused by this pandemic. Thus, there is an essential need to assemble and understand the importance of emerging technologies to open all possible doors to handle the devastating situation caused by COVID-19. This chapter reviews the technologies to combat previous epidemics such as Ebola and SARS. It provides a significant insight into emerging technologies used to combat with COVID-19. It classifies the technology into five major groups and then discusses its use in the least developed, developing, and developed countries.

**Corresponding author*: nusratrouf@bgsbu.ac.in (ORCID ID: 0000-0002-9989-2357)
†*Corresponding author*: sahbran8@gmail.com (ORCID ID: 0000-0002-9305-3835)

Abhinav Juneja, Vikram Bali, Sapna Juneja, Vishal Jain and Prashant Tyagi (eds.) Enabling Healthcare 4.0 for Pandemics: A Roadmap Using AI, Machine Learning, IoT and Cognitive Technologies, (117–142) © 2021 Scrivener Publishing LLC

***Keywords*:** COVID-19, emerging technologies, IoT, AI, robotics, telemedicine, pandemic

7.1 Introduction

Novel corona-virus or COVID-19 marked its first appearance in Wuhan City of China in December 2019 [1]. It was declared as a public health emergency of international concern by the WHO, World Health Organization on 30th January 2020 [2]. COVID-19 has a ripple effect on everyone all over the world with its exponential spread to more than 160 countries. It engulfed whole world and was declared as a global health crisis on 11 March 2020. It has affected almost every country and currently the most affected country is the US (United States). The number of confirmed cases has reached a peak of 33.7 million and the death toll has reached 1.01 million as of 30 September 2020 [3]. As of now vaccine is unavailable and stakeholders worldwide are working day and night to develop a vaccine. To restrict the spread of this fatal disease WHO has given some guidelines to prevent the spread of this deadly virus that has forced several countries to adopt travel restrictions, lockdowns, social distancing, and many other precautionary measures [4, 5]. Due to the adaption of these measures, the workforce across all sectors has reduced and that has greatly impacted socio-economic relations across the globe. The current crisis has built up enormous loads on our lives, economies, and social stratum. Researchers across the globe are joining hands to develop an effective strategy to come over this crisis. WHO has always been at the forefront in inspiring countries worldwide to develop smart planning to mitigate the deadly impact of this outbreak.

Innovative technological advances are emerging with a rapid pace to mitigate the consequences beforehand and obtain new capacities to construct a more secure world. According to the reports published by the United Nations, digital technologies are advancing at such a pace that it has transformed 50% of societies of the developing world in a mere time of two decades. McKinsey recommends that by 2030, about 800 million jobs would be lost to digitization, and the majority of job seekers would fear that they don't have enough skills to get a satisfactory job [6]. The current crises constantly push the field of science and technology to emerge with innovative solutions to mitigate the devastating effects of this pandemic. Technological innovations are profoundly novel, growing at a constant pace, and becoming eminent with time, subsequently, have a considerable effect on social and financial domains [7]. Technologies are penetrating our daily lives to meet our necessities and are becoming vital with each passing day. The exponential growth of digital technologies is continuously replacing existing work practices. The current crisis has paralyzed various sectors of life, including business, pharmaceuticals, banking, tourism, etc. As humans are adaptive in nature, various countries across the globe have adapted to rely on emerging technological solutions to minimize the loss of life and economy [8]. The last decade has seen rapid growth in interest towards emerging technologies and has prominently impacted policy formulators and socio-economic fields [7]. The integration of emerging technologies and healthcare provides a great opportunity to come over the current crisis [9]. The integration of IoT (Internet of Things) gadgets in healthcare institutions encourages the foundation of a profoundly interconnected digitized healthcare system. The big data generated from these institutions can be utilized by AI (Artificial Intelligence) and deep learning systems to get more insights and anticipate the causes and predict the outcomes associated with the diseases (nature healthcare). As we are stuck in a difficult time, digital innovative technologies can come to our rescue and help us to mitigate the challenges posed by this fatal disease. The majority of countries that switched to the technological solution were successful in fighting with this devastating disease. Figure 7.1 represents the confirmed cases of the top 10 worst-hit COVID-19 countries.

While surfing the internet with all relevant keywords to explore the technological solutions to fight against the pandemic, it is evident that most of the search results are webpages, blogs, white papers, press releases.

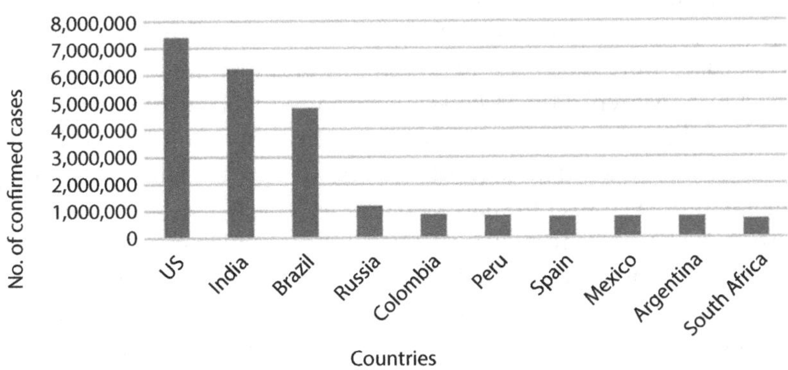

Figure 7.1 Total confirmed cases of top 10 worst-hit countries.

As it is vital to get insights into the technological advances; peer-reviewed research papers, chapters, and experimentations play a great role in building integrity and confidence in these areas. This chapter reviews the technologies to combat previous epidemics such as Ebola and SARS. It provides significant insights into emerging technologies used to combat with COVID-19. It classifies the technology into five major groups and then discusses its use in the least developed, developing, and developed countries.

7.2 Review of Technologies Used During the Outbreak of Ebola and SARS

This section reviews the technological strategies and tools that were deployed during the outbreak of Ebola and SARS. The technologies employed during these outbreaks remained effective in mitigating the ill effects posed by these epidemics and controlling their spread. Traditional responses to these outbreaks were greatly strengthened by the use of emerging technologies in an effective way. Organizations like the UN and WHO successfully helped the underprivileged countries especially in Africa to form an effective response to these situations.

7.2.1 Technological Strategies and Tools Used at the Time of SARS

In November 2002 epidemic SARS marked its appearance in the southern Chinese province of Guangdong. The impact of this virus was from November 2002 to August 2003. The outbreak was widespread in China, Hong Kong, Taiwan, Canada, Singapore, Vietnam, and the US. Total affected cases were 8,089 out of which 774 had lost their lives to this epidemic. On 17 March 2003, WHO called upon 11 laboratories in 9 countries to join a collaborative multi-center research project on SARS diagnosis. This network took advantage of modern communication technologies (e-mail; secure web site) to share outcomes of investigation of clinical samples from SARS cases in real-time [10]. Table 7.1 discusses the technological solutions that were adopted by various countries to limit the spread of Ebola. Table 7.2 discusses the tools and their use during the outbreak of Ebola and Table 7.3 discusses the future technologies that can be deployed to limit the spread of similar type diseases.

Table 7.1 Technological strategies adopted by various countries during the outbreak of SARS.

Country name	Technological strategies	Description
USA	Protective Equipment Negative Pressure Wards	In Hunting Hospital, Pasadena health workers used special protective equipment like goggles, masks, and gowns. Specially designed negative pressure wards were designed for isolated patients to help keep the SARS from spreading.
China	Infra-red Sensors Genome Sequencing Mapping technology	An infra-red sensor was invented that detected body temperature without physical touch. China also did the sequencing of genomes of various strains of SARS. China used mapping technology to physically show the case distribution.
Taiwan	Grid Computing	Used grid computing to securely share and store the patient information [11].
Singapore	Telehealth	Singapore General Hospital, during the SARS crisis, introduced an online physiotherapy program allowing physical therapists to remotely monitor patients in their homes. Using a webcam, patients could communicate with their therapists, who could in turn show their patients new exercises and give them feedback on their progress [12].

7.2.2 Technological Strategies and Tools Used at the Time of Ebola

In December 2013 epidemic Ebola marked its appearance in West Africa. The impact of this virus was from December 2013 to June 2016. The outbreak was widespread in Guinea, Sierra Leone, and Liberia. Total affected cases were 13,500 out of which 4,900 had lost their lives to this epidemic [14]. Table 7.3 discusses the technological solutions that were adopted

Table 7.2 Technologies and their use during the outbreak of SARS.

Technology	Description	Use
Healthcarelink	Detection of SARS before the occurrence of symptoms and prediction of bioterror attacks.	Patients upload their daily reports of temperature through smartphones or the internet. The website continuously publishes reports and graphs based on the given data [12].
Medday	Swedish company MedDay developed a website to predict the early breakout of the disease [13].	People enter their symptoms through smartphones or PDAs and that data is transferred to infectious-disease-center. It is believed that by the collection of data through this mechanism early breakout of diseases can be detected. The company also rebranded its software namely PharmaPoint into RegPoint so that the stakeholders may use this software to track the health situations of the population [12].
SMS service	A Hong Kong-based smartphone operator company developed an SMS service that would alert subscribers whenever they are within a kilometer range of a SARS infected person.	The subscribers received an SMS alerting them that they are near an infected SARS instance.
Electronic Tracking Systems	Contact tracing using wearable RFID cards.	Singapore health officials developed a wearable tracking system based on RFID (Radio Frequency Identification). Visitors and health workers wore credit card sized RFID chips round their necks. The sensors were hidden in the ceilings of the hospitals. These RFID cards were used to monitor the visitors and internal staff of the hospital [12].

Table 7.3 Technological strategies adapted by various countries during the outbreak of Ebola.

Country name	Technological strategies	Description
USA	Nebraska Medicine developed face shields hands-free medicine, Bluetooth stethoscopes, wireless X-rays [15]. Use of webcams [16].	Health workers used Protective equipment like triple-layered gloves and others mentioned so as to protect themselves from the spread of the virus. Webcams were used for patient monitoring.
Sierra Leone	Data sharing was hectic due to redundancy of names of villages, spelling mistakes, smartphones or GPS (Global Positioning System) enabled devices were not effective due to poor internet connectivity. These gadgets were ineffective due to the use of PPE (Personal Protection Equipment) kits by health workers. Google came to the rescue by funding Whitespell to develop an Ebola proof tablet.	Tablet was waterproof, chlorine resistant, and had the function of wireless charging. Its software and design were made open-source to encourage other humanitarian organizations and business units to develop similar kinds of equipment. It was used to record data in offline mode that could later have been uploaded to a common platform. Accurate data collection was done with respect to GPS coordinates of a particular area using GPS enabled smartphones [17].

(Continued)

Table 7.3 Technological strategies adapted by various countries during the outbreak of Ebola. (*Continued*)

Country name	Technological strategies	Description
Africa	Kobo Toolbox	Digital data collection was done using different digital forms such as the Kobo Toolbox that collected data and did its error checking.
	Local Wi-Fi	Relatives of patients were allowed to connect to isolated patients through video calls using local Wi-Fi.
	m-HERO	Sharing and receiving of Ebola information with health workers using SMS service such as m-HERO [18].

by various countries to limit the spread of Ebola. Table 7.4 discusses the tools and their use during the outbreak of Ebola and Table 7.5 discusses the future technologies that can be deployed to limit the spread of similar type diseases.

7.3 Emerging Technological Solutions to Mitigate the COVID-19 Crisis

In this section, we have classified the emerging technologies into five major categories Artificial Intelligence, IoT, and Robotics, Telemedicine, Innovative Healthcare, and Nanotechnology. We have discussed the current deployment of these technologies in least developed, developing and developed countries to fight COVID-19. Figure 7.2 shows the classification of Emerging technology into five major groups.

7.3.1 Artificial Intelligence

AI is changing our way of life aspiring to imitate human intelligence by a machine in comprehending different issues. At first, AI was intended

Table 7.4 Technologies and their use during the outbreak of Ebola.

Technology	Description	Use
DHIS2 (District Health System 2)	DHIS2 (District Health System 2) is an open-source web-based information system used in 49 countries. It was adapted by the Liberian Ministry of Health and Social Welfare prior to the Ebola crisis. Its visualization features include dashboards, GIS (Geographical Information System), charts, and pivot tables.	Data collection and sharing in near real-time.
RAPID PRO	This SMS providing tool was supported by UNICEF. It was easy to use tool and quickly created communication campaigns and monitored programs and activities. It collected critical indicators in specifically designated areas such as critical medicines.	Data collection and sharing in near real-time.
WHO DCP (World Health Organization data coordination platform)	WHO and UNICEF jointly developed an effective tool for countering Ebola and was used for data collection and management targeting health workers and their safety. It was a part of the m-HERO tool [19].	Data collection and sharing in near real-time.
HealthMap	This tool collects data from crowd-based informal sources and is used for surveillance and monitoring outbreaks in real-time using the web platform healthmap.org and mobile app Outbreaks NearMe.	Mapping and geolocation of Ebola technologies.
OpenStreetMap	The tool that utilizes satellite technology and on-ground volunteers spread around the globe to develop maps of streets and roads of specific towns that help in mapping the outbreak.	Mapping and geolocation of Ebola technologies.

Table 7.5 Future technologies that can be deployed to limit the spread of similar type diseases.

Technology	Description	Use
i callQ	This biosensor is a smartphone-based tech tool that quantifies, stores, and does the interpretation of specific diagnostic tests and shares information to a common centralized platform.	Point of care diagnostics.
Fionet	It is a system developed for health workers and it utilizes cloud technology for data storage and provides real-time data mining for rapid diagnostic tests. Fionet can provide an effective response against Ebola by helping in contact tracing, efficient online working, and providing relevant information to program managers and other stakeholders.	Point of care diagnostics and contact tracing.
Novarum DX	This mobile app is another mobile point-of-care diagnostic technological solution for health workers that enables them to do rapid testing and provide a real-time record to health experts using a smartphone. The information provided helps to develop a geo-referenced map that can help health workers and managers to provide an effective response against area-specific Ebola outbreak.	Point of care diagnostics.

to beat fewer complex issues like dominating a chess match, among others. With the innovative progressions, AI is playing a the role of game-changer and is currently being applied to every field of study due to its proficiency in tackling complex issues. In the current health crisis, AI has played a significant role to mitigate the issues in a better way. AI is being used in contact tracing, tracking down the high-risk patients, predicting the hotspots, drug discovery, and controlling the outbreak in real-time. By analyzing the previous patient datasets it can also be used to predict the mortality risk [20]. AI helps us in fighting the current crisis by quick screening and fast treatment of patients, prediction of infection, and mortality rate [21]. WHO, CDC (Centers for Disease Control and Prevention), ECDC (European Centers for Disease Control and Prevention), and many

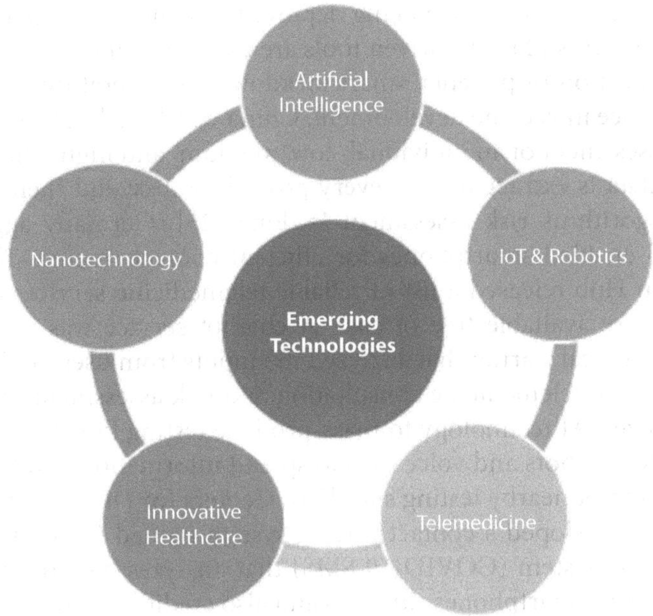

Figure 7.2 The classification of Emerging Technologies.

others provide free access to COVID-19 statistical data in real-time all over the world. The researchers can access this data and develop an AI-based collaborative model to handle the current crisis. Unsupervised learning on textual data from social media platforms generates valuable and predictive insights [5]. AI-based advanced methods and algorithms help in the development of vaccines, it also enables us to perceive the effectiveness of a particular measure taken against COVID-19. AI has also revolutionized education and financial sectors. UNESCO supported the Quebec Institute of Artificial Intelligence in developing AI-enabled mobile App solutions to counter the COVID-19 crisis. These apps were specially developed in accordance to the fundamental rights of the people.

7.3.1.1 Application of AI in Developed Countries

In Canada, an AI-driven surveillance system named BlueDot predicted the outbreak of pandemic nine days before WHO released the statement alerting people about novel coronavirus [22]. In China, AI diagnostic tool helps in distinguishing COVID-19 form other pneumonic diseases by analyzing the CT scan chest images. Chinese E-commerce Company Alibaba developed an AI-based diagnostic system that diagnoses COVID-19 in seconds [23].

AI thermal cameras are also being deployed in China to keep a check on potential patients [24]. AI-driven tools are used to facilitate fast diagnosis and classification of patients, smart lockdowns, temperature monitoring, and assistance in vaccine development. China developed a Health Barcode for risk assessment of an individual- low, medium, and high. The potential patients' data is extracted from every possible source and then by applying AI algorithms risk assessment is done [25]. Germany aggressively used GPS enabled smartphones for efficient contact tracing. The health innovation Hub released a list of reliable telemedicine services and most of them were available free of cost. A chatbot service was provided by DOCYET, a local startup that analyzed the inputs from users and provides the options for telemedicine consultation and risk assessment [26]. South Korea utilized AI technology to mass-produce testing kits. It also utilized AI-enabled chatbots and voice calls to spread information and help in the identification of nearby testing sites [24]. Centers for Disease Control and Prevention developed a contact tracing system named COVID-19 Smart Management System (COVID-19 SMS) that analyzes data from CCTVs, GPS data from smartphones, and cars and also credit card transaction data to trace the infected patient's movement [25]. South Korea adopted a policy of strict quarantine for the people that were actively involved in health services and warned the violators of facing serious consequences like jail [27]. Dubai has used the Dubai Mobile App that allows its users to access 160 health and utility services. This App has been a success in achieving its mission. Also, a nation-wide 'Digital Signature' was introduced as a secure and trusted way to digitally sign the documents, this has allowed multiple firms to participate in public tenders through the internet [28].

7.3.1.2 Application of AI in Developing Countries

India's All India Institute of Medical Sciences (AIIMS), Delhi has received AI-driven tools and equipment from the Israeli embassy to fight against COVID-19. It includes innovative products that are designed to give contact-free access to a patient's heart rate and respiratory rates. It also includes tools for 24 × 7 patient surveillance [29]. TCS (Tata Consultancy Services) in collaboration with CSIR (Council of Scientific and Industrial Research) is using AI to develop new drugs for SARS CoV-2. A company [30]. Indian companies such as Qure.ai and Tata Consultancy Services are using AI in chest X-rays for the diagnosis of COVID-19 and the extent of infection in the lungs [31]. The app known as Aarogya Setu [32] is widely used for contact tracing and spreading awareness among the masses in India. This app uses Bluetooth and GPS services to alert the user about nearby COVID-19 patients. This app is similar to the TraceTogether app that is used in Singapore. South African government has also partnered with an online health platform, 'HelloDoctor' to give its citizens free access to its services [24]. Pakistan has been relatively successful in curbing the COVID-19 crisis. Recently it has developed an AI-based system to do the risk assessment of regions [33]. The system analyzes 10 factors including social distancing, mask adherence, and other factors and helps area authorities in strengthening their SOP (standard operating procedure) implementation strategy. The government of Sindh in collaboration with Aga Khan University has developed an App named CoronaCheck using AI-driven chatbot that enables masses to keep a check on their symptoms and assist them in a timely manner [34]. This app is similar to Canada's Alberta Health Services. Two students from Ghulam Ishaq Khan Institute developed an AI-driven deep learning model for the detection of COVID-19 from CT scan of lungs that has an accuracy of 92% [35].

Least developed countries especially in Africa are utilizing their past experiences with epidemics to form an effective response with respect to AI in fighting the COVID-19.

7.3.2 IoT & Robotics

IoT is considered as a prime building block for developing the smart strategy to combat COVID-19. IoT enabled healthcare systems to allow continuous surveillance of patients and assist potential patients during their quarantine period. IoMT (Internet of Medical Things) and IoHT (Internet of Healthcare Things) are deployed for real-time biometric measurements such as heart rate, respiratory rate, etc. Since the early phase of the pandemic, WHO has continuously issued guidelines to take proper care of sanitization and cleanliness. Autonomous robots are being deployed for this task so as to limit physical contact. Robots may appear as an individual entity but in actual they extensively use IoT. Ultraviolet radiations are being generated by robots to decrease the outbreak of this virus. Robots have been deployed in vulnerable environments such as hospitals, quarantine centers, and on airplanes to help in sanitization.

IoMT would not only serve to help with the current pandemic, but also could be implemented to prevent future outbreaks as well. Unmanned Aerial Vehicles (UAVs) or drones can identify potential COVID-19 carriers. UAVs have the capacity to detect ground surface temperatures from a certain height above the ground and send the measured data, captured thermal images, and optical images along with GPS location, to a server [36]. Also, in some countries, different emerging technologies and AI-based information retrieving gadgets like wrist bands, GPS based smartphones, and CCTV cameras are being utilized for tracking the infected patients and monitoring people under quarantine. Monitoring the Credit card transactions of suspected cases serves the same purpose [37]. AI cameras are being used to check whether social distancing is respected in public places [24]. Bluetooth technology has also been jointly utilized by Apple and Google to develop a mobile Bluetooth based contact tracing [24].

7.3.2.1 Application of IoT and Robotics in Developed Countries

In China's Wuhan, a smart field hospital deployed robots to assist health-care workers in the treatment of potential patients [38]. Some of the robots are used to fulfill the daily needs of patients and some are used for sanitization of the hospital. Pudu technology delivered its catering robots to more than 40 hospitals in China [39]. The concerned authorities have used drones fitted with cameras and speakers to alert masses from gathering and to adapt strict lockdowns [39]. Other IoT devices that are utilized include smart bracelets and rings that continuously monitor temperature, respiratory rate, and heart rates of patients [40]. In the US, the GermFalcon robot that uses UVC radiations is currently being deployed to sanitize airports [41]. Companies such as Demir UVC innovations, Xenex Disinfection Services, and PDI healthcare are currently focusing on making more robots so as to mark their contribution in fighting COVID-19 [38]. Robots are currently utilized to deliver the daily needs for survival to the masses. UK (United Kingdom) is aggressively using robots for delivery of medicine, PPE kits, and other vital supplies so as to make faster deliveries and reduce the vulnerability of medical staff and workers to this virus [42]. Vodafone has introduced heat cameras to detect the temperature of people entering the buildings. These cameras have a capacity to measure temperatures of 100 people in a minute. In Singapore robot equipped with numerous sensors and cameras is deployed to maintain social distancing in parks. Whenever a robot detects violations in social distancing it broadcasts warnings. Singapore government with the assistance of IoT devices developed a smart system to deliver the correct information regarding COVID-19 and curb misinformation [43]. It also used TraceTogether Bluetooth based app to trace contacts. Recently, the first Internet of Things buttons was designed which are being used by hospitals in Canada. It addresses the need for rapid deployment in a facility of any size and sends rapid alerts to management notifying of any cleaning or maintenance issues that may pose risks to public safety [44]. Robots have been used by multiple nations around the world primarily in order to maintain social distancing. Countries like China are using robots for various medical operations like sample collection, medical testing, stethoscope usage, etc. In Europe, countries like Italy are using robots as food delivery systems and health checking systems [45].

7.3.2.2 Application of IoT and Robotics in Developing Countries

The UN (United Nations) launched "solidarity flights" to airlift medical equipment and supplies for developing nations to help them against COVID-19 [46]. In India, IoT-based fever detection thermal cameras have been developed by experts that measure the body temperature of people that pass in the range of the camera [47]. The research team from LPU (Lovely Professional University) has developed an IoT device called '20Sec4Life' that glows and plays music for 20 seconds to help masses in proper handwashing [48]. India is continuously using drones for monitoring and alerting people to maintain social distancing and to disinfect public places [42]. South Africa uses WhatsApp messenger to deliver informative messages to millions of its users in five languages. They have implemented the drone technology of flying towers for network connectivity so as to facilitate communications with far-flung areas [42]. UNESCO (United Nations Educational, Scientific, and Cultural Organization) also partnered with Innovation for Policy Foundation (i4Policy) and launched an online campaign #DontGoViral in Africa to counter the misinformation. Artists and cultural entrepreneurs were actively involved in the campaign to spread awareness in local African languages [49]. Mongolia is using drones for surveillance, to enforce strict lockdowns. It is also using mass broadcast drones to aware people of about social distancing measures, preventive measures and inform them about the nearest available medical facilities [42].

Mapping of medical supplies in the least developed countries ought to be done using the data-sharing technologies like Frontline SMS which reports the supply distribution of critical medical equipment to a common internet-platform. This distribution is then to be represented on a map. This use of technology can help local manufacturers, budding entrepreneurs, and business units to respond to an area-specific medical shortage and improve their economic opportunity [65].

7.3.3 Telemedicine

Telemedicine is an innovative provision where the health workers abide by social-distancing rules and provide medicinal help to patients. The major risk in the spread of the virus is in the Healthcare emergency institutions.

The current crisis has led to various innovations and telemedicine is one of them. It is highly recommended to make use of contactless health consultations so as to limit the spread of the virus. The developed countries have deployed telemedicinal facilities to keep health workers secure from virus [50]. Social platforms are now being used for patient–doctor interactions. The adaption of lockdowns, quarantines, isolations, and social-distancing has triggered mental health issues such as anger, frustrations, and fear, so, teleconsultation facilities provide vital services of online counseling [51]. Telemedicine services can be utilized to provide staff training in remote areas [36]. The use of telehealth services lowers down the costs of transportation and improves the quality of service in remote areas.

7.3.3.1 Application of Telemedicine in Developed Countries

Ref. [52] has shown an increase in the interest of the US in telehealthcare facilities. It has further revealed that around 60% of US healthcare institutions have deployed telemedicine services. Various healthcare institutions in the US including McLeod Health offer telehealth services free of cost since the beginning of March for COVID-19 screening. In China, 18 workgroups were employed by NTCC (National Telemedicine Center of China) in collaboration with Huawei Technologies and China Mobiles to help set up telemedicine services in Isolation wards. NTCC has provided fast services to diagnose and assist potential patients in need during the crisis [53]. An E-commerce giant, Alibaba has developed a teleconsultation platform where expert consultants that were at the forefront during the initial outbreak in Wuhan, are available for the Chinese people living abroad [54]. Singapore has adopted the telehealth services to take care of isolated patients. Telepresence robots are used in Alexandra Hospital to assist isolated patients by delivering daily food, medicines to them and also help doctors and healthcare workers to have contactless communication with them [55]. In response to the increased use of telehealthcare facilities, Singapore Medical Association in February 2020, issued guidelines on usage of telemedicine during the COVID-19 crisis and also published the guidelines to use already available telemedicine systems for health workers that were unfamiliar with the services [56]. The Australian government has come up with an idea of funding telemedicine service providers to fight against the COVID-19 crisis. People there are aggressively using virtual healthcare facilities, and healthcare practitioners are actively involved in providing services. The Australian government has issued an advisory to physicians, psychiatrists, and other health practitioners to actively participate in providing telehealth services to isolated patients [57].

7.3.3.2 *Application of Telemedicine in Developing Countries*

The majority of the population in developing countries is concentrated in rural areas. However, qualified doctors tend to live in urban areas that lead to geographical in-equilibrium in the availability of healthcare professionals [58]. During the current crisis, such services can minimize the workload of health professionals and risk of causalities by making services available to remote areas. India has released an advisory to healthcare experts to leverage the use of telemedicine facilities in the current crisis. It also includes the guidelines to use existing tele-platforms and tools to provide healthcare services [57]. Tele-platform named Practo has been used extensively since early March. There is an increase of 50% of health practitioners joining Practo. Other teleconsultation platform named as ForeignOPD, has been continuously providing service to the masses to help fight the COVID-19 crisis. The developers are currently working on the development of a mobile application [59]. The Government of Pakistan in collaboration with the private sectors has developed various platforms for telehealth services such as the Telehealth portal by the federal government, helplines by various state governments, Marham, and others to help people in the current crisis [60]. People access such facilities through websites, social media platforms, SMS, and telephonic services. Marham has been one of the most successful telehealth platforms that allow the masses to use health services by giving access to health professionals. Marham is also using the social media platform to spread awareness among the masses and allow people to directly pose queries related to COVID-19. This platform has also its own official YouTube channel that makes people aware regarding of the current crisis [60]. Currently, 12K health professionals are registered with Marham. Due to the not availability of 3G/4G network connectivity in remote and rural areas due to the non-implementation of laws supporting telehealth in developing countries these services can't fully be explored [61]. The governments in developing countries should fund and assist healthcare agencies in developing telehealth services and enforcing laws that support the implementation of telehealth [62]. The integration of existing healthcare services and telehealth in the current crisis will minimize the rate of mortality and will help in limiting the spread of this virus [61].

7.3.4 Innovative Healthcare

Strong healthcare forms the backbone of COVID-19 effective response. The present pandemic has exposed the healthcare of many developed nations. Some of the Latin American and Asian nations have also had a poor response to this pandemic. It explains the motivation and the necessity for innovation in the field of healthcare. Innovative healthcare includes progressive healthcare policies, improved and updated medical systems, efficient medical chains, embedding modern technologies in the health sector, and improved services. WHO has also established a group named WHIG (WHO Health Innovation Group) that actively engages in Innovative healthcare. Innovative healthcare majorly includes Scientific Innovation, Social Innovation, and Business Innovation [63].

7.3.4.1 Application of Innovative Healthcare in Developed Countries

Developed countries should mobilize their resources and machinery to develop a network in stockpiling the supplies [24]. Development of innovative devices like wrist-mounted sprays, specialized wristbands that buzz on face-touch, hands-free door-openers, etc. can help in effectively containing the pandemic [67]. Companies like Dyson (UK) and Ford (US) are using 3D printing technology to produce much-needed medical equipment [67]. Virustatic Shield (UK) produced a snood mask that is equipped with an anti-viral coating effective against COVID-19 [67]. Doctors from Glangwill Hospital, Carmarthen, Wales (UK) designed a simple and effective model of a basic ventilator to specifically help patients suffering from COVID-19 symptoms [67]. Effective, efficient, and mass-producible test methods need to be developed. Companies like Mammoth Biosciences (US) and GlaxoSmithKline (UK) have been successful in this field and have developed a 20-minute CRISPR (Clusters of Regularly Interspaced Short Palindromic Repeats) based test that can dramatically increase our testing capabilities. In the coming time masks containing biosensors sensitive to COVID-19 can greatly help the health workers in their practice [68]. Companies like Mercedes Formula One (UK) have partnered with UCL (University College London) professionals to produce a Continuous Positive Airway Pressure system that helps in pushing oxygen to the patient's lungs without the use of a ventilator. This particular model is 70% more efficient in oxygen consumption [45].

7.3.4.2 Application of Innovative Healthcare in Developing Countries

South African missile manufacturer Denel has reinvented itself by shifting its production to manufacture ventilators and redeveloped armored trucks into ambulances [46]. Turkey has developed an AI-based stethoscope that checks the specific sounds and identifies the potential patients [64]. Open-source local manufacturing by different organizations like Field Ready can help to easily produce humanitarian supplies that are cheap and in bulk. Governing bodies should also ensure that various industries and machinery like 3D Printing should be designated as "critical infrastructure" so that essential items and spare parts are 3D printed and supplies match the demand [65]. Tech Access Partnership (TAP), a program started by United Nations Technology Bank (UNTB) is helping the developing nations by creating a digital warehouse of manufacturing and design specifications, technical knowledge, and information required to increase their capacity to produce equipment to counter COVID-19. TAP has forged relations with local business units and manufacturers to help them in developing affordable and efficient technologies to counter the COVID-19 [66].

7.3.4.3 Application of Innovative Healthcare in the Least Developed Countries

Governments across the world especially in Africa have developed innovative ways to reinvent the factories. Many manufacturing units have been successful in producing the much-needed medical equipment. Countries like Kenya have successfully utilized their companies to produce relevant supplies. Kenya's textile industry, KICOTEC (Kitui County Textile Center) has shifted its production from uniform-production to face-masks and scrubs. Also, Kenyan state-owned oil company has been mass-producing sanitizers and distributing them free to help contain the COVID-19 threat [46]. Nigeria is working with car companies to manufacture locally produced ventilators [46]. Many African countries have set up public hand-washing stations with suitable sanitizers or soaps at important points like building entrances and transport centers [72]. These centers were primarily used to counter Ebola in countries like Liberia and Sierra Leone [46]. Médecins Sans Frontières (MSF) has also set up multiple points for hand-washing in Nigerian Migrant camps and the health facilities of Mozambique [46].

7.3.5 Nanotechnology

Nanotechnology has become the backbone of emerging technologies. New materials and techniques have given us the power to develop unique substances with amazing properties. In containing the spread of a pandemic like COVID-19, nanotechnology offers the best set of solutions that have the potential to dramatically reverse the effects of these crises. Advanced nanomaterials are helping in the development of therapeutics, efficient diagnostic kits, development of a vaccine, and production of new types of PPEs [24]. An Italian company named Nanotech Surface developed a sanitizer based on advanced nanomaterials that remains effective on the surface for months. Also, the Czech Respilon Group designed a nanofiber-based mask that has the potential to kill the trapped virus [24]. Nano-medicine also offers a powerful way to help in COVID-19 therapeutics. Therapeutics based on nanocarriers can help us in overcoming the challenges like poor solubility and less bio-availability [69]. Drug-delivery systems having nanocarriers help in preventing premature drug release, hence, increasing the half-life of biologicals. Nano-science can also be utilized in chemically altering and re-engineering drugs [69]. In vaccine development, virus mimicking macro-molecular complexes called Virus Like Particles (VLPs) is the most common methodology employed to develop safe nano-sized vaccines [70]. Vaccine Adjuvant Nanoparticles (VANs) can help in the mass production of COVID-19 vaccines by effectively and safely reducing the antigen dose [69]. Nanotechnology plays a vital role in diagnostics, drug delivery, and bio-markers. Bio-compatible and functionalized nanoparticles can act as broad-spectrum anti-virals. Nanomaterials like metal-based nanoparticles and graphene having antipathogenic properties that are responsible for causing the inactivation of pathogens can help in development in the self-disinfecting surfaces that are effective in containing COVID-19 in health workers. Nanostructured copper can also increase the anti-microbial activity. Graphene, a famous and emerging 2D allotrope of carbon can form an effective protective barrier for the antigens (with size greater than 300 nm) in critical medical equipment like masks, gloves, and PPEs. Biosensors based on nanomaterials can effectively replace classical laboratory tools for different types of analyses [71].

7.4 Conclusion

COVID-19 has a ripple effect on everyone all over the world with its exponential spread to more than 160 countries. The outbreak of this virus has escalated the concerns of all agencies worldwide. Due to the current crisis, various sectors such as import and export, education, transportation, healthcare, industries, etc. are either staggering under pressure or are in a deadlock state. People find it difficult to combat with COVID-19 due to insufficient availability of resources and expertise. Innovative technological advances are emerging at a rapid pace to mitigate the consequences beforehand and obtain new capacities to construct a more secure world. Emerging technologies are playing a major role in managing the current situation. This chapter reviews the technologies to combat previous epidemics such as Ebola and SARS. It provides significant insights into emerging technologies used to combat with COVID-19. It classifies the technology into five major groups and then discusses its use in based in least developed, developing, developed countries.

References

1. Wu, F. *et al.*, A new coronavirus associated with human respiratory disease in China. *Nature*, 579, 7798, 265–269, 2020.
2. *Coronavirus disease 2019*, [Online]. Available: https://www.who.int/emergencies/diseases/novel-coronavirus-2019. [Accessed: 30-Jun-2020].
3. *Coronavirus Update (Live): 33.7M Cases and 1.01M Deaths from COVID-19 Virus Pandemic—Worldometer*, [Online]. Available: https://www.worldometers.info/coronavirus/?zarsrc=130. [Accessed: 30-September-2020].
4. *Centers for Disease Control and Prevention*, https://www.cdc.gov/ (accessed Sep. 07, 2020).
5. Khanday, A.M.U.D., Rabani, S.T., Khan, Q.R. *et al.* Machine learning based approaches for detecting COVID-19 using clinical text data. *Int. J. Inf. Tecnol*,. 12, 731–739, 2020. https://doi.org/10.1007/s41870-020-00495-9.
6. *The Impact of Digital Technologies | United Nations*, https://www.un.org/en/un75/impact-digital-technologies (accessed Sep. 07, 2020).
7. Agarwal, S., Punn, N.S., Sonbhadra, S.K., Pandian, K.K.S., Saxena, P., Unleashing the power of disruptive and emerging technologies amid COVID-19: A detailed review. 2020, arXiv:2.
8. Vaishya, R., Haleem, A., Vaish, A., Javaid, M. Emerging Technologies to Combat the COVID-19 Pandemic. *J. Clin. Exp. Hepatol.*, 10, 2–4, 2020.
9. McKibbin, W. and Fernando, R., The global macroeconomic impacts of COVID-19: Seven scenarios. *Asian Econ. Pap.*, 1–55, 2020. https://doi.org/10.1162/asep_a_00796.
10. WHO, *WHO collaborative multi-centre research project on Severe Acute Respiratory Syndrome (SARS) diagnosis*, [Online]. Available: https://www.who.int/csr/sars/project/en/. [Accessed: 20-Aug-2020].
11. Larkin, M., Technology confronts SARS. *Lancet Infect. Dis.*, 3, 7, 453, Jul. 2003.
12. Eysenbach, G., SARS and population health technology. *J. Med. Internet Res.*, 5, 2, e14, Jun. 2003.
13. *News & Events—MedDay Pharma*, https://www.medday-pharma.com/news-and-events/ (accessed Aug. 20, 2020).
14. *Ebola data and statistics*, WHO, Accessed: Aug. 20, 2020. [Online]. Available: https://apps.who.int/gho/data/node.ebola-sitrep.quick-downloads?lang=en.

15. *4 Technologies Developed in Light of Ebola and Other Health Scares*, https://healthinformatics.uic.edu/blog/4-technologies-being-developed-in-light-of-ebola-and-other-broad-scale-health-scares/ (accessed Aug. 20, 2020).
16. *Treating Ebola: The Bluetooth Method*, https://www.nationalgeographic.com/news/2014/11/141106-science-ebola-cure-medicine-health-africa-disease-technology/ (accessed Aug. 20, 2020).
17. *The technology helping to fight Ebola*, World Economic Forum, https://www.weforum.org/agenda/2015/05/the-technology-helping-to-fight-ebola/ (accessed Aug. 20, 2020).
18. *6 Ways Technology is Helping to Fight Ebola*, TechChange, The Institute for Technology and Social Change, https://www.techchange.org/2014/10/08/ebola-technology-ict/ (accessed Aug. 20, 2020).
19. *Overview: The Ebola Outbreak Use Of Technology In The Ebola Response In West Africa Technology Use In The Ebola Response*, Accessed: Aug. 20, 2020. [Online]. Available: https://www.msh.org/sites/default/files/technology_and_ebola_response_in_west_africa_technical_brief_final.pdf.
20. Vaishya, R., Javaid, M., Khan, I.H., Haleem, A., Artificial Intelligence (AI) applications for COVID-19 pandemic. *Diabetes Metab. Syndr. Clin. Res. Rev.*, 14, 4, 337–339, 2020.
21. Dananjayan, S. and Raj, G.M., Artificial intelligence during a pandemic: The COVID-19 example. *Int. J. Health Plan. Manag.*, 35, 5, 1260–1262, 2020.
22. *BlueDot used artificial intelligence to predict coronavirus spread*, [Online]. Available: https://www.cnbc.com/2020/03/03/bluedot-used-artificial-intelligence-to-predict-coronavirus-spread.html. [Accessed: 18-Aug-2020].
23. *Alibaba's new AI system can detect coronavirus in seconds with 96% accuracy*, https://thenextweb.com/neural/2020/03/02/alibabas-new-ai-system-can-detect-coronavirus-in-seconds-with-96-accuracy/ (accessed Sep. 07, 2020).
24. *Using the Fourth Industrial Revolution to fight COVID-19 around the world*, https://www.brookings.edu/techstream/using-the-fourth-industrial-revolution-to-fight-covid-19-around-the-world/ (accessed Aug. 20, 2020).
25. Lin, L. and Hou, Z., Combat COVID-19 with artificial intelligence and big data. *J. Travel Med.*, 27, 5, taaa080, 2020.
26. *How Germany Leveraged Digital Health to Combat COVID-19—The Medical Futurist*, https://medicalfuturist.com/how-germany-leveraged-digital-health-to-combat-covid-19/ (accessed Sep. 07, 2020).
27. *South Korea warns of deportation, jail for quarantine violators*, Reuters.com, https://www.reuters.com/news/picture/south-korea-warns-of-deportation-jail-fo-idUSKBN21D06C.
28. *Digital Technologies and the COVID-19 pandemic*, Accessed: Aug. 20, 2020. [Online]. Available: https://www.uclg.org/sites/default/files/eng_briefing_technology_final_x.pdf.
29. *Israel AI-based technologies to help tackle COVID-19—The Hindu*, https://www.thehindu.com/news/cities/Delhi/israel-ai-based-technologies-to-help-tackle-covid-19/article32329689.ece (accessed Sep. 07, 2020).

30. *These three Indian IT firms are developing tech tools to fight COVID-19. TechGig*, https://content.techgig.com/these-three-indian-it-firms-are-developing-tech-tools-to-fight-covid-19/articleshow/75067278.cms.
31. *How Artificial Intelligence is Helping to Fight against Coronavirus in India?*, https://www.analyticsinsight.net/artificial-intelligence-helping-fight-coronavirus-india/ (accessed Sep. 07, 2020).
32. Aarogya Setu, https://aarogyasetu.gov.in/.
33. *Pakistan develops AI system to measure Covid risk*, The Express Tribune, https://tribune.com.pk/story/2259538/pakistan-develops-ai-system-to-measure-covid-risk (accessed Sep. 07, 2020).
34. *Pakistan's CoronaCheck app to help fight COVID-19*, https://www.geospatialworld.net/apps/covid-19/pakistans-coronacheck-app-to-help-fight-covid-19/ (accessed Sep. 07, 2020).
35. *In Pakistan, digital platform offers a baseline to fight COVID-19 | 2020-05-28 | BioWorld*, https://www.bioworld.com/articles/435383-in-pakistan-digital-platform-offers-a-baseline-to-fight-covid-19 (accessed Sep. 07, 2020).
36. Tsikala Vafea, M., Atalla, E., Georgakas, J. *et al.*, Emerging Technologies for Use in the Study, Diagnosis, and Treatment of Patients with COVID-19. *Cel. Mol., Bioeng.*, 13, 249–257, 2020, https://doi.org/10.1007/s12195-020-00629-w.
37. *Embracing tech to tackle coronavirus*, The Commonwealth, https://thecommon wealth.org/media/news/embracing-tech-tackle-coronavirus (accessed Aug. 20, 2020).
38. *Open source underpins coronavirus IoT and robotics solutions*, Opensource.com, https://opensource.com/article/20/5/robotics-covid19.
39. *How countries are using technology to fight coronavirus*, https://economictimes.indiatimes.com/tech/software/how-countries-are-using-technology-to-fight-coronavirus/articleshow/74867177.cms.
40. *How China is using robots and telemedicine to combat the coronavirus*, https://www.cnbc.com/2020/03/18/how-china-is-using-robots-and-telemedicine-to-combat-the-coronavirus.html. (Accessed on: Aug. 20,2020)
41. *Company offers germ-killing robot to airports to address coronavirus outbreak*, https://www.therobotreport.com/company-offers-germ-killing-robot-to-airports-to-address-coronavirus-outbreak/ (accessed Sep. 07, 2020).
42. GSMA, How the emergence of connected drones is helping the fight against COVID-19. *Internet Things*, https://www.gsma.com/iot/drones/how-the-emergence-of-connected-drones-is-helping-the-fight-against-covid-19/ (accessed Sep. 07, 2020).
43. *The five: robots helping to tackle coronavirus, Technology*, The Guardian, https://www.theguardian.com/technology/2020/may/31/the-five-robots-helping-to-tackle-coronavirus.
44. *How IoT can help fight COVID-19 battle*, Geospatial World, https://www.geospatialworld.net/blogs/how-iot-can-help-fight-covid-19-battle/ (accessed Aug. 19, 2020).

45. *3 key areas innovative tech is helping during the COVID-19 pandemic—ITU News*, https://news.itu.int/3-ways-innovative-tech-is-helping-during-the-covid-19-pandemic/ (accessed Aug. 20, 2020).
46. *6 Ways To Fight Coronavirus In The Developing World: Goats and Soda: NPR*, https://www.npr.org/sections/goatsandsoda/2020/04/26/844207862/6-solutions-to-beat-covid-19-in-countries-where-the-usual-advice-just-wont-work (accessed Aug. 20, 2020).
47. *The role of AI and IoT technologies in the COVID-19 situation—NASSCOM Community*, The Official Community of Indian IT Industry, https://community.nasscom.in/communities/covid-19/the-role-of-ai-and-iot-technologies-in-the-covid-19-situation.html (accessed Sep. 07, 2020).
48. *COVID-19: Novel IoT device may help people clean hands properly, India News*, Times of India, https://timesofindia.indiatimes.com/india/covid-19-novel-iot-device-may-help-people-clean-hands-properly/articleshow/76685968.cms.
49. *Fighting COVID-19 through digital innovation and transformation*, https://en.unesco.org/covid19/communicationinformationresponse/digitalinnovation (accessed Aug. 20, 2020).
50. Mahmood, S., Hasan, K., Colder Carras, M., Labrique, A., Global Preparedness Against COVID-19: We Must Leverage the Power of Digital Health. *JMIR Public Health Surveill.*, 6, 2, e18980, Apr. 2020.
51. Rajkumar, R.P., COVID-19 and mental health: A review of the existing literature. *Asian J. Psychiatr.*, 52, 102066, March 2020.
52. Hong, Y.-R., Lawrence, J., Williams, D., Jr, Mainous, A., III, Population-Level Interest and Telehealth Capacity of US Hospitals in Response to COVID-19: Cross-Sectional Analysis of Google Search and National Hospital Survey Data. *JMIR Public Health Surveill.*, 6, 2, e18961–e18961, Apr. 2020.
53. Zhai, Y., *et al.*, From Isolation to Coordination: How Can Telemedicine Help Combat the COVID-19 Outbreak?, medRxiv; 2020.
54. *Global MediXchange for Combating COVID-19—Alibaba Cloud*, https://www.alibabacloud.com/covid-19-global-medixchange.
55. Ahmed, S., Sanghvi, K., Yeo, D., Telemedicine takes centre stage during COVID-19 pandemic. *BMJ Innov.*, 6, 252–254, 2020.
56. *Singapore Medical Association—For Doctors, For Patients*, https://www.sma.org.sg/ourvoice/index.aspx?ID=375.
57. *Telehealth in the era of COVID-19—Economist Intelligence Unit*, https://www.eiu.com/n/telehealth-in-the-era-of-covid-19/.
58. Kadir, M.A., Role of Telemedicine in Healthcare During COVID-19 Pandemic in Developing Countries. *Telehealth Med. Today*, 5, 2020.
59. *COVID-19 lockdown 2.0: Telemedicine in India to see continued growth*, Health News, ET HealthWorld, https://health.economictimes.indiatimes.com/news/health-it/covid-19-lockdown-2-0-telemedicine-in-india-to-see-continued-growth/75172147.

60. *How Telemedicine Has Helped Pakistan Combat COVID-19 Pandemic | Business*, https://ipsnews.net/business/2020/07/17/how-telemedicine-has-helped-pakistan-combat-covid-19-pandemic/.
61. Keshvardoost, S., Bahaadinbeigy, K., Fatehi, F., Role of Telehealth in the Management of COVID-19: Lessons Learned from Previous SARS, MERS, and Ebola Outbreaks. *Telemed. J. E. Health*, 26, 7, 850–852, 2020.
62. Bokolo, A. Jnr., Use of Telemedicine and Virtual Care for Remote Treatment in Response to COVID-19 Pandemic. *J. Med. Syst.*, 44, 7, 132, 2020. https://doi.org/10.1007/s10916-020-01596-5.
63. *WHO Health Innovation Group*, Accessed: Aug. 20, 2020. [Online]. Available: https://www.who.int/phi/1-health_innovation-brochure.pdf.
64. *Turkish university develops tool to diagnose COVID-19*, https://www.aa.com.tr/en/latest-on-coronavirus-outbreak/turkish-university-develops-tool-to-diagnose-covid-19/1912645 (accessed Aug. 20, 2020).
65. *How can we help beat coronavirus in developing countries?*, World Economic Forum, https://www.weforum.org/agenda/2020/05/five-ways-collective-intelligence-can-help-beat-coronavirus-in-developing-countries/ (accessed Aug. 20, 2020).
66. *UN rolls out new technology initiative to help developing countries fight COVID-19—The National*, https://www.thenational.ae/business/technology/un-rolls-out-new-technology-initiative-to-help-developing-countries-fight-covid-19-1.1018936 (accessed Aug. 20, 2020).
67. *COVID-19 innovation: These gadgets were designed to fight the pandemic*, World Economic Forum, https://www.weforum.org/agenda/2020/04/coronavirus-covid19-pandemic-gadgets-innovation-technology/ (accessed Aug. 20, 2020).
68. Sheridan, C., COVID-19 spurs wave of innovative diagnostics. *Nat. Biotechnol.*, 38, 7, NLM (Medline), 769–772, Jul. 01, 2020.
69. Chauhan, G., Madou, M.J., Kalra, S., Chopra, V., Ghosh, D., Martinez-Chapa, S.O., Nanotechnology for COVID-19: Therapeutics and Vaccine Research. *ACS Nano*, 14, 7, 7760–7782, Jul. 2020.
70. Palestino, G., García-Silva, I., González-Ortega, O., Rosales-Mendoza, S., Can nanotechnology help in the fight against COVID-19?, *Expert Rev. of Anti-Infect. Ther.*, 18, 9, 849–864.
71. Weiss, C. *et al.*, Toward Nanotechnology-Enabled Approaches against the COVID-19 Pandemic. *ACS Nano*, 14, 6, 6383–6406, Jun. 2020.
72. *COVID-19 and the least developed countries*, Department of Economic and Social Affairs, https://www.un.org/development/desa/dpad/publication/un-desa-policy-brief-66-covid-19-and-the-least-developed-countries/.

8

Advances in Technology: Preparedness for Handling Pandemic Challenges

Shweta Sinha* and Vikas Thada

Amity University Haryana, Gurgaon, India

Abstract
High transmissibility and lack of effective vaccine have made the control of disease spread a challenge, and eventually, they take the form of a pandemic. The uncontrollable spread of virus creates challenges not only for the social or health front but also on the global economy. This chapter discusses the social, health and economic difficulties due to pandemic. The claims are validated with reference to the present-day epidemic the COVID-19. Technology promises to make life easier. The role of technology in government coordinated efforts to the response and preparedness is discussed in the chapter. Forecasting the spread pattern helps in readiness to handle the severity. Undoubtedly the technological advancements have led several changes to the society leading to a comfortable lifestyle even during the challenging times. The discussion here outlines the role of these advancements during the time of the pandemic. As digital technology intervenes to control the disastrous effect on humankind, it simultaneously introduces several challenges that are highlighted in the chapter.

Keywords: Pandemic, COVID-19, digital technology, regression, forecast, digital technology challenges

8.1 Introduction

Pandemics are the diseases that spread their wings across countries and continents. Undoubtedly, these diseases are infectious and spread from one person to another. Time and again, the world have been hit by

**Corresponding author*: meshweta_7@rediffmail.com

Abhinav Juneja, Vikram Bali, Sapna Juneja, Vishal Jain and Prashant Tyagi (eds.) Enabling Healthcare 4.0 for Pandemics: A Roadmap Using AI, Machine Learning, IoT and Cognitive Technologies, (143–162) © 2021 Scrivener Publishing LLC

pandemics. Epidemics like H1N1, Ebola, Flu influenza and many more have shown their existence in the past. After every encounter with these potentially devastating threats, the human race is learning to manage and handle them. Human experts, with their intelligence and hard work, come up with drugs to fight these diseases. But, for infections that spread quickly from one person to the other require rapid control and novel ways to cope up. This century has witnessed the outbreak of coronavirus disease 2019 (COVID), a condition stemming from SARS-COV-2 [1]. This began in the year 2019 December in Wuhan, China and has since spread to over 300 thousand people in over 200 countries around the world. The statistics show that COVID-19 has rapidly emerged as a global threat.

Due to the Genomic sequence similarity of SARS-CoV-2 with that of SARS-CoV and MERS-CoV, several countries have started taking measures based on past experiences. The spread of COVID-19 is primarily due to droplets of saliva and other body secretions of an infected person [2]. As there is no known clue to this disease till date and the research labs are putting up continuous efforts to come up with vaccines at the earliest, till then the only and the best way is to practice social distancing and hygiene. Many countries have implemented lockdown for several days to enforce social distancing. On the one hand, this effort works well to flatten the disease growth curve, but on the other hand, it takes a toll on the economy of the world, which may have devastating outcomes. With the failure to overcome the loss due to this pandemic quick adaptation of healthcare systems became evident. Digital health solutions have been identified as one of the most promising approaches to address this challenge in society.

Out of all the reported pandemic like Influenza, MERS (Middle East Respiratory Syndrome), SARS (Severe acute respiratory syndrome) or Ebola [3], COVID-19 is unique in its own ways. This can be measured in terms of clinical severity, the number of infected patients and the transmission ability of the virus as compared to the easier ones. Also, it can be marked as the first pandemic in the era of technology [4]. It is perceived that digital health solutions, an outcome of massive technological growth will indeed play its role in the containment of the disease. Apart from identifying and tracking transmissions, creating virtual venues for day-to-day operations the digital technology can facilitate the widespread rapid distribution of information and provide telemedicine for patients to avoid the spread of disease due to crowd [5]. More advanced and aware countries such as South Korea have integrated digital technology into containment and mitigation process of the government to provide a higher rate of curve flattening [6]. Prediction methods have been utilized by researchers to predict the growth curve [7]. This similar trend has been observed in Japan and other technologically advanced countries.

This chapter propounds the framework for the application of digital technology in the crisis due to present-day pandemic. To start with, we identify the impact of disease and the issues and challenges associated with it. Then the role of technology in preparedness to handle the epidemic is discussed. This chapter further talks about the applications of advanced technology to curb the menace of the pandemic. And in the end, it concludes after highlighting the risks associated with digital technology for handling the present situation.

8.2 Issues and Challenges Due to Pandemic

The exact definition of the term pandemic is missing from many of the medical textbooks, but there are some key features of a pandemic including wide geographic extension, disease movement, novelty and high attack risks etc. [8]. These features point to the fact that any epidemic that occurs worldwide or impacts population across the international boundary cab be termed as pandemic [9]. Pandemics like Cholera, the Black Death and Spanish Flu have also shown their impact on the human race in the past [10]. The present-day pandemic- the COVID-19 is assumed to be the most contagious, and despite so much development in healthcare and technology, still, no solution is available. Owing to its devastating impact the human race is suffering a lot. The effect of pandemics on different facets of society is majorly influenced by a few factors, such as:

- The workforce to which the pandemic impacts the most.
- The requirement and structure of economic lockdown.
- The state and the standards of healthcare.

It is important to identify the effect of the pandemic on the different age group. If the disease influences the people in the age group to which the maximum workforce belongs more as compared to a child or the old age people, then it will have a severe impact on the economy. Also, the requirement of economic lockdown, its duration and scope will produce an adverse impact on society. As compared to the previous major pandemic, the COVID-19 has worst hit the economy, and the fact lies behind the globalization that has boosted the world economy in recent times. The state of healthcare, in terms of availability and advancements, also impacts the mortality rate. Undoubtedly, during the present pandemic, the healthcare

Table 8.1 A quantitative measure of pandemics based on crucial factors.

Factors	Major devastating pandemics		
	The Black Death	**Spanish Flu**	**COVID-19**
Impact on workforce	Very High	Very High	Moderate
Economic Lockdown	Yes	Yes	Yes
Healthcare Standards	Low	Moderate	High

system is more advanced as compared to past, and technological growth is the primary factor behind it. Based on these three factors, the pandemic that has shown the worst impact on the society are compared quantitatively to identify their effect on health, economy and social issues. Table 8.1 presents the comparison of Black death, Spanish Flu and COVID-19.

In the past, as well as the COVID-19 has created a massive health crisis at the global level. The confinement of people within their houses and a total physical cut off from the society creates a significant burden at the psychological and mental status of individuals. The social and cultural influence due to pandemic creates substantial challenges. The striking impact on the global economy can be one of the immense economy shocks and may require years to revive. This section covers the influence and challenges faced by society due to pandemic. Substantial evidence from the COVID-19 situations are used to strengthen this belief.

8.2.1 Health Effect

The direct impact of a pandemic on health can be catastrophic. It has influenced millions of people, causing a high mortality rate and severe illness. During Black death around 30–50% of the workforce was killed [11] and then the Spanish Flu caused around 30 million deaths [12], and till date, COVID-19 has taken approximately 1 million lives, and across the globe, the number is still growing. Not only the physical effects are essential, also the mental impact of the disease is problematic [13]. The requirement of social distancing, confinement to limited geographic locations, all these have created anxiety, stress, stigma. In light of the widening economic crisis and uncertainties related to the cure and control of the disease, it has become essential to train the health workers to take care of the emotional and psychological issues. To help people deal with mental health issues, the WHO has come up with several policies and platform [14]. Figure 8.1

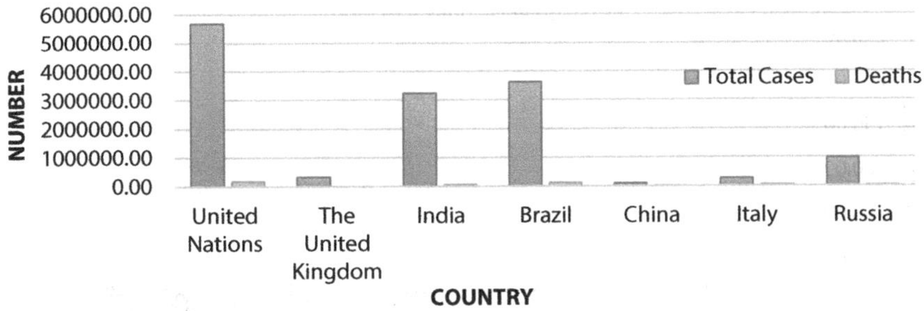

Figure 8.1 Impact of COVID-19 on health.

presents the statistics of Coronavirus cases and death in a few severely affected countries of the world based on the data from WHO [15]. The number of deaths as compared to the number of cases is significantly low, and this is undoubtedly due to the technological advancements of medical technology. The same reason can also be attributed to the lesser number of deaths with COVID-19 as compared to the death toll in the Black Death and Spanish Flu.

8.2.2 Economic Impact

Pandemic causes serious threats not only to the health of individuals but also adversely affects the economy of the world. The adversity can result in economic instability. Several factors such as direct cost, indirect cost and the long-term burden on the economy influence the intensity of the crisis. The direct cost associated with the healthcare systems includes hospitals, staff, maintenance of quarantine centers and medication, the indirect costs impact the GDP of the country due to loss incurred by several service sectors influenced due to lockdown. The long-term burden due to the untimely death of the workforce severely impacts the economy. Its contribution to the economic downfall can be long term. These factors may have varying impact on the economy of several sectors, and their impact can be short term as well as long term. Undoubtedly, in today's era of globalization, the influence of economic downfall in one part of the world impacts the other part, but it also helps in faster recovery. Figure 8.2 represents the change of share index price of the world developing economy based on data from Ref. [16].

The trend highlights the adverse impact of COVID-19 during its spread across the world. However, as the lockdown from several parts of the world have been removed or eased, the economy has started to revive. It may take several years to reach back to the original state.

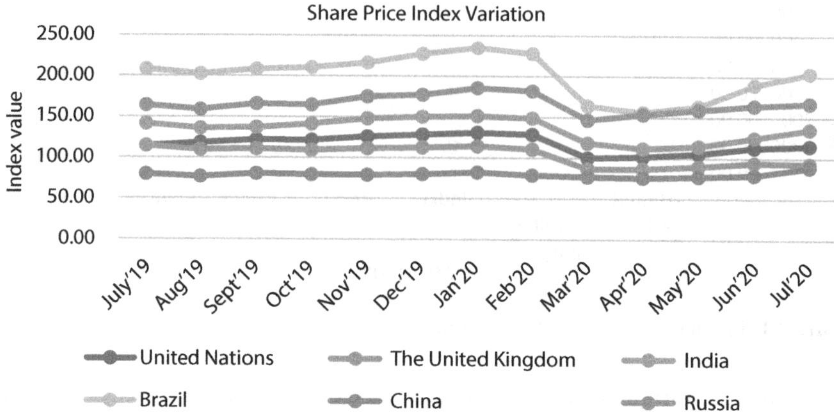

Figure 8.2 Global economy impact due to COVID-19.

8.2.3 Social Impact

The pandemic has shown an adverse effect on all segment of society and is particularly detrimental to people living in poverty. Also, the ones who are physically disabled, youth and old age people all have to face the ill effect in one way or the other. The impact of the pandemic on the overall society can be felt due to constrained movement, fewer options for employability and closure of academic activities. The spread of disease creates mental stress to homeless, refugees and migrant people who may have aftermath impact. The statistics available for the COVID-19 situation highlights the 100% increase in domestic violence cases in India, and this increasing trend is similar worldwide [17]. The search on social media handles for domestic violence has increased manifolds [18]. This increase in domestic violence has created mental health issues. Children have been adversely impacted due to pandemic, and this impact may last long. During COVID-19 itself almost 188 countries have imposed complete closure of schools, and it definitely exacerbates the academic crisis. Being at home, these children are more vulnerable to exploitation, violence at home and abuse. No doubt, these phenomena are mainly prevalent among poor families, but they cannot be ignored [19]. Due to loss of income, the household may suffer from food crunch and may lead to malnutrition of children in poor families and also poses a threat to the survival of child in few families. Reports by several agencies highlight that unemployability has increased by 27% during COVID-19. Also, the migrants of society are poorly affected. Survival without family, susceptibility to the spread of disease, unemployability all have ill-effects psychologically, and these create challenges for the society.

After the discussion on the misfortune caused by the pandemic, the point to ponder is to look for the solutions that can be of help to handle these hardships. In the era of technological advancements, the whole world looks towards the technology development that can ease their life during these difficult times. Apart from medical science digital technology also has many roles to play during this difficult time.

8.3 Digital Technology and Pandemic

Data from the previous pandemic highlights that life during a pandemic and after it has changed a lot as compared to life before the pandemic. The tough time during pandemic brings in light the strengths and weaknesses of the system. It forces us to look for new ways of working, living and interacting. The COVID-19 epidemic has also brought several changes. The demand for social distancing to reduce the disease spread has forced us to decide the priorities of life in the light of future needs. The scale at which COVID-19 has spread in such a small duration has forced to think about working with the technology to handle upcoming challenges. The advancements in technology, especially digital technology, are considered as a gateway to support the new ways of living and respond to the crisis. It is believed that technology can help reduce the harmful effects of the pandemic on health, society and economy. Apart from being the gateway to solve the COVID-19 crisis, digital technology can handle challenges related to socioeconomic interactions, maintaining essential services and providing information relevant to disease protection.

Although the dominant digital divide within the society poses challenges for the technology, efforts have been continuing to overcome them and utilize digital technology in several walks of life. Figure 8.3 identifies the role of digital technology for the easement of living, especially during the pandemic time. This section discusses these six roles of digital technology, and undoubtedly, the technology has to play many more such roles during the tough times to tackle the disease spread and help in the new way of living.

8.3.1 Digital Healthcare

After frontline warrior technology is the greatest weapon against the pandemic, especially COVID-19. The research community is putting up all their efforts to come up with some innovative techniques and tools to fight COVID-19. In a short span after the outbreak of COVID-19, several

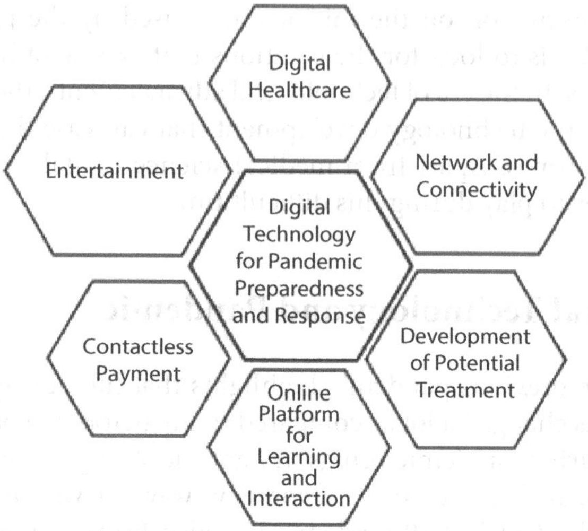

Figure 8.3 Role of digital technology during pandemic.

research works have been reported on this epidemic. The research has done covers publications on symptoms and complications [20, 21] which presents anemia, respiratory distress syndrome, headache, fever and cough as the most common symptoms. The virus mutation is reported to be very fast. Under this circumstance development of targeted vaccine seems to be the most effective measure in halting this epidemic, but since the overall process of trial and approval takes months/years, it seems to be very difficult in the near future.

All these factors highlight the fact that the control for the spread of disease is a challenge, and it becomes essential to converge digital technology with healthcare to provide precise and more personalized healthcare services. Computational technologies and smart devices can help monitor the patient. Starting with planning and contact tracking to clinical management and screening of infection, all these can be handled by digital technology. Implementation of Telehealth services that provide health-related services through electronic communication has helped dissipate disease-related information to distant individuals [22]. Also, online doctor–patient interactions have helped in receiving services without visiting the hospitals and have helped in maintaining social distancing. The text-based telemedicine services have made the interaction ubiquitous, and also, kiosk-based telemedicine through designated pharmacy shops have provided convenience for the patient-doctor interactions. The use of sensing technology has also been reported during the time of

COVID-19. The use of camera, microphones, temperature and inertial sensors to collect data and apply machine learning techniques to detect the disease has also been reported [23]. IoT-enabled systems for early and quick diagnosis of the disease are in use [24]. The software application for the mobile devices provides online monitoring and location tracking facility along with treatment.

8.3.2 Network and Connectivity

The need for pandemic management requires social distancing. In general, countries implement full or partial lockdown for a few days to control the spread. Similar norms have been followed during COVID-19 also. The lockdown in around 200 countries across the globe has forced the people to be confined within their houses. But the life has to move, and the lockdown cannot impose a total shutdown of several activities like shopping, education and healthcare as these are the essential services for the economic and social health of the mankind. To continue with these services while staying within the house, an online platform that can network several services and provide efficient connectivity with the end users are required. These telecommunication and connectivity have become essential than ever before. The high-speed network provides quality services for analysis of real time data of patient's audio or video. The need is for more secure and reliable connectivity.

8.3.3 Development of Potential Treatment

The pandemics are often caused due to viruses that are new and whose characteristics are not entirely known. Due to these limitations, the development of vaccines to treat them becomes a challenge. The advancements in artificial intelligence and availability of massive data related to disease spread, symptoms etc. help in identifying the spread pattern and behavior of the virus. Big Data technology provides ways to handle the humongous data generated through apps and sensing devices and provide ways to store data in the format that can be effectively used and processed for disease management. The development of robot interaction makes the collection of data easy; Drones can be used as a logistic provider and also serve the purpose of remote area surveillance. The Blockchain technology can provide realtime information in a secure manner for strategic control and management of the disease. All these technologies combined together can help in developing potential treatments for the cure with the help of spread pattern detection.

8.3.4 Online Platform for Learning and Interaction

The online platform offers a wealth of information, and during the time of crisis, they play a vital role in providing necessary information access as well. These platforms provide opportunities for collaborative working and skill sharing across the globe. People can showcase their creativity and culture while staying inside their house. The communication technology has provided ample options for telecommuting and online education, along with webinars and workshops through virtual labs. The application like Zoom, Microsoft Team, Cisco Webex etc. have helped in the continuous learning process even during the difficult times. These tools have made it possible to map almost all the real-time activity to the virtual platform without compromising with the work process.

8.3.5 Contactless Payment

To avoid the spread of the virus it is desirable to avoid any physical contact. Transaction of money cannot be stopped as it is the backbone of the economy. It was essential to develop platforms that provide contactless money transfer to maintain the flow of money. Applications like Google Pay, Paytm etc. provide digital money transfer platform that enables transaction without involving physical currencies. Apart from these facilities like net banking and phone banking also offer contactless payments. These services have helped people to continue their financial activities without fear. All these have only been possible due to advancement in digital technology.

8.3.6 Entertainment

With the limitations imposed on physical, social activities due to confinement within the houses, people have moved towards the digital media for entertainment. The over-the-top (OTT) platform, online gaming and television have eased the life of people during the time of crisis. Applications like Netflix, Amazon Prime and others provide a multitude of entertainment options at a very reasonable cost while maintaining physical distancing norms. The COVID-19 times have seen a surge in the demand of at-home digital media. Post COVID-19 also it is assumed that the attraction towards in-house entertainment medium is going to persist. Technological development can further play a pivotal role in the outreach of the digital entertainment platform to the consumer's place.

The role of artificial intelligence and smartphone apps in the period of crisis can never be overlooked. Be it disease management and control or self-isolation and quarantine or, making the life easy during lockdown AI and smartphone apps are prevalent everywhere.

8.4 Application of Technology for Handling Pandemic

The healthcare services are highly data-driven, and data management is a critical challenge. The availability of smartphone Apps, GPS monitoring and wearable devices has increased the data generation many folds. Use of these data by advanced technology after thorough mining can provide great offerings to both the provider and the consumer. The digital ecosystem enables interaction of service provider and consumers through a digital platform. During COVID-19, this ecosystem has been thoroughly explored to monitor and control the disease. It is essential to curb the infection by preventing the spread and providing proper care to infected individuals. But it is equally necessary to be prepared in advance to handle the worst situation. These quick-spreading diseases demand comprehensive management of resources ranging from high expense services like hospital beds and ventilators to basic essential requirements of masks, sanitizers, gloves etc. This preparedness becomes easy if some forecast about the disease is available. The compartmental models like the SIR, SEIR and SEIS models and their variants used for mathematically modeling the disease have been utilized by ML techniques for forecasting the disease spread [25, 26]. These forecasts help in preparedness and decision making.

8.4.1 Technology for Preparedness and Response

The present-day pandemic COVID-19 has emerged as highly contagious. To reduce cluster creation, the WHO has advised following the strategy of detection, testing, isolation, tracing and mobilization. Till the time any vaccine is available, the best weapon to handle this disease is to follow public health strategies. Besides treatments and other clinical processes, technological interventions are required to implement these strategies effectively. Countries like South Korea have integrated the digital technology with the regular containment strategies used by the government and are able to contain the disease spread and the death rate [6]. Table 8.2 highlights the role and application of emerging digital technology that can be used for control, tracking and management of COVID-19.

Table 8.2 Digital technology for COVID-19 management.

Sl. no.	Activity	Purpose	Digital technology involved	Limitation
1	Tracking	Identify real-time status of disease activity, its spread in real-time for forecast and resource management	Machine learning can be applied upon real-time data from smartphone applications such as maps and wearable devices to identify the spread.	Highly cost-oriented, breach of privacy
2	Screening of suspected individuals	Preliminary check to identify the prevalence of disease and individuals for further treatment and isolation.	AI techniques along with a thermal camera, sensor-based digital thermometer and mobile apps.	Privacy breach, high cost and failure to identify asymptomatic cases
3	Contact Tracing	Identify the individuals who came into contact with the infected person	GPS system and Bluetooth technology in smartphones	Privacy concern, dependent upon the availability of network and hand held devices.
4	Isolation	Identify the infected individuals and put them to isolation or quarantine	AI, Digital Camera, quick response codes	Fails to work if the isolated person moves out without the code or device.
5	Mobilize	Provide timely clinical treatment to infected individuals through proper clinical management or telemedicine.	AI for diagnostics and ML for virtual care and treatment	Privacy breach and diagnosis may be incorrect.

8.4.2 Machine Learning for Pandemic Forecast

Since Artificial Intelligence attributes to new standards for healthcare, several machine learning (ML) algorithms can be employed to strategically manage and curb the spread of disease along with modeling and predicting number of cases. In this dimension, most of the research published studies on statistical data to expect the surge in a number of patients affected by this virus [27]. The objective was to identify the current situation and predict the demands and future conditions. Mathematical models are available to project the progression of infectious diseases, and the statistics available is used to find parameters that help in measuring the effect of interventions. Researchers have estimated the timings of the surge and clinical demand using Monte-Carlo simulation on SIR (susceptible, infected, removed) model [28]. Lopez and Rodo in Ref. [29] applied the SEIR model with some modifications to predict the COVID-19 outbreak in Italy and Spain. Most of the mathematical models used for analysis are subject to potential bias.

Technology can participate in handling the problems related to COVID-19, and AI is the front runner in this regard. The present-day AI mainly evolves around ML. The ML algorithms look for patterns in the chronicled information. This information is utilized as training data for the machine, and then the model developed can be used with some other inputs also. The data assembled under the current condition of a pandemic can work as the base for drawing theoretical information about the disease that can be utilized while accumulating newly generated data. Models based on ML algorithms and artificial neural networks curve fitting techniques are defined in Ref. [30] to forecast the spread of COVID-19 in India and USA. ML techniques have been applied on chest computed tomography pictures in Ref. [31] to identify the first stage of COVID-19. A novel methodology based on hybrid CNN structure called GSA-DenseNet121 is proposed in Ref. [32]. Exploratory data analysis is used in Ref. [33] to report COVID-19 situation for the first quarter of 2020. A more accurate result is presented in Ref. [34] using regression models.

Regression models are statistical processes that deal with the relationship between independent and dependent variables. It predicts the relationship by fitting a curve along with the dataset. It has many variants like stepwise regression, linear regression or polynomial regression. In this section, the prediction of COVID-19 is presented using regression technique. Regression is used to forecast the infection along with the recovery and death cases prediction for August. Initially, the statistics of daily cases from mid of April till July middle is represented to highlight the growth rate (Figure 8.4). This is then followed by the prediction graphs representing

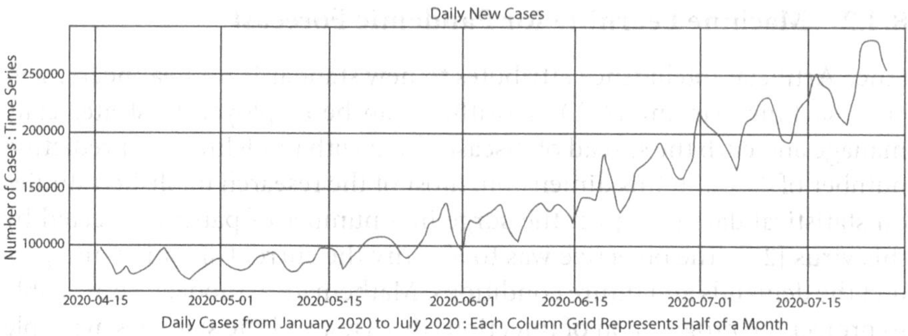

Figure 8.4 Daily cases from 15 April to July 2020.

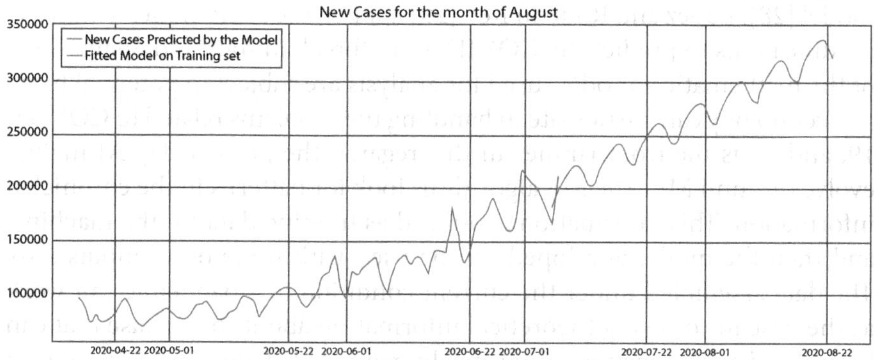

Figure 8.5 New cases predicted for August 2020 based on training data from April to July 2020.

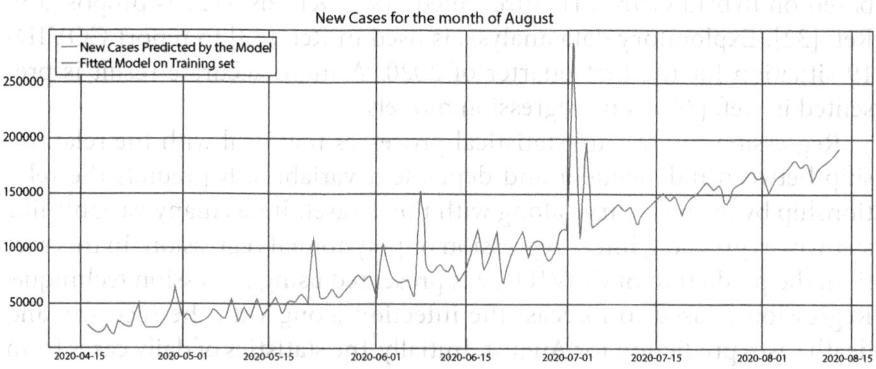

Figure 8.6 Recovery prediction for August based on the training set from April to July 2020.

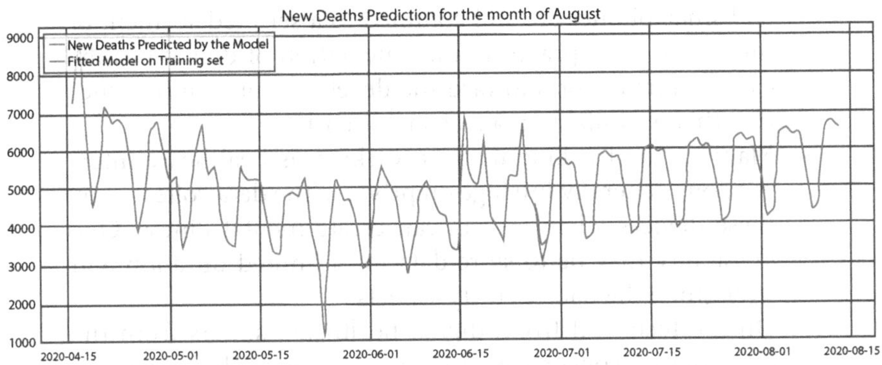

Figure 8.7 Death prediction for August based on the training set from April to July 2020.

the forecast of infection spread (Figure 8.5), forecast of recovery in August (Figure 8.6) and forecast of death in August (Figure 8.7). The training data is the data used until the first week of July. For forecasting fbprophet model from library fbprophet in Python is used along with pandas, matplotlib and NumPy to obtain the time series analysis.

All representations are based on the dataset taken from the Ministry of health and family welfare updates.

8.5 Challenges with Digital Healthcare

The potential of digital healthcare to radically improve the condition of the healthcare ecosystem is beyond doubt. But, there are several challenges on the societal front as well as the technical front that creates challenges for the implementation of digital healthcare. This section discusses a few societal and technical issues that need attention to exploiting the potential of digital healthcare.

- The digital divide across the globe is the biggest hurdle in providing efficient healthcare support. Part of the world cannot till date avail simple network facility on the digital platform, accessing healthcare through the internet is a distant dream for them. In the current digital divide scenario, these digital healthcare initiatives will further amplify the healthcare disparity and widen the socioeconomic differences. The access to smart wearable devices, faster broadband signal and smartphones are still confined to a selected segment of the society. The practical implementation of digital healthcare requires efforts toward the development of infrastructure that is available at a reasonable cost.

- Many of the tracking devices working as healthcare interventions generally infringe on privacy. The data collected by these devices when leaked, can create mental illness. One possibility may be to store data for a limited duration and strengthen the data security aspects.
- On the technical front, digital healthcare suffers from the challenges associated with data processing. The enormous data collected by hospitals and sensing and wearable devices are a challenge to process and analyze using standard technology. Robust AI systems are needed to handle and utilize these data.
- Another technical challenge is associated with the security of data due to a high volume of data breaches. The vulnerabilities may be due to excessive user permissions, user authentication and data leakage. Internet of medical things (IoMT) devices can further increase the chances of a data breach.

8.6 Conclusion

The technological advancements have played an essential role during a pandemic. The current epidemic has initiated a dramatic digital transformation into society. The use of technology for entertainment, education or other activities has made life more comfortable during the time of crisis. The integration of digital technology into government policies for pandemic control has helped in controlling the spread—all these demands for good internet connectivity. Technological developments have somehow tried to meet the demand of end-users. Availability of telemedicine has made the patient-doctor interactions easier. Be it a text-based of video-based interaction both have generated convenience along with avoiding crowd exposure. Technologies like AI and ML, along with data science, can utilize the vast data to come up with predictions on different fronts. The forecast highlights the trend and becomes helpful in the preparedness of disease handling. Undoubtedly, at one end the society is getting benefitted with the advancements of technology, and at the other end, the prevailing digital inequalities become evident in creating health inequalities. Also, the intervention of digital technology into the life of people brings along the challenges concerning to privacy infringement and data breach. Undoubtedly, the need is to take up the challenges to make the technology more secure.

References

1. NUMBERS, S.I. and ASSESSMENT, W.R., Coronavirus disease 2019 (COVID-19). *Americas*, *10*, 2, 1, 2020.
2. World Health Organization: https://www.who.int/news-room/commentaries/detail/modes-of-transmission-of-virus-causing-covid-19-implications-for-ipc-precaution-recommendations; accessed on 10-July-2020.
3. Centers for disease control and prevention: https://www.cdc.gov/vhf/ebola/about.html; Accessed on 10-July-2020.
4. Teles, M., Sacchetta, T., Matsumoto, Y., COVID-19 Pandemic Triggers Telemedicine Regulation and Intensifies Diabetes Management Technology Adoption in Brazil. *J. Diabetes Sci. Technol.*, 14, 4, 797–798, 2020.
5. Fagherazzi, G., Goetzinger, C., Rashid, M.A., Aguayo, G.A., Huiart, L., Digital health strategies to fight COVID-19 worldwide: Challenges, recommendations, and a call for papers. *J. Med. Internet Res.*, 22, 6, e19284, 2020.
6. Whitelaw, S., Mamas, M.A., Topol, E., Van Spall, H.G., Applications of digital technology in COVID-19 pandemic planning and response. *Lancet Digit. Health*, 2, 8, e435–e440, 2020.
7. Kolhe, L., Pingle, Y., Kadam, P., Jain, V., Prediction of Coronavirus COVID-19 cases using Linear Regression and Support Vector Machine. *Int. J. Adv. Sci. Technol.*, 29, 5s, 1911–1924, 2020.
8. Green, M.H., Emerging diseases, re-emerging histories. *Centaurus*, *62*, 2, 234–247, 2020.
9. Qiu, W., Rutherford, S., Mao, A., Chu, C., The pandemic and its impacts, in: *Health, Culture And Society*, vol. 9, pp. 1–11, 2017.
10. Snowden, F.M., *Epidemics and society: From the black death to the present*, Yale University Press, London, UK, 2019.
11. Karlsson, G., Plague without rats: The case of fifteenth-century Iceland. *J. Mediev. Hist.*, 22, 3, 263–284, 1996.
12. Taubenberger, J.K. and Morens, D.M., 1918 Influenza: The mother of all pandemics. *Rev. Biomed.*, 17, 1, 69–79, 2006.
13. Wason, R., Rana, P.S., Jain, V., Real-Time Mental Health Monitoring: The Indian Scenario, in: *Applications of Deep Learning and Big IoT on Personalized Healthcare Services*, IGI-Global, Hershey, Pennsylvania, 2020.
14. Torous, J., Myrick, K.J., Rauseo-Ricupero, N., Firth, J., Digital mental health and COVID-19: Using technology today to accelerate the curve on access and quality tomorrow. *JMIR Ment. Health*, 7, 3, e18848, 2020.
15. World Health Organization: https://covid19.who.int/; Accessed on: 18-Aug-2020.

16. Statista business data platform: https://www.statista.com/statistics/1034575/share-price-index-in-major-developed-and-emerging-economies/; Accessed on: 20-Aug-2020.
17. United Nations—Un Women 2020. Violence Against Women and Girls: the Shadow Pandemic. https://www.unwomen.org/en/news/stories/2020/4/statement-ed-phumzile-violence-against-women-during-pandemic; Accessed on 03-05-2020.
18. Moutafis, R., *The Shocking Correlation Between Quarantine and Domestic Violence*, Medium Women, San Francisco, 2020, https://medium.com/@rheamoutafis/the-shocking-correlation-between-quarantine-and-domestic-violence-b40425eff605. Accessed on 03-05-2020.
19. Taub, A., *A new COVID-19 crisis: Domestic abuse rises worldwide*, p. 6, New York Times, New York City, 2020.
20. Huang, C., Wang, Y., Li, X., Ren, L., Zhao, J., Hu, Y., Zhang, L., Fan, G., Xu, J., Gu, X., Cheng, Z., Clinical features of patients infected with 2019 novel coronavirus in Wuhan, China. *Lancet*, 395, 10223, 497–506, 2020.
21. Wang, D., Hu, B., Hu, C., Zhu, F., Liu, X., Zhang, J., Wang, B., Xiang, H., Cheng, Z., Xiong, Y., Zhao, Y., Clinical characteristics of 138 hospitalized patients with 2019 novel coronavirus-infected pneumonia in Wuhan, China. *Jama*, 323, 11, 1061–1069, 2020.
22. Dinesen, B., Nonnecke, B., Lindeman, D., Toft, E., Kidholm, K., Jethwani, K., Young, H.M., Spindler, H., Oestergaard, C.U., Southard, J.A., Gutierrez, M., Personalized telehealth in the future: A global research agenda. *J. Med. Internet Res.*, *18*, 3, e53, 2016.
23. Maghdid, H.S., Ghafoor, K.Z., Sadiq, A.S., Curran, K., Rabie, K., A novel ai-enabled framework to diagnose coronavirus COVID-19 using smartphone embedded sensors: Design study. In *2020 IEEE 21st International Conference on Information Reuse and Integration for Data Science (IRI), IEEE,* Las Vegas, pp. 180–187, 2020.
24. Wason, R., Singh Rana, P., Jain, V., Real-Time Mental Health Monitoring: The Indian Scenario, in: *Applications of Deep Learning and Big IoT on Personalized Healthcare Services*, IGI-Global, Hershey, Pennsylvania, 2020.
25. Bai, L., Yang, D., Wang, X., Tong, L., Zhu, X., Zhong, N., Bai, C., Powell, C.A., Chen, R., Zhou, J., Song, Y., Chinese experts' consensus on the Internet of Things-aided diagnosis and treatment of coronavirus disease 2019 (COVID-19). *Clin. eHealth*, 3, 7–15, 2020.
26. Lalmuanawma, S., Hussain, J., Chhakchhuak, L., Applications of machine learning and artificial intelligence for COVID-19 (SARS-CoV-2) pandemic: A review. *Chaos, Solitons Fractals*, 139, 110059, 2020.
27. Poirier, C., Liu, D., Clemente, L., Ding, X., Chinazzi, M., Davis, J., Vespignani, A., Santillana, M., Real-time forecasting of the COVID-19 outbreak in Chinese provinces: Machine learning approach using novel digital data and estimates from mechanistic models. *J. Med. Internet Res.*, 22, 8, e20285, 1–15, 2020.

28. Weissman, G.E., Crane-Droesch, A., Chivers, C., Luong, T., Hanish, A., Levy, M.Z., Lubken, J., Becker, M., Draugelis, M.E., Anesi, G.L., Brennan, P.J., Locally informed simulation to predict hospital capacity needs during the COVID-19 pandemic. *Ann. Intern. Med.*, 173, 1, 21–28, 2020.
29. López, L. and Rodó, X., The end of social confinement and COVID-19 re-emergence risk. *Nat. Hum. Behav.*, 4, 7, 746–755, 2020.
30. Tamang, S.K., Singh, P.D., Datta, B., Forecasting of COVID-19 cases based on prediction using artificial neural network curve fitting technique. *Glob. J. Environ. Sci. Manag.*, 6, Special Issue (COVID-19), 53–64, 2020.
31. Öztürk, Ş., Özkaya, U., Barstuğan, M., Classification of Coronavirus (COVID-19) from x-ray and CT images using shrunken features. *Int. J. Imaging Syst. Technol.*, 31, 1, 5–15, 2021.
32. Ezzat, D., Hassanien, A.E., Ella, H.A., An optimized deep learning architecture for the diagnosis of COVID-19 disease based on gravitational search optimization. *Appl. Soft Comput.*, 98, 106742, 1–13, 2020.
33. Gupta, R. and Kumar, S., Trend Analysis and Forecasting of COVID-19 outbreak in India. *medRxiv*, 1–19, 2020, https://doi.org/10.1101/2020.03.26.20044511.
34. Bagal, D.K., Rath, A., Barua, A., Patnaik, D., Estimating the parameters of susceptible-infected-recovered model of COVID-19 cases in India during lockdown periods. *Chaos Soliton Fract.*, 140, 110154, 1–12, 2020.

9

Emerging Technologies for COVID-19

Rohit Anand[1]*, Nidhi Sindhwani[2], Avinash Saini[1] and Shubham[1]

[1]*ECE Department, G.B. Pant Engineering College, New Delhi, India*
[2]*ECE Department, Amity University, Noida, India*

Abstract
This chapter discusses the ideas that have emerged from infectious diseases like COVID-19. This chapter talks about solutions to avoid and manage the uncertainty of infectious diseases like COVID-19 for the global public health. Through this chapter, we will discuss about the emerging technologies for handling the pandemic challenges. The emerging technologies that can tackle these key challenges are the technologies like Blockchain, Drone facilities, Mobile APK, Wearable Sensing, Internet of Healthcare Things, Artificial Intelligence, 5G and Virtual Reality. Soon these technologies will be seen to manage the pandemic challenges. We will also discuss the comparison of these technologies with the help of their applications, challenges and their solutions in context with COVID-19.

Keywords: COVID-19, pandemic, emerging technologies, challenges

9.1 Introduction

A disease that becomes prevalent over the entire world is referred to as pandemic. The Coronavirus (COVID-19) as a consequence of novel severe coronavirus has affected the whole world so badly that the World Health Organization (WHO) has marked this epidemic as 'Pandemic'. The coronavirus is a highly infectious disease that attacks on the respiratory system of the human body. It spreads from one person to the other one via very small droplets from the noise or mouth when a human with COVID-19 exhales. The most popular warning sign of COVID-19 are fever, dry cough

**Corresponding author*: roh_anand@rediffmail.com; https://orcid.org/0000-0002-3782-0163

Abhinav Juneja, Vikram Bali, Sapna Juneja, Vishal Jain and Prashant Tyagi (eds.) Enabling Healthcare 4.0 for Pandemics: A Roadmap Using AI, Machine Learning, IoT and Cognitive Technologies, (163–188) © 2021 Scrivener Publishing LLC

and tiredness while the less common symptoms are headache and pain, diarrhea, sore throat, loss of taste and rashes on skin etc. Some serious symptoms are problematic breathing, chest pain and loss of moment. The impact of COVID-19 varies from meager illness to critical illness. The number of patients suffering from COVID-19 is continuously growing across the world. Many efforts are being put by the various Governments to mitigate the severe impact of COVID-19 [1–3].

A very acute care or medical attention provides the diagnosis, observation and treatment of the patient suffering from COVID-19. Important points are: (1) To ask for urgent medical care if a person has severe symptoms. (2) On average, it takes 5–6 days from when someone is suffered with Coronavirus for the symptoms to appear. Though, it may take up to 14 days. The question is: 'How the corona virus is spreading in all over world. (1) This infection spreads mainly through droplets release from the nose when a contaminated person coughs or sneezes. It attacks on the respiratory system of the human body. (2) This virus can spread from one object to other objects or things. The droplets after being discharged from the nose from any infected person and land on any object or surface around the person.

As we know that many of the technologies have quite significant effects on human's life. All of these technologies are based upon various techniques, skilled methods and production for good services. To palliate the COVID-19 pandemic, large number of papers has been published in past few months. Various kinds of machines, instruments, devices and weapons are technology tools [4]. These technologies are also used for the various challenges in COVID-19 (i.e. pandemic). One of the important techniques is Blockchain Technology [5] in which the patients may collect their medical data automatically. All the blockchain system records may have digitized medical data. The drones [6] also provide an efficient healthcare to the patients from any distance by tele-monitoring in the remote areas. They may cloud deliver the medicines to the patients and deliver the patient's health data to the medical professional. The drones have the ability to capture the image, real-time video and streaming. The mobile application techniques also called Mobile APK techniques [7] that are based upon application code, resources and manifest file are also used for the medical emergencies like COVID-19. The wearable sensors [8], made as a result of developments in the microelectronics and material science can be fixed on the human body so as to be used for the processing of the collected data to provide the healthcare of human being. Internet of Healthcare Things (IoHT) is an integration of smart and intelligent health monitoring devices and software computing technologies. It can also be used for the diagnosis of COVID-19 patients from a remote location [9].

Besides, Artificial Intelligence (AI) techniques are incredible to mitigate the effects of COVID-19 pandemic by early detection. These techniques are used for tracking and foreseeing the patients [10]. By integrating 5G technology with various other tools, an efficient system may be designed to detect the infection and provide the treatment without the human intervention [11]. The concept of Virtual Reality (VR) may also be used to handle the belongings of COVID-19. This VR technology is attracting many healthcare professionals due to its benefits [12]. All of these technologies will be discussed in detail in this article.

There are various adverse effects of COVID-19. The fear of illness/death and the loss of sense of personal safety can invoke the feeling of anxiety that may interfere with the daily activities. The types of anxiety may be panic disorder, phobia, social anxiety, illness anxiety disorder and separation anxiety disorder. So, anxiety management techniques are very helpful in such cases to manage or treat the anxiety in pandemic COVID-19 [13].

This whole work is structured as follows. Later section represents the related work for COVID-19. This section indicates what types of latest technologies have been suggested to combat this pandemic. The subsequent section represents the description of the various thrust areas that may be implemented to tackle and battle against COVID-19. The various challenges and their solutions are also discussed in this section. Next section presents the comparative analysis of the various contemporary techniques in terms of the various aspects. At last, the conclusion is drawn.

9.2 Related Work

The authors in Ref. [1] introduced a review on the state-of-the-art solutions in the fight against the pandemic of COVID-19. First, they presented an outline to the COVID-19 infection and motives of Artificial Intelligence (AI) as well as Big Data for discovering quickly and efficient solutions that can effectively fight the COVID-19 illness. The applications of Artificial Intelligence and big data for diagnosis and detection, tracking and forecasting outbreaks for COVID-19 are also reviewed in this paper. The authors in Ref. [2] have explicitly concentrated on the wearable devices appropriate for tracking the people at danger and those in isolation, both for the evaluation of the health status of administrators and for improving the triage procedures for patient admission. Remote monitoring and treatment of COVID-19 and associated diseases by telehealth technologies has also been discussed. The advanced technology and fast-tracking developments have been used in Ref. [12] to put an end to this threat. Virtual

Reality (VR) is also very crucial to combat against COVID-19 through the communication in audio or video mode. This method offers a broad-edge for defending and confronting the current epidemic of COVID-19 by enhancing skills, trust, performance and effectiveness. An innovative model namely Assisted Reproduction Treatment (ART) has been proposed by the authors in Ref. [14] that reduces the number of medical clinic visits, reduces the cost of medical services, improves the patient care and reduces the costs as well as inconveniences. In Ref. [15], there has been proposed some new solutions using Bluetooth technology and GPS anonymously, which can be used on smartphones or bracelets to prepare the maps for quarantine monitoring, touch tracking, tracking of movement, statistics of social distance and density. This article presents the various applications that have been introduced to fight COVID-19 and the associated confidentiality concerns of the personal data that will happen in the post-coronavirus period. The authors in Ref. [11] have addressed in-depth analysis of COVID-19 itself, in which its clinical characteristics, relaying mechanisms and diagnostic measures are analysed. After stages of spread that the disease is going through is also mentioned. There has also been mentioned the different prevention attempts that are being done to end to the epidemic and precautionary steps that are to be taken. This discussion focuses primarily on using emerging technologies like Internet of Things, UAVs, Artificial Intelligence, 5G etc. to mitigate the effect of the COVID-19 pandemic. In Ref. [16], the author has shed light on some of the problems and challenges affecting to the adaptation of mobile contact tracking to combat the pandemic. The aim of the mobile contact tracing is to make the process of contact tracing faster based on a manual interview in order to contain an outbreak efficiently and quickly. A healthcare system allowed by the Internet of Things (IoT) has been proposed by the authors in Ref. [9] that is quite suitable for remote monitoring of COVID-19 patients, using an unified framework. This platform benefits in improving the patient satisfaction and decreases the rate of readmission in hospital. It is useful for network of management of patients, doctors, surgeons and hospitals.

9.3 Technologies to Combat COVID-19

Some of the important ingenious technologies that can be powered to battle against COVID-19 are shown in Figure 9.1. All of these will be explained in detail in context with COVID-19.

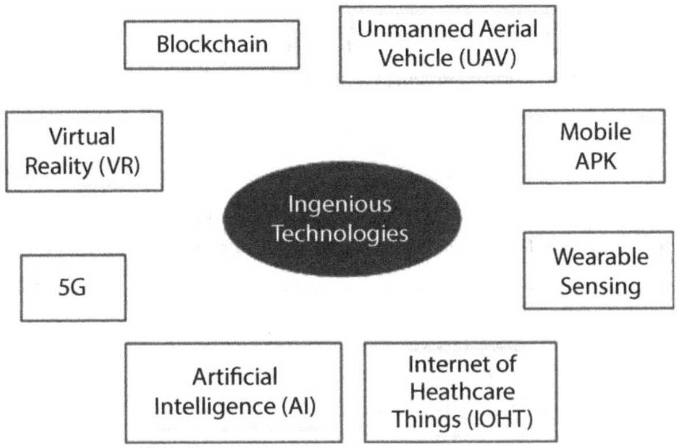

Figure 9.1 Some ingenious technologies to fight against COVID-19.

9.3.1 Blockchain

Block chain [5, 17] is a method of recording information in a way that it is impossible or very difficult to modify, hack or cheat. It is a digital collection of transactions which works as a tool to help some of the healthcare industry problems that are concerned with wasteful spending and highest cost for providers and patients. Block chain platform permits the patients to allocate the access rules for the medical data. The patients may connect to others and can collect their medical data automatically. It is a distributed network development for the purpose of accountability, authentication and reliability in the past information protection that highlights on discretion, integrity and availability of the data. Telehealth and telemedicine solutions in general are gaining popularity in healthcare. Figure 9.2 shows the integration of block chain and AI technologies for pandemic challenges.

The architecture shown is categorized into four parts as shown. First, the data from hospitals, labs and various other sources are combined to develop the big data. This data is to be secured via blockchain. The advantage of the blockchain is that it is decentralized, secure, immutable and completely transparent technology [18]. Blockchain provides various solutions to the various services related to coronavirus. The data hence collected from blockchain may be inspected using AI functions. At the top of the network is stakeholder layer that includes Governments, Public etc. who may take benefits from this network.

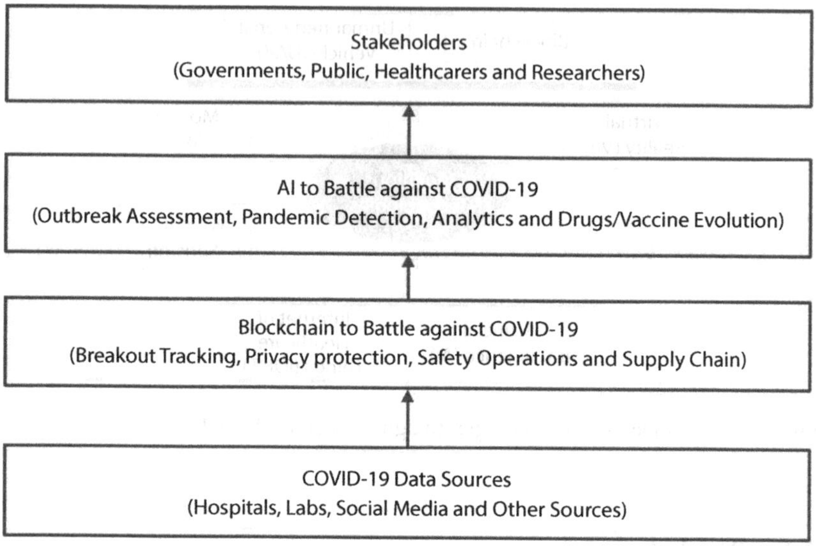

Figure 9.2 Blockchain and AI for battling against COVID-19.

9.3.1.1 Challenges and Solutions

The first and foremost challenge in the implementation of blockchain is the unawareness regarding blockchain and its usage. Moreover, there are several uncertainties concerning the usage of blockchain because people link blockchain only with malicious and duplicitous activities. Next challenge is that the blockchain-based implementations frequently incur from their nonexistence of scalability. The present calamity demands an extremely accessible solution because almost every human in the world is affected by this. Currently, a few platforms related to blockchain are present and most of them have inherent scalability limitations [17]. Lastly, the ongoing pandemic needs the merging of the various emergent and latest technologies. Since blockchain platform is quite novel and undeveloped, its potential needs to be explored. Therefore, it is tough to merge the blockchain applications with other latest algorithms. There are some issues of blockchain integration with facial recognition algorithms and computer vision regarding the colour and gender of people [19].

Though these challenges can easily be resolved by providing the awareness to the people, Government should authorize some rules and regulations in order to design and develop the blockchain implementation.

9.3.2 Unmanned Aerial Vehicle (UAV)

A drone known as unnamed aerial vehicle (UAV) [6] is a technology that has the ability to work as transport in medical services, in military services and to live stream any fixed public area etc. It has the ability to offer real time video [20]. No pilot is needed in the drones that are controlled by remotes, computer, mobile or tablet. These are having software to pre-program specific GPS coordinates and create a specific path for drones. They can communicate with cellular, satellite, drone and ground.

Drones are working just like flying robots that are controlled autonomously or remotely through the software-controlled flight plan in the embedded system with the sensors and GPS system. The major components of UAV system are speed controller, flight controller, GPS module, battery, antenna, receiver, cameras, sensors, accelerometer and altimeter.

These UAVs are used in trouble sites and areas of biological and chemical hazards. They can track the spread of diseases (i.e. pandemic in the present case). They can get the information about the patients and their needs. These are used for the medical emergencies such as aerosols, heavy metals and radiation. These are mainly used to find the radiation in air, trace the gas level in air and map out the nuclear radiation [21]. In the pandemic emergencies, these drones are used as telemedicine or to transfer the samples in laboratories or to supply the vaccine to some place [22]. They may sanitize the various public areas. Drones are used to communicate with the patients and gather their information and telemonitor in certain remote areas [23].

9.3.2.1 Challenges and Solutions

There are several profits that drones can offer in response to the health emergencies; still this drone technology is provoked by certain challenges.

The amalgamation of drones in the COVID-19 influences the response system in various cities due to the dearth of clearances of government regulations. Due to the susceptibilities in the operation of drone such as GPS jamming and hacking, drone becomes a striking panorama for the malevolent handlers to conduct the illegitimate actions. At present, several companies have raised their voice about the security risks related to drones [24]. Even though a lot of significant paces have been made in the improvement of drone technology at present, till the Visible Line of Sight (VLOS) drone operations continue to some extent safe. But there is need for some hi-tech functional rules to license the harmless actions of UAVs [25]. UAVs face numerous restraints in terms of battery life and load capacity i.e. they can't lift heavy weights, which hinders their ability to cover the long distances and make manifold carriages at a time. Moreover, Drone's rotors have limited flying time and also landing of drone is also difficult.

Because of the several challenges, the countless potential that a UAV grips in regard to the healthcare support cannot be ignored. In order to resolve the problems, Government Regulatory should cautiously gather and analyse the data concerning earlier UAV implementations and try to motivate people to put some additional effort into UAV research and implementation.

9.3.3 Mobile APK

The app which is used for android mobile is mobile apk [7, 16]. These are designed to run on mobile or phone tablets. For making these apk files, first android is compiled using android studio. For medical emergencies like COVID-19 the most commonly useful app is 'Aarogya Setu'. This app uses mobile phone's Bluetooth and GPS abilities. This app has the capacity to record the data of other apps users and to detect the nearby Bluetooth users. The user can change the latitude or longitude to get the data at multiple locations. This application may be used to stop the spread of coronavirus. If any corona patient and non-corona patient are in contact with each other, then the app gives warning to pay the attention which means that it keeps track of other app users. This application has a fixed range which it can control or monitor. It can take only one of the given values 500 m, 1 km, 2 km, 5 km and 10 km.

The recorded data of the phone is stored till any person tests positive or asserts indications of COVID-19 in a self- assessment investigation in the mobile app. If any person is not a patient of COVID-19, then it shows that 'you are safe'. It is shown in Figure 9.3. This app also asks the questions to manage and monitor the current health crises and research to stop the spreading of coronavirus.

9.3.3.1 Challenges and Solutions

There are several challenges offered by Mobile APK. The concerns related to the respective user confidentiality linked with the usage of contact tracing apps, numerous problems with regard to precision as well as consistency also hinder their behavior. These tracking applications are insignificant unless persons are enthusiastic to apply them whenever they move from their houses. In the near future, the measures appraised by the

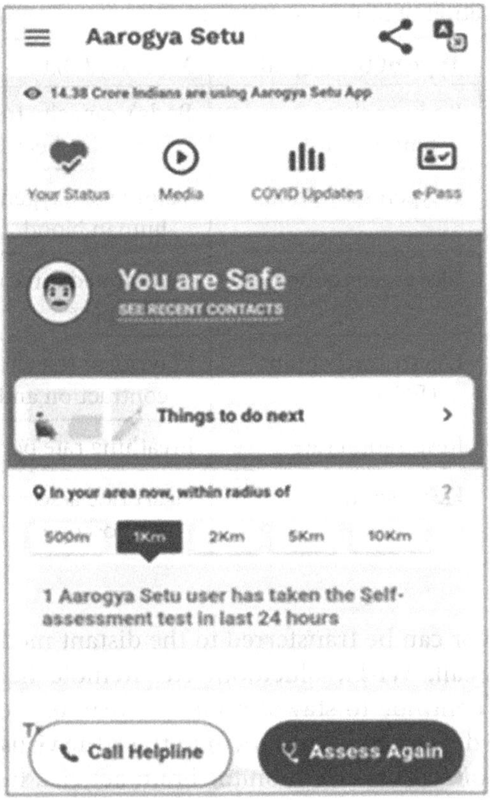

Figure 9.3 Aarogya Setu Mobile App.

administrations as well as other humans would affect the amount of the chaos caused by the epidemic [26].

To tackle the challenges, the app providers must ensure an adequate level of security by using encryption so as to minimize the chances of any data leakage and manipulation by the untrusted third parties.

9.3.4 Wearable Sensing

Rapid growth in the telecommunications, Very Large Scale Integration (VLSI), sensing technology and material science makes novel opportunities for the collaboration between human body and wearable sensors. Wearable technology in healthcare include the electronic devices that consumer can wear (like smart watches) and are designed to collect the data of personal health and exercise for a user or patient [8]. Data collected

Table 9.1 Classification of bio-sensors.

Type of sensor	Type of bio-signal	Measured data
Temperature sensor	Body or skin temperature	Body's capacity to generate and eliminate heat
Pulse oximeter	Oxygen saturation	Volume of oxygen provided by human blood
Accelerometer	Movement of body	Accelerated force analysis in 3D-space
Chest or skin electrode	Electrocardiogram (ECG)	Waveform test showing heart rate contraction and relaxation
Piezo sensor	Respiration rate	Breathing rate per unit of time
Piezo cardio graph	Heart sound	Heart rate assessment using stethoscope

from the bio-sensor can be transferred to the distant medical station [27] directly through call, Wi-Fi, Bluetooth etc. Remote health monitoring allows people to continue to stay at home. A wearable sensor is attained to body wearable devices to permit them to track the virus activity in such a way that most of sensors can monitor brain activity, heart activity and muscle activity. These devices collect the data for body health which helps to monitor the clinical health.

The different sensors are classified on the basis of bio-signal and data they can measure. This is shown in Table 9.1.

9.3.4.1 Challenges and Solutions

Even though wearables have contributed substantially in the competition against the epidemic, it is important to consider that some of the restrictions incumber the usage of wearable devices during this current health emergency [28]. Due to shutdowns in many factories in this current pandemic situation, the supply chain is interrupted and hence the delivery of the various wearable devices is very tough in several parts of the world [29]. Further, the battery life of these intelligent devices is generally an eye opener. The monotonous challenge of charging devices again and again frequently discourages persons from purchasing those [16]. One more challenge is that there are no well-known guidelines from the Government authorities regarding the collection of secrete using these wearable devices which increases the security and confidentiality concerns.

The possible solution is that while developing these devices, the designing firm should preserve the confidentiality and security of users while using the device.

9.3.5 Internet of Healthcare Things

Internet of Things is the system of unified devices conformed with the various constituents such as hardware part, software, network connection and personal computer/laptop that eventually makes them approachable by providing data exchange and collection [30–32]. IoT may be employed to handle the various challenges during the shutdowns circumstances. IoT idea makes the reachability to the ill patients quite easily as it provides the proper care so that they can easily get out of this disease. As we know due to present epidemic condition, the number of person infected due to disease is cumulative day by day, therefore there is a requirement to exploit the suitable amenities offered with IOT approach.

IoT is an advanced technique which confirms that all the humans infected due to this coronavirus are in self-isolation. The tracking of patients having high danger can be easily done using networking. This technique is employed for the measurement of blood pressure, blood glucose level and heartbeat monitoring. During the treatment of disease, IoT connects all the medical machinery and equipment through internet which transmit the real-time data.

The Internet of Healthcare Things (IoHT) [9, 33] also mentioned as the Internet of Medical Things (IoMT) is an integration of smart and intelligent health monitoring devices and software computing technologies. In Current Scenario, IoHT has achieved a rise in the number of its various promising applications. The rise is due to increasing number of NFC reader mobile devices that allow the various devices to communicate with each other [33]. The applications of IoHT include remote monitoring and diagnosis of patients from a remote location, tracking of medical related supplies and transmission of patient data to doctors through various wearables devices due to efficient collection, analysis and transmission of health related information and records [34]. Among the current epidemic situation, many researchers, medical administrations and government authorities are observing to influence IoHT technology along with sensors in order to lessen the load on the various medicare systems. With the appropriate use of IOMT technology infected people can be remotely monitored properly with high-tech tele-devices. It tackles all issues quickly to issue the facility to the patients and healthcare practitioners. It provides an excellent solution in the screening of the infected patients. By using a numerical-based approach, IoHT would help in predicting an imminent condition of this illness.

The various tools used for the functioning of IoHT are mentioned below:

(i) Digital Thermometer: A device that can measure the temperature (coldness or hotness) or temperature gradient of a human's body uses infrared technology as a thermometer. It is mainly used for checking fever in COVID-19 pandemic disease. It has two elements which are needed for the thermometer to measure the temperature: (a) thermometer sensor, (b) mercury in glass thermometer or pyrometric sensor in an infrared thermometer [35]. It measures the temperature without having contact with the patient. With the help of touchless thermometers, one can measure the infrared (heat) radiation given off by objects without even touching them. These thermometers are connected to Android app, which permits them to communicate their readings to the concerned authority.

To measure the temperature of any surface the thermometer emits the heat in the form of IR rays. It will measure the temperature difference (i.e. gradient) between surface and objects in Fahrenheit and Celsius including the temperature of the surrounding environment. The gradient will be measured and used.

(ii) IoT Buttons: To continue hygienic environment and bound the number of Infections in hospitals, many medicare centers have mounted IoT buttons [36] that work on battery. These buttons issue the various kinds of alert messages to administration regarding sanitation and maintenance issue.

(iii) Telemedicine: The exercise of using IoHT technologies to enable monitoring and diagnosis of patients at remote locations is known as Telemedicine [23]. Using this practice, the healthcare professionals can easily access, diagnose, and provide treatment to sick people even without any physical communication with them. The availability of these technologies such as digital thermometers and smart wearables devices is worthless unless people are eager to apply them to combat the pandemic. The usage of telemedicine platforms is insignificant unless sick people are enthusiastic to have faith on their healthcare professionals.

9.3.5.1 *Challenges and Solutions*

The major challenge in IoHT is related to the safety and privacy issues in healthcare data. Further, patient data may be misused. Lastly, the process of data collection is very much challenging [33].

The challenges may be overcome by using some novel solution to connect all the medical devices through internet. There may be used some statistical technique to envisage the critical situations.

9.3.6 Artificial Intelligence

Artificial Intelligence (AI) plays a substantial role to combat against the pandemic. Deep Learning (DL) & Machine Learning (ML) are the two major techniques used in AI [1]. DL can easily solve the complicated systems after being trained from the elementary representations while ML indicates the capability to take out the useful patterns from the entire database. The efficiency of the various ML algorithms depends upon how the various features are represented.

Artificial Intelligence is a very robust tool to battle against COVID-19. For example, a DL model can recognize which type of the existing drug can be used for the infected patients [37]. Although the various findings in this direction are yet to be approved, still it can open some new doors to combat COVID-19. Similarly, an ML model may also be used for the modelling and simulations to get some new compounds for fighting with COVID-19 [38]. However, currently, AI techniques are still in the prefatory phases. AI may be integrated with the blockchain technology. This integration concept has already been explained through Figure 9.2 in the earlier section.

9.3.6.1 *Challenges and Solutions*

There are various challenges and drawbacks incumbering the application of AI in COVID-19. AI modeling requires significant amount of training of data in order to get consistent and accurate results. However, due to the unique feature of the epidemic, there is a lack of the previous data on which training of Artificial Intelligence models can be done. The absence of open data has also introduced a challenge to the competent use of Artificial Intelligence algorithms [10]. Further, AI analytics for the crowdy place is realized by many people as an opening of privacy. Although in today's scenario, people have apprehended the fact that health concern of human is more important than data confidentiality; the secrecy drawbacks related with the use of AI have inculcated wisdom of anxiety among the people that administrations may track any time. Another restraint of AI is that it depends on human acquaintance. Human proficiency plays a very crucial role in the implementation of AI algorithms and makes a substantial contribution against the COVID-19 pandemic.

Several high-tech solutions have been suggested for mitigating these challenges. By joining and encouraging the various communities on multi-disciplinary groups and by establishing the partnerships, the various gaps in health system using AI may be filled.

9.3.7 5G

The integration of 5G technology with UAVs, robots, and telemedicine tools makes an competent system for monitoring the crowdy places, identifying infection among persons, and offering treatment to them, all without the necessity of human intervention. Though, currently, the deployment of 5G networks suffers various pitfalls, few of them are mentioned below.

9.3.7.1 Challenges and Solutions

The distribution of 5G networks is currently in emerging phases; the most important drawback is the non-existence of set-up to accommodate the functioning of networks [11]. Moreover, the establishment and perpetuation of 5G networks requires a high cost. Its wide-scale distribution is tough for the governments and telecom operators. 5G networks themselves cannot transform the healthcare industry. For getting the better results, it needs to be employed in parallel with the emergent techniques like Internet of Things, Artificial Intelligence and cloud computing. Currently, no well-known guidelines are available that give permission regarding the use of a patient's private information obtained using 5G technology. Moreover, data privacy and many other issues related to security are also linked with the usage of 5G [39].

The various challenges imposed by using 5G technologies may be overcome by introducing security and privacy in the machine learning algorithms.

9.3.8 Virtual Reality

Virtual Reality (VR) [12] plays a prime role in the efficient handling of the continuing epidemic belongings. It can treat ill people and it can provide the awareness about the disease using image acquisition and proper communication. Virtual Reality concept is proved for providing a large number of medical applications and hence it is attracting a large number of healthcare professionals. There are many ways in which the idea and methodology of VR are helpful in framework to alleviate the effects of pandemic. Some of the techniques are in starting phase while others have been proved very well.

9.3.8.1 *Challenges and Solutions*

The challenges and competition for the virtual reality concept are its effectiveness, precision and accuracy. The foremost non-technical drawback is the challenge in terms of the psychological behaviour of person. After passing through such an extreme pressure of epidemic like COVID-19, the patients also experience some psychosomatic disturbances [12]. More imagination and intelligence while applying these concepts and realities of virtual reality in the actual database environment would always be challenge. Another challenge is that the virtual reality application should be battered over the development of specifically planned rooms providing with numerous bigger screen fronts in addition to the currently existing small camera screen front in the virtual reality environment.

The challenges may be overcome in many ways. The proper staff training can make the healthcare professionals quite aware to the real case and the condition to be handled [40]. A more analogous environment can be created where the doctors and medical staff can learn more rapidly and positively to tackle the problems with care and proper training. Further, there is a need to practically employ the virtual reality culture planning to deliver the excellent quality training for the handling of surgery cases. With the help of suitable virtual training and learning environment, VR helps in managing the pain and providing the physical therapy.

9.4 Comparison of Various Technologies to Combat COVID-19

The various technologies discussed in the earlier section may be compared with respect to each other (as shown in Table 9.2).

Table 9.2 Comparison of various technologies.

Technology	Application	Challenges	Solution
Blockchain	(i) It effectively monitors the quarantine cases at home or at medical facilities (ii) It tracks the location of a patient by real-time testing and block recording without interference with data privacy	(i) It is still an innovation. Building trust in the network is a challenge for blockchain. (ii) Many blockchains on the market consume a large amount of resources. This technology requires a high amount of computing power to solve complex mathematical model (iii) Lack of expertise on blockchain	(i) There should be some procurement process to implement blockchain applications by government agencies (ii) Blockchain research and growth should be promoted to concentrate on workforce and student skills (iii) Regulatory and policy considerations are required for the development of a vibrant blockchain ecosystem

(Continued)

Table 9.2 Comparison of various technologies. (*Continued*)

Technology	Application	Challenges	Solution
UAV	(i) It is used for the surveillance to ensure quarantine and mask wearing (ii) It is used to carry out the tasks without any external entity having an impact (iii) It is used for the deployment of robots to patrol the areas and ensure that citizens are following the lockdown instructions (iv) It is used to provide the support to the medical staff by monitoring of remote patients	(i) Security problems are mainly associated with the resource constraints along with UAV delay constraints (ii) Confidentiality, authentication and non-repudiation properties on the contact networks are also challenges (iii) Avoid the drone usage over the residential areas, which leads to the violations of confidentiality by irresponsible behavior, as the captured footage can be used either for cheating and/or fraud	(i) By granting rights to UAV-controlled staff. (ii) Ensure multifactor authentication using something we know (constantly changing password), something we have (username), what we are (biometric assets)) (iii) By monitoring and arresting legal proprietors of drones/UAV in the event of malicious happenings

(*Continued*)

Table 9.2 Comparison of various technologies. (*Continued*)

Technology	Application	Challenges	Solution
Mobile APK	(i) It does the app monitoring to understand population movement and lockout consequences (ii) It determines the proximity of productive persons to COVID-19 (iii) It is a collection of user data for statistical analysis (iv) High Speed Network is used to track strategic locations, infected patients and monitor data and model disease outcomes	(i) The challenge is that such programs also need to be used by a certain proportion of the population in the war against the virus to be genuinely of value (ii) It is a compromise of rapidly launching a new application to maximize its effect in helping to stop the spread of the virus while maintaining a robust and tested security/privacy strategy is a challenge	(i) The tempt developers should not disclose the true purpose of the app (ii) App providers must ensure an adequate level of security, possibly by using encryption, to avoid any data leaks and manipulation by untrusted third parties

(*Continued*)

Table 9.2 Comparison of various technologies. (*Continued*)

Technology	Application	Challenges	Solution
Wearable Sensing	(i) The person under observation is monitored continuously through wearable sensors (ii) The workplace device is secure for COVID-19 (iii) It uses Contact and Proximity tracing (iv) It monitors physiological signs and wellbeing habits, (v) By pattern recognition, behaviour prediction and disease growth may be obtained	There are no guidelines from the government authorities regarding the collection of secrete using these wearables devices, which increases the security and confidentiality concerns	The designing firm should preserve the confidentiality and security of users while using the device
IOHT	(i) It gives the notification to Medical Staff in case of Emergency (ii) It provides the intelligent Tracking of Infected Person	(i) There are safety and privacy issues of data (ii) There may be misuse of records of patient (iii) The process of data collection is very hard	(i) The creative approach is to connect all medical equipment and resources through the Internet (ii) On the basis of available data, any predictive method must be used to forecast future situations

(*Continued*)

Table 9.2 Comparison of various technologies. (*Continued*)

Technology	Application	Challenges	Solution
AI	(i) It may find early infection detection and diagnosis (ii) It reduces the healthcare workers' workload (iii) It predicts the future course of the disease (iv) It develops the effective treatment regimens, preventive approaches, product discovery and vaccine	(i) Risk and mortality data are not sufficiently disaggregated by sex, race, or ethnicity. (ii) Racial and ethnic data are incomplete, and the terms and labels are inconsistent. (iii) Pandemic data tracking systems do not capture data on immigrants and other marginalized populations	(iii) There is a demand for transparency and explanation of the Artificial Intelligence system. (iv) People should join and encourage working groups or committees on multidisciplinary ethics to inform the response to the pandemic. (v) The partnerships to fill gaps in health data in ways should be established that secure and authorize the local communities

(*Continued*)

Table 9.2 Comparison of various technologies. (*Continued*)

Technology	Application	Challenges	Solution
5G	High-speed network enables video and audio quality data in real-time for patients' data analysis, telemedicine, diagnostic and surgical intervention	(i) 5G must effectively distribute IoT Network resources. A lack of scalability would be one of the big problems with such networks (ii) Second, how to interconnect multiple heterogeneous networks with the current 5G networks is a big challenge (iii) Massive numbers of IoT devices linked to heterogeneous networks present new risks and security challenges. The risks could be smart meter hacking, malicious code attacks, sniffing, and Denial of Service (DoS) attacks	5G technology implementation algorithms by updating security machine learning algorithms are needed

(*Continued*)

Table 9.2 Comparison of various technologies. (*Continued*)

Technology	Application	Challenges	Solution
Virtual Reality	(i) It is used to concentrate on something entirely different to make medical care less stressful (ii) There must be planned the complicated surgeries pertaining to vital organs and many other unique cases (iii) Virtual reality-based glasses can help to eliminate any stress caused by staying in the hospital	(i) While passing through such an extreme pressure of epidemic like COVID-19, patients also experience some psychosomatic disturbances (ii) More imagination and intelligence are required in actual data base	(i) The proper staff training can make the healthcare very much professional (ii) There is a need to practically employ the virtual reality culture planning to deliver the excellent quality training for the handling of surgery cases.

9.5 Conclusion

Through this article, the various technologies to fight with infectious diseases like COVID-19 have been discussed. We have discussed the brief idea and related work related to pandemic COVID-19. Subsequently, the various thrust technologies for handling the pandemic challenges have been discussed. Soon these technologies will be seen to handle the various challenges related to pandemic. At last, the comparison of all the technologies with the help of their applications, challenges and their solutions related to COVID-19 have been discussed.

References

1. Pham, Q.V., Nguyen, D.C., Hwang, W.J., Pathirana, P.N., Artificial Intelligence (AI) and Big Data for Coronavirus (COVID-19) Pandemic: A Survey on the State-of-the-Arts. *IEEE Access*, 8, 130820–130839, 2020.
2. Ding, X.R., Clifton, D., Nan, J.I., Lovell, N.H., Bonato, P., Chen, W., Xu, K., Wearable Sensing and Telehealth Technology with Potential Applications in the Coronavirus Pandemic. *IEEE Rev. Biomed. Eng.*, 14, 48–70, 2020.
3. Hussain, A.A., Bouachir, O., Al-Turjman, F., Aloqaily, M., AI Techniques for Covid-19. *IEEE Access*, 8, 128776–128795, 2020.
4. Bain, R., Technology and state government. *Am. Sociol. Rev.*, 2, 6, 860–874, 1937.
5. Puppala, M., He, T., Yu, X., Chen, S., Ogunti, R., Wong, S.T., Data Security and Privacy Management in Healthcare Applications and Clinical Data Warehouse Environment. *2016 IEEE-EMBS International Conference on Biomedical and Health Informatics (BHI)*, Las Vegas, USA, pp. 5–8, 2016.
6. Yaacoub, J.P. and Salman, O., Security Analysis of Drones Systems: Attacks, Limitations, and Recommendations. *Internet Things*, 11, 100218, 2020, https://doi.org/10.1016/j.iot.2020.100218.
7. Mateless, R., Rejabek, D., Margalit, O., Moskovitch, R., Decompiled APK based Malicious Code Classification. *Future Gener. Comput. Syst.*, 110, 135–147, 2020.
8. Yuce, M.R., Implementation of Wireless Body Area Networks for Healthcare Systems. *Sens. Actuators A: Phys.*, 162, 1, 116–129, 2010.
9. Singh, R.P., Javaid, M., Haleem, A., Suman, R., Internet of things (IoT) Applications to Fight against COVID-19 Pandemic. *Diabetes Metab. Syndr.: Clin. Res. Rev.*, 14, 4, 521–524, 2020.
10. Vaishya, R., Javaid, M., Khan, I.H., Haleem, A., Artificial Intelligence (AI) Applications for COVID-19 Pandemic. *Diabetes Metab. Syndr.: Clin. Res. Rev.*, 14, 4, 337–339, 2020, https://doi.org/10.1016/j.dsx.2020.04.012.

11. Chamola, V., Hassija, V., Gupta, V., Guizani, M., A Comprehensive Review of the COVID-19 Pandemic and the Role of IoT, Drones, AI, Blockchain, and 5G in Managing its Impact. *IEEE Access*, 8, 90225–90265, 2020.
12. Singh, R.P., Javaid, M., Kataria, R., Tyagi, M., Haleem, A., Suman, R., Significant Applications of Virtual Reality for COVID-19 Pandemic. *Diabetes Metab. Syndr.: Clin. Res. Rev.*, 14, 661–664, 2020.
13. Boettcher, J., Åström, V., Påhlsson, D., Schenström, O., Andersson, G., Carlbring, P., Internet-based Mindfulness Treatment for Anxiety Disorders: A Randomized Controlled Trial. *Behav. Ther.*, 45, 2, 241–253, 2014.
14. Domínguez, D., Morales, L., Sánchez, N., Navarro-Pando, J., IoMT-driven e-Health: A Technological Innovation Proposal based on Smart Speakers, in: *Bioinformatics and Biomedical Engineering*, Lecture Notes in Computer Science, vol. 12108, I. Rojas, O. Valenzuela, F. Rojas, L. Herrera, F. Ortuño, (Eds.), Springer, Cham, 2020, https://doi.org/10.1007/978-3-030-45385-5_33.
15. Borra, S., COVID-19 Apps: Privacy and Security Concerns, in: *Intelligent Systems and Methods to Combat Covid-19*, A. Joshi, N. Dey, K.C. Santosh, (Eds.), pp. 11–17, Springer, Singapore, 2020, https://doi.org/10.1007/978-981-15-6572-4_2.
16. Dar, A.B., Lone, A.H., Zahoor, S., Khan, A.A., Mir, R.N., Applicability of Mobile Contact Tracing in Fighting Pandemic (COVID-19): Issues, Challenges and Solutions. *Comput. Sci. Rev.*, 38, 1–14, 2020, http://dx.doi.org/10.2139/ssrn.3683404.
17. Nguyen, D., Ding, M., Pathirana, P.N., Seneviratne, A., *Blockchain and AI-based Solutions to Combat Coronavirus (COVID-19)-like Epidemics: A Survey*, Preprints, USA, 2020.
18. Peck, M.E., The bitcoin arms race is on! *IEEE Spectr.*, 50, 6, 11–13, 2013.
19. Hasan, H. R., Salah, K., Jayaraman, R., Arshad, J., Yaqoob, I., Omar, M., Ellahham, S. Blockchain-based Solution for COVID-19 Digital Medical Passports and Immunity Certificates. *IEEE Access*, 8, 222093–222108, 2020.
20. Chan, K.W., Nirmal, U., Cheaw, W.G., Progress on drone technology and their applications: A comprehensive review. *AIP Conference Proceedings 2030*, 2018, https://doi.org/10.1063/1.5066949.
21. Tang, X.B., Meng, J., Wang, P., Cao, Y., Huang, X., Wen, L.S., Chen, D., Efficiency Calibration and Minimum Detectable Activity Concentration of a Real-time UAV Airborne Sensor System with Two Gamma Spectrometers. *Appl. Radiat. Isot.*, 110, 100–108, 2016.
22. Martin, P.G., Payton, O.D., Fardoulis, J.S., Richards, D.A., Scott, T.B., The use of unmanned aerial systems for the mapping of legacy uranium mines. *J. Environ. Radioact.*, 143, 135–140, 2015.
23. Breen, G.M. and Matusitz, J., An evolutionary examination of telemedicine: A health and computer-mediated communication perspective. *Soc Work Public Health*, 25, 1, 59–71, 2010.
24. Angurala, M., Bala, M., Bamber, S.S., Kaur, R., Singh, P., An Internet of Things Assisted Drone Based Approach to Reduce Rapid Spread

of Covid-19. *J. Saf. Sci. Resilience*, 1, 1, 31–35, 2020, DOI: https://doi.org/10.1016/j.jnlssr.2020.06.011.

25. Kumar, S., Raut, R.D., Narkhede, B.E., A Proposed Collaborative Framework by using Artificial Intelligence-Internet of Things (AI-IoT) in COVID-19 pandemic situation for healthcare workers. *Int. J. Healthc. Manage.*, 13, 1–9, 2020.
26. Bassi, A., Arfin, S., John, O., Jha, V., An Overview of Mobile Applications (apps) to Support the Coronavirus Disease-2019 Response in India. *Indian J. Med. Res.*, 151, 5, 468–473, 2020.
27. Mosenia, A., Sur-Kolay, S., Raghunathan, A., Jha, N.K., Wearable Medical Sensor-based System Design: A Survey. *IEEE Trans. Multi-Scale Comput. Syst.*, 3, 2, 124–138, 2017.
28. Weizman, Y., Tan, A.M., Fuss, F.K., Use of Wearable Technology to Enhance Response to the Coronavirus (COVID-19) Pandemic. *Public Health*, 185, 221–222, 2020, https://doi.org/10.1016/j.puhe.2020.06.048.
29. Kapoor, A., Guha, S., Das, M.K., Goswami, K.C., Yadav, R., Digital healthcare: The Only Solution for Better Healthcare during COVID-19 Pandemic? *Indian Heart J.*, 72, 61–64, 2020, https://doi.org/10.1016/j.ihj.2020.04.001.
30. Gupta, A., Srivastava, A., Anand, R., Tomažič, T., Business Application Analytics and the Internet of Things: The Connecting Link, in: *New Age Analytics*, G. Shrivastava, S.-L. Peng, H. Bansal, K. Sharma, M. Sharma, (Eds.), pp. 249–273, Apple Academic Press, Canada, 2020.
31. Anand, R., Sinha, A., Bhardwaj, A., Sreeraj, A., Flawed Security of Social Network of Things, in: *Handbook of Research on Network Forensics and Analysis Techniques*, G. Shrivastava, P. Kumar, B.B. Gupta, S. Bala, N. Dey, (Eds.), pp. 65–86, IGI Global, Hershey, Pennsylvania, USA, 2018.
32. Gupta, A., Srivastava, A., Anand, R., Cost-Effective Smart Home Automation using Internet of Things. *J. Commun. Eng. Syst.*, 9, 2, 1–6, 2019.
33. Swayamsiddha, S. and Mohanty, C., Application of cognitive Internet of Medical Things for COVID-19 Pandemic. *Diabetes Metab. Syndr.: Clin. Res. Rev.*, 14, 5, 911–915, 2020.
34. Mbunge, E., Integrating Emerging Technologies into COVID-19 Contact Tracing :Opportunities, Challenges and Pitfalls, Diabetes & Metabolic Syndrome. *Clin. Res. Rev.*, 14, 1631–1636, 2020, https://doi.org/10.1016/j.dsx.2020.08.029.
35. Bigotti, F., The Weight of the Air: Santorio's Thermometers and the Early History of Medical Quantification Reconsidered. *J. Early Mod. Stud.*, 7, 1, 73–103, 2018.
36. Chai, P.R., Zhang, H., Baugh, C.W., Jambaulikar, G.D., McCabe, J.C., Gorman, J.M., Landman, A., Internet of Things Buttons for Real-time Notifications in Hospital Operations: Proposal for hospital implementation. *J. Med. Internet Res.*, 20, 8, e251, 2018.
37. Beck, B.R., Shin, B., Choi, Y., Park, S., Kang, K., Predicting Commercially Available Antiviral Drugs That May Act on the Novel Coronavirus

(SARS-CoV-2) through a Drug-target Interaction Deep Learning Model. *Comput. Struct. Biotechnol. J.*, 18, 784–790, 2020, https://doi.org/10.1101/2020.01.31.929547.

38. Zhavoronkov, A., Zagribelnyy, B., Zhebrak, A., Aladinskiy, V., Terentiev, V., Vanhaelen, Q., Bishop, M., *Potential Non-covalent SARS-CoV-2 3C-like Protease Inhibitors Designed using Generative Deep Learning Approaches and Reviewed by Human Medicinal Chemist in Virtual Reality*, Hong Kong, vol. 307, p. 2, E1, Insilico Medicine Hong Kong Ltd A, 2020.
39. Saeed, N., Bader, A., Al-Naffouri T.Y., Alouini, M.S., When Wireless Communication Responds to COVID-19: Combating the Pandemic and Saving the Economy. *Frontiers in Communications and Networks*, 1, 1–15, 2020.
40. Wang, S.S., Teo, W.Z., Teo, W.Z., Chai, Y.W., Virtual reality as a bridge in palliative care during COVID-19. *J. Palliat. Med.*, 23, 6, 2020, https://doi.org/10.1089/jpm.2020.0212.

10

Emerging Techniques for Handling Pandemic Challenges

Ankur Gupta[1]* and Puneet Garg[2]

[1]*Dept. of Computer Science and Engineering, Vaish College of Engineering, Rohtak, India*
[2]*J.C. Bose University of Science and Technology YMCA, Faridabad, India*

Abstract
The world right now is dealing with a nightmare in the form of Corona virus disease. COVID-19 has been declared a pandemic by the WHO. It's an infectious disease caused by virus called SARS-CoV-2. The symptoms of the disease range from fever, dry cough, headaches to difficulty in breathing. Technology has been making it out lives easier and how. The healthcare system also incorporates technology everywhere. We can use latest technologies to deal with crisis situations such as pandemic. Remote healthcare monitoring is the process of monitoring patients in a non-clinical environment. The patients can be provided with sensors and wearable's to monitor them from afar. The devices range from wearable health monitors to fit bits. Artificial Intelligence is the future, everyone says. With help of technology, devices can check that people are maintaining social distancing and have their masks on. The data collected can be used to make people aware during a pandemic situation. It can be psychologically disturbing and stir up all sorts of feelings, like unreasonable fear and stress. Online counseling also proves helpful to those who shy way in going to hospitals to discuss issues such as depression. It also breaks the barrier of stigma among the patients.

Keywords: COVID-19, pandemic, emerging techniques, healthcare

**Corresponding author*: ankurdujana@gmail.com

Abhinav Juneja, Vikram Bali, Sapna Juneja, Vishal Jain and Prashant Tyagi (eds.) Enabling Healthcare 4.0 for Pandemics: A Roadmap Using AI, Machine Learning, IoT and Cognitive Technologies, (189–210) © 2021 Scrivener Publishing LLC

10.1 Introduction to Pandemic

A disease which spreads all over the word becomes famous in the form of pandemic [1]. Outbreak of influenza takes place in a situation where a latest virus related to influenza comes in to existence and it spreads internationally. When the outbreak of influenza takes place the maximum number of people all over the world does not have enough immunity to fight with the virus. Outbreaks which have taken place in previous years mainly come out of animal viruses.

Most of the symptoms observed at the time of influenza outbreak are almost equivalent to regular influenza but some symptoms are different. Let us explain this point with the help of an example. In case of regular and outbreak, symptoms appear in all age groups and most of them becomes well without taking any diagnosis. At the same time, in case of regular influenza only those people died whose age are above sixty and suffering from other disease.

In comparison to this, when an outbreak takes place, in addition to elder people, it affects those people which are still in its early stage. In comparison to normal influenza, at the time of outbreak more people get infected. Several researches are leveraging emerging technique in the post-pandemic workplace [4].

All of us know that whenever an outbreak takes place, to handle this outbreak in addition to healthcare department involvement of common man is required.

In the year nineteen ninety nine guidance required at the time of outbreak is prepared by WHO which are modified in two thousand and five. In 2005, there have been advances in many areas of preparedness and response planning.

10.1.1 How Pandemic Spreads?

Separation of virus entirely depends upon different parameters. When these parameters are manipulated they will bring different consequences. These consequences are following the pattern of logical curve. These curves are S-shaped which define growth of population and viruses. In present situation, corona virus which cause breathing problem in human beings has triggered a panic situation all over the world. It happens because its outbreak is already organized in the form of pandemic. Research community provides guidance about this virus growth on regular basis. In addition research community and scientific community also provide significant contributions. Let us understand this point with the help of an example. With the help of program given below it becomes possible to determine the extent of this virus distribution over a population. Whenever an infected person comes in close contact with a healthy person, he will deliver virus in the direction of healthy person. But the healthy person did not get disease if his immunity is strong. Because of that, it becomes possible to transmit this virus to other people.

Transmission of a virus mostly depends upon four factors which are as follows:

- total number of people available;
- considerable amount of epidemic days;
- number of human being to whom an infected person meets;
- chance of virus transmission when an infected person meets with a healthy population.

10.1.2 Background History

Whenever a disease spreads in the population of a particular natural region in an uncontrolled manner, it becomes a pandemic. At the same time, it becomes a worldwide pandemic when it spreads all over the world in international boundaries. For example, the "Black Plague" comes into occurrence in the 1300s, remains restricted to Europe, where as the epidemic Spanish Flu which occurred in 1918 transmitted internationally.

The Antonine Plague (165–180)

This epidemic comes into existence when European army comes back from the Near East. This epidemic creates smallpox. In first stage, nearly fifty lakes of people died at the time of next explosion which took place in between third era, it was estimated that five thousand people died with each passing day in Rome.

Cholera

First explosion of this deadly disease took place in India in 1816. It became an epidemic when its transmission started from Bengal to all over India, and to China and the Caspian Sea. In its subsequent explosion which took place in the end of 1820 produced effect on the European and North

American population. After that, five more outbreaks related to this disease took place. Last explosion of this disease took place in the middle of 1961–66 in Indonesia, which spread to Bangladesh, India, and the Soviet Union.

The Spanish Flu Pandemic (1918)
It took place in 1918 in Kansas. Its first patient came into existence at the army base camp of Fort Riley on 11 March 1918, followed by one hundred and seven patients before noon that same day. Out of twenty six thousand men, 1,127 were infected, out of which 46 were found in critical condition.

It was believed that this epidemic was transmitted from a bird to human. The first infected person left the base camp in order to take part in World War I. This disease was spread by them at every stoppage point, due to which it transmitted all over the world. The number of people who died because of this disease was higher than the number of soldiers who died at the time of war. It was estimated that nearly 5 lakh U.S. citizens died because of this epidemic and in between ten to hundred million people died all over the world.

Explosion of Asian Flu (1957–58)
In comparison to 1918 virus, virus which brought this disease in 1957 was identified very early because of scientific development. Explosion of this virus took place in China. Formation of vaccine and its supply in small quantity starts till this virus reaches to America. Still near about seventy thousand U.S citizens died whereas all over of word twenty lakh people died.

10.1.3 Corona

It is a communicable disease which comes into existence from the latest breed of a corona virus. Several research are preparing for the perpetual issues of pandemics of infections by corona virus with special focus [3]. It is already noticed that most of corona patients will experience normal symptoms which go away with time by taking domestic treatment. In some cases these symptoms diminish in the absence of diagnosed moderate respiratory and recover without needing particular treatment. Serious symptoms are shown in people whose ages are above sixty and people who are suffering from some other type of diseases such as blood pressure, sugar, incurable breathing disease and cancer. Everyone knows the manner in which the virus of this pandemic transmits. The best possible methods by which the transmission rate of coronavirus is slowed down are also known to every individual. These methods protect yourself and others by maintaining a safe distance, wash hands with soap regularly for

Table 10.1 Total reported cases and death cases due to Corona Virus are shown below.

Location	Confirmed	Recovered	Deaths
Haryana	47,153 1,860	39,601 1,562	538 21
Maharashtra	596K 5,218	417K 3,653	20,037 175
Tamil Nadu	338K 4,982	278K 4,101	5,766 85
Andhra Pradesh	290K 5,869	201K 4,075	2,650 54
Karnataka	227K 3,543	141K 2,209	3,947 62
Uttar Pradesh	154K 756	100K 492	2,449 12
Delhi	153K 8,038	138K 7,247	4,196 221
West Bengal	116K 1,290	86,771 961	2,428 27
Chennai	115K 16,260	102K 14,322	2,434 343
Bihar	104K 1,049	72,324 730	461 5
Telangana	92,255 2,621	70,132 1,993	703 20
Mumbai	84,524 27,395	55,884 18,112	4,899 1,588
Gujarat	78,680 1,255 +1,121	61,512 981	2,785 44 +20
Assam	76,875 2,484 +1,317	55,215 1,784	189 6 +7

(*Continued*)

Table 10.1 Total reported cases and death cases due to Corona Virus are shown below. (*Continued*)

Location	Confirmed	Recovered	Deaths
Odisha	62,294 1,425 +2,244	42,277 967	353 8 +10
Rajasthan	61,296 890	46,604 676	876 13
Thane	47,935 4,334	18,156 1,642	1,270 115
Madhya Pradesh	45,455 620	34,038 464	1,105 15
Kerala	44,415 1,276 +1,530	28,894 830	156 4 +10
Punjab	31,206 1,115 +1,165	19,431 694	812 29 +41

at least 20 s, do not touch your face, nose and eyes and put sanitizer on hands in which alcohol level is more than 70%. As tabulated in Table 10.1, a comparison of recovered patients and dying patients is shown over total patient reported.

Corona virus mostly transmits through an infected person to a healthy person when the saliva drops of infected person discharges either through mouth at the time of cough or nose at the time of sneeze. Therefore, obeying the protocol related to respiratory becomes essential. Up to this point of time, neither a vaccine nor a tablet has been developed for the diagnosis of Corona virus. But, scientific community works very hard in the field of vaccine development.

10.2 Technique Used to Handle Pandemic Challenges

10.2.1 Smart Techniques in Cities

Smart (Canny) techniques [4] get great support from China at the starting of 2000 when they were introduced in their latest policy. Techniques that came in trend are Online shopping using Robot Deliveries, Digital as well as Contactless Payments, working remotely, distance learning, tele-health, entertainment online, supply chain, fifth generation and information and communications technology [5], Block chain technologies to nanotechnology [6]. These techniques were used in support of good governance. On the basis of statistical records which were collected in 2015, it was brought into limelight that population of metropolitan cities in China is almost 56% to the country overall population. It was considered, that if this population rose up to 76% in the coming twenty years, the level of Chinese people living becomes better and additional career options were developed. Opportunities in cities, is supposed to rise exponentially in the next 2 to 76%. To deal with this growing population, Chinese started to build canny cities. In these cities latest techniques were implemented in order to provide support in the direction of urbanized government. According to a study about 500 smart cities were available in China at an international level. The city from where the pandemic of corona virus started is a smart city. In the primary stage of coronavirus people of this city were highly affected. In its twelfth five year plan which was made available to the public in 2010, China committed to develop smart cities. A design in the support of social economic and political intentions was made with regard to the subsequent five years. The country latest urbanization design which was started in 2014 took the responsibility of developing smart cities. This program will be completed in twenty. In this design existing cities are also designed in the form of smart cities. Additionally, in the 2015 Li Keqiang, who was the ex-prime minister of China highlighted, canny cities and latest techniques that provided a significant contribution in the growth of any country. In the next five-year design, concept of building canny cities was considered in a more serious way. This was the first design which was put forward under the leadership of President Xi Jinping's. According to this design they were not only promoting them but it is also creating inter-city infrastructures. It is also building partnership in between them. It would provide additional support in the favor of national government. Centralization of state government in the central government and its controlling power on cities make arrangements in a very speedy way. Engineering related to IoT is much used in China even at smallest level that the bus tickets are charged on the basis of traveler facial identification. In addition to this, canny hardwares are also linked with dustbin in such a way that delivers signal to a system in an electronic way whenever a dustbin completely fills. Therefore the environment of developed cities are made in such a way that people of these cities use the growing application of IoT for the last one decade.

Because of this, China becomes most refined industry in relation to IoT technology. All the credit is being given to the desire of Chinese people in support of developing smart cities. Most number of new technologies is also developed in China. Maintain continuous observations, provide disaster signals and making of decisions in a fastest way become possible for cities when technologies like big data, artificial intelligence and IoT are implemented. In a similar way the field related to medical science also gets significant contribution when they used latest technologies. All these things made China highly powerful countries which can control the explosion of any outbreak in a very speedy way in comparison to other countries.

10.2.2 Smart Technologies in Western Democracies

In contrast with China, distribution of power in the governments of metropolitan and local areas in Western democracies is equal in the company of centralized governments. Like Chinese contextual relationship, cities were developed due to the increment of urbanized population. It seems to be happening in North American and European countries because they start to implement the engineering of canny city. Community of Europe started with different plans in which the plan of canny cities, council initiative, and the plan of introducing partnership in support of Smart Cities are included. With the help of these initiatives, European cities required facilities on the behalf of European government which allowed then to convert their cities into smart cities. The countries which are highly affected by the pandemic of coronavirus in Western surroundings are already famous because of their high tech cities. A strong relationship exists in the middle of these countries because of similar environment conditions and business connectivity with China. This business connectivity in relation to China becomes the most relevant reason of coronavirus transmission. IoT provides canny solutions in support of city wise concerns because it is connected to mankind and medical sector. Corona virus put a great effect on New York City, but the way in which it uses IoT application for the collection of detailed knowledge out of communities sets an example in front of whole world. In addition to cities like LA, Boston, Denver, Seattle, some other cities of the United States of America come under the category of canny cities. Let us talk about European countries. In European countries a city of Spain called Barcelona, is one of the highly affected cities, also developed the supporting infrastructure of their smart city in order to use its application in an improved way.

10.2.3 Techno- or Human-Driven Approach

Developments of canny cities are progressing in China and Western democracies with a very speedy rate. But, still human driven method is used by the smart cities in the management of state affairs. This method identifies the manner in which they implement latest techniques in order to communicate with their population. This method gives significant support to technologies in order to make the technology dependent on people. In this method environmental conditions are not taken into consideration. This method comes across in the company of difficult technological prospect. Depending upon human requirement they consider latest engineering techniques which contribute significantly in the arrangement of public systems. Challenges and issues faced by governments can be easily resolved when the internal abilities of these latest techniques are used. Technology driven method becomes very useful in imposing the government rules and regulations. But, at the same time, it affects human freedom, increase restrictions and bring ethical queries whereas human driven method are used in condition when use of technologies becomes impossible. Therefore it will not affect human freedom. They come across in the company as a simple technological outlook. Every person retains agency in determining technological use. With the help of this method, governments improve public and private capital in the middle of their population. It gives permission in the direction of developing technologies depending upon human's requirements. The difference in the middle of these methods potentially holds a key to determining the standard of canny techniques implemented in setting of Chinese and Western democracies to manage the spread of Corona virus.

10.3 Working Process of Techniques

Technology has played, and would continue to play a significant role in supporting efforts to track, identify and combat this virus [8]. The working process of different techniques used to restrict corona are explained in this section. There are several emerging techniques to tackle and manage Corona virus Pandemic Corona virus [9, 10]. However several countries have used AI technology to figure out corona virus [12].

a) Face Mask Detector

At some places the neural classifier technology has been used to confirm the presence of mask on the face [13] of entering persons (see Figure 10.1). The camera captures the face of person then semantic segmentation [14]

Figure 10.1 Face mask detection from group of people.

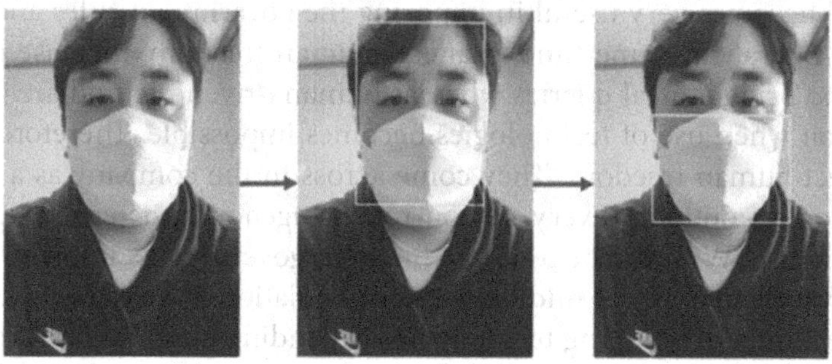

Figure 10.2 Face mask detections.

takes place. Neural classifier [15] may be used to detect the mask shape on person face (see Figure 10.2).

Smart video surveillance system [17, 18] is connected to face mask detection system. This helps in implementing IoT based notification system in case of absence of mask [16]. Cameras are connected to internet for security purposes [19]. If mask pattern is not found then the alarm is triggered using IoT devices to represent present of person without mask. Intelligent CCTV Surveillance Systems [20–23] are getting popular day to day.

b) IoT Based Camera Surveillance System

IoT has been integrated to camera surveillance system [24–26] and has improved their utility. Such systems are frequently used in order to track the status of density of people at public place. More over this system are capable to notify or trigger the alarm in case of any person at crowdie place is found without face mask or people are situated at less distance.

c) Smart Sanitization

Smart sanitization allows sanitization without any touch in order to reduce the probability of virus spreading [11]. Several sensor based sanitization equipment are frequently used in public places to avoid infection spreading (see Figure 10.3). Even surveillance cameras are also set in order to confirm whether entering person has sanitized there hand or not.

d) Use of AI Based Techniques for Healthcare

Artificial intelligence based healthcare system could be found helpful for medical prescription [2]. It has been observed that the people who are suffering from other diseases cannot visit the hospital or clinics frequently. Moreover there is chance of infection too. Thus the intelligent medicine prescription system could diagnose them considering their problems. In this way the healthcare services could be provided using AI in era of COVID-19.

e) COVID-19 Tracker

After regular test the positive cases are uploaded on the server that helps in identification of infected persons. Another person around infected person gets the status of infected person around them and this helps them to take preventive measures. IoT technology [7] could play significant role in isolation of infected person. In India government launched 'AarogyaSetu App' (as shown in Figure 10.4) to track COVID-19.

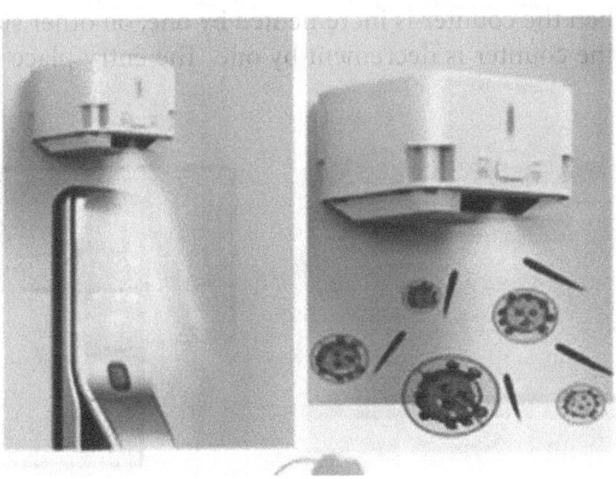

Figure 10.3 Smart sanitizations.

Figure 10.4 COVID-19 tracking applications.

f) Social Distancing

Mechanism to count the number of entering person and exiting person has been built to reduce presence of huge number of persons. When person enters then the counter is incremented by one, on other side if person exists then the counter is decrement by one. The entry place is restricted

Figure 10.5 Occupancy representation systems.

when the number of count reaches its maximum. The entry is allowed only after exiting of any person (Figure 10.5).

10.4 Data Analysis

As shown in Figures 10.6 to 10.23, Dataset of 3,290 records has been considered from 17 April 2020 to 20 July 2020. This data is representing total test, positive and negative cases at different dates. The states considered in present research are Haryana, Punjab, Utter-Pradesh, Rajasthan, Delhi, Maharashtra, Gujarat, Madhya Pradesh, and Bihar.

Analyzing the Total Sample and Positive Cases of Corona in different State of India

Haryana: Following chart is representing the total sample taken and positive cases in April, May, June and July in Haryana.

Punjab: Following chart is representing the total sample taken and positive cases in April, May, June and July in Punjab.

Uttar Pradesh: Following chart is representing the total sample taken and positive cases in April, May, June and July in Uttar Pradesh.

Rajasthan: Following chart is representing the total sample taken and positive cases in April, May, June and July in Rajasthan.

Bihar: Following chart is representing the total sample taken and positive cases in April, May, June and July in Bihar.

Delhi: Following chart is representing the total sample taken and positive cases in April, May, June and July in Delhi.

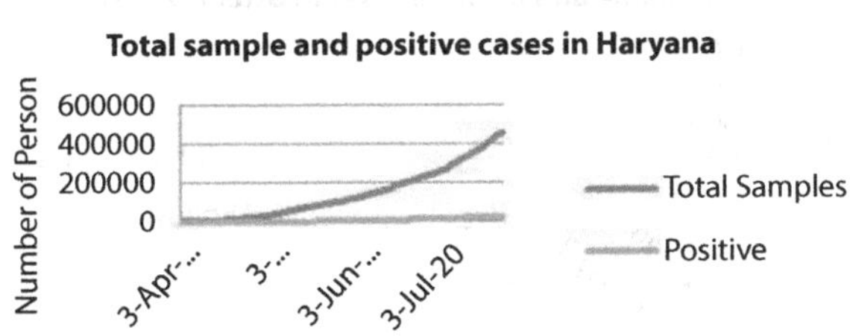

Figure 10.6 Total sample and positive cases in Haryana.

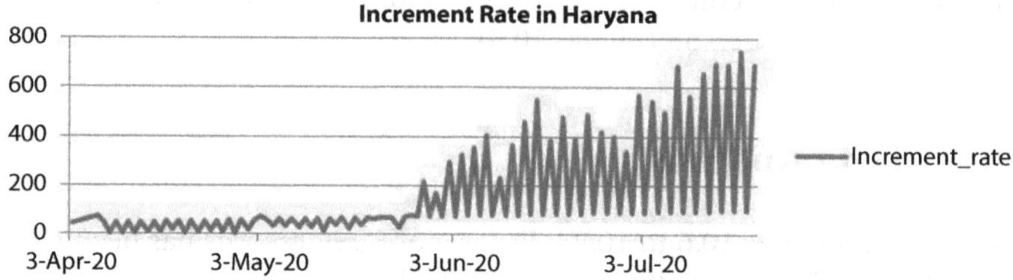

Figure 10.7 Increment rate in Haryana.

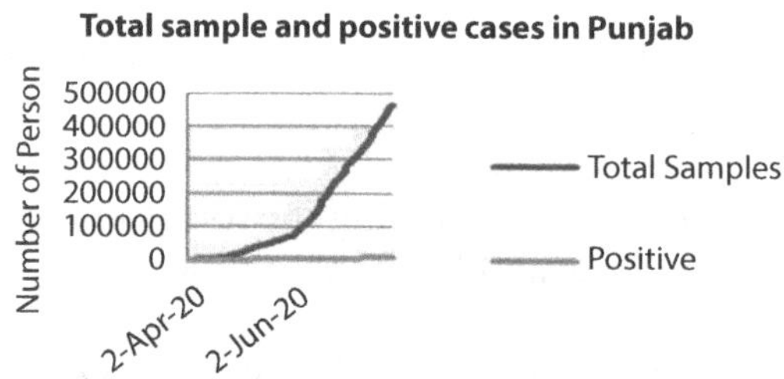

Figure 10.8 Total sample and positive cases in Punjab.

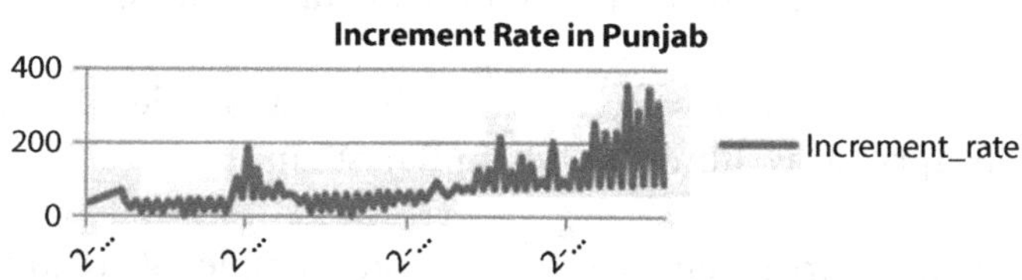

Figure 10.9 Increment rate in Punjab.

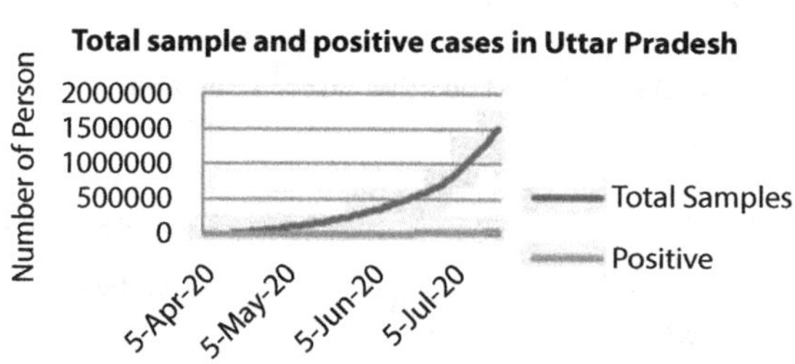

Figure 10.10 Total sample and positive cases in Uttar Pradesh.

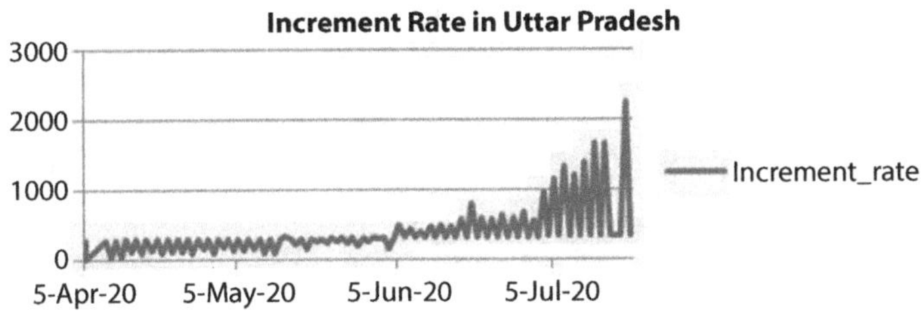

Figure 10.11 Increment rate in Uttar Pradesh.

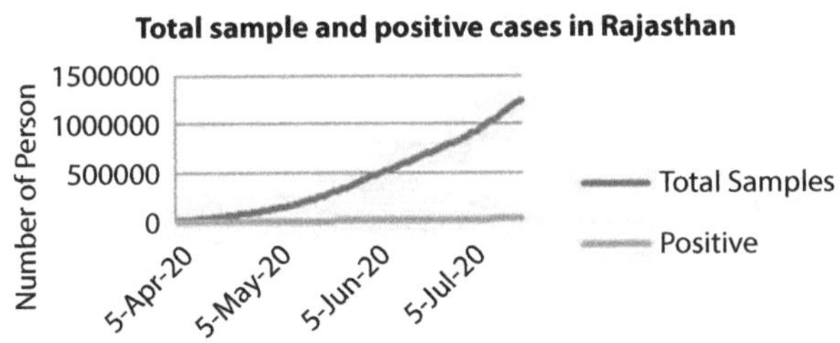

Figure 10.12 Total sample and positive cases in Rajasthan.

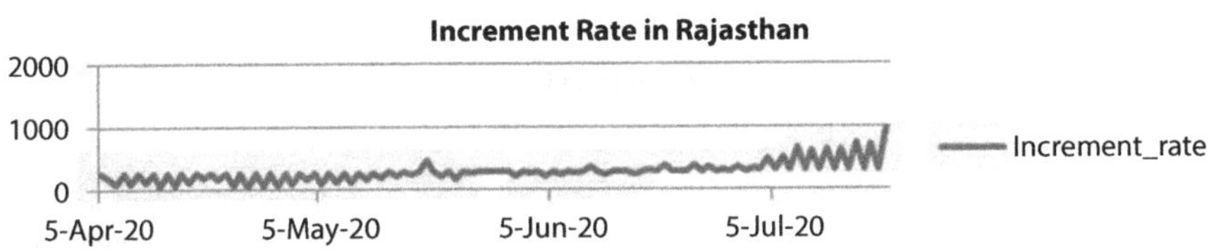

Figure 10.13 Increment rate in Rajasthan.

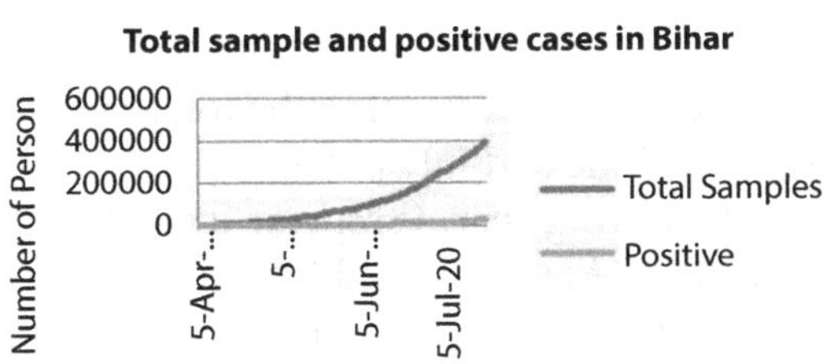

Figure 10.14 Total sample and positive cases in Bihar.

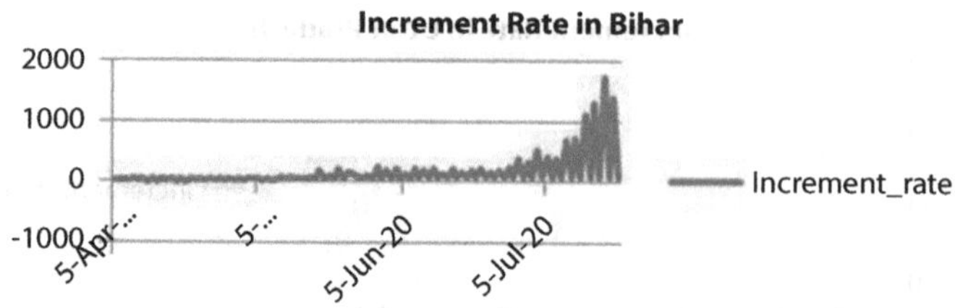

Figure 10.15 Increment rate in Bihar.

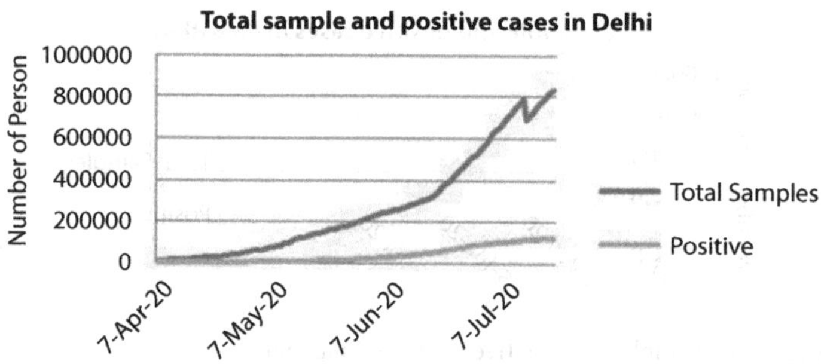

Figure 10.16 Total sample and positive cases in Delhi.

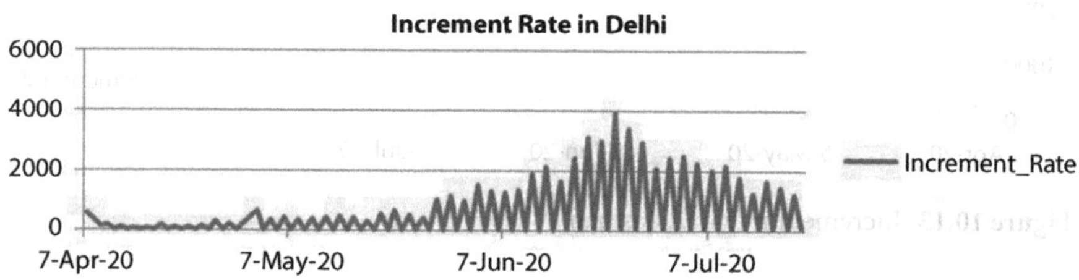

Figure 10.17 Increment rate in Delhi.

Gujarat: Following chart is representing the total sample taken and positive cases in April, May, June and July in Gujarat.

Madhya Pradesh: Following chart is representing the total sample taken and positive cases in April, May, June and July in Madhya Pradesh.

Maharashtra: Following chart is representing the total sample taken and positive cases in April, May, June and July in Maharashtra.

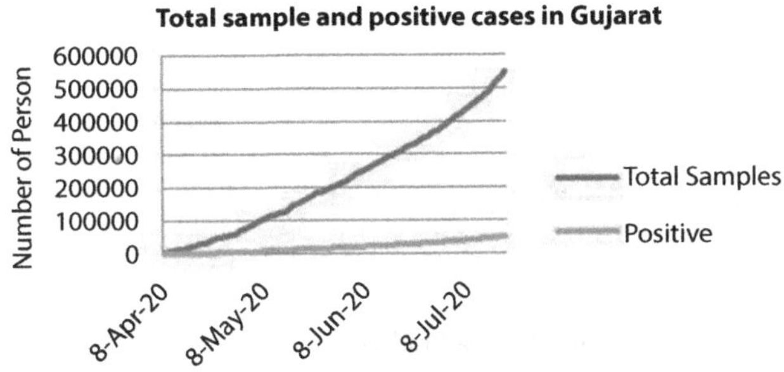

Figure 10.18 Total sample and positive cases in Gujarat.

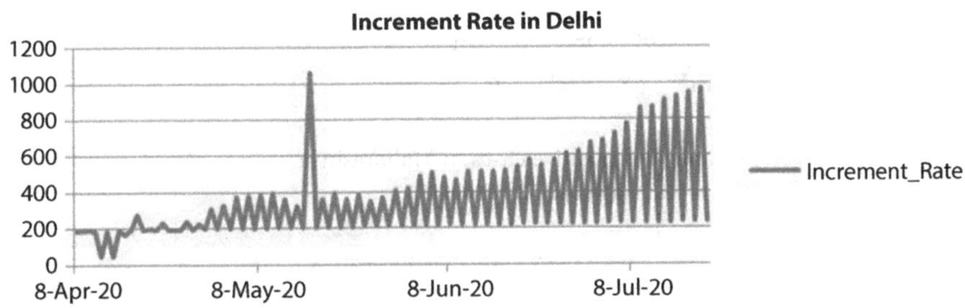

Figure 10.19 Increment rate in Gujarat.

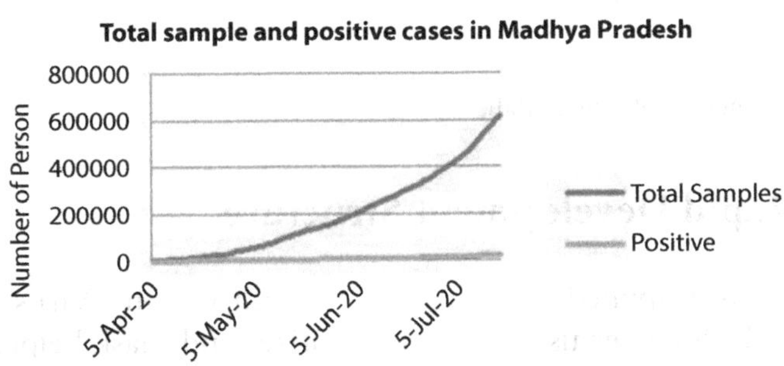

Figure 10.20 Total sample and positive cases in Madhya Pradesh.

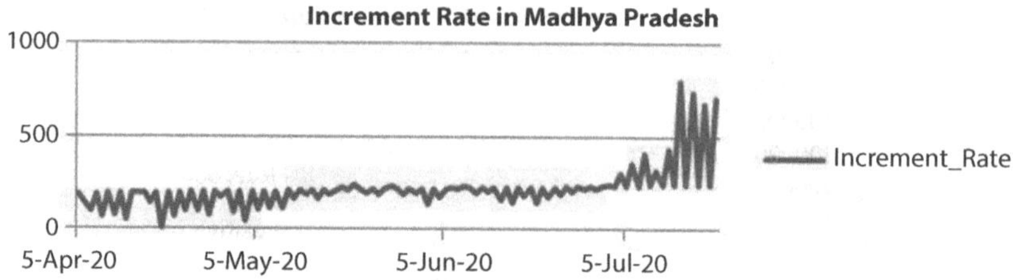

Figure 10.21 Increment rate in Madhya Pradesh.

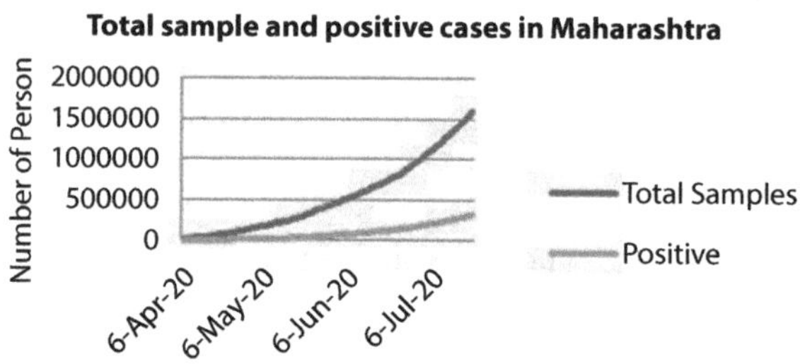

Figure 10.22 Total sample and positive cases in Maharashtra.

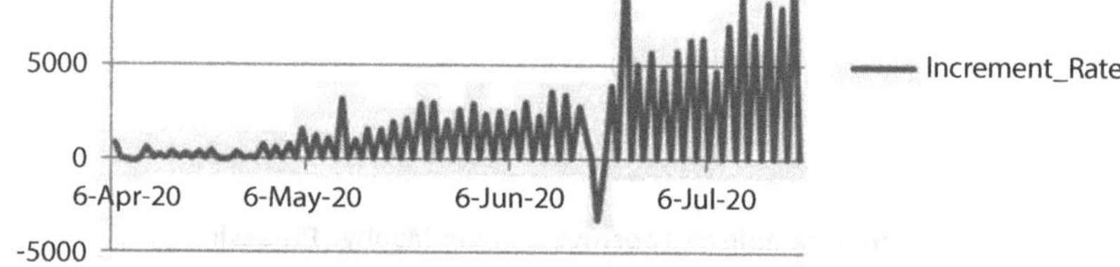

Figure 10.23 Increment rate in Maharashtra.

10.5 Rapid Development Structure

The mechanism applied in India to deal with Corona Virus is mainly "Lockdown". Moreover use of regular sanitizer and mask helped in dealing with Corona. The use face mask and sanitizer would be continuing from initial face to forever. But regular test and isolation of corona patient is essential. In India "LOCK OUT" has played significant role in

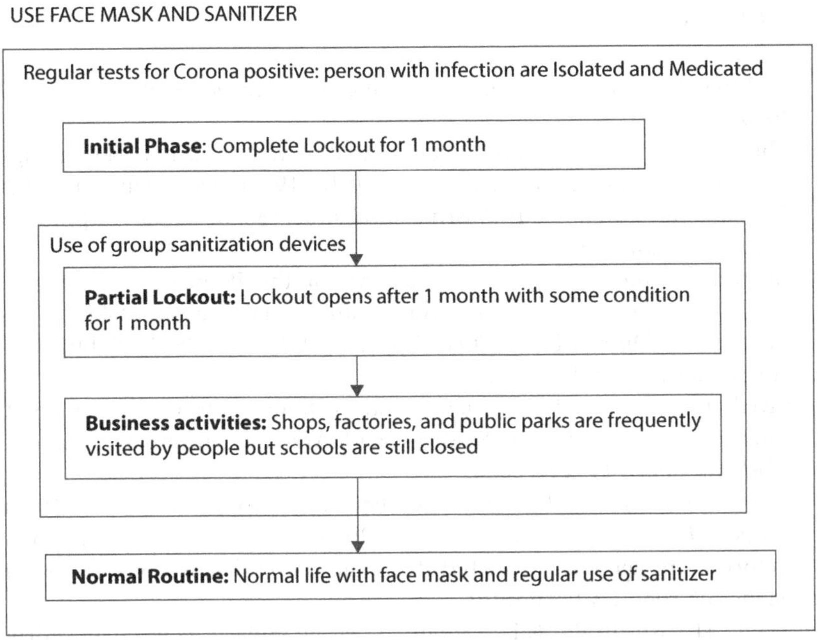

Figure 10.24 Proposed rapid development structure.

handling cases. The developed countries such as USA, ITALY suffered a lot from Corona. India has limited medical facilities still due to immediate lockout the Indian medical facilities could get time for upgradation. The rapid development structure is mentioned in Figure 10.24.

10.6 Conclusion & Future Scope

The research is going to play a significant role in considering the solution to handle the corona. The impact of prevention mechanism considered has influenced the different states in different ways. The area density, life style of people and prevention mechanism make the differences. The social distancing, use of face mask, sanitizer and work from home have played best role during corona situation. On other hand the use of technology enabled people to fulfill their regular needs. The use of IoT and artificial with camera surveillance is supposed to provide efficient and flexible approach in order to achieve objective. The use of IoT application to notify the infected person nearby would reduce the probability of expansion of disease.

References

1. Crabtree, J., How To Manage a Pandemic. *MIT Technol. Rev.*, 123, 3, 28–33, 2020.
2. Chettri, Sarat and Debnath, Dipankar and Devi, Pooja, Leveraging Digital Tools and Technologies to Alleviate COVID-19 Pandemic (June 11, 2020). Available at SSRN: https://ssrn.com/abstract=3626092 or http://dx.doi.org/10.2139/ssrn.3626092
3. Chawla, S. and Saxena, S.K., Preparing for the Perpetual Challenges of Pandemics of Coronavirus Infections with Special Focus on SARS-CoV-2, Coronavirus Disease 2019 (COVID-19), 2019, 1, 165–186, 2020, https://doi.org/10.1007/978-981-15-4814-7_14.
4. Sayed, E., How AI, Data Science and Technology Is Used to Fight the Pandemic COVID-19: Case Study in Saudi Arabia Environment. *Research in World Economy*, 11, 409, 2020.
5. Xiao, Y. and Fan, Z., 10 technology trends to watch in the COVID-19 pandemic. *The World Economic Forum*, 2020, Retrieved from https://www.weforum.org/agenda/2020/04/10-technology-trends-coronavirus-covid19-pandemic-robotics-telehealth/.
6. Khan, H., Kushwah, K.K., Singh, S. *et al.* Smart technologies driven approaches to tackle COVID-19 pandemic: a review. *3 Biotech*, 11, 50, 2021. https://doi.org/10.1007/s13205-020-02581-y
7. Kummitha, R.K.R., Smart technologies for fighting pandemics: The techno- and human-driven approaches in controlling the virus transmission. *Gov. Inf. Q.*, 37, 3, 2020, https://doi.org/10.1016/j.giq.2020.101481.
8. Yan, Z., Gaspar, R., Zhu, T. How humans behave with emerging technologies during the COVID-19 pandemic?, *Human Behavior and Emerging Technologies*, 3, 1, 5–7, 2021.
9. Alsunaidi, S. J., Almuhaideb, A. M., Ibrahim, N. M., Shaikh, F. S., Alqudaihi, K. S., Alhaidari, F. A., Khan, I. U., Aslam, N., & Alshahrani, M.S., Applications of Big Data Analytics to Control COVID-19 Pandemic. *Sensors* (Basel, Switzerland), 21(7), 2282, 2021, https://doi.org/10.3390/s21072282
10. Nasajpour, M., Pouriyeh, S., Parizi, R.M. *et al.* Internet of Things for Current COVID-19 and Future Pandemics: an Exploratory Study. *J. Healthc. Inform. Res.*, 4, 325–364, 2020. https://doi.org/10.1007/s41666-020-00080-6.
11. Kumar, A., Gupta, P. K., Srivastava, A., A review of modern technologies for tackling COVID-19 pandemic. *Diabetes Metab. Syndr.*, 14, 4, 569–573, 2020. https://doi.org/10.1016/j.dsx.2020.05.008.
12. Vaishya, R., Javaid, M., Khan, I. H., Haleem, A., Artificial Intelligence (AI) applications for COVID-19 pandemic. *Diabetes Metab. Syndr.*, 14, 4, 337–339, 2020. https://doi.org/10.1016/j.dsx.2020.04.012
13. Meenpal, T., Balakrishnan, A., Verma, A., Facial Mask Detection using Semantic Segmentation, 2019 4th International Conference on

Computing, Communications and Security (ICCCS), 1–5, 2019, 10.1109/CCCS.2019.8888092.

14. Meenpal, T., Balakrishnan, A., Verma, A., Facial Mask Detection using Semantic Segmentation. *2019 4th International Conference on Computing, Communications and Security (ICCCS)*, Rome, Italy, pp. 1–5, 2019.
15. Martin-Gonzalez, A., Baidyk, T., Kussul, E., Makeyev, O., Improved neural classifier for microscrew shape recognition. *Opt. Mem. Neural Networks (Information Optics)*, 19, 220–226, 2010, 10.3103/S1060992X10030033.
16. https://www.leewayhertz.com/face-mask-detection-system/
17. Gulve S.P., Khoje S.A., Pardeshi P., Implementation of IoT-Based Smart Video Surveillance System. In: Computational Intelligence in Data Mining. Advances in Intelligent Systems and Computing, Behera H., Mohapatra D. (eds) vol 556, pp. 771–780, Springer, Singapore, 2017. https://doi.org/10.1007/978-981-10-3874-7_73.
18. Patil, N., Ambatkar, S., Kakde, S., IoT based smart surveillance security system using raspberry Pi, International Conference on Communication and Signal Processing, 0344-0348, India, 2017. 10.1109/ICCSP.2017.8286374.
19. Valente, J., Koneru, K., Cardenas, A., Privacy and Security in Internet-Connected Cameras. *2019 IEEE International Congress on Internet of Things (ICIOT)*, Milan, Italy, pp. 173–180, 2019.
20. Ibrahim, S., A comprehensive review on intelligent surveillance systems. *Commun. Sci. Technol.*, 1, 7–14, 2016, 10.21924/cst.1.1.2016.7.
21. Hampapur, A., Brown, L., Connell, J., Pankanti, S., Senior, A., Tian, Y., Smart surveillance: Applications, technologies and implications. in: Fourth International Conference on Information, Communications and Signal Processing, 2003 and the Fourth Pacific Rim Conference on Multimedia. Proceedings of the 2003 Joint, 2, 1133–1138, 2004, 10.1109/ICICS.2003.1292637,.
22. Zabłocki, M., Gościewska, K., Frejlichowski, D., Hofman, R., Intelligent video surveillance systems for public spaces—A survey. *J. Theor. Appl. Comput. Sci.*, 8, 13–27, 2014.
23. Davies, A. and Velastin, S., A Progress Review of Intelligent CCTV Surveillance Systems,, Paper for IDAACS'05 Workshop –Sofia, pp. 1-6, September 2005. 10.1109/IDAACS.2005.283015.
24. SyadusSefat, Md., Khan, A.M., Shahjahan, Md. A., Implementation of vision based intelligent home automation and security system. *3rd International Conference on Informatics, Electronics & Vision*, 2014.
25. Ramakrishna, U. and Swathi, N., Design and Implementation of an IoT Based Smart Security Surveillance System. *IJSETR*, 05, 04, 0697–0702, February-2016.
26. Deshmukh, A., Wadaskar, H., Zade, L., Dhakate, N., Karmore, P., Webcam Based Intelligent Surveillance System. *IJES*, 2, 8, 38–42, 2013.

Part 3

ALGORITHMIC TECHNIQUES FOR HANDLING PANDEMIC

11

A Hybrid Metaheuristic Algorithm for Intelligent Nurse Scheduling

Tan Nhat Pham and Son Vu Truong Dao*

International University, Vietnam National University, Ho Chi Minh City, Vietnam

Abstract

In this work, we address the staff scheduling problem in hospitals. The challenge is to assign nurses into various shifts over a certain planning period to meet a number of constraints such as the contractual working time, maximum working time per day and so on. We proposed a method by grouping nurses into clusters, then each cluster is served by a schedule optimized by a hybrid metaheuristic which is a combination of Particle Swarm Optimization (PSO) and Grey Wolf Optimizer (GWO). We obtain the results from the hybrid algorithm and compare them with those from the standard PSO, GWO, and a linear programming formulation using IBM CPLEX Studio, to evaluate the effectiveness of our algorithm.

***Keywords*:** Nurse scheduling problem, grey wolf optimization, particle swarm optimization, metaheuristic, hybrid

11.1 Introduction

The main purpose of all nurse scheduling problems is to create the schedules that both satisfy the fit constraints for nurses and the purposes that the hospital would like to achieve. There are 3 shifts for a nurse to work: morning, evening, night shift, and day off. For circumstances happen in all corners of the world today, the COVID-19 pandemic, almost all hospitals have faced a huge shortage of nurses and doctors, which leads to the fact

**Corresponding author*: dvtson@hcmiu.edu.vn

Abhinav Juneja, Vikram Bali, Sapna Juneja, Vishal Jain and Prashant Tyagi (eds.) Enabling Healthcare 4.0 for Pandemics: A Roadmap Using AI, Machine Learning, IoT and Cognitive Technologies, (213–236)

that they have to stay at hospitals without coming back home for over a month. This work aims to solve that problem once it happens again.

Nurse Scheduling Problem (NSP) (or Nurse Rostering Problem-NRP) [1], is the operation of finding the best assignmentof attendants to work shifts, regularly with a set of difficult imperatives which all substantial arrangements must take after, and some of delicate limitations which characterize the quality of substantial arrangements. NSP can be applied to other fields as well. Since before 1969, this type of problem has been studied and is known to have an NP-hard difficulty [2]. NSP is previously solved using linear [3] or quadratic programming [4] depending on the constraints. They may also be formulated and solved using search methods, including tabu search [5].

Grey Wolf Optimizer (GWO) [6] is a recently introduced metaheuristic which simulates how a pack of wolf goes hunting. It had shown good results on many continuous and combinatorial optimization problems, such as 3D Stacked SoC [7], Job Shop [8], Clustering WSN [9], Prediction [10]. Several variants of the GWO have also been proposed to either enhance its performance or solve a particular problem, namely binary GWO, GWO-DE, GWO-GA, GWO with opposition-based strategy, modified GWO (mGWO) [11–15].

Particle Swarm Optimization (PSO) [16] is also a popular metaheuristic and famous for its simplicity, convergence speed, and global searching capability. PSO was also successfully implemented to solve many combinatorial optimization problems [17–19]. Due to its simple mechanism, many researchers have tried to combine it with other algorithms to solve complicated problems. Notable variants are PSO-GA, PSO-ACO, PSO-DE, and recently, PSO with Gravitational search algorithm (PSO-GSA), PSO with backpropagation (PSO-BP), PSO with modified velocity, PSO with the simplex method, PSO-SA, or PSO-BFOA [20–28].

In this work, we develop a hybrid combinatorial PSO-GWO to solve NSPs by minimizing the number of nurses needed for the allocation of shift. We also compare the results with those of GWO, PSO, and exact solution.

11.2 Methodology

11.2.1 Data Collection

This paper uses the data sets which are being reputable and public internationally, containing 24 instances, obtained from Ref. [29]. Based on these instances, we create multiple scenarios featuring different combinations of shift types and the number of available nurses. A mathematical model is developed and solved by IBM CPLEX to get the exact solution. By challenging the collection of benchmark test instances selected from several sources, we can test and develop the APGWO algorithm, especially in some fields of industrial collaborators and scientific publications, which is the main purpose of these data sets.

11.2.2 Mathematical Model Development

To solve NSP means satisfying the demand, which is the most important thing, and other requirements such as the number of consecutive shifts and days or minimum and maximum working days.

One day has 3 shifts: morning (7:00–16:00), evening (16:00–23:00), and night (23:00–7:00).

Index:

i: index of nurse $i = 1 \ldots I$

d: index of day $d = 1 \ldots D$

D: number of days in the scheduling period

I: number of nurse

Parameters:

M_d: number of nurses required for morning shift d

E_d: number of nurses required for evening shift d

N_d: number of nurses required for night shift d

Decision variables:

XM_{id} binary variable $XM_{id} = 1$ if nurse i is assigned to morning shift d, otherwise $XM_{id} = 0$.

XE_{id} binary variable $XE_{id} = 1$ if nurse i is assigned to evening shift d, otherwise $XE_{id} = 0$.

XN_{id} binary variable $XN_{id} = 1$ if nurse i is assigned to night shift d, otherwise $XN_{id} = 0$.

XR_{id} binary variable $XR_{id} = 1$ if nurse i is off on day d, and 0 otherwise.

$Y_i = 1$ if nurse i is used, and 0 otherwise.

C_i is the cost for nurse i, \$100, \$150, \$200 and \$0 for morning, evening, night and day-off, respectively.

Objective function: Minimize the cost based on the number of nurses needed

$$\textbf{\textit{Minimize}} \sum_{i=1}^{I} C_i Y_i \tag{11.1}$$

Constraint:

Demand constraints: Each shift must be enough for the minimum coverage demanded of nurses

$$\sum_{i=1}^{I} XE_{id} = E_d, \forall d \tag{11.2}$$

$$\sum_{i=1}^{I} XM_{id} = M_d, \forall d \tag{11.3}$$

$$\sum_{i=1}^{I} XN_{id} = N_d, \forall d \tag{11.4}$$

The consecutive shift constraints:

One nurse cannot work 2 consecutive shifts and at most two shifts a day. Nurse working at night shift cannot work morning shift.

$$XE_{id} + XM_{i,d+1} = 1 \tag{11.5}$$

$$XE_{id} + XN_{id} = 1 \tag{11.6}$$

$$XN_{id} + XM_{i,d+1} = 1 \tag{11.7}$$

One nurse cannot work at most 6 consecutive days and 5 shifts per week.

$$\sum_{t=0}^{t=6} XR_{i,d+t} \geq 1, \forall i, d = 1 \ldots D-6 \tag{11.8}$$

$$\sum_{t=0}^{t=6} XM_{i,d+t} + \sum_{t=0}^{t=6} XE_{i,d+t} + \sum_{t=0}^{t=6} XN_{i,d+t} \leq 5, \forall i, d = 1,8,15,22\ldots \tag{11.9}$$

If the nurse i is used then $Y_i = 1$

$$Y_i \geq XM_{id}, \forall i, d \tag{11.10}$$

$$Y_i \geq XE_{id}, \forall i, d \tag{11.11}$$

$$Y_i \geq XN_{id}, \forall i, d \tag{11.12}$$

$$Y_i \geq \sum_{d=1}^{D} XM_{id} + \sum_{d=1}^{D} XE_{id} + \sum_{d=1}^{D} XN_{id}, \quad \forall i \tag{11.13}$$

11.2.3 Proposed Hybrid Adaptive PSO-GWO (APGWO) Algorithm

APGWO aims at using GWO to enhance the overall performance of PSO, this algorithm was first introduced in Refs. [30, 31]. In PSO, there are two acceleration coefficients, which are c_1 and c_2.They control the global searching (exploration) and local searching (exploitation) phases of the algorithm. To get a balance between these two aforementioned phases, c_1 and c_2 are usually equal to 1 or 2, these are found after several experiments. The following formulas propose a modification to the coefficients:

$$c_1^t = 1 - \frac{fit\left(x_k^t\right)}{f(gBest)} \tag{11.14}$$

$$c_2^t = 1 + \frac{fit\left(x_k^t\right)}{fit(gBest)} \tag{11.15}$$

where c_1^t and c_2^t stand for the values of the coefficients at iteration t; $fit\left(x_k^t\right)$ is the fitness value of particle k at iteration t, and $fit(gBest)$ is the best fitness of the swarm. These formulas make the particles focus on exploration in the early iterations, then force them converge to a good optimum near the end. The formula for inertia is also modified as follows:

$$w_t = (maxIter - t) \times \frac{w_{max} - w_{min}}{maxIter} + w_{min} \tag{11.16}$$

This formula aims at reducing the inertia value gradually during the iteration process, thus reduce the global search procedure at the latter stage of the iteration process. Then the velocity, and position of particles are updated as follows:

$$\begin{aligned} v_k^{t+1} = w_t \times v_k^t + c_1^t \times rand \times \left(pbest_k^t - x_k^t\right) + \\ c_2^t \times rand \times \left(gBest - x_k^t\right) \end{aligned} \tag{11.17}$$

$$x_k^{t+1} = x_k^t + v_k^t \tag{11.18}$$

A probability of mutation $P_m = 0.5$ is also introduced in this algorithm, which triggersa loop of GWO in the PSO main loop, and the best solution found by the GWO (the Alpha wolf) would be added to the swarm. Figure 11.1 presents the pseudocode of this algorithm.

The proposed algorithm is tested on 30 CEC2014 benchmark functions [32]. These functions have many local optima, which makes them suitable for testing metaheuristic algorithm's performance. All algorithms are set to have 30 search agents and carry out 2,000 iterations and they are run 20 times. The dimension of the functions is 30. The "Best" value is the best result of each function that can be found after 20 runs. The accuracy and stability of the algorithm are indicated by the "mean" value and the "standard deviation" value. APGWO showed competitive results compared to GWO and PSO as shown in Table 11.1.

```
Initialize the swarm and parameters
while (t< Max number of iteration)
for each particle with position X_p
        evaluate fitness value f(X_p)
        if f(X_p) is better than pbestp then
                pbest_p ← X_p
        endif
        if f(pbest_p) is better than gbest then
                gbest ← pbest_p
        endif
end for
update w according to equation (16)
for each particle with position X_p
        calculate c_1, c_2 by equation (14), (15)
        update velocity of each particle by equation (17)
        re-calculate position of each particle by equation (18)
end for
if rand (0,1) < P_m
        run GWO
        X_p = position of the best wolf
endif
t=t+1
end while
return gbest
```

Figure 11.1 Pseudocode of APGWO.

11.2.4 Discrete Version of APGWO

The original formulations PSO and GWO need to be modified to solve combinatorial optimization problem such as the NSP. To apply GWO to NSP, we define the following terminology:

- Search agent/Particle: a random schedule of all nurses.
- Global Best: the minimum cost of all schedules.
- Fitness: total cost of a schedule that satisfies all the constraints.

11.2.4.1 Population Initialization

The assignment of nurses is randomly generated; each random schedule represents one search agent. The search space is a matrix with size $N \times D$, in which N is the number particles/search agents and D is the schedule period, measured in days. The three best schedules having three best

Table 11.1 Benchmark results of APGWO vs GWO and PSO.

Function	Actual optimum	Best			Mean			Standard deviation		
		GWO	PSO	APGWO	GWO	PSO	APGWO	GWO	PSO	APGWO
1	100	541,853.43	**4,457.0149**	429,898.9	8,051,833	**40,995.91**	560,747.4	6,761,371	**35,685.89**	91,832.02
2	200	5,302.3764	**284.58493**	864,650.77	5,4364,509	**880.8021**	1,216,169	1.09E+08	**642.7583**	388,493.2
3	300	841.97732	**334.59629**	2,127.458	3,449.915	**2,050.401**	2,938.121	2,440.022	2,778.795	**659.5567**
4	400	434.84534	**401.76255**	402.13124	436.0521	**402.4887**	403.2791	1.170979	**0.976123**	1.131843
5	500	520.35384	520.00107	**500**	520.465	520.1011	**500.845**	**0.061153**	0.064878	1.076095
6	600	601.33284	601.52137	**600.12196**	602.5458	603.6156	**600.5849**	0.765965	1.872383	**0.336801**
7	700	700.72122	700.0886	**700.08112**	701.4034	**700.1837**	700.2808	0.402896	**0.09175**	0.138014
8	800	805.03879	815.91931	**800.99496**	813.7657	826.6649	**802.3879**	7.216458	6.46033	**1.014662**
9	900	907.96623	910.94454	**902.98488**	913.4785	932.6345	**903.5819**	4.059425	14.21636	**0.795967**
10	1,000	1,064.0438	1,608.1865	**1,046.7706**	1,433.25	1,739.096	**1,070.353**	241.6405	101.1183	**19.30522**
11	1,100	1,481.3056	1,580.6532	**1,168.135**	1,701.301	1,969.914	**1,251.046**	185.8108	209.5975	43.0474

(Continued)

Table 11.1 Benchmark results of APGWO vs GWO and PSO. (*Continued*)

Function	Actual optimum	Best			Mean			Standard deviation		
		GWO	PSO	APGWO	GWO	PSO	APGWO	GWO	PSO	APGWO
12	1,200	1,200.0978	1,200.0303	**1,200.0109**	1,200.716	1,200.104	**1,200.052**	0.664353	0.060397	**0.032872**
13	1,300	1,300.1341	1,300.107	**1,300.0256**	1,300.167	1,300.225	**1,300.053**	0.028156	0.075829	**0.020723**
14	1,400	1,400.1633	1,400.2972	**1,400.0843**	1,400.387	1,400.366	**1,400.132**	0.228733	0.047151	**0.038344**
15	1,500	1,500.7659	**1,500.2591**	1,501.2338	1,502.456	**1,500.756**	1,501.525	1.031319	0.326846	**0.234661**
16	1,600	**1,601.2501**	1,602.1364	1,601.7002	1,602.571	1,603.04	**1,601.958**	0.730544	0.475096	**0.183149**
17	1,700	2,909.4626	**2,213.6314**	3,003.0344	126,989	3,377.313	**3,283.403**	242617.4	1,626.933	**154.111**
18	1,800	2,228.2805	4,491.3362	**1,888.1617**	9,948.118	18,064.67	**2,019.54**	5768.639	9,429.341	**105.1583**
19	1,900	1,901.8021	1,903.0322	**1,901.4933**	1,902.844	1,903.548	**1,901.618**	0.907356	0.633904	**0.139151**
20	2,000	2,161.182	**2,075.2267**	2,082.3693	9,162.69	5,295.131	**2,118.444**	3,665.498	5,088.438	**28.79687**
21	2,100	6,328.0984	**2,236.7397**	2,626.2765	8,166.474	3,061.773	**2,734.821**	3,009.836	976.9794	**101.3707**
22	2,200	2,238.8862	2,237.0641	**2,220.6132**	2,272.099	2,326.381	**2,221.104**	43.24327	61.45893	**0.641267**
23	2,300	2,630.5239	2,629.4575	**2,300.0004**	2,634.758	2,629.457	**2,497.676**	2.138504	**0.46523**	161.3989

(*Continued*)

Table 11.1 Benchmark results of APGWO vs GWO and PSO. (*Continued*)

Function	Actual optimum	Best			Mean			Standard deviation		
		GWO	PSO	APGWO	GWO	PSO	APGWO	GWO	PSO	APGWO
24	2,400	2,535.0616	2,567.0412	**2,500**	2,543.287	2,587.136	**2,506.439**	8.389232	15.89373	**3.842239**
25	2,500	2,698.9678	2,670.1593	**2,619.6281**	2,701.162	2,693.142	**2,622.811**	**1.651654**	11.70806	1.893998
26	2,600	2,700.1397	2,700.111	**2,700.0359**	2,720.131	2,700.208	**2,700.051**	39.93461	0.081562	**0.012753**
27	2,700	3,007.7234	3100	**2,702.3648**	3,053.12	3,144.606	**2,703.175**	32.1715	53.02392	**0.503434**
28	2,800	3,169.5748	3,305.0835	**3,050.0333**	3,247.929	3,714.568	**3,077.562**	49.49617	370.8018	**15.98732**
29	2,900	3,227.3655	**3,103.7644**	3,176.9238	3,96405	**3,129.471**	3,209.633	785,576.4	35.82135	**26.44029**
30	3,000	3,887.7169	4,458.0453	**3,557.3951**	4,310.933	5,047.121	**3,600.961**	438.8744	417.9484	**27.21439**

fitness values are defined as wolf α, β, and δ, whose positions are X_α, X_β, and X_δ. The shifts are denoted by number: number 1 stands for the morning shift (M), while numbers 2, 3, 4 represent evening shift (E), night shift (N), and day off (O), respectively. If there are 10 nurses, N and the schedule period is 14 days, then the search space matrix would have 10 × 14 = 140 elements. Elements 1–14 represents the schedule of nurse 1, 15–28 for nurse 2, 29–42 for nurse 3, and so on. This encoding process is shown in Table 11.2.

11.2.4.2 Discrete Search Operator for PSO Main Loop

Eddaly *et al.* proposed a transformation formula for the PSO, which we also utilized for our hybrid version [19]. Let y_{ij}^t be a variable to transform the particles' position from continuous state to combinatorial state and vice versa, where t denotes the current iteration, i is the index of particle ith, j is the index of the jth element in the particle's position. We have:

$$y_{ij}^t = \begin{cases} 1 \quad \text{if } x_{ij}^t = gbest_j^t \\ -1 \quad \text{if } x_{ij}^t = pbest_j^t \\ -1 \text{ or } 1 \text{ randomly if } x_{ij}^t = pbest_j^t = gbest_j^t \\ 0 \quad \text{otherwise} \end{cases} \tag{11.19}$$

Table 11.2 Example of the initial solution.

Search agent (Particle)	(1,1)	...	(1,14)	(2,15)		...	(2,28)	...	(N,N×D)
Agent 1	M	...	N	N		...	E	...	M
⋮	A	...	A	O		...	E	...	N
Agent 2	O	...	O	E		...	M	...	N
⋮	O	...	M	A		...	A	...	E
Agent i	A	...	M	O		...	O	...	A
⋮	E	...	E	O		...	O	...	E
Agent N	E	...	N	M		...	M	...	M

Then the velocity would be calculated as:

$$v_{ij}^{t+1} = w \times v_{ij}^{t} + c_1 \times rand \times \left(-1 - y_{ij}^{t}\right) + c_2 \times rand \times \left(1 - y_{ij}^{t}\right) \tag{11.20}$$

where c_1, c_2, and w are calculated by Equations (11.14), (11.15), and (11.16).
The new position of a particle would be updated as follows:

$$\lambda_{ij}^{t+1} = y_{ij}^{t} + v_{ij}^{t} \tag{11.21}$$

$$y_{ij}^{t} = \begin{cases} 1 & if\ \lambda_{ij}^{t} > \alpha \\ -1 & if\ \lambda_{ij}^{t} < \alpha \\ 0 & otherwise \end{cases} \tag{11.22}$$

$$x_{ij}^{t+1} = \begin{cases} gbest_j^{t} & if\ y_{ij}^{t} = 1 \\ pbest_j^{t} & if\ y_{ij}^{t} = -1 \\ a\ random\ number & otherwise \end{cases} \tag{11.22}$$

11.2.4.3 Discrete Search Strategy for GWO Nested Loop

In this work we employed a discrete operator based on the crossover and mutation inspired from genetic algorithm. Let X_k^t be the solution of the *k*th wolf; X_α^t, X_β^t, and X_δ^t define the solutions of wolf α, β and δ at iteration *t*; and let *f* be the crossover operation, and *rand* be a random number in range [0,1]. Then we have the following position updating process:

$$X_k^{t+1} = \begin{cases} f\left(X_k^t, X_\alpha^t\right), if\ rand \le \frac{1}{3} \\ f\left(X_k^t, X_\beta^t\right), if\ \frac{1}{3} < rand \le \frac{2}{3} \\ f\left(X_k^t, X_\delta^t\right), if\ rand > \frac{2}{3} \end{cases} \tag{11.23}$$

The procedure of the crossover operation is as follows:

- Divide search agents by half into two subsets.
- Randomly select two search agents to be the parents.
- Choose a random crossover-point.
- Copy the first part of Parent 1 and merge with the second part of Parent 2 to create new solution, called Child 1, and vice versa to create Child 2.

In this work, we implemented both one and two-point crossover operators. The mechanism is shown in Figures 11.2 and 11.3. During the main loop of the algorithm, each operator is chosen with a probability of 0.5, to enhance the diversity of the population.

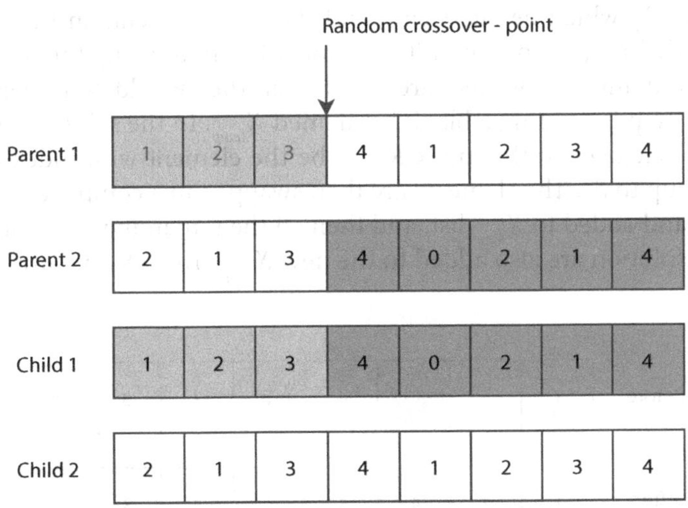

Figure 11.2 One-point crossover operation.

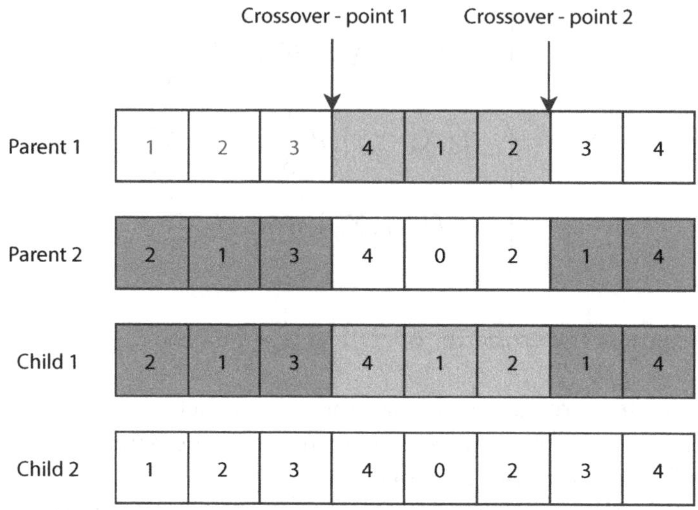

Figure 11.3 Two-point crossover operation.

In GWO, the three best (α , β and δ) guide all search agents towards the optimum. We perform a neighborhood search (NS) on the three best individuals. NS can improve the search by changing the neighborhood structures. Figure 11.4 illustrates how NS is performed. Firstly, a random number n is generated in between 1 and the length of the solution. Then n points would be randomly chosen to be swapped by picking n random numbers R_1, R_2, ... R_n, which lie between 0 and the total elements in the solution list after defining a function initialization with input being the number of solutions. If any two of them are equal, then they would be re-generated. The next step is creating a blank list named X_{temp}. In the solution array, let A_1 be the element in the index R_1, A_2 be the element with index R_2, and similarly up to A_n. The elements are then swapped in a completely random manner and added to X_{temp} list, and then all the remaining elements of the original solution are also added to the new X_{temp}. The NS operator are also

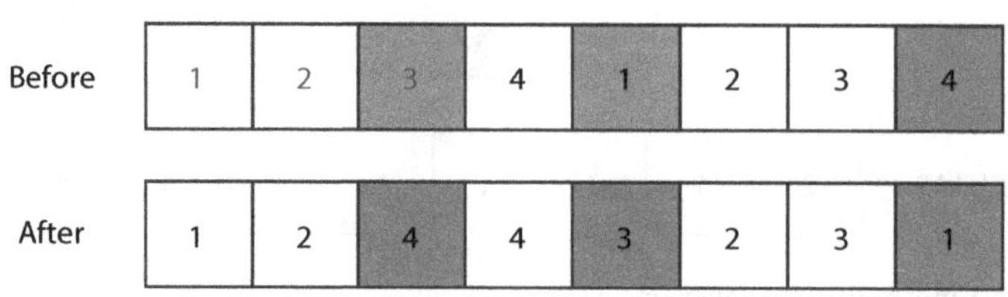

Figure 11.4 Creating a neighborhood solution.

Table 11.3 Summarized results (rounded up).

Instance	Demand	# Nurse	#Day	Cost by GWO	Cost by PSO	Cost by APGWO	Cost by CPLEX
1	(5,0,0)	8	14	8,350	8,550	7,250	7,000
2	(0,5,4)	14	14	21,850	22,350	21,800	21,700
3	(3,5,3)	20	14	27,050	29,100	25,150	23,100
4	(3,0,3)	10	28	28,650	25,900	27,800	25,200
5	(6,0,4)	16	28	39,350	42,300	39,250	39,200
6	(4,3,4)	18	28	47,050	48,250	47,050	46,200
7	(4,5,2)	20	28	48,900	54,000	46,750	43,400
8	(4,4,3)	30	28	76,650	85,900	76,650	44,800
9	(4,4,3)	36	28	51,650	104,300	48,250	44,800
10	(5,6,2)	40	28	65,600	121,000	55,000	50,400
11	(9,11,9)	50	28	132,550	148,000	132,000	121,800
12	(10,11,11)	60	28	166,400	178,200	145,050	135,800
13	(17,17,18)	120	28	338,150	365,700	270,100	219,800
14	(5,5,4)	32	42	126,450	150,150	96,450	86,100

(*Continued*)

Table 11.3 Summarized results (rounded up). *(Continued)*

Instance	Demand	# Nurse	#Day	Cost by GWO	Cost by PSO	Cost by APGWO	Cost by CPLEX
15	(8,5,5)	45	42	187,950	201,700	110,950	107,100
16	(3,5,3)	20	56	100,750	112,600	98,500	92,400
17	(5,6,5)	32	32	93,900	115,400	85,150	76,800
18	(3,5,3)	22	48	94,850	106,750	89,150	79,200
19	(7,6,7)	40	48	186,500	192,400	150,150	144,000
20	(5,15,5)	50	104	536,550	574,000	565,450	390,000
21	(5,5,6)	100	104	790,650	803,650	790,150	655,200
22	(3,3,3)	50	208	1,135,500	1,820,700	1,135,000	1,123,200
23	(11,14,11)	100	208	1,155,000	1,215,500	1,144,550	1,123,200
24	(15,19,14)	150	208	1,523,100	1,809,300	1,523,150	1,487,200
25	(3,3,3)	24	14	18,950	19,450	18,950	18,900
26	(4,3,4)	28	14	23,250	23,500	23,250	23,100
27	(4,4,4)	28	14	25,400	25,650	25,350	25,200
28	(1,1,1)	10	14	8,050	27,450	8,000	6,300

(Continued)

Table 11.3 Summarized results (rounded up). (*Continued*)

Instance	Demand	# Nurse	#Day	Cost by GWO	Cost by PSO	Cost by APGWO	Cost by CPLEX
29	(2,1,2)	10	14	10,600	25,150	10,500	10,500
30	(3,1,3)	20	14	20,300	27,150	18,150	14,700
31	(3,2,3)	20	14	21,750	27,200	20,350	16,800
32	(11,20,11)	100	104	1,103,550	Infeasible	1,103,550	Infeasible
33	(8,8,8)	50	208	1,251,400	Infeasible	1,241,400	Infeasible
34	(9,9,9)	50	14	135,450	Infeasible	128,450	Infeasible
35	(10,10,10)	50	14	Infeasible	Infeasible	156,500	Infeasible
36	(11,11,11)	40	14	Infeasible	Infeasible	166,450	Infeasible
37	(12,12,12)	80	14	Infeasible	Infeasible	195,500	Infeasible
38	(10,11,12)	80	14	Infeasible	Infeasible	210,500	Infeasible
39	(13,13,13)	80	14	Infeasible	Infeasible	245,650	Infeasible
40	(13,13,13)	80	14	Infeasible	Infeasible	315,450	Infeasible

used during the main loop to further increase the diversity, triggered by a probability $P_n = 0.3$, this value is found by empirical study.

11.2.4.4 Constraint Handling

All the solutions' fitness values are calculated using the objective function and violation of constraints is also being checked. If there are violated constraints, a penalty value is added to the objective function so that the algorithm will discard the bad solution.

11.3 Computational Results

In this part, the solution found by APGWO is compared with ones found by IBM CPLEX, PSO, and GWO. The demand for each instance is written in the form of (x, y, z), which means it requires x nurses for the morning shift, y nurses for the evening shift and z nurses for the night shift. Both CPLEX and Python programs are run on a PC with an Intel Core i7 CPU at 3.40 GHz with 16 GB of RAM. The average result of 5 consecutive runs by GWO and PSO are recorded in Table 11.3.

The gap from the metaheuristic's results with respect to the exact solution is calculated by:

$$\frac{\textit{Results obtained by metaheuristic} - \textit{Results obtained by CPLEX}}{\textit{Results obtained by CPLEX}} \tag{11.24}$$

The gap is presented in Table 11.4.

Table 11.4 Summarized gap.

Instance	Gap (GWO-CPLEX) (%)	Gap (PSO-CPLEX) (%)	Gap (APGWO-CPLEX) (%)
1	19.29	22.14	3.57
2	0.69	3.00	0.46
3	17.10	25.97	8.87

(Continued)

Table 11.4 Summarized gap. (*Continued*)

Instance	Gap (GWO-CPLEX) (%)	Gap (PSO-CPLEX) (%)	Gap (APGWO-CPLEX) (%)
4	13.69	2.78	10.32
5	0.13	7.91	0.13
6	1.84	4.44	1.84
7	12.67	24.42	7.72
8	71.09	91.74	71.09
9	15.29	132.81	7.70
10	30.16	140.08	9.13
11	8.83	21.51	8.37
12	22.53	31.22	6.81
13	53.84	66.38	22.88
14	46.86	74.39	12.02
15	75.49	88.33	3.59
16	9.04	21.86	6.60
17	22.27	50.26	10.87
18	19.76	34.79	12.56
19	29.51	33.61	4.27
20	37.58	47.18	44.99
21	20.67	22.66	20.60
22	1.10	62.10	1.05
23	2.83	8.22	1.90
24	2.41	21.66	2.42
25	0.26	2.91	0.26
26	0.65	1.73	0.65
27	0.79	1.79	0.60

(*Continued*)

Table 11.4 Summarized gap. (*Continued*)

Instance	Gap (GWO-CPLEX) (%)	Gap (PSO-CPLEX) (%)	Gap (APGWO-CPLEX) (%)
28	27.78	335.71	26.98
29	0.95	139.52	0.00
30	38.10	84.69	23.47
31	29.46	61.90	21.13
32	–	–	–
33	–	–	–
34	–	–	–
35	–	–	–
36	–	–	–
37	–	–	–
38	–	–	–
39	–	–	–
40	–	–	–

11.4 Conclusion

The solutions show that the proposed APGWO outperformed PSO and GWO almost in all instances, although for complicated cases the solution found by GWO is still far from optimum. One worth noting point is that for large instances such as instances 32 and 33, PSO and CPLEX cannot find feasible solutions. On average, GWO's solution is approximately 20.4% larger than the exact solution, while the mean gap of the solution found by PSO is about 53.8%, and that of APGWO is 11.38%. For many instances such as instance 2, 5, 26, 27, or 29, APGWO provides solutions that are very close to the exact solution. It can be clearly seen that APGWO is more stable and better at avoiding local optima, at which PSO usually cannot escape from. Besides saving the budget of the hospital, this can allocate the good schedules in a short time rather than manually assigning shifts to each nurse as a lot of hospitals have been doing right now. Besides, PSO can only solve the small case in a suitable time; however, with the instance with a large number of nurses and schedule period, it took too much time to run the same number of iterations as APGWO. Also, there were still complicated instances that APGWO and GWO outperformed exact method. Therefore, this work considers helping the future research of APGWO as well as healthcare system. This work proposed a new meta-heuristic approach to solve Nurse Scheduling Problem which has never been used in this field. The results demonstrate that APGWO gives a much better total cost compared to that using PSO and GWO. Furthermore, results obtained using APGWO are relatively close to the exact solution using CPLEX for small case studies. However, for large case studies, due to the combinatorial nature of NSP, there is no solution available using the exact method and our APGWO provides the best results. In future works, we would like to extend our work by working with other scheduling scenarios with more practical constraints and involved other variants of APGWO.

References

1. Ernst, A.T., Jiang, H., Krishnamoorthy, M., Sier, D., Staff scheduling and rostering: A review of applications, methods and models. *Eur. J. Oper. Res.*, 153, 1, 3–27, Feb. 2004.
2. Solos, I., Tassopoulos, I., Beligiannis, G., A Generic Two-Phase Stochastic Variable Neighborhood Approach for Effectively Solving the Nurse Rostering Problem. *Algorithms*, 6, 2, 278–308, May 2013.
3. Trilling, L., Guinet, A., Le Magny, D., Nurse Scheduling Using Integer Linear Programming And Constraint Programming. *IFAC Proc. Vol.*, 39, 3, 671–676, Jan. 2006.
4. Miller, H.E., Pierskalla, W.P., Rath, G.J., Nurse Scheduling Using Mathematical Programming. *Oper. Res.*, 24, 5, 857–870, Oct. 1976.
5. Dowsland, K.A., Nurse scheduling with tabu search and strategic oscillation. *Eur. J. Oper. Res.*, 106, 2–3, 393–407, Apr. 1998.
6. Mirjalili, S., Mirjalili, S.M., Lewis, A., Grey Wolf Optimizer. *Adv. Eng. Software*, 69, 46–61, 2014.
7. Zhu, A., Xu, C., Li, Z., Wu, J., Liu, Z., Hybridizing grey Wolf optimization with differential evolution for global optimization and test scheduling for 3D stacked SoC. *J. Syst. Eng. Electron.*, 26, 2, 317–328, 2015.
8. Jiang, T. and Zhang, C., Application of Grey Wolf Optimization for Solving Combinatorial Problems: Job Shop and Flexible Job Shop Scheduling Cases. *IEEE Access*, 6, 26231–26240, 2018.
9. Sharawi, M. and Emary, E., Impact of grey Wolf optimization on WSN cluster formation and lifetime expansion, in: *9th International Conference on Advanced Computational Intelligence, ICACI 2017*, pp. 157–162, Jul. 2017.

10. Wang, M. *et al.*, Grey wolf optimization evolving kernel extreme learning machine: Application to bankruptcy prediction. *Eng. Appl. Artif. Intell.*, 63, 54–68, Aug. 2017.
11. Emary, E., Zawbaa, H.M., Hassanien, A.E., Binary grey wolf optimization approaches for feature selection. *Neurocomputing*, 172, 8, 371–381, 2016.
12. Zhu, A., Xu, C., Li, Z., Wu, J., Liu, Z., Hybridizing grey Wolf optimization with differential evolution for global optimization and test scheduling for 3D stacked SoC. *J. Syst. Eng. Electron.*, 26, 2, 317–328, Apr. 2015.
13. Tawhid, M.A. and Ali, A.F., A Hybrid grey wolf optimizer and genetic algorithm for minimizing potential energy function. *Memet. Comput.*, 9, 4, 347–359, Dec. 2017.
14. Zhang, S., Luo, Q., Zhou, Y., Hybrid Grey Wolf Optimizer Using Elite Opposition-Based Learning Strategy and Simplex Method. *Int. J. Comput. Intell. Appl.*, 16, 2, 1750012:1–1750012:37, Jun. 2017.
15. Mittal, N., Singh, U., Sohi, B.S., Modified Grey Wolf Optimizer for Global Engineering Optimization. *Appl. Comput. Intell. Soft Comput.*, 2016, 1–16, 2016.
16. Kennedy, J. and Eberhart, R., 47-Particle Swarm Optimization Proceedings, IEEE International Conference. *Proc. ICNN'95 - Int. Conf. Neural Networks*, vol. 4, pp. 1942–1948, 1995.
17. Wu, T.H., Yeh, J.Y., Lee, Y.M., A particle swarm optimization approach with refinement procedure for nurse rostering problem. *Comput. Oper. Res.*, 54, 52–63, Feb. 2015.
18. Hannan, M.A., Akhtar, M., Begum, R.A., Basri, H., Hussain, A., Scavino, E., Capacitated vehicle-routing problem model for scheduled solid waste collection and route optimization using PSO algorithm. *Waste Manage.*, 71, 31–41, Jan. 2018.
19. Eddaly, M., Jarboui, B., Siarry, P., Combinatorial particle swarm optimization for solving blocking flowshop scheduling problem. *J. Comput. Des. Eng.*, 3, 4, 295–311, Oct. 2016.
20. Esmin, A.A.A., Lambert-Torres, G., Alvarenga, G.B., Hybrid evolutionary algorithm based on PSO and GA mutation, in: *Proceedings—Sixth International Conference on Hybrid Intelligent Systems and Fourth Conference on Neuro-Computing and Evolving Intelligence, HIS-NCEI 2006*, p. 57, 2006.
21. Holden, N. and Freitas, A.A., A Hybrid PSO/ACO Algorithm for Discovering Classification Rules in Data Mining. *J. Artif. Evol. Appl.*, 2008, 1–11, 2008.
22. Niu, B. and Li, L., A novel PSO-DE-Based hybrid algorithm for global optimization, in: *Lecture Notes in Computer Science (including subseries Lecture Notes in Artificial Intelligence and Lecture Notes in Bioinformatics)*, vol. 5227 LNAI, pp. 156–163, 2008.
23. Mirjalili, S. and Hashim, S.Z.M., A new hybrid PSOGSA algorithm for function optimization, in: *Proceedings of ICCIA 2010—2010 International Conference on Computer and Information Application*, pp. 374–377, 2010.

24. Zhang, J.R., Zhang, J., Lok, T.M., Lyu, M.R., A hybrid particle swarm optimization-back-propagation algorithm for feedforward neural network training. *Appl. Math. Comput.*, 185, 2, 1026–1037, Feb. 2007.
25. Yu, S., Wu, Z., Wang, H., Chen, Z., A hybrid particle swarm optimization algorithm based on space transformation search and a modified velocity model, in: *Lecture Notes in Computer Science (including subseries Lecture Notes in Artificial Intelligence and Lecture Notes in Bioinformatics)*, vol. 5938 LNCS, pp. 522–527, 2010.
26. Ouyang, A., Zhou, Y., Luo, Q., Hybrid particle swarm optimization algorithm for solving systems of nonlinear equations, in: *2009 IEEE International Conference on Granular Computing, GRC 2009*, pp. 460–465, 2009.
27. Kathpal, S., Vohra, R., Singh, J., Sawhney, R.S., Hybrid PSO—SA algorithm for achieving partitioning optimization in various network applications. *Proc. Eng.*, 38, 1728–1734, Jan. 2012.
28. Abd-Elazim, S.M. and Ali, E.S., A hybrid particle swarm optimization and bacterial foraging for power system stability enhancement. *Complexity*, 21, 2, 245–255, Nov. 2015.
29. Curtois, T. and Qu, R., *Computational results on new staff scheduling benchmark instances*, Technical report, ASAP Research Group, School of Computer Science, University of Nottingham, NG8 1BB, Nottingham, UK 2014, Accessed: Aug. 20, 2020. [Online]. Available: http://schedulingbenchmarks.org/papers/computational_results_on_new_staff_scheduling_benchmark_instances.pdf.
30. Pham, T.N., Van Tran, L., Dao, S.V.T., Early Disease Classification of Mango Leaves Using Feed-Forward Neural Network and Hybrid Metaheuristic Feature Selection. *IEEE Access*, 8, 189960–189973, 2020.
31. Son, D. and Tan, P.N., Capacitated Vehicle Routing Problem—A New Clustering Approach Based on Hybridization of Adaptive Particle Swarm Optimization and Grey Wolf Optimization, in: *Evolutionary Data Clustering: Algorithms, and Applications*, Springer, Springer Singapore, 2019.
32. Liang, J., Qu, B.Y., Sunganthan, P.N., *Problem definitions and evaluation criteria for the CEC 2014 special session and competition on single objective real-parameter numerical optimization*, Technical Report 201311, Computational Intelligence Laboratory, Zhengzhou University, Zhengzhou China and Technical Report, Nanyang Technological University, Singapore, 2013.

12

Multi-Purpose Robotic Sensing Device for Healthcare Services

HirakRanjan Das[1], Dinesh Bhatia[2*], Ajan Patowary[1] and Animesh Mishra[3]

[1]*Department of Mechanical Engineering, Royal Global University, Guwahati, India*

[2]*Department of Biomedical Engineering, North Eastern Hill University, Shillong, India*

[3]*Department of Cardiology, North Eastern Indira Gandhi Regional Institute of Health and Medical Sciences, Shillong, India*

Abstract

The whole world at present is under the grasp of a pandemic termed as COVID-19. The World Health Organization (WHO) guidelines suggest that the social distancing norms are followed with contactless operations as far as possible. Therefore, the population around the world is turning towards efficient modes of operating the daily work with minimal human contact. To contain the spread of the novel coronavirus or COVID-19, it is important and suitable to deploy machinery for operating in conditions wherever social distancing is required. The multipurpose robot makes it feasible to minimize human contact and carry out operations without the risk of the spread of the virus. This chapter aims at the fabrication of a robot that can have multiple utilities and is employed in different areas as per the requirement of the user.

Keywords: Multipurpose, machine learning, Internet of Things (IoT), sensors, robot

**Corresponding author*: bhatiadinesh@rediffmail.com

Abhinav Juneja, Vikram Bali, Sapna Juneja, Vishal Jain and Prashant Tyagi (eds.) Enabling Healthcare 4.0 for Pandemics: A Roadmap Using AI, Machine Learning, IoT and Cognitive Technologies, (237–250) © 2021 Scrivener Publishing LLC

12.1 Introduction

A multipurpose robot as the name suggests is a robot that could perform several tasks to assist the medical personnel and patients in the hospitals during their routine daily life and especially during the present pandemic Coronavirus crisis. Till the availability of any suitable COVID vaccine or drugs to kill the virus, most nations are requesting their citizens to strictly follow social distancing norms, regular washing of their body, and keeping their surroundings hygienic to avoid the spread of infection from an infected person to a healthy person. To prevent the spread of this rapidly spreading communicable disease it is utmost necessary to avoid close physical contact with anyone who is infected [1, 2]. These multipurpose robots are equipped with different types of sensors and features to monitor the medical equipment with the help of equipped cameras and send the information to the doctors and supporting hospital staff so that abnormalities can be checked in real mode or offline. With the help of these devices patients and healthcare service providers can be in constant touch and interact among themselves.

Several old aged or incapacitated persons globally suffer from loneliness and lack desire to lead a healthy normal life. The number of people suffering from depression and loneliness has increased tremendously across all age groups during the present pandemic situation leading to suicidal tendencies in such a population. These patients require frequent monitoring that could be time-consuming activity due to the heavy burden on medical institutions and healthcare providers due to the present pandemic. Companion robots are a solution to these problems that could make life easier and safer for a lot of people globally. The developed robotic device is made with readily available materials that would result in lesser production costs and eventually make them more efficient than other available robots in the market. The robots that could be designed with ease can incur lower maintenance costs and function well without any technical manpower support thereby reducing usage costs and involved human errors. The present chapter would highlight the deployment and use of multi-purpose robotic devices with a sensory system incorporating artificial intelligence, machine learning, and the internet of things (IoT) that would be helpful in patient care and improved healthcare efficiency [3, 4].

12.2 Background and Objectives

In the healthcare sector, social distancing is quite crucial but not feasible when it comes to dealing with patients or treating them. The PPE kits are mandatory for the medical personnel as it protects them from the infection spreading from an infected person and working without fear when dealing with such population. However, the complete possibilities of getting exposed to the virus cannot be nullified by the use of such kits only. So, it is necessary to find ways of reducing contact with an infected person whenever possible. Therefore, the inclusion of multipurpose robots in the healthcare sector paved the way for contactless services to the patients and safeguards the medical personnel to some extent. It reduces the workload and stress on the medical workers and operations can be handled with convenience from a remote location [5]. The objective of the multipurpose robot is to minimize human contact for certain instances and its application for that purpose. To reduce the stress and the phobia associated with the manpower involved to provide essential services for certain tasks such as delivering medicines, food, documents from one point to another in a controlled environment the robotic device may be utilized [7, 8]. The robot can be used as monitoring devices too in serious cases where remote monitoring of the patient is mandatory. It can be used to receive and deliver information several times from the doctor and the patient. The robot is a programmed to follow a dedicated path marked on the floor or ceiling. Usually, the marked line is the path which the robot follows that maybe a black line on a white surface but it can be another way around with white line on a black surface. Based on software programming, the robot will move from certain preset points to complete an assigned task and return to its home position [6, 9].

12.3 The Functioning of Multi-Purpose Robot

The fundamental robot structure consists of cameras, stepper motors, servo motors, connecting pins, springs, sensors, and Raspberry Pi as the main controller [7, 8]. The robot is usually equipped with different types of sensors to sense and monitor different user parameters. The routes and trajectory will be preset with the help of geo-mapping to track the robotic path [9, 10]. The Raspberry Pi board will control the cameras with the help of stepper motors and actuators along with the servo motors. The Raspberry Pi will control every element as per instructions in the structured program [11]. The sensors will sense the information coming from the sender and will process the information. The robot will then move to the sender's location and ask for inputs to perform the task as directed. It will have the voice recognition feature to avoid any sort of contact with them and prevent the spread of virus or disease. The sender will select the option and upon confirmation, the robot will set its path and trajectory to the location assigned to do the task. If it is asked to bring medicines, it will move to the storeroom and pick up the required medicines with its automated arms or with minimal assistance. Then it will again move to the sender's location to deliver those medicines. Once the task is completed and upon confirmation from the patient, it will return to its home location. The robot will be equipped with sensors to detect temperature to prevent doctors from coming nearby of an infected patient. Assistive robots are programmed to perform several supporting tasks as per need employing embedded tools. This helps robot to be in synchrony with the ambient conditions (temperature, humidity etc.) while performing assigned tasks which is an important requirement. The ambient information helps the robotic device to prepare precise maps of the impending conditions in its surroundings while carrying out any assigned task [12, 14]. It will also be able to measure the blood pressure of patients and print the result in real-time mode.

The robot can be used in the hospitals to monitor the medical equipment with the help of equipped cameras and send the information to the doctors thereby allowing them to check for abnormalities in real mode or offline. The patients can record their message and send it to the doctors if they face any health-related issue or require nursing assistance. The robot can have automatic sanitizing units so that it can help to sanitize the hospital infrastructure without human involvement [13]. It can also be equipped

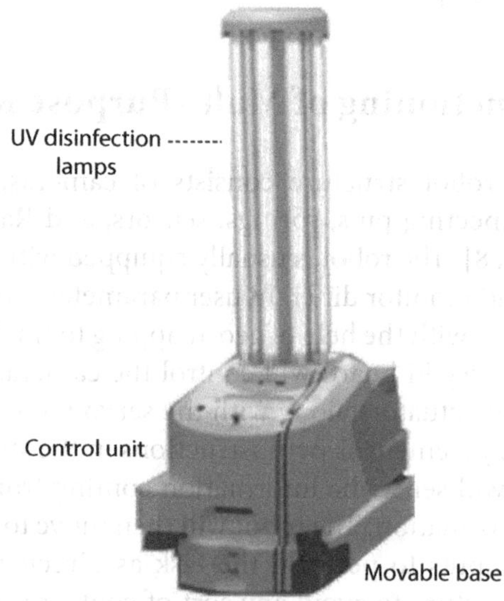

Figure 12.1 UV disinfection robot.

with ultraviolet (UV) ray emitter to disinfect metal surfaces or sterilize the medical equipment being utilized for patient care [14]. UVD Robots as shown in Figure 12.1, are deployed in hospitals to disinfect patient rooms and operating theaters. These robots are a subsidiary of Blue Ocean Robotics. Multiple lidar sensors comprising of short wavelength ultraviolet C (UVC) light arrays are mounted on the robot's mobile base. The robot is deployed with the help of a computer. The robot creates a digital map by analyzing the ambient environment with the help of lidars which can be controlled by an operator. Following that, the simultaneous localization and mapping (SLAM) make the robot capable of navigating through the given dimension.

A robotic system that can disinfect large surfaces and control the spread of coronavirus was developed by a team from the Artificial Intelligence Laboratory at MIT in collaboration with the Ava Robotics as shown in Figure 12.2. The mobile base was developed by Ava Robotics which was integrated with a customized ultraviolet fixture designed by the MIT laboratory. In case of humans being exposed to unsafe areas, the ultraviolet (UV-C) light would get activated to disintegrate and kill viruses and bacteria on the surface. Human supervision is not required for Ava's telepresence robot. The telepresence top is substituted and for disinfecting surfaces a UV-C array is used. The DNA of microorganisms is disrupted to kill the virus by the use of short-wavelength UV light and the process is known as

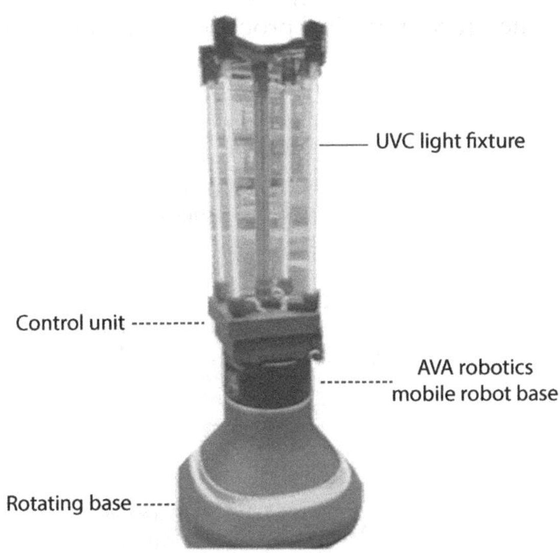

Figure 12.2 Telepresence robot.

ultraviolet germicidal irradiation. The complete robot system can map the area and navigate between waypoints and other specified areas. A UV-C dosimeter is used while testing the system model to verify the expected dosage delivery required disinfecting the surfaces.

Xenex's LightStrike is a disinfection robot made by Xenex Disinfection Services LLC as shown in Figure 12.3. A xenon lamp is used to generate bursts of high-intensity UVC light which is more intense than sunlight of full germicidal spectrum (200–315 nm). The company claims that LightStrike is a unique pulsed xenon UV device and the other devices available are mercury UV devices. They claim that it can lead to a reduction of 53 to 100% infections acquired in hospitals as per findings published in different peer-reviewed journals. The LightStrike robot destroyed SARS-CoV-2 in 2 min in a recent test performed at the Texas Biomedical Research Institute achieving a four-log (99.99%) reduction during the test.

The biggest benefits of robots are speed and accuracy, two features that are quite important to pharmaceutical stores in the hospital. The robots will be equipped with printing systems so that real-time prescriptions can be printed and medicines can be delivered accordingly to the patients with a record of inventory. This will result in faster service and more organized delivery with the less human intervention [15].

Robotic-assisted surgeries deploy the use of robots to perform minimally invasive complex surgical procedures with better flexibility, accuracy, and precision. These surgeries provide spatial accuracy in reaching region of interest thereby reducing blood loss and minimize damage to surrounding tissues during surgical procedure. One such device developed

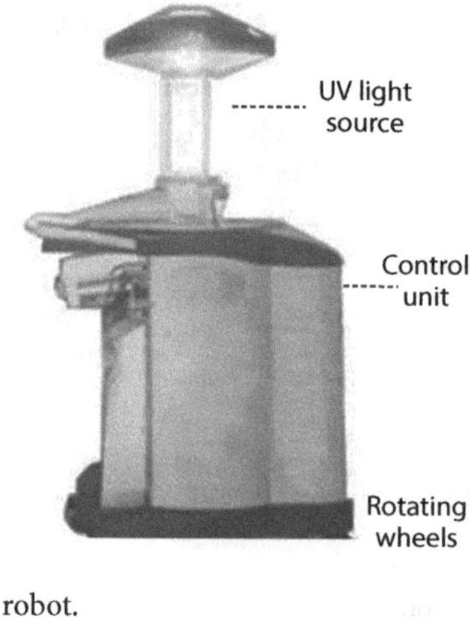

Figure 12.3 Disinfection robot.

by IBM for total hip-replacement procedures known as ROBODOC system is shown in Figure 12.4 which was employed in several surgical procedures in Germany from 1994 until 1998. This system comprises of three major components, namely, the workstation for procedure planning, the control unit to provide guidance during procedure and the robot itself to perform the surgery [16].

With advancement in technology, improvements in the robotic devices with new enhancements are being researched and developed. Researchers at the Eberhard Karls University developed a master-slave robotic device called as ARTEMIS for performing minimally invasive surgeries. A surgeon controls the robotic arms of the system from a control console. The device functions by employing slow vacuum movements for suction with remaining procedure similar to a conventional colonoscopy system. The endoscopist with the assistance of this system can directly supervise the endoscope to employ its use in endoluminal diagnosis and surgery. The device can be employed for precise spatial location of the surgical devices in their marked anatomy. Light-emitting diodes (LEDs) are used in opto-electronic tracking hybrid systems combining surgical instruments and cameras to monitor the LEDs. The mechanical tracking systems comprise of joint-angle sensors (encoders) equipped on a mechanical linkage that can locate and calculate the end point of the linkage. Since these systems are not powered mechanically they are not considered as robots. Robotics

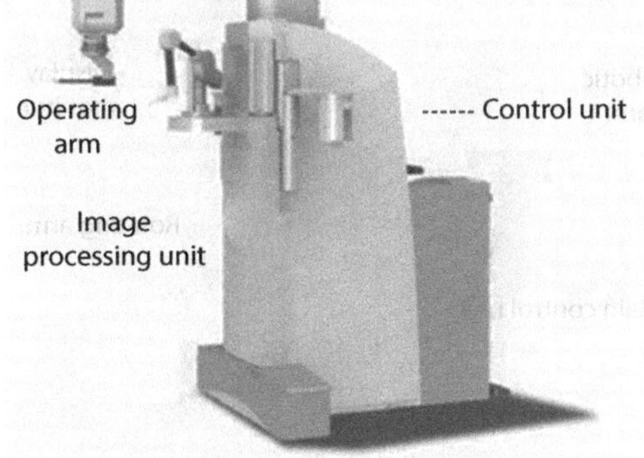

Figure 12.4 Surgery assisting robot.

are associated with the domain of computer-aided surgery [17] and considered to be useful in overcoming limitations of laparoscopic procedures. These systems increase dexterity with better coordination, ergonomic location and improved visualization. Besides, they allow technically difficult surgeries or previously not possible to be feasible. Dexterity is enhanced in several ways because of these systems providing higher degrees of freedom to the surgeon to perform the procedure with convenience and ease. They help in minimizing tremor in surgeon movements while performing surgical procedure with help of available system device features. One additional feature of these systems is that it could provide better control grip and spontaneous movements to surgeons by eliminating fulcrum effect thereby reducing unnecessary movements inside the patient. These systems help in avoiding awkward instrument movements and help the surgeon to better visualize the monitor from their remote workstation. Additionally, they allow enhanced vision which is quite remarkable to perform the procedure. The conventional laparoscopic camera views are enhanced due to 3D view with better depth perception. As the magnification is increased and maneuverability is enhanced, the surgeons are capable of directly controling a stable visual field. All these systems combine to create high-resolution images with enhanced dexterity and freedom of movements augmenting the surgeon's ability to locate and operate on anatomic structures at minute scales [18]. ROSA or Robotic Operating Surgical Assistant is used in neurosurgery to carry out less invasive procedures in the brain as shown in Figure 12.5. It is equipped with a robotic arm that is capable of producing detailed pictures of the brain. Minerva is a neurosurgery robot which is programmed and manufactured for abnormal brain surgeries and works

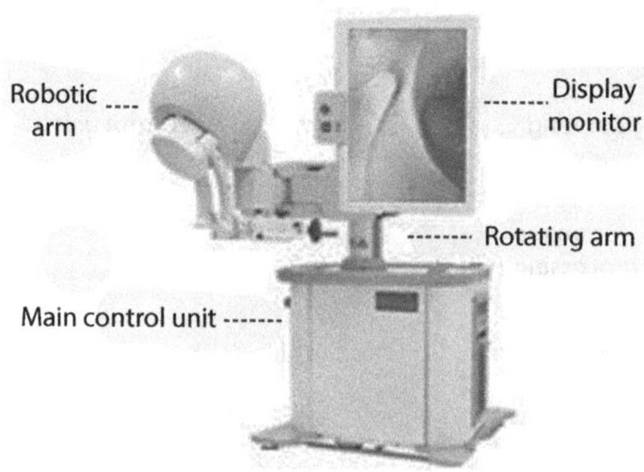

Figure 12.5 Neurosurgery assisting robot.

within the CT scanner. It allows tracking of real-time position of instruments by the surgeon on successive scanner images and also facilitates the control of different surgical interventions such as biopsy and cyst aspiration etc. The operations like incisions in the skin, drilling of bones, dura insertion, and probe navigation are performed by robotic device. This allows surgeon to focus their attention on device control for performing the surgical procedures and avoid the repetitive tasks to focus their attention on doing clinical evaluation of the patient.

Antibacterial nanorobots are smaller machines that are manufactured from gold nanowires and platelets are used for the coating the red blood cells (RBCs) which help in removing bacterial infections directly from the patient's blood. So, a bacterium (and its toxins) target is being mimicked and when the bacteria gets near it ensnares them in their nanowire mesh. To speed up the clearance process, specific targeting through ultrasound could be utilized to treat localized infections. Nanorobots can potentially be the alternative for broad-spectrum antibiotics due to the natural response of the bacteria towards them which could help in their removal from the body system. This indirectly supports the fight against antibiotic resistant bacteria and diseases [19–21]. Bone drilling manipulations are quite common in orthopedic surgery requiring skill, precision and dexterity to execute the procedure successfully. As the recovery of the patient depends on the operation performance, therefore robotics extensively assist in the process. The requirement of higher precision and surgical manipulations which are accurate can be achieved by using robots for bone drilling applications in orthopedic trauma surgery [22]. Several old aged or incapacitated persons globally suffer from loneliness and lack desire to lead a healthy normal life. These patients require frequent monitoring that could be time-consuming activity due to the heavy burden on medical institutions and healthcare providers. Friendly robots are therefore making life convenient and safer for a lot of people by solving both of these problems at once. The robot will be made with readily available materials which will result in lesser production costs and eventually will be less costly than other available robots in the market. These devices aid in completing supporting tasks as performed by surgical trainees or nursing staff during the main surgical procedure to assist the surgeon. Few examples of such tasks include positioning, still holding of camera during procedure or retraction. The deployment of such systems can be justified by (a) less expenditure due to reduced manpower during surgery, (b) better patient access, and (c) less errors due to human fatigue and boredom during carrying out of surgical procedure. The challenge in developing such systems is that they should precisely follow surgeon's command, should be inexpensive and not attract undue attention. The devices that can provide better surgical assistance than humans could lead to a shift in the cost–benefit balance [23, 24]. The robots nowadays are designed simply so that maintenance costs are low, reduce errors, and require less technical support. The present chapter would highlight the deployment and use of multi-purpose robotic devices with a sensory system incorporating artificial intelligence [25] which makes it possible for the robot to have a computer vision, navigate and process information. It also focuses on machine learning which allows the robot to acquire the novel skills and adapt to the changing or dynamic environment. Recently, machine learning has been used to develop robotic assistive technologies which comprise integrating these machines with anatomy, for example, the MICO robotic arm (configured at Northwestern University) which is enabled to make observations of the surroundings through supporting sensors. Due to partial autonomy and control sharing between the robot and the user, these devices are able to adapt easily to the requirements of the user. With advances machine learning technology, several applications of robotics in different domains is progressing, however, fewer applications have found implementation in the medical world due to regulatory norms and clearances. The Smart Tissue Autonomous Robot (STAR) employs machine learning technology developed by a collaboration between researchers at different institutes, selected physicians and the Centre for Automation and Learning for Medical Robotics (Cal-MR). Using the technology, the artificial intelligence (AI) systems are trained and tested several times till desired precision and accuracy is achieved to perform the task better than a humans. This provides support to humans in performing mundane tasks with accuracy, one such example being the FDNA system which can screen patients for over 8,000 diseases by using facial recognition and rare genetic disorders and it is worth mentioning that the system is highly accurate. The Magnetic Resonance Imagining and Ultrasound Robotic Assisted Biopsy (MURAB) project employs minimally invasive technique which is useful in early cancer diagnosis. In this system, the robotic device is guided by combining magnetic resonance imaging and ultrasound to the relevant biopsy site for performing the procedure. The 3D image is created from the biopsy site helping the surgeon to choose the relevant region where the procedure needs to be performed. Post completion of the procedure, the robotic device can be removed and it leaves a minor incision or cut at the biopsy region [26]. Besides, the internet of things (IoT) is proving to be helpful in patient care and improved healthcare efficiency. The combination of IoT clinical devices paves the way for intelligent and clever associated gadgets, which facilitates the screening of the patient's strength and makes the patient aware of the beginning of any infection. IoT finds a wide application in healthcare for patients in the form of wearables with blood pressure monitors, oximeters, and heart rate monitoring cuffs. Wearables find applications in screening the wellbeing state of interminable patients, facilitate taking readings, watch designs, and imparting caution. The information gathered from these systems finds its utilization in the conclusion, improved treatment, and enhanced patient care.

These devices can be worn by the patient, guardian and emergency clinical staff comprising of unique identification number which would help in smooth administration and patient handling by the medical staff. Medical devices and gadgets are being used to keep a track of the utilization of the hardware for every patient and highlight the information with gained understanding and check their status. When the framework is followed and the wearable marks are coordinated with the ongoing area have the potential to improve the communication between the healthcare providers and the patients and take time-efficient actions that are necessary. The patient's health could be monitored employing the data available from these wearable medical devices to keep a track about patient's health condition by the physicians facilitating clinical decision making for patient treatment and outcome evaluation. Several medical devices such as wheelchairs, defibrillators, heart and oxygen monitoring devices can be equipped with IoT sensors, and thus effective asset management can be achieved. Fraud claims can be detected from the data captured from monitoring equipment to maintain transparency between the healthcare insurance providers and the patients [27, 28]. The obstructions in the growth of healthcare systems include the rapidly increasing population, non-availability of proper infrastructure and fewer medical professionals, quality healthcare not being accessible in remote and rural areas, increasing occurring rate of chronic disease, and expensive healthcare facilities. The connectivity of Internet of Things (IoT) has enabled to improve the deteriorating healthcare system into a unified, structured, and patient-friendly system. IoT has been playing a vital role in tracking the progression of diseases and their treatment, monitoring health conditions of the patients and alter medication levels if necessary as well as tracking the usage of medicines to make sure that the patient adheres to the plans of treatment as set by the healthcare providers. It also makes them capable of receiving real-time information on symptoms. IoT also is turning healthcare technology into user-friendly for people, with easily understandable interfaces which make the users understand what an application can do for them in their everyday lives. The Internet of things is playing a key role in removing several healthcare issues and providing support especially in remote regions where scarcity of resources and manpower exists. The healthcare solutions should be customized as per needs of the patient(s) and the healthcare provider(s). Application of IoT for personalized care provides opportunity to service providers to customize solution based on the patient's health history and living style to achieve effective treatment. The main objective of IoT in healthcare is to build patient confidence in the healthcare system, support clinicians, reduce costs and provide quality services for the patients as well as the healthcare service providers. To improve efficiency and reduce overall costs in the IoT network, it is imperative to have a well-defined role of sensors with transmission and reception of the data when required [29, 30].

12.4 Discussion and Conclusions

The guidelines advised by the World Health Organization (WHO) to control the present pandemic include following social distancing norms and contactless operations to prevent the spread of infectious disease. New ways and means are being explored to carry out routine mundane jobs through different available efficient modes with minimal human contact to prevent the risk and safety of people. The multipurpose robot is one such device that is finding widespread our age in different fields and operating in conditions wherever social distancing is required. These devices help in reducing the pressure on healthcare personnel by providing support, performing routine mundane tasks, provide safety with help of multiple sensors such as light, torque, position and acquire patient health parameters through bio-sensors. These devices help in overcoming limitations and disadvantages of present healthcare system to provide better patient care, reduce costs, ensure transparency, help in data storage and analysis, easier payment procedures with seamless smooth integrated healthcare services benefitting the patients as well as the healthcare service provider [27, 28, 30]. In the present Chapter, we discussed the fabrication of the different types of multipurpose robot(s) which can perform several daily tasks and are employed in different areas as per the requirement of the user. Many of these devices are presently in use and the future holds promise for such technologies to support mankind. With the advent of artificial intelligence, Internet of Things (IoT) and machine learning such devices would become more efficient and smart shortly. The overall healthcare solutions should be as per the requirement of the patient with reduced costs, the defined role of sensors and ability to transmit and receive data appropriately [28, 29].

References

1. Geospatial World, Dasgupta, S., How robots are helping in the fight against COVID-19, https://www.geospatialworld.net/blogs/covid-19-how-robots-help-in-fight-against-covid-19/, 2020.
2. The Indian Express, Jha, A., Humanoid robots are here to help doctors in COVID-19 fight, https://indianexpress.com/article/lifestyle/health/covid-19-coronavirus-robots-hospital-humanoid-robots-are-here-to-help-doctors-diagnose-patients-6497840/, 2020.
3. The Economic Times, COVID-19: Robots to deliver food and medicines to patients at Chennai Hospital, https://economictimes.indiatimes.com/news/politics-and-nation/covid-19-robots-to-deliver-food-and-medicines-to-patients-at-chennai-hospital/robot-zafi-in-chennai/slideshow/75026241.cms, 2020.
4. Robotics Research, Delivery robots move medical supplies in COVID-19 response, https://www.roboticsresear.ch/articles/20545/delivery-robots-move-medical-supplies-in-covid-19-response, 2020.
5. Circuit digest June, Line follower robot using Arduino https://circuitdigest.com/microcontroller-projects/line-follower-robot-using-arduino, 2018.
6. Electronics Hub, How to make Arduino line follower robot, https://www.electronicshub.org/arduino-line-follower-robot/, 2017.
7. Instructables circuits, IOT Lunar Rover Raspberrypi + ArduinoURL https://www.instructables.com/id/IOT-Moon-Rover/, 2018.
8. Sciencing, Frank, B., The main parts of a Robot, https://sciencing.com/main-parts-robot-7403157.html, 2018.
9. Kemper, R., Latecki, L., Sun, X., Geometric robot mapping, 1, 1–12, 2005.
10. Baizid, K., Lozenguez, G., Fabresse, L., Intelligent Robotics and Applications 9th International Conference. *Proceedings, Part I.* pp. 418–429, ICIRA 2016, Tokyo, Japan, August 22-24, 2016.
11. Dexter Industries, Raspberry Pi Robot Projects, https://www.dexterindustries.com/old-projects/.
12. Palacin, J., Clotet, E., Martinez, D., Moreno, J., Tresanchez, M., Automatic Supervision of Temperature, Humidity, and Luminance with an Assistant Personal Robot, 2017, 1480401, 1–7, 2017.
13. Tectales, Keutel, S., Disinfection robots fighting the coronavirus. https://tectales.com/bionics-robotics/9-disinfection-robots-fighting-the-coronavirus.html.
14. Robotics Technologies, Saltmarsh, A., COVID-19: Disinfection robots are being deployed, http://emag.medicalexpo.com/disinfection-robots-against-covid-19/.
15. Azorobotics, Kaur, K., Automated delivery robots for hospital use, https://www.azorobotics.com/Article.aspx?ArticleID=111.
16. Cleary, K. and Nguyen, C., State of the art in surgical robotics: clinical applications and technology challenges. *Comput. Aided Surg.*, 6, 1, 312–328, 2001.

17. Camarillo, D.B., Krummel, Salisbury, J.K., Robotic technology in surgery: Past, present, and future. *Am. J. Surg.*, 188, 4, 2–15, 2004.
18. Lanfranco, A.R., Castellanos, A.E., Desai, J.P., Meyers, W.C., Robotic surgery: A current perspective. *Ann. Surg.*, 239, 1, 14–21, 2004.
19. Glauser, D., Fankhauser, H., Epitaux, M., Hefti, J.-L., Jaccottet, A., Neurosurgical robot Minerva: First results and current developments. *J. Image-Guid. Surg.*, 1, 5, 266–272, 1995.
20. Varma, T. and Eldridge, P., Use of the NeuroMate stereotactic robot in a frameless mode for functional neurosurgery. *Int. J. Med. Rob. Comput. Assisted Surg.*, 2, 2, 107–113, 2006.
21. Kwoh, Y.S., Hou, J., Jonckheere, E.A., Hayati, S., A robot with improved absolute positioning accuracy for CT guided stereotactic brain surgery. *IEEE Trans. Biomed. Eng.*, 35, 2, 153–160, 1988.
22. Kotev, V., Boiadjiev, G., Mouri, T., Delchev, K., Kawasaki, H., Boiadjiev, T., A Design Concept of an Orthopedic Bone Drilling Mechatronics System. *Appl. Mech. Mater.*, 302, Trans. Tech. Publ., 248–251, 2013.
23. Preising, B., Hsia, T., Mittelstadt, B., A literature review: Robots in medicine. *IEEE Eng. Med. Biol. Mag.*, 10, 2, 13–22, 1991.
24. Taylor, R.H., Robots as surgical assistants: Where we are, wither we are tending, and how to get there, in: *6th Conference on Artificial Intelligence in Medicine (AIME)*, vol. 1211, pp. 1–11, Springer Verlag, Grenoble, France, 1997.
25. Udacity, Artificial intelligence for robotics, https://www.udacity.com/course/artificial-intelligence-for-robotics–cs373.
26. Emerj, Machine Learning in Robotics, https://emerj.com/ai-sector-overviews/machine-learning-in-robotics/.
27. Wipro, what can IoT do for healthcare, https://www.wipro.com/en-IN/business-process/what-can-iot-do-for-healthcare-/.
28. Beasley, R.A., Medical robots: Current systems and research directions. *J. Rob.*, 2012, 401613, 1–14, 2012.
29. Optum, Internet of healthcare things in India: Changing the landscape, http://www.optum.in/thought-leadership/library/internet-healthcare-things.html.
30. Finoit, A., The role of IoT in healthcare: Applications and Implementations, https://www.finoit.com/blog/the-role-of-iot-in-healthcare-space/.

13

Prevalence of Internet of Things in Pandemic

Rishita Khurana* and Madhulika Bhatia†

Department of Computer Science and Engineering, Amity School of Engineering and Technology, Noida, India

Abstract

The current COVID-19 pandemic has created several problems now-a-days.

All these problems point to the inability to examine and scale the situation according to the intensity of the outbreak. Along with creating problems, this pandemic has exceeded many boundaries such as the provincial, radical, conceptual, spiritual, social, and educational. It has changed the fundamental nature of our society.

For controlling such a pandemic situation, a collection, analysis, elucidation of data on regular basis regarding the spreading disease trends should be done in order to predict the outbreak of major health related symptoms. A proper surveillance is required to cure any type of disease.

Surveillance-collection of data can be performed best with the assistance of technology like Internet of things.

As "Internet of things is an idea which comprises of interconnected frameworks which has the ability of finding data about a specific thing with the assistance of extraordinary identifiers and detecting capability."

The technological platform of IoT connected with the healthcare system is helpful in observing the infected people. This monitoring is done by the interconnected network offered by IoT [1].

Implementation of such a technology will help to decrease the healthcare expenses and enhance treatment of the infected patients.

**Corresponding author*: rishitaakhurana14@gmail.com

†*Corresponding author*: madhulikabhatia@gmail.com

Abhinav Juneja, Vikram Bali, Sapna Juneja, Vishal Jain and Prashant Tyagi (eds.) Enabling Healthcare 4.0 for Pandemics: A Roadmap Using AI, Machine Learning, IoT and Cognitive Technologies, (251–274) © 2021 Scrivener Publishing LLC

***Keywords*:** Internet of Things, healthcare, IoT in COVID-19, COVID-19, hospitals, pandemic, IoT applications, IoT devices

13.1 Introduction

Pandemics cannot be predicted much but least one can do is to be prepared for it.

The current wave of COVID-19 pandemic has already damaged the growth engines of the world such as China, U.S.A., Italy and India badly.

Many countries of the world are battling economic fatigue and declining growth as they are paying precious resources to fight with COVID-19 which includes public lockdowns. These lockdowns are going to trigger the economy of many countries.

As countries around the world are struggling every day to contain the virus, the deaths and infections are continuously rising.

According to Worldometers, the number of corona cases crossed 950,000 while the number of deaths crossed 48,000 on March 31, 2020. Although, it is widely believed that China has hidden its true numbers from the world.

However, there are many photos coming out of Wuhan which shows that the actual death count in Wuhan alone may be in tens of thousands.

When the entire world is battling a similar foe, we have all needed to grasp and embrace new advancements in technology and find their advantages, despite the fact that there is as yet far to go.

Technology plays a significant role in beating irresistible diseases, and the IoT is a significant piece of our innovation stockpile. Cost decrease, self-governing and remote providing care and analysis, just as recently accessible patient information are only a couple of the ways that the IoT is changing human services. What's more, with regards to disease control, remote and IoT advancements offer incredible arrangements and solutions. Thus, COVID-19 has been the epitome of the Internet of Things (IoT).

This term which is called as "Internet of Things" was framed by Sir Kevin Ashton in the year 1998 when he was talking at the Massachusetts Institute of Technology. However, International Telecommunication Union in 2005 officially presented this term [2].

The IoT was originally described and called as RFIT (radio-frequency identification technology). It was merged with the Internet which was based on the communication protocol agreement in order to accomplish administration of the information insightfully. But this idea has been broadened and deepened today.

In this technology, the Internet is utilized to connect various devices such as sensors, machines, individuals, and things to accomplish the relationship among individuals and things, things and things, individual based data, remote control and management [3].

We frequently consider IoT a system of sensors and remote microcontrollers, yet this is just the physical layer of IoT. Comprehensively, the IoT is circulated registering for a huge scope. They evaluated 24 billion brilliant associated gadgets of the IoT which can gather and perform calculations on exceptional measures of information.

Experts have also stated that the IoT market was worth about $150 billion in the year 2019 and now it is expected that it is going to worth $243 billion by the year 2021 as shown in the Figure 13.1 [4].

IoT has already found its way in the healthcare sector with numerous applications in this era of coronavirus, for example, telemedicine, connected imaging, virtual monitoring of patients, connected health, connected worker, connected ambulance etc. because various life conforming benefits are being offered by IoT in healthcare which makes it an appropriate technology to put forward in difficult times like pandemic such as the

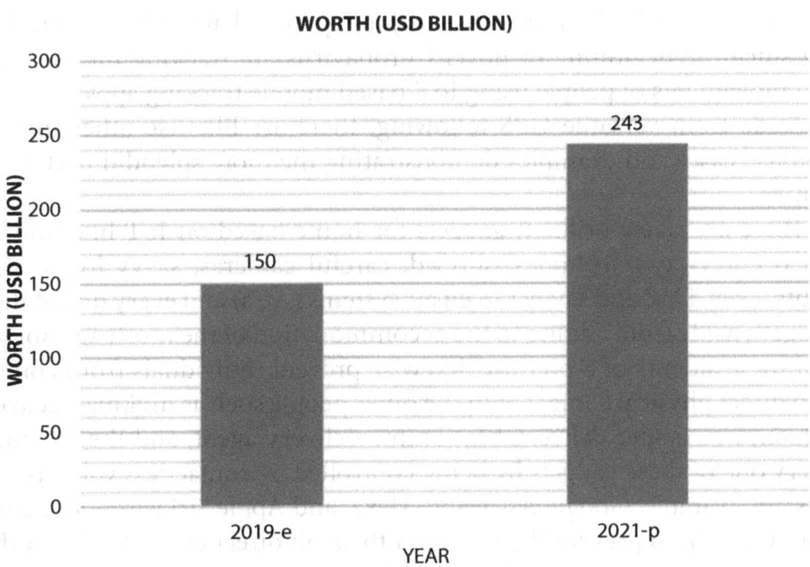

Figure 13.1 Impact of COVID-19 on IoT market. e: estimated; p: projected.

recent COVID-19. “Health 4.0” was just conceivable gratitude to a few IoT applications.

Interconnecting imaging and radiology hardware or remotely screen patients is conceivable, for instance—and from that point a genuine “Health 4.0” is conceived. Freestyle’s Libreview is probably the best case of this kind of 4.0 innovations. It is a product that permits access to records put into any glucometer of the brand. NFC technology is used at different levels and also the Blood glucose reader works using NFC and when the blood glucose reader is connected with the Freestyle’s Libreview then, the patient simply moves towards the reader via the sensor. And, because of this the doctor can see the blood glucose at any instant. Charts are also available regarding the blood glucose level on a daily basis which gives a complete statistical data to the doctors as well as the patients.

Internet of Things can, therefore, be called an innovative and astounding technology which is providing information and monitoring several important things during the current pandemic COVID-19.

As in the contemporary difficult position, the number of infected people is getting increased daily so there is a huge need to use well sufficient, sorted out facilities. Internet of things essentially implies better dynamic and better reaction plans by providing more information. Both are indispensable in forestalling and controlling the spread of disease. Moreover, IoT has just been utilized to fulfil the asked needs in various areas.

Along with this, there are other major key roles that IoT have been playing since the beginning of novel Coronavirus are tracking the locations and movements of people using IoT-based mobile tracking apps.

Aside from versatile GPS following, there are likewise other innovation use cases and examples demonstrating the more splendid part of the matter.

There are a few brilliant gadgets for home based on IoT like brilliant video entryway telephones, shrewd, careful cameras, savvy locks, keen lights, keen TVs, and savvy forced air systems (ACs) and every one of these gadgets, aside from adding to the accommodation of the mortgage holders and the residents of a premise, likewise prevent individuals from coming into direct physical contact with the other people such as milkman delivery person, newspaper delivery boy, online delivery agent, and the postman. Every one of these gadgets by being controlled by contactless voice associates, for example, Google Assistant, Alexa, and Apple Siri without much of a stretch help to prevent the infection through direct contact. Many other innovative applications are launched by various enterprises in this era of infection and will be discussed in this chapter. For example, SYOOK has launched a login-free “Social Distancing” App.

The demand for IoT is likewise increasing in the major APAC (Asia Pacific countries), such as China, India and Australia. As the COVID-19 outbreak has slowed down the economy of the countries, technological advancements will keep up the demand for IoT in major verticals like healthcare and utilities.

Apart from the applications launched, the disruption caused by COVID-19 in the economy will trigger a blast in the market of IoT.

A lot of big companies such as Infosys, Citius Tech, Tata Communications, Thought works and Hero Electronics are wagering on these right set of circumstances and a new study from Juniper Research has also found that the economic disruption which is caused by COVID-19 pandemic can also be overcome by the IoT market [5].

Therefore, the ultimate goal of this research-based chapter is to highlight the prevalence of IoT in pandemic; various applications developed to stop and lessen the spread of the novel Corona virus using IoT, advantages and disadvantages of the applications and other necessary findings related to IoT and healthcare.

13.2 What is IoT?

The power of the internet to collect the data using the sensing capability of devices and machines without human to the PC or human to human interconnection is called as Internet of Things.

It is a characterized plan of interdependent figuring strategies, advanced, and machine-like gadgets having the capability of conveyance of data over the system. This plan does not involve any human association at any extent.

All these examined gadgets are linked to their specific new distinctive confirmation numbers or codes. IoT is currently demonstrated development which sets about as a convergence to the countless strategies, prompt investigation, the reasoning of AI, tactile items, and so on. Additionally, IoT in every day working is perceived as the utility of the items or the machines serve the genuine prerequisites of individuals in different methods such as lighting apparatuses, indoor controllers, and other home machines that help in essential framework [6].

13.2.1 History of IoT

In the year 1982, the principle idea of the system of smart devices was discussed with an amended Coca-Cola vending machine at a private University in Pittsburgh-Carnegie Mellon, turning into the crucial machine related to

Internet, prepared to report its stock. It also tells and notifies whether late stacked drinks were cold or not.

Mark Weiser produced the modern vision of the IoT on ubiquitous computing paper in 1991, "The Computer of the 21st Century", as well as academic venues, for example, UbiComp and PerCom [7].

Reza Raji depicted the idea in IEEE Spectrum as "[moving] little bundles of information to an enormous course of action of centers, so as to fuse and automate everything from home mechanical assemblies to entire processing plants" in the year 1994.

The term "Internet of Things" was framed by Sir Kevin Ashton in the year 1998 when he was talking at the Massachusetts Institute of Technology. However, it was officially presented by the International Telecommunication Union in 2005.

Since the conceptualization of IoT in 2005, the advancement of smart devices having sensing, communication and inciting capabilities quickened development in the previous years. Metal oxide semiconductor field-effect transistor is indeed the key driving force behind the IoT.

Sir Mohamed M. Atalla and DawonKahng invented the MOSFET in 1959 at the Bell Laboratory.

The MOSFET is the central structure square of most present-day equipments which is comprised of personal computers, mobile phones, and many other organizations. MOSFET downsizing at a pace foreseen by Dennard scaling and Moore's law has been the primary purpose behind mechanical advances in the gadgets business since the late 20th century. MOSFET scaling has been connected into the mid-21st century with propels, for instance, reducing power usage, creation of silicon-on-separator (SOI) on semiconductor gadgets and multi-focus processor advancement, preparing to the Internet of things, which is being driven by MOSFETs cutting back to nano-electronic levels with diminishing essentialness utilization [8].

13.2.2 Background of IoT for COVID-19 Pandemic

Internet of Things (IoT) is a creative innovation which is providing data and observing framework during COVID-19 scourge.

Furthermore, it is beyond to an idea that builds up the general design foundation which eventually permits the assimilation and exchange of important information or data between the individual and organizations. In the present circumstance, the majority of the issues are emerging on the grounds that the non-successful attainability to the infected people. This is the subsequent significant issue after the worry of antibody development [9].

The utilization of the Internet of Things makes the attainability to the infected people very useful, and eventually they are provided with care and help so that they can escape the disease or pandemic.

13.2.3 Operations Involved in IoT for COVID-19

IoT is a creative innovative stage to battle with COVID-19 pandemic and can satisfy huge difficulties during the lockdown circumstance. This innovation is useful to catch the ongoing information and other important data of the infected individual [10].

- In the first step, the health data of people is monitored using remote monitoring system.
- In the second step, the virtual management is done through meetings and communications.
- The third step consists of analysis and controlling of the information gathered.
- At last, the report is attained and followed.

Figure 13.2 shows the noteworthy procedures utilized by IoT for COVID-19.

13.2.4 How is IoT Helping in Overcoming the Difficult Phase of COVID-19?

1. Remote working via IoT.

The standard for some organizations throughout the previous hardly any months was Remote working and will keep on being so at every possible opportunity.

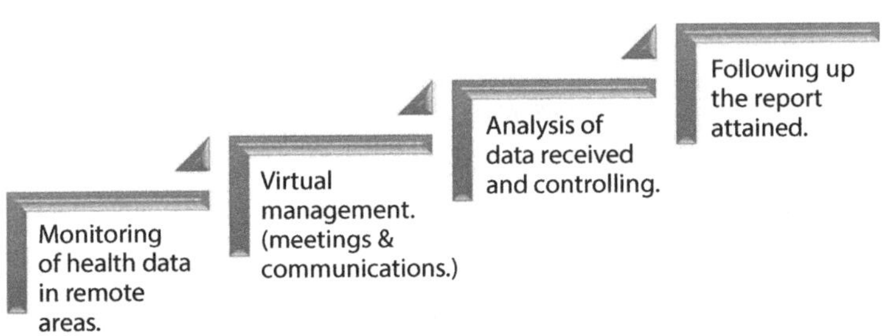

Figure 13.2 Processes utilized by IoT for COVID-19.

Obviously, remote working is the same old thing, and it was at that point a developing pattern for a few reasons. Greater adaptability, permits organizations to save money on physical spaces, groups occupied in various areas working on specific issues and finding solutions are some of the benefits offered to us.

Indeed, even before the occurrence of the current pandemic, the IoT innovations that were of most enthusiasm to organizations are described below in the pie-chart (Figure 13.3) [11].

Most likely it could never have been conceivable to keep frameworks operating without all the innovation we have embraced as of late: distributed computing, collective apparatuses, (for example, videoconferencing programming, venture the board, talks), remote PC access and gadget synchronisation, VPN, and portable first applications. What's more, it's actually this sort of arrangement that, as indicated by gauges, will become the most somewhere in the range of 2020 and 2021.

2. Using smart robots based on IoT for delivering essential materials.

For mechanical support administrators, meeting social separation on a sequential construction system is a test. Numerous production lines should re-examine their design to fulfil all wellbeing guidelines, while others should work with diminished groups. For this not to prompt a breakdown underway, numerous organizations should depend on IoT to endure and mechanize forms.

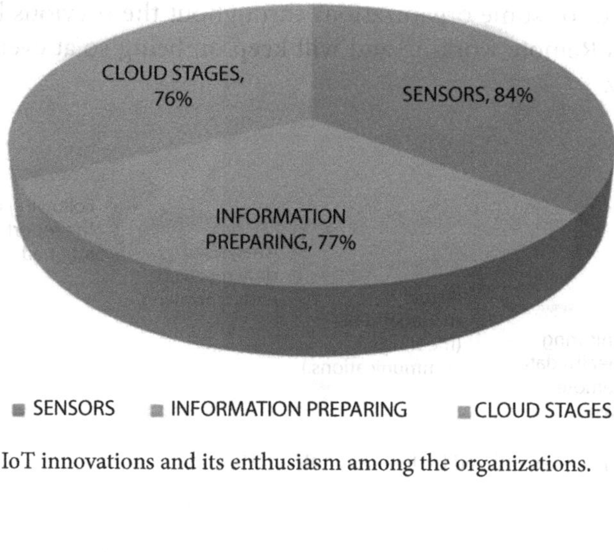

Figure 13.3 IoT innovations and its enthusiasm among the organizations.

Smart robots can be utilized, for instance, to convey important materials and food as now it is the situation to prevent infection in certain emergency clinics. A few organizations are utilizing automatons to make conveyances which are safe to be used at home. XAG and Huawei have changed over robots and automatons used to spread farming composts into disinfectant showers [12].

3. Controlling of stock.

With the interruption of conveyance chains, control of stock was probably the greatest test for retailers and wholesalers which they faced in the lock-down period. Also, this trouble may proceed until the year's end. In any case, without a doubt, organizations that were at that point utilizing NFC marks to control stock all through distribution centers made their tasks simpler.

Furthermore, the systems based on trace and track utilized by several carrier companies have demonstrated the need to keep the online business in full activity and to deal with the deferrals in conveyances progressively.

Therefore, IoT has become an approach to offer a quicker and progressively straightforward support of the final shopper.

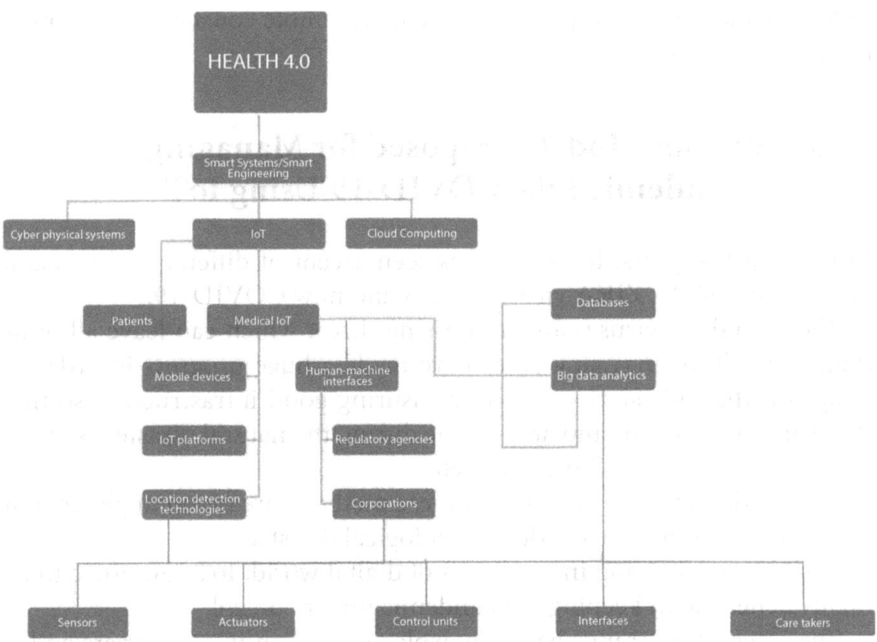

Figure 13.4 Healthcare framework based on IoT.

4. IoT and Health 4.0.

The healthcare sector has a lot to pick up from mechanical & technological advancements.

Starting today, we can discuss "telemedicine" and "intelligent medication" to go with patients who are at home or who can't make a trip to the clinic. A portion of the advances we apply in Industry 4.0 likewise have applications here. Interconnecting imaging and radiology gear or remotely screen patients is conceivable, for instance—and from that point a genuine "Health 4.0" is conceived.

There is this framework of healthcare developed in the current era using IoT and is given in Figure 13.4 [13].

5. Digital connectivity of hospital during COVID-19 pandemic using IoMT.

IoMT technique permits the Healthcare and clinical work force to use its very much associated system of administrations and offices while providing treatment to the infected. These interconnected administrations incorporate the very much organized channel of efficient advances, a computerized checking framework, smart medical care, information examination apparatuses, cloud-based processing, smart bed offices, filtering machines, and so forth and these all offices are additionally adjusted with the genuinely necessary internet based plans in particular; remote constancy, Bluetooth, modem, and so on.

13.3 Various Models Proposed for Managing a Pandemic Like COVID-19 Using IoT

In the past few years, the world has seen ascent of different viruses and diseases like SARS, ZIKA virus, EBOLA and now COVID-19.

These kinds of viruses are an uprising threat which can leave all of us shattered. Although, many cities have made a huge progress in order to safeguard their physical systems by ensuring good infrastructure so that they can stay vigorous and anti-fragile during the natural disasters such as earthquakes, tsunamis, hurricanes etc.

But pandemics have shown that these methods are not enough when it comes to access our society during biological disasters.

Now as we are living in a new era of digital world, IoT can prove to be highly beneficial in keeping the pandemic under control.

The Internet of Things has seen explosive growth in some years and is making great growth in the healthcare industry as well.

Grand View Research stated that the world's largest and most trusted Business Intelligence enabled market research database-IoT market for healthcare will reach USD 534.3 billion by the year 2025.

Many researches have been done on potential of IoT in managing a pandemic. The various techniques that have been proposed are demonstrated below.

13.3.1 Smart Disease Surveillance Based on Internet of Things

The Central health ministry needs to keep a proper check on the cases reported in order to know and be aware of the current situation during a pandemic.

For this, a proper surveillance is required for the regular collection and analysis of data. The smart disease surveillance system which is based on IoT is proposed to make disease surveillance more efficient, accurate and successful and this proposal can also help in determining and identifying the various disease trends [14].

This proposal was proposed in 2015 and it is mainly for a vast network of innovative and smart devices which can naturally process and examine the information which is put into it.

Further, the-devices-can process the-data and send it to-the central health ministry. The data which is expected to be amended regarding the-spreading-of-the disease is only sent.

As soon as the central health ministry gets the data it can further take the necessary steps to prevent the spreading of disease.

This will likewise assist the individuals to conclude about the quickly spreading-disease.

13.3.1.1 Smart Disease Surveillance

"Smart disease surveillance is an-innovative-proposal to improve and accelerate the current procedure of surveillance and furthermore making it exact at national level timely."

The components of Smart Disease Surveillance are depicted in Figure 13.5.

The-primary part of IoT is Radio frequency identification (RFID).

It can quickly recognize-the moving or still-entities. The primary point of IoT is to monitor the objects with the help of internet. One active RFID sensor fitted main server will be registered with the health ministry. This server is a smart IoT device which will analyse the data entered [15].

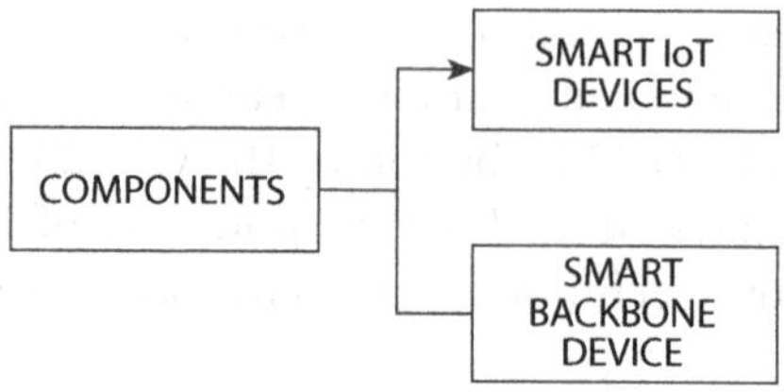

Figure 13.5 Components of Smart disease surveillance.

The server has the following tasks:

- Gathering the trending symptoms from the information entered.
- Analysing the information and making reports out of it.
- Checking if aggregate indications can be an indication of another malady.

After gathering the data, reports are created by the smart devices and then the results are passed to the health ministry through the mode of internet.

The Central Health Ministry will henceforth get a more precise study and malady surveillance using IoT based Smart-disease-surveillance-system depicted in the Figure 13.6.

The smart servers will continue to pass the data to the backbone which will help the Ministry in making decisions so as to prevent the upcoming disease.

In the network, there are different nodes formed by several smart devices

Source node: The node through which the data is being sent currently.

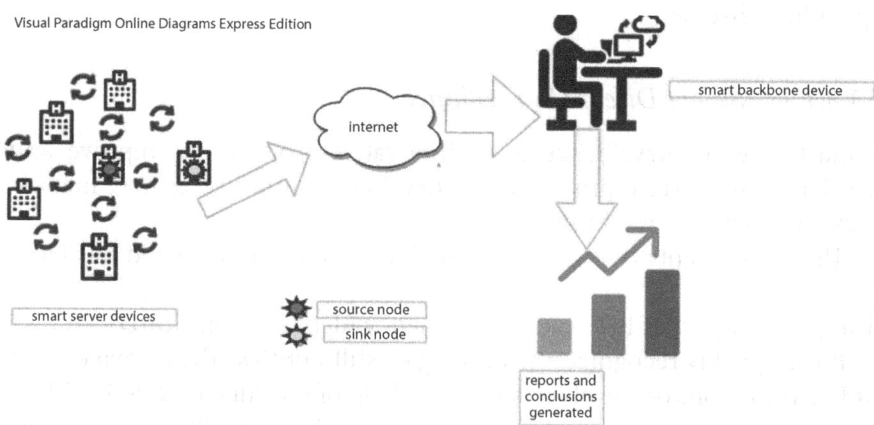

Figure 13.6 Conceptual view of Smart disease surveillance system.

Sink node: The node which accepts the data and transfers into the internet is the sink node. It can also manage higher data rate and it can also pass the data timely to the internet.

If the present scenario of the country-INDIA is considered then it can be concluded that a need for proficient disease-surveillance-system is there.

The above explained-system based on IoT will be a significant advancement in the fields of science & technology.

13.3.2 IoT PCR for Spread Disease Monitoring and Controlling

Dengue, which is a mosquito borne viral disease having the potential of producing a pandemic developed as a genuine general wellbeing concern. According to WHO, the number of people getting affected has increased 30 times in the past fifty years. Various zones in Eastern and Southeast Asia, are getting influenced by this DENV [16].

During such sort of virus outbreaks, specific areas are required to be screened by the disease control centers. Numerous endeavors have been done for improvement of compact, easy to use, and worthwhile frameworks for point-of-care (POC) diagnostics. This would likewise make an Internet of Things (IoT) for medicinal services by means of a worldwide system.

What is an IoT PCR?
An internet associated simple to use PCR designed by high scholars. PCR is a technique which is used to amplify specific parts in a DNA molecule.

The IoT system presented here is a low cost DNA replication connected to the internet. This is a compact-system-which weighs 170 g and the physical measurements are approximately equal to $60 * 100 * 34\ mm^3$ outfitted with-Bluetooth between the android remote instrument and PCR. The researchers used it to test complementary DNA of a DENV template (MCA) which further could-also-be-utilized-for the-detection of RNA. The unit sent this information once the DENV was detected including the GPS coordinates-to-a-centralized-location-through the network, consequently helping the specialists to map-the-spread of virus [17].

Two basic experiments were performed; first was conducted with 4 samples mixed with contents of the cDNA of DENV. This experiment was performed to verify-the-PCR-system while the-second-experiment-consisted-of-actual-field-test-having-3-samples-and-NTC. The output amplification data was displayed along with PCR unit number, time of test finish and GPS coordinates and transferred to the smartphone via Bluetooth. Figure 13.7 shows a complete setup of PCR based IoT system.

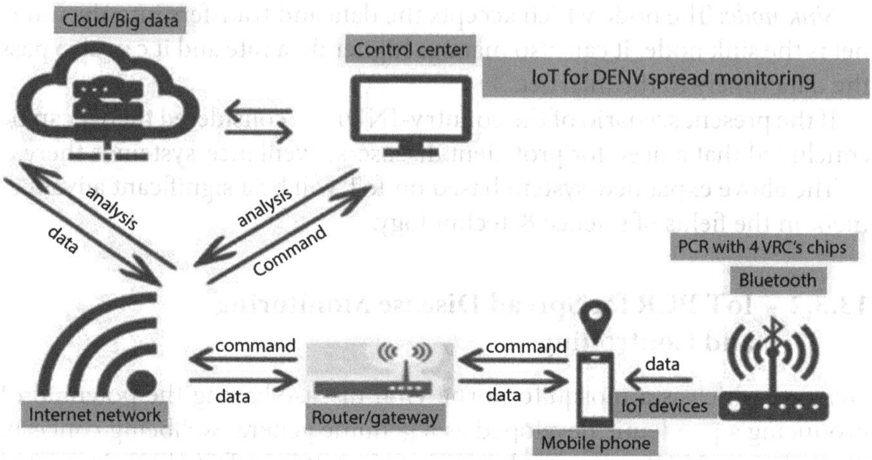

Figure 13.7 The conceptual diagram shown above demonstrates the integrated IoT system that is based on PCR. The results originated from the detection are uploaded automatically with the help of a Bluetooth interface to the mobile phone. With this framework, coordinates of the test spot are sent by the means of world-wide system. The outline showing spreading of disease in different zones is generated in few seconds.

13.4 Global Technological Developments to Overcome Cases of COVID-19

Hence, to endure and make the normal individuals logically careful about the ongoing pandemic, the legislature of India has impelled an application. The application is named as—Arogya Setu which is a mobile phone app, intended to produce a relationship among the huge possible human administrations organizations and the citizens of India. Likewise, the versatile app called as—Close Contact is impelled for its customary people living in China. This app educates the app user regarding the closeness to the crown constructive person.

With the objective that an extra thought can be considered while going out. The government of United States of America is before long going to dispatch a comparative sort of portable application for its regular folks toward the finish of April 2020.

Taiwan was the most unsurprising to have progressively number of instances of COVID-19 after China. In any case, Taiwan promptly prepared and initiated crystal clear approaches for any possible COVID-19 case noticeable evidence, covering, and asset arrangement to watch the stability of the network. Taiwan incorporated its national medical coverage database with its movement office and took index to incite the production of enormous data for assessment. They have likewise utilized this most recent innovation. The innovation incorporates checking of travel history, QR code, and so on for the supposable identification of the contaminated ones [18].

13.4.1 Noteworthy Applications of IoT for COVID-19 Pandemic

While everyone around the globe is finding different ways to fight with the pandemic, here we take some time to discuss the prevalence of IoT technology in pandemic. The IoT is now paving way for new revenue streams by providing real time tracking of vehicles and monitoring feeds of passengers. This helps in knowing about the travel histories of the passenger and identifies if the passenger needs to be isolated or not. The two developed countries China and South Korea are as of now tracking and examining the movement of the infected patients and furthermore of the people who have been in contact with the bearers of the deadly disease. Also, many companies are using devices such as drones as another method of delivering the food supplements are other essentials to the patients. Many apps have been developed and are being developed through IoT so as to manage the pandemic remotely [19].

In 2011, an app called Fluphone was created at Cambridge University to track where and with whom the potential flu carriers had been.

The China's Alibaba has built up Alipay health code app, which each citizen of china needs to introduce on their telephones. The app uses a 3-color code to inform the user if he or she can have a free movement in public spaces or transportation. The green shows that they are allowed to do so while the yellow color depicts limited movement and red color shows total quarantine.

IoT research specialist Dilip Sarangan suggests that the world health organization should start pressurizing the nations to execute the use of IoT devices at the very beginning of an infectious disease outbreak before they become into a pandemic. Although, we can find that IoT applications are being used well in most of the developed and developing countries such as India in order to monitor public's health.

The governments are now finding new ways to deal with COVID-19. They are relying on different instruments such as sensors and powerful algorithms instead of flesh and blood spooks. The government is implementing these new surveillance tools based on IoT so as to fight with COVID-19. The health specialists are motivating patients to interface with the doctors remotely via an app so that the doctors can guide them further.

An application called as MaNaDr, is helping patients in Singapore to check in with their doctors on regular basis and report them about their symptoms. Also, if their condition is getting worse the healthcare providers can call for an ambulance.

One of the smartest cities, Singapore, which is also called as the hub for technology and healthcare innovations, has witnessed a number of innovations based on the Internet of Things which are helping to cope up with the COVID-19 crisis. Some of them are listed below:

1. *IoT enabled Tele-Ventilator*

A company named as ABM Respiratory Care which is a medical device company has showed their creativity and intelligence by developing an innovative ventilator which helps the healthcare specialists in monitoring the device from anyplace on the planet.

Due to the COVID-19 pandemic a problem has been highlighted regarding the shortage in number of ventilators and also there are less healthcare professionals to manage the ventilators. As the chances of spread of virus increases if the healthcare professionals check the patients manually through their frequent visits, so this ABM's Tele ventilator solves this issue by empowering the medicinal services experts to screen the patients and alter the ventilator settings through their online site from anywhere. This device enables several important characteristics which are usually required in connectivity systems such as time-valuable, sensible, consistent telemetry and enormous scale secure access without complex set-up [20].

2. *Employee screening*

One of the several companies Ramco systems is exploring new methods to reduce the COVID-19 "surface area" in the environment of office.

Currently, an innovation lab in Singapore has found and developed a RamcoGEEK-facial recognition-based time and attendance system.

This system consists of recording of temperature with the help of thermal imaging technology. This technology is inserted into an access control screen and IoT door. Therefore, it can restrict the people who have high temperature from entering the office. Along with this, it also sends alerts to the manager if the staff is moving with high temperature in the office [21].

3. Mitigating virus spread

Pensees is an IoT company which has released a really efficient Non-contact Body Temperature Monitoring system. Pensees has developed this system so that the spread of COVID-19 can be lessened.

As fever is the most common symptom of this virus, so becomes the most important alternative to detect the infected person.

This non-contact body temperature tracking device includes infrared thermal body temperature measuring and an intelligent FR access with an integrated temperature screening module.

It also comprises of convenient warm temperature screening framework with FR ability.

As tracking the quarantined people within the homes, offices or other places have become a challenge for the authorities, so people-tracking-and historic-contact tracing solution based on IoT technology for manufacturing companies and IT companies is given by SenseGiz. This helps in tracing the employees if they have been in contact with another employee who was diagnosed as COVID-19 positive.

This alert helps in enforcing social distancing, prevents over-crowding and also enforces geo-fencing in some areas [22].

4. Contact tracing

Nodle.io launched coalition is an IoT start-up which is a contact tracing application. This app safeguards privacy of the user.

This coalition works on Nodle's Bluetooth low-energy powered network in order to communicate with the nearby devices.

As soon as one downloads the application and turns the Bluetooth on the application begins to record one's encounters with other's coalition users nearby. And to keep up the privacy these encounters are stored locally on the cell phone [23].

5. Connected thermometers

These thermometers are being used to screen patients by the hospital staff. This device is built up by VivaLNK's which is a California-based health start-up. This gadget utilizes IoT Access regulator by cassia to get constant information of patients from the sensors. These sensors wirelessly transmit the data for remote monitoring to the nurse's station.

SPHCC—Shanghai Public Health Clinical Centre in China is currently using the temperature sensors to monitor COVID-19 patients. There are 7 more hospitals which are using the same concept [22, 23].

6. IoT Buttons

IoT buttons are designed by Visionstate which are being used in hospitals of Vancouver. Instant alerts are sent by the IoT buttons to the management regarding cleanliness and maintenance issues that may post danger to the public.

This technology empowers tracking of alerts and staff response and also empowers monitoring of cleaning activities in high-traffic areas.

The IoT buttons operates on battery and are automatically connected to the network. The IoT buttons can be used in nurse's room, rest rooms, common areas etc. [17, 18].

A new smart device called Soapy care has developed and called as "Smart Sinks", which adheres to the WHO hand hygiene guidelines and obtains real time hand washing reports for all the users.

These smaller scale stations which are somewhat water coolers use IoT sensors to apportion off the specific measure of cleanser or sanitizer that ought to be expected to wash the hands and also set the temperature of water required to wash the hands appropriately.

Soapy care's systems can-be-found-in-United states, Africa, Asia and since the COVID-19 pandemic their cell phones are not being stop ringing.

A field emergency hospital was set up in Wuhan, China during the outbreak and this hospital was staffed fundamentally with IoT robots so these IoT robots could deliver clean and sterilize meds to the patients and furthermore take their body temperature.

This whole set up helped the hospital staff to lessen the chances of spreading the virus.

Mayo Clinic in U.S.A is talking to the "producers of remote screening tools about ways to keep nearer tabs on patients with COVID-19 who do not need intensive care."

Also, to keep the non COVID patients protected and sound at home different other IoT gadgets measure "wellbeing measurements, for example: internal heat level, pulse and glucose a few times each day and are put away on the cloud with the goal that the specialists can keep a check if the readings are anomalous."

Along with collecting the data related to individual health statistics, the IoT is tracking the community level data which gives a wider view of evolution of the virus.

Such wellbeing following applications introduced on cell phones which examine the information patterns like an ascent in internal heat level in the topographical region can give pieces of information to developing groups of cases.

The "U.S. Health weather map" which is raised up by the kinsa insights provides a representation of amassed information on influenza disease. Healthcare specialists can therefore use the maps in order to distinguish the topographical zones where there is an increment in disease and look as if protective precautions are being taken to slow the spread of COVID-19 [24].

An article named "IoT to track urban mobility changes during pandemic" was published by Matt Johnson on May 4, 2020.

This article expressed that another organization between the University of Wollongong and Meshed IoT is set up to enable the policymakers to see how individuals are responding to the changing limitations forced by the legislature as the nation is presently coming out of disengagement [25].

13.4.2 Key Benefits of Using IoT in COVID-19

IoT is an inventive advancement as it confirms and ensures that every single contaminated person suffering from this virus is isolate. It is useful for a legitimate checking framework to track patients during quarantine. All most at risk patients are followed efficiently using the web based system. This advancement is used for the biometric estimations like pulse, heartbeat and glucose level [26]. Figure 13.8 shows some key merits of utilizing IoT.

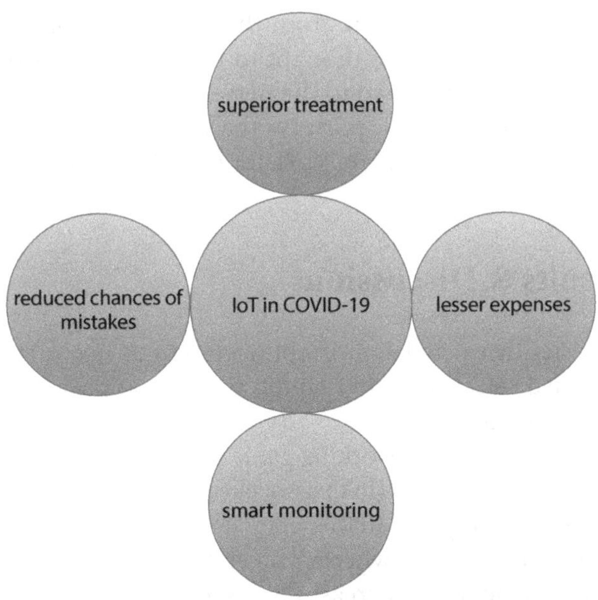

Figure 13.8 Key merits of IoT.

13.4.3 A Last Word About Industrial Maintenance and IoT

Maintenance disappointments can be lethal for the individuals who are attempting to keep themselves under control. In the event that you can't hazard more personal time this year, prescient support merits your consideration. As we know, for instance, that various sensors such as temperature and acoustic estimation sensors are compelling at distinguishing issues. This permits the experts to examine the outcomes and settle on increasingly emphatic choices about the work they have to perform and with what seriousness. Another favorable position of a significant number of these prescient upkeep strategies is that, when connected to cloud-based support programming, they additionally permit reviews to be made distantly—virtual examinations—to show up at a determination without truly getting to the site. Additionally, all breakdowns and appoint undertakings can be followed by the support administrator distantly with the help of computerized maintenance management system associated with the cloud [27].

13.4.4 Issues Faced While Implementing IoT in COVID-19 Pandemic

The major concern while utilizing Internet of Things in the on-going pandemic circumstance is majorly about the security of the data. The sending and receiving of data should be done effectively so as to preserve its privacy. This is important and basic from the perspective of wellbeing. The other major point is about the thought to be taken while organizing the data from the devices connected to the network.

The Figure 13.9 given below portrays the summarized point of view on issues and difficulties in actualizing IoT for COVID-19 pandemic [28].

13.5 Results & Discussions

"IoT has consistently existed as a computerization device yet this interruption has upgraded selection of IoT simply as it accomplished for collective virtual gathering stages".

The quick move to remote working game plans has additionally observed the ascent of internet of things (IoT) associated gadgets all the more conspicuously not long previously, and in the repercussions of, the current pandemic.

A prolonged time period wherein "social distancing" transforms into the standard will achieve increasingly imperative reliance of mechanized arrangements in a scope of businesses. On the other hand, many

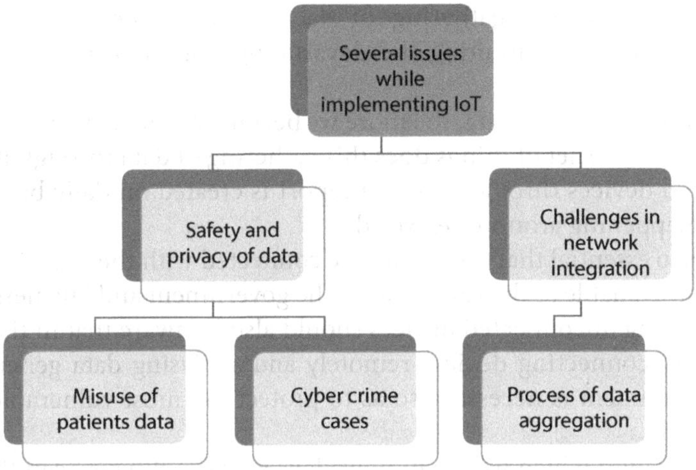

Figure 13.9 Issues in implementing IoT.

restrictions are imposed in the countries which also include movement restrictions. The offices are shut and people are getting used to the term called as "Work from Home".

In such kind of scenario, the time frame for a return to the normal living which includes office-working is highly uncertain. By and by, the governments and organizations are thinking of returning to the normality. They will consider measures to prevent the spread of COVID-19. The move from biometric that is finger-or thumb-based staff support/get the opportunity to control systems to those subjected to touch-less advances, for instance, facial acknowledgment based on IoT is one of the potential examples we may observe [29].

Obviously, the impact of IoT on the COVID-19 pandemic has quite recently begun and is most likely to go up in coming months. While much is up 'til now dark on how this condition will spread out, clearly advancement is all around arranged to help attempts, governments and society take on the risk. In any case, what is critical to note for both the venture and purchaser is that IoT isn't just about interfacing gadgets, it is tied in with utilizing and breaking down the information these gadgets gather to accomplish a result [30].

13.6 Conclusion

The problematic situation of COVID-19 which we are facing nowadays is not totally prevented but restricted to least harm using the technology, Internet of Things.

We all know that gathering of data from all the corners of the world is essential in limiting the devastating impact of this and future pandemics.

The more we gather data, the more we become efficient at handling such pandemics. Internet of things does this gathering of data through its interconnected devices through which a report is created on daily basis about what is happening around the world.

It is also essential that those who are connected with these devices make their data available to the researchers. The government and businesses who are managing unconnected devices should also be aware that in this modern world, connecting devices remotely and analysing data generated in safe environment is necessary so as to protect the most vulnerable in the society [31].

The situation which we are in nowadays would not have been the same without the fruitful innovations made using the IoT technology.

With legitimate execution of this innovative technology, we can make a more secure condition to battle with pandemics.

References

1. Singh, R.P., Javaid, M., Haleem, A., Suman, R., Internet of Things (IoT) applications to fight against COVID-19 pandemic. *Diabetes Metab. Syndr.: Clin. Res. Rev.*, 14, 521–524, 2020.
2. Al-Fuqaha, A., Guizani, M., Mohammadi, M., Aledhari, M., Ayyash, M., Internet of things: A survey on enabling technologies, protocols, and applications. *IEEE Commun. Surv. Tutorials*, 17, 2347–2376, 2015.
3. Bai, L., Yang, D., Wang, X., Tong, L., Zhu, X., Bai, C., Powell, C.A., Chinese experts' consensus on the Internet of Things-aided diagnosis and treatment of coronavirus disease 2019. *Clin. eHealth*, 3, 7–15, 2020.
4. Onag, G., *Analysts say COVID-19 pandemic will spur IoT adoption*, 2020, https://futureiot.tech/analysts-say-covid-19-pandemic-will-spur-iot-adoption/.
5. Lohchab, H., ET Bureau, *COVID-19 disruption creates market boom for IoT*, connected tech, India, 2020, https://economictimes.indiatimes.com/tech/internet/new-normal-creates-market-boom-for-iot-connected-tech/articleshow/76125002.cms.
6. Lee, I. and Lee, K., The Internet of Things (IoT): Applications, investments, and challenges for enterprises. *Bus. Horiz.*, 58, 4, 431–440, 2015.
7. Sharma, N., Shamkuwar, M., Singh, I., The history, present and future with IoT, in: *Internet of Things and Big Data Analytics for Smart Generation*, pp. 27–51, Springer, Cham, 2019.

8. Mattern, F. and Floerkemeier, C., From the Internet of Computer to the Internet of Things (PDF). *Informatik-Spektrum*, 6, 242–259, 2010.
9. Wang, Y., Hu, M., Li, Q., Zhang, X.P., Zhai, G., Yao, N., Abnormal respiratory patterns classifier may contribute to large-scale screening of people infected with COVID-19 in an accurate and unobtrusive manner. *arXiv preprint arXiv*:2002.05534, Extended version accepted in IEEE Internet of Things Journal, 2, 1–6, 2020 Feb 12.
10. Allam, Z. and Jones, D.S., On the coronavirus (COVID-19) outbreak and the smart city network: Universal data sharing standards coupled with artificial intelligence (AI) to benefit urban health monitoring and management. *Healthcare*, 8, 1, 46, Multidisciplinary Digital Publishing Institute, 2020 Mar.
11. Rahman, Md S. *et al.*, Defending against the Novel Coronavirus (COVID-19) Outbreak: How Can the Internet of Things (IoT) help to save the World? *Health Policy Technol.*, 9, 136–138, 2020.
12. Dewey, C., Hingle, S., Goelz, E., Linzer, M., Supporting clinicians during the COVID-19 pandemic. *Ann. Intern. Med.*, 172, 752–753, 2020 Mar 20.
13. Estrela, V.V., Monteiro, A.C.B., França, R.P., Iano, Y., Khelassi, A., Razmjooy, N., Health 4.0: Applications, management, technologies and review. *Med. Technol. J.*, 2, 4, 262–276, 2018.
14. Tan, L. and Wang, N., *Future Internet: Internet of Things*, IEEE paper, Computer Science & Technology Dept., East China Normal Univ., Shanghai, China, 2010.
15. Mathew, A., SA, F.A., Pooja, H.R., Verma, A., Smart disease surveillance based on Internet of Things (IoT). *Int. J. Adv. Res. Comput. Commun. Eng.*, 4, 5, 180–183, 2015.
16. WHO, *A Global Brief on Vector-borne Diseases*, WHO, Geneva, 2014.
17. Zhu, H., Podesva, P., Liu, X., Zhang, H., Teply, T., Xu, Y., Niculescu, A., IoT PCR for pandemic disease detection and its spread monitoring. *Sens. Actuators B: Chem.*, 303, 127098, 2020.
18. Wang, C.J., Ng, C.Y., Brook, R.H., Response to COVID-19 in Taiwan: Big data analytics, new technology, and proactive testing. *J. Am. Med. Assoc.*, 323, 14, 1341–1342, 2020.
19. Zheng, S.Q., Yang, L., Zhou, P.X., Li, H.B., Liu, F., Zhao, R.S., Recommendations and guidance for providing pharmaceutical care services during COVID-19 pandemic: A China perspective. *Res. Soc. Adm. Pharm.*, 17, 1819–1824, 2020 Mar 26.
20. Ghosh, A., Gupta, R., Misra, A., Telemedicine for diabetes care in India during COVID19 pandemic and national lockdown period: Guidelines for physicians. *Diabetes Metab. Syndr.: Clin. Res. Rev.*, 14, 4, 273–276, 2020.
21. Roy, D., *Singapore demonstrates innovative IoT uses*, 2020, https://www.geospatialworld.net/blogs/singapore-demonstrates-innovative-iot-uses-during-covid-pandemic/.
22. Choudhary, M., *How IoT can help fight COVID-19 battle*, 2020, https://www.geospatialworld.net/blogs/how-iot-can-help-fight-covid-19-battle/.

23. Gupta, R., Ghosh, A., Singh, A.K., Misra, A., Clinical considerations for patients with diabetes in times of COVID-19 epidemic. *Diabetes Metab. Syndr., Clin. Res. Rev.*, 14, 3, 211–212, 2020.
24. O'Malley, M., *Will IoT get us through the COVID-19 pandemic*, 2020, https://securityboulevard.com/2020/04/will-iot-get-us-through-the-covid-19-pandemic/.
25. Johnson, M., *IoT to track urban mobility changes during pandemic*, 2020, https://www.itnews.com.au/news/iot-to-track-urban-mobility-changes-during-pandemic-547692.
26. Singh, R.P. *et al.*, Internet of things (IoT) applications to fight against COVID-19 pandemic. *Diabetes Metab. Syndr.: Clin. Res. Rev.*, 14, 521–524, 2020.
27. Parpala, R.C. and Iacob, R., Application of IoT concept on predictive maintenance of industrial equipment. *MATEC Web of Conferences*, vol. 121, EDP Sciences, 2017.
28. Siripongdee, K., Pimdee, P., Tuntiwongwanich, S., A blended learning model with IoT-based technology: Effectively used when the COVID-19 pandemic? *J. Educ. Gift. Young Sci.*, 8, 2, 905–917, 2020.
29. Swayamsiddha, S. and Mohanty, C., Application of cognitive Internet of Medical Things for COVID-19 pandemic. *Diabetes Metab. Syndr.: Clin. Res. Rev.*, 14, 911–915, 2020.
30. Chaudhari, S.N. *et al.*, Role of Internet of Things (IOT) In Pandemic COVID-19 Condition, *International Journal of Engineering Research and Applications (IJERA)*, 10, 57–61, 2020.
31. Rakhra, A., Jain, I., Gupta, R., Bhatia, M., Predicting the Prevalence Rate of COVID-19 Falsity on Temperature. In *2021 11th International Conference on Cloud Computing, Data Science & Engineering (Confluence)*, pp. 327–331, IEEE, 2021, January.

14

Mathematical Insight of COVID-19 Infection—A Modeling Approach

Komal Arora[1], Pooja Khurana[2*], Deepak Kumar[2] and Bhanu Sharma[2]

[1]Department of Biotechnology, Manav Rachna International Institute of Research and Studies, Faridabad, India
[2]Department of Applied Science, Manav Rachna International Institute of Research and Studies, Faridabad, India

Abstract
Application of mathematics has gotten progressively abundant in epidemic disease research. The complexity of disease is appropriate to quantitative methodologies as it gives difficulties and chances to new turns of events. Thusly, computational modeling demonstrating to epidemiology research by assisting with clarifying components and by giving quantitative expectations that can be approved. The ongoing extension of quantitative models tends to numerous inquiries with respect to Epidemic disease (COVID-19) inception, and treatment reactions and opposition. These models have allowed researchers to better understand the physical phenomena. Computational models can supplement exploratory and clinical investigations, yet additionally challenge flow standards, reclassify our comprehension of systems driving epidemiology and shape future research.

Keywords: COVID-19, epidemiology, mathematical modeling, pandemic disease, viral infection

14.1 Introduction

Viruses are parasitic organisms and are thought to be not as important as plants in human life. They lack the ability of reproducing by their own, but once they penetrate the susceptible cell, they take over the host machinery

**Corresponding author*: pooja.fet@mriu.edu.in

Abhinav Juneja, Vikram Bali, Sapna Juneja, Vishal Jain and Prashant Tyagi (eds.) Enabling Healthcare 4.0 for Pandemics: A Roadmap Using AI, Machine Learning, IoT and Cognitive Technologies, (275–298)

and divide rapidly. They possess genetic material either in the form of RNA or DNA [1]. As reported in CGHR report, 2017, low mortality rate has been observed due to viral infections as compared to the diseases like cardiovascular diseases, TB, cancer due to which many researchers and funding organizations underestimated the consequences of viral infection on the health of humans and on the security socio-economic factor. No research has been done on the drug designing or other medical facilities by the scientists related to viral disease such as flu and its clearly visible from the real time situation the rapid pace of spreading viral diseases that is causing serious health implications and bringing down the economy of various countries. Change in the climate quickens the process of the viral spread by increasing the number of vectors. Thus, climatic variations is one of the reason that is causing surge in viral epidemics' outbreak [2]. Viruses such as ebola, influenza, smallpox, HIV, rabies have been documented as yet for causing the outbreaks in different countries of the world and corona virus is also one of the deadliest viruses belonging to the same category of causing serious health implications. This COVID-19 outbreak has changed everyone's perspective as it affecting the human life at an exponential rate.

14.1.1 A Brief on Coronaviruses

Coronaviruses are RNA (plus strand) viruses of genomic size 27–32 kb with an outer covering or envelop, belonging to the *Coronaviridae* family and Nidovirales order [3, 4]. There are six species of coronavirus that have been reported and are associated in causing disease to humans, out of which four are prevailing or endemic and cause symptoms like common cold [5, 6]. The other two species viz. MERS-CoV and SARS-CoV transmit from non-human to human (zoonotic in origin) and are known to cause fatal sickness sometimes [7]. SARS-CoV strain was responsible for causing the "Severe Acute Respiratory Syndrome" epidemics happened in China (Guangdong Province) in the years 2002 and 2003 while strain MERS-CoV was the contributing factor to cause acute respiratory illness pandemic in the Middle East in year 2012 [8–11]. International Committee on Taxonomy of Viruses on February 11, 2020 named novel COVID (coronavirus) as SARS-COV2 [12]. SARS-COV-2, (Severe acute respiratory syndrome coronavirus 2), the causative agent of disease coronavirus (COVID-19), is found to be of great concern for public health globally. Virus attacks respiratory system of human and has been associated with the outbreak happen in Wuhan, China reported first on December 31, 2019 [13, 14]. It belongs to group 2B of betacoronavirus sharing at least 70% similarity of genetic sequences with SARS-CoV. It is the seventh species of coronavirus family infecting humans [4, 5, 15].

14.2 Epidemiology and Etiology

COVID-19 has been announced pandemic by WHO after confirmed infected cases reached to above 200,500 and more than 9,000 deaths has been reported across 115 countries [16]. COVID-19 outbreak originated in China from a local seafood market and has been increased greatly affecting not only China but the individuals worldwide. The first occurrence/cases of infection of COVID-19 were documented in December 2019 [17] and in end of January, the very first expression of novel virus infection was revealed in India. As of August 30, 2020, the virus infected 3,544,486 people in India with 63,688 deaths reported [18]. It has been recorded from the period of December 18 to 29, 2019 that five patients of having viral infection symptoms were hospitalized and one of these 5 patients died [19]. About 41 patients who got admitted to hospital by January 2, 2020 were identified as Corona positive [20]. Dry cough, dyspnea (problems in breathing), fever, fatigue, headache, diarrhea, production of sputum, pneumonia are the symptoms associated with this disease. Progression in the disease may lead to the failure of respiratory system resulting in Acute respiratory distress syndrome and even death. Clinical symptoms like rise in the temperature of body, low count of lymphocytes and WBC's identified by clinicians led them to know that the disease is associated with virus-induced pneumonia. These symptoms seem after the completion of 5.2 days of incubation/latency period of 2019-nCoV [21]. The infection lasts from 6 to 41 days starting from the beginning of symptoms till death with an average of 14 days. This interval is based on the patient's age and the efficiency of immune system to tackle the infection. The shorter interval has been reported for the patients that belongs to the age group more than 70 as compared to the patients that are under the age of 70 [22]. Various similarities have been observed in the symptoms of novel coronavirus and previous betacoronavirus like dry cough, fever, breathing problems, however, sneezing, sore throat, rhinorrhea are the unique symptoms showed by SARS-COV 2 [20, 23, 24].

14.3 Transmission of Infection and Available Treatments

Though early cases of COVID-19 had a zoonotic origin, however, current situation is linked to the disease succession through human contacts as well [25], and is transmitting at a very high pace. The spread of infection can take place through airborne molecules (if an infected person is at the distance less than 1meter to an uninfected person), or via an infected person's droplets since virus remains alive for many in droplets on the surfaces. Once it infects the host, it starts dividing itself in the body, and the body stores viral molecules and hence becomes the reservoir [13]. This transmission of infection led to the patients in isolation and undergone a variety of treatments. Currently, no potential therapy for the infection available that can challenge the infection completely, however, the use of antiviral broad-spectrum drugs such as HIV protease inhibitors is the only option that could reduce the viral effect [26]. This treatment of preexisting antiviral drugs has been tried on 75 patients. 75 mg of oseltamivir (administered orally for every 12 h), 500 mg tablets of ritonavir and lopinavir (administered orally for two times a day) and 0.25 g of ganciclovir (administered intravenously for every 12 h was included in the course of treatment. The total time period of this antiviral treatment ranged from 3–14 days [12]. The results of another study reported the highly efficacious activity of chloroquine and remdesivir that could help to prevent SARS-COV 2 viral infection *in vitro*. These drugs can be therapeutically considered as great candidate for treating this novel virus infection [27]. Additionally, EIDD-2801 compound (that have a high potential against pandemic infections caused by influenza virus) could be considered to combat the infection [13, 28]. Moreover, the latest plasma therapy where convalescent plasma that is a product highly rich in antibodies donated by people who have recovered from COVID-19 can be one of the potential treatments [29]. However, scientists across the world are working hard in order to develop a candidate model to check the sensitivity of the kits designed and to understand main pathophysiology behind the COVID-19 infection. In addition to this, extensive research is ongoing for the development of a potent vaccine that can fight the battle against coronavirus completely. In order to combat this novel infection, interdisciplinary approach towards research should be adopted which involves contributions from biologists, mathematicians, data scientists, clinicians present all over the world. Multidisciplinary approach can be helpful in the discovery or designing of drug and other methods for the permanent cure against this epidemic. Government has made policies and taken appropriate measures for the citizens in controlling the infection to an extent, arranging test kits and setting testing centers and isolation rooms for patients. Besides all the efforts undergoing for the development of vaccine by researchers and the unlimited support from the government, we as an individual have to take care of all the factors such as hygiene, maintaining social distancing, staying home, strengthen immune system and thus by doing this we can do our part in making this rising curve a little flat.

14.4 COVID-19 Infection and Immune Responses

When viral particles penetrate the susceptible cell either through eyes, nose or mouth, they take over the host machinery and divide rapidly. 2019-nCoV hijack the host's machinery by lift out the protein ACE 2 (Angiotensin-converting-enzyme-2) present on the surface of the lung cells with the help of its spike proteins. Virus particles when bind to the receptor, they get recognized as foreign by the immune system and thus immune system starts the mechanism of antibodies production. Binding of viral particles to receptors generates some signals that alert the immune system to release the specialized cells that destroy the foreign viral particles. The signals also trigger the release of cytokines and chemokines that results in the inflammation in the cells. This inflammation results in the runny nose in order to imprison the foreign particles. Inflammation of sinuses results in the headache and the inflammation of hypothalamus causes fever. The virus, SARS-COV-2 penetrates deep inside the lungs where the inflammation activates fluid (residue of a host of specialized cells—including T cells) which causes damage to the body's self-cells and foreign viral particles and due to this process, symptoms like dry cough, fever appears. The infection in alveoli and air sacs by virus prevents the lungs to carry out their core function of oxygen extraction from air, and eventually, results in breathlessness.

Due to inherent malfunctioning in the immune system of the people of old age (above 50 years) or the individual with the existing diseases like cardiovascular, diabetes, they are more prone to develop viral infection or even its very difficult for them to combat that infection caused due to 2019-nCoV.

The novel strain, SARS-COV 2 invade the cell by scoop out the protein ACE 2 present on the surface of lung cell with the help of its spike proteins and releases its RNA inside the cell where some of the RNA is translated into viral proteins. The proteins thus formed generate a replication complex that

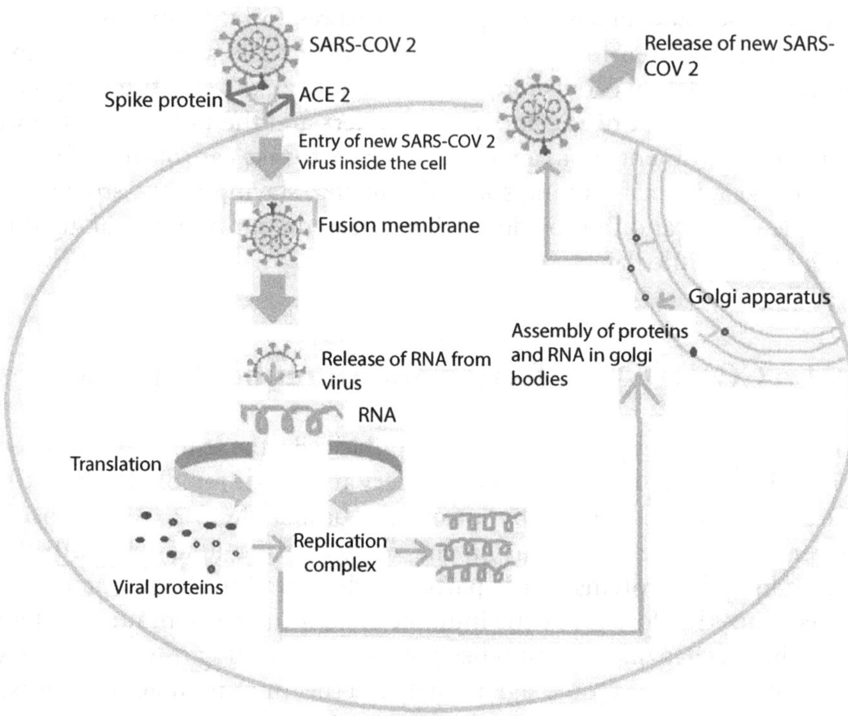

Figure 14.1 Mechanism of infection resulting from SARS-COV 2 infection [6].

work to produce more RNA. Finally, after the assembly of both proteins and RNA in Golgi bodies, the new virus released (as shown in Figure 14.1).

14.5 Mathematical Modeling

Mathematical modeling is a key template that can act as a decision tool for controlling or preventing diseases caused in humans and animals. Models generated mathematically have been used since long to reveal the information quantitatively and have the potential of managing outbreaks and pandemics by providing guidelines that is helpful for both researchers and common man. The mathematical models are also valuable to comprehend the nature of a viral infection upon its entry into a network and explore the conditions under which the particular virus will be cleared out or proceed further.

COVID-19, a novel virus and a totally novel condition [30], has been declared by WHO as International concern for public health emergency on January 30, 2020 [31]. Many mathematical models have been designed or proposed and available in the prior art describing the evolution, transmittance of SARS-COVID 2. Epidemic development of COVID infection has been investigated by Yang *et al.* in China using model-S: Susceptible, E: Exposed, I: Infected, R: Recovered [32]. Using same SEIR model, transmission effectiveness of COVID-19 infection in China has been described by Wu *et al.*, where they predicted the spread of infection nationally and globally [33]. One study reported the effective reduction in reproduction number and risk of transmission that was done by Tang *et al.* by taking into account the parameters like disease's clinical progression, epidemiological status of an individual and measures of intervention (such as isolation and quarantine) into their model [34]. Roosa *et al.* [35] presented the three models whose validation has been done on the basis of epidemics of diseases other than COVID-19, where they have been tried to create and examine the estimates of the collective cases that were reported till that date. Kucharski *et al.* [36] proposed SEIR model with slight modifications and stochastic components were included in some of the works.

Since biological characteristics of each disease is different, selection of an appropriate model is a necessary criterion that in each specific case it is capable of challenging the real time circumstances. Brief description of most of mathematical models have been listed below:

14.5.1 Simple Mathematical Models

14.5.1.1 Basic Model

However, the infection of SARS-CoV-2 is a self-limiting communicable disease. Maximum cases SARS-CoV-2 have mild (symptoms) and can recover in 7 to 14 days. There are 5 possibilities or outcomes of SARS-CoV-2 infection. These outcomes are 1.2% asymptomatically infected persons; 80.9% mild to medium cases; 13.8% severe cases; 4.7% critical cases; and 2.3% death.

TR (Transmission Rate), MR (Mortality Rate) and RR (Recovery Rate) are helpful in understanding the chances of favorable and unfavorable outcomes.

$$\mathrm{TR}\,(\%) = \frac{\mathrm{I}}{\mathrm{N}} \times 100$$

$$\mathrm{MR}\,(\%) = \frac{\mathrm{D}}{\mathrm{I}} \times 100$$

$$\mathrm{RR}\,(\%) = \frac{\mathrm{R}}{\mathrm{I}} \times 100$$

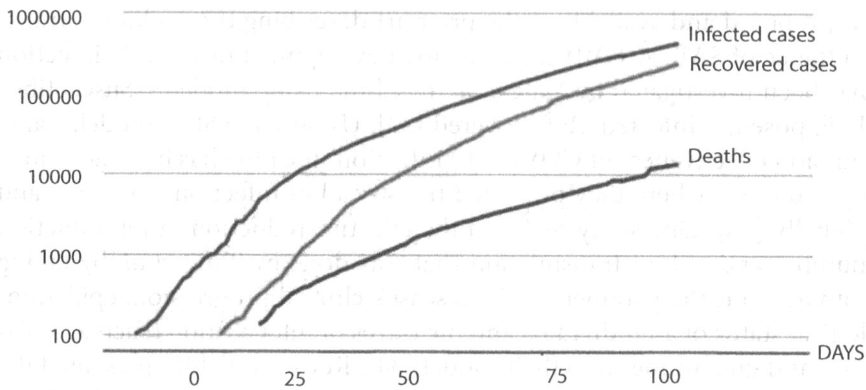

Figure 14.2 Source: India's Ministry of Health and family welfare [37].

Where,

I represents the cases of infected patients

N represents the number of those in population who are at risk of infection,

D represents to the quantity of passing because of infection

R represents the cases of recovered individuals.

All these percentages will change with more testing and data. The transmission of contagious and infectious agent is measured as the basic reproduction number R_0. An outbreak is likely to persist if $R_0 > 1$ and to end if $R_0 < 1$. For all newly emerged infectious diseases, usually, the R_0 values are high initially, as no one is immune.

The above graph represents the number of infected, recovered and removed (due to death) cases per unit time (Figure 14.2) [37].

14.5.1.2 Logistic Model

This model is predominantly utilized to study the transmission of disease. It is often used to investigate the hazardous or risk factors associated with the specific disorder and also to anticipate the likelihood of event of a specific infection in consonance with the associated risk factors. The logistic model is chosen to express the law of infectious diseases' spread and to contemplate the components that prevent, control and influence the spread of SARS-COV 2 infection.

$$C_t = \frac{m}{1 + e^{n - l(t - t_0)}}$$

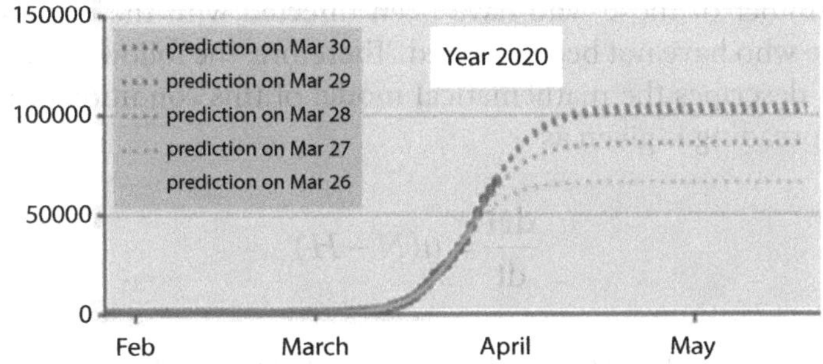

Figure 14.3 Logistic growth of COVID-19 infection for Germany [40].

Where, C_t indicates the aggregate of confirmed cases (deaths)
m Indicates the predicted maximum of confirmed cases (deaths)
n and l = constant.
t = the number of days since the first case
t_0 = the time when the first case occurred [38, 39].

The graph represents the logistic model fit to forecast the cumulative figure/number of novel SARS-COV2 infection confirmed cases (Figure 14.3) [40].

14.5.2 Differential Equations Models

14.5.2.1 Temporal Model (Linear Differential Equation Model, Logistic Model)

This involves the investigation of the pandemic course which is dependent on the data that the spreading rate of no. of individuals who got infected with the infection (time dependent) is directly proportional to the product

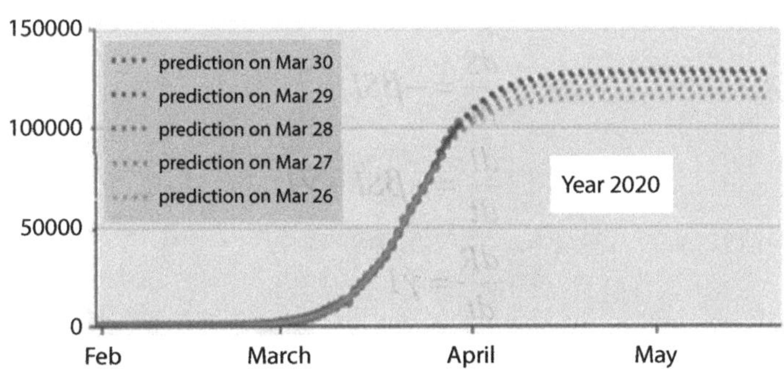

Figure 14.4 Logistic growth of COVID-19 infection for Italy [40].

of the number of those who have been infected with the contamination and those who have not been infected. Therefore, the following differential equation describes the mathematical model of this condition. The rate of disease spreading is given as

$$\frac{\mathrm{dH}}{\mathrm{dt}} = \mu(N - H)$$

Where, time in days (t), number of patients $H(t)$, includes all the factors influencing the rate of spreading (μ), for a region (city, country) with a population N [41].

The graph represents the increment in growth of spreading infection rate in a time dependent fashion (Figure 14.4).

14.5.2.2 SIR Model

It is termed as 'Susceptible-Infectious-Removed' model. Despite the fact that SIR model is a basic/preliminary model for an infectious disease, it tends to be justifiably utilized at various levels for the management of medical care framework in the current situation. The various implementations can be executed at district level based on the predictive results obtained via this model. This model has been used by Nesteruk in order to predict statistically the biological characteristics of novel coronavirus rolling out in mainland China.

The basic mathematical model is used to measure the characteristic features of the coronavirus outbreak in China. The group of susceptible (person at risk of infection), the number of infected (those who are sick and transmit the infection) and removed (individuals who are dead and recovered from hospital after treatment) [42].

$$\frac{dS}{dt} = -\beta SI$$

$$\frac{dI}{dt} = -\beta SI - \gamma I$$

$$\frac{dR}{dt} = \gamma I$$

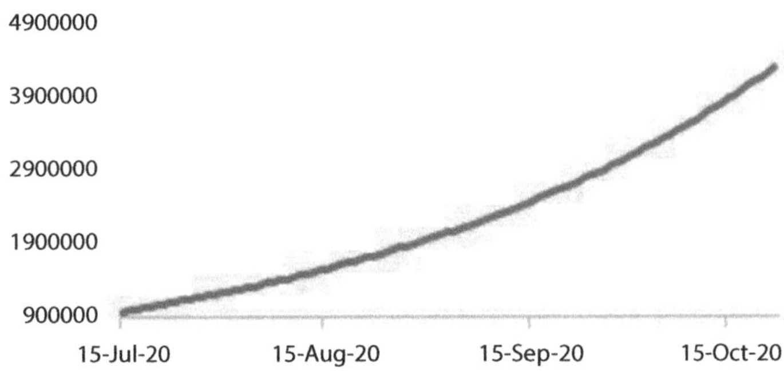

Figure 14.5 Growth of Corona patients in India [41].

Kermack and Mckendrick discussed SIR model in 1927 [43]. Also, numerous mathematical models have been examined, discussed and evaluated by different mathematicians to explore the various phases of epidemiological diseases along with the serious consequences on the living things [44].

The above graphs describe the change in the compartment from susceptible to infective to recover over the period of time (Figure 14.5).

14.5.2.3 SEIR Model

The SEIR system controls the rate-history of an infectious epidemic. Within the initial formulation, it represents people's interpersonal and competitive communication amongst four different contexts, the susceptible (S), the exposed (E), the infective (I) and the recovered (R). S represents all those

Table 14.1 Significant countries affected by the CODIV-19 pandemic [16].

Country	**β (Transmission rate)**	**γ (Recovery rate)**	**$R_0=\beta/\gamma$ (Reproduction Number)**
Japan	0.00002856	0.29819303	0.00009578
South Korea	0.00001297	0.00000001	1297.49430758
Italy	0.00001582	0.00000001	1581.92377423
Iran	0.00006294	0.39999237	0.00015735

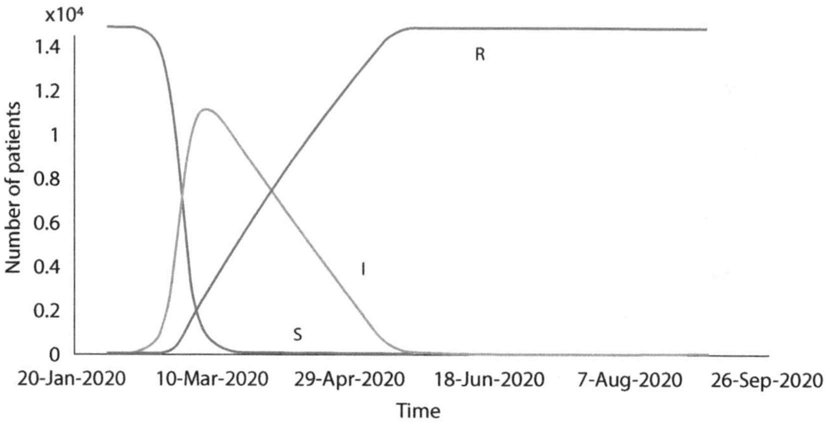

Figure 14.6 SIR model for Japan [16].

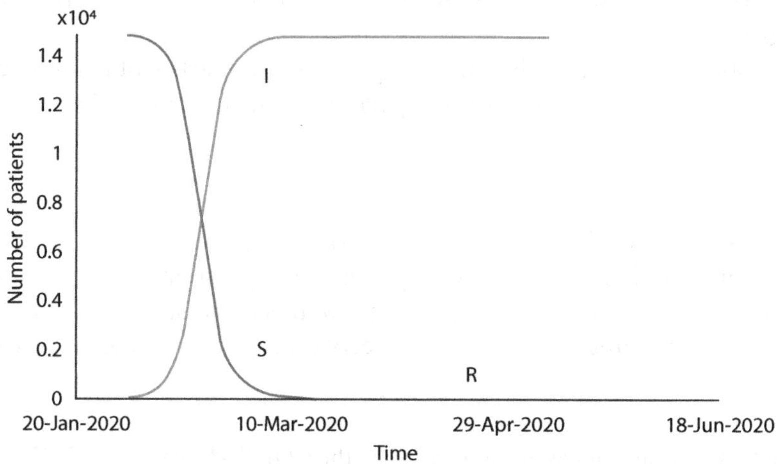

Figure 14.7 SIR model for Italy [16].

who are prone to disease out of whole population; I represent the class of infected persons who come from class of S, R represents class of recovered persons who get excluded form infection class and E represents exposed persons who come in contact with infected class I of persons (Table 14.1, Figure 14.6 and Figure 14.7).

The ODEs of SEIR model is defined as follows:

$$\frac{dS}{dt} = -\beta I\left(S/N\right)$$
$$\frac{dE}{dt} = \beta I\left(S/N\right) - \sigma E$$
$$\frac{dI}{dt} = \sigma E - \mu I - \gamma I$$
$$\frac{dR}{dt} = \mu I + \gamma I$$

β – Represents the rate of infection,

σ – Represents the rate of changing the status of infected persons from exposed to infectious.

μ – Represents therate of recovery i.e. the status of infected persons from infected to recovered,

γ – Represents the rate of demise.

The advantage of SEIR model has always been that the sum of the four main categories S, E, I, R is equivalent to the combined population N [45].

14.5.2.4 *Improved SEIR Model*

The improved SEIR ('Susceptible-Exposed-Infectious-Removed') model for an infectious disease is structural concise and it effectively apprehend the regimen of the coronavirus epidemic. Thusly, this model reveals insight into understanding the patterns of the viral epidemic. This work adopts the 'Susceptible-Exposed-Infectious-Removed' (SEIR) concept of the worldwide population dimension. The number of susceptible (person who are on risk of infection)—*S*, group of exposed individuals—*E*, group of people infected (those ones who are ill and transmit the infection)—*I* and, removed (individuals who are dead and recovered from hospital after treatment)—*R*, the total size of population—*N*, ($S + E + I + R = N$). "*D*" imitating the communal viewpoint of likelihood and risk in regard to the number of serious cases and number of demises, Also (2) "C" depicting the overall net cases for either of published and not published data.

$$\frac{dS}{dt} = -\frac{\beta_0 SF}{N} - \frac{\beta SI}{N} - \mu S$$

$$\frac{dE}{dt} = \frac{\beta_0 SF}{N} + \frac{\beta SI}{N} - (\sigma + \mu)E$$

$$\frac{dI}{dt} = \sigma E - \mu I - \gamma I$$

$$\frac{dR}{dt} = \gamma I - \lambda R$$

$$\frac{dR}{dt} = -\mu N$$

$$\frac{dD}{dt} = d\gamma I - \lambda D$$

$$\frac{dC}{dt} = -\sigma E$$

Where, β–is the rate of transmission,

μ–is the natural natality (birth) and mortality (death),

σ–is the rate of changing the status of infected camels from exposed to infectious,

γ–is the rate of changing the status of infected camels from infected to recovered,

λ–is the rate of recovery and,

d–Proportion of severe cases.

14.5.3 Stochastic Models

14.5.3.1 Basic Model

If we conduct a large number of experiments or carry out a big number of surveys under same initial conditions, we find the population size at a time 't' is not uniquely determined and keeps on fluctuating randomly means we require probability distributions are called stochastic models. Statistical methods in various sorts of epidemiological studies are shown through examples with real or imaginary ("fictive") data. Essential measures of recurrence and impact will be presented. Distinctive relapse models will be introduced as instances of sophisticated systematic strategies.

Basic Equation:

$$\frac{dp_n}{dt} = -p_n \sum_{j \neq 0} f_j(n) + \sum_{j \neq 0} p_{n-j} f_j(n-j)$$

Multiplying by x^n, summing for all n and using the definition of probability generating function

$$\phi(x,t) = \sum_{n-0}^{\infty} p_n(t) x^n$$

Where p_n—Probability of n susceptible persons and $f_j(n)$—Probability that the number changes to $n + j$ in the time interval $^{t+\Delta t}$, n and j-integer.

14.5.3.2 *Simple Stochastic SI Model*

Susceptible and infective individuals represented by the process (S_t, I_t) at time t [46].

At time interval [t,t + Δt], infection's probability and the complementary probability is defined as:

$$P((S_{t+\Delta t}, I_{t+\Delta t}) - (S_t, I_t)) = (-1,1) = \beta \frac{S_t I_t}{N} \Delta t + o(\Delta t)$$

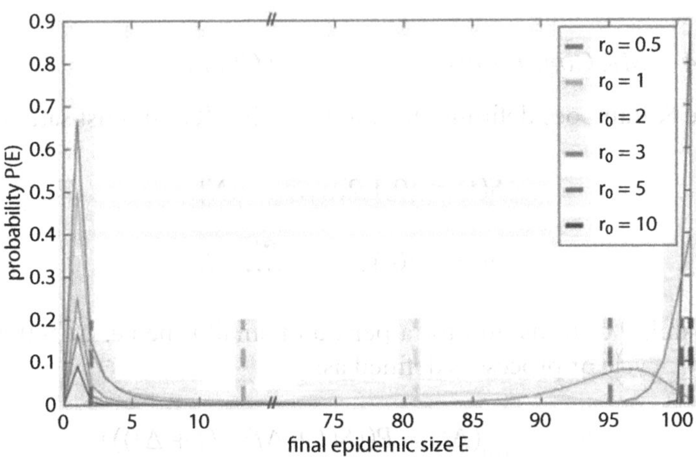

Figure 14.8 Distribution of probability of last scale of the outbreak [48].

$$P((S_{t+\Delta t}, I_{t+\Delta t}) - (S_t, I_t)) = (0,0) = 1 - \beta \frac{S_t I_t}{N} \Delta t + o(\Delta t)$$

Each susceptible individual can contact one and all at the rate β in the entire population and a proportion of the pathogens (as depicted in Figure 14.8).

14.5.3.3 SIR Stochastic Differential Equations

SIR stochastic differential equation model is based on the principle of diffusion process (Allen [47]). The variables i.e. time $t \in [0, \infty)$ and states $S(t)$, $I(t)$ and $R(t)$ are random and continuous, described as:

$$S(t), I(t), R(t) \in [0, N)$$

The advantage of SIR model has always been that the sum of the three main categories S, I, R is equivalent to the combined population N. Also

$$\frac{dS(t)}{dt} + \frac{dI(t)}{dt} + \frac{dR(t)}{dt} = 0$$

One or two diffusion coefficients can be added in SIR stochastic differential equation model

$dI(t)$, upon adding of diffusion coefficient can be r

α = constant, W_t = One-dimensional Wiener process.

14.5.3.4 SIR Continuous Time Markov Chain

Discrete & Ran does defining this model within $[0, \infty)$ must satisfy

$$S(t) \in \{0,1,2,\ldots\ldots\ldots.N\}.$$

$$I(t) \in \{0,1,2,\ldots\ldots\ldots.N\}$$

Probability of transition for a period of small time i.e. $\Delta t > 0$ with the stochastic cycle or process is defined as:

$$p_{(s,i),(s+k,i+j)}(\Delta t) = P((S(t+\Delta t), I(t+\Delta t))) = (s+k, i+j)/(S(t),I(t)) = (s, i)).$$

Where s and i are the DRVs, $s, i \in N$

ODE model for SIR:

$$p_{(s,i),(s+k,i+j)}(\Delta t)=\begin{cases} \beta i\frac{s}{N}\Delta t+o(\Delta t), & (k,j)=(-1,+1) \\ \gamma i\Delta t+o(\Delta t), & (k,j)=(0,-1) \\ 1-\left(\beta i\frac{s}{N}+\gamma i\right)\Delta t+o(\Delta t), & (k,j)=(0,0) \\ o(\Delta t), & Otherwise \end{cases}$$

The dependence of these transition probabilities is on Δt—period in between incidents and not on t (specific time). Furthermore, there is no dependence of the present state of t, and the near term State: $t + \Delta t$ upon times preceding t. This is referred to as Markov property. For the purpose of comparison, the adaptation probabilities have been described in respect to rates in the above model [47].

14.5.3.5 Stochastic SIR Model

As we know in SIR model the sum of these three classes = N, total population. Therefore, for the interval of time [t,t + Δt], infection's probability = β SI N Δt + o(Δt), where S is getting decreased by *1* and *I* is getting increased by *1*. Also probability of recovery = γIΔt + o(Δt), where γ is recovery rate and *R* is getting increased by *1*.

At time interval [t,t + Δt], the infection and recovery's probability is defined as

$$P((S_{t+\Delta t},I_{t+\Delta t})-(S_t-I_t)=(-1,1))=\beta\frac{S_tI_t}{N}\Delta t+o(\Delta t)$$

$$P((S_{t+\Delta t}, I_{t+\Delta t}) - (S_t - I_t) = (0, -1)) = \gamma I_t\Delta t + o(\Delta t)$$

$$P((S_{t+\Delta t},I_{t+\Delta t})-(S_t-I_t)=(0,0))=1-\left(\beta\frac{S_t}{N}+\gamma\right)I_t\Delta t+o(\Delta t)$$

Plot of probability distribution P(E) representing susceptible and infective individuals in the stochastic model and 0.15 has been set as the recovery rate (γ) while the range of reproductive number (r_0) may vary from 0.5–10. Dashed lines are used to represent the corresponding deterministic results/outcomes.The probability distribution P(E) has been depicted for just a population of hundred initial contagious and one infectious in the stochastic model.

14.5.3.6 Stochastic SIR With Demography

In Stochastic SIR model with demography, means when births and deaths of individuals, are both considerable where humans being born in the prone class and demise cases being considered, in the three compartments at the same rate per individual.

The events' probabilities are as follows:

$$P((S_{t+\Delta t}, I_{t+\Delta t}) - (S_t, I_t) = (1,0)) = P((S_{t+\Delta t}, I_{t+\Delta t}) - (S_t, I_t) = (-1,0)) = \mu N\Delta t + o(\Delta t)$$

$$P((S_{t+\Delta t}, I_{t+\Delta t}) - (S_t, I_t) = (-1,1)) = \beta \frac{S_t I_t}{N} \Delta t + o(\Delta t),$$

$$P((S_{t+\Delta t}, I_{t+\Delta t}) - (S_t, I_t) = (0,-1)) = (\gamma + \mu) I_t \Delta t + o(\Delta t).$$

14.6 Conclusion

Coronaviruses are RNA (plus strand) viruses of genomic size 27-32 kb with an outer covering or envelop, belonging to the *Coronaviridae* family and Nidovirales order. Accurate prediction of the nature, dynamics and transmission of virus is very important for the pharmaceutical industries since it help them to develop an effective medicine or vaccine. Mathematical models are being employed as a tool for controlling or preventing epidemic diseases and also to comprehend the nature of a viral infection well upon its entry into a network and explore the conditions under which the particular virus will be cleared out or proceed further. Also, these numerical models can be utilized to represent COVID-19 infected patients in terms of susceptible, recovered and removed as well as the number of people that have been checked or tested. Constant improvement and advancement in the mathematical models have picked up great fascination for the prevention and management of infectious and epidemic diseases. This paper listed most of the possible mathematical models that can supplement exploratory and clinical investigations, yet additionally challenge flow standards, reclassify our comprehension of systems driving epidemiology and shape future research.

References

1. Gelderblom, H.R., Structure and classification of viruses, in: *Medical Microbiology*, 4th edition, University of Texas Medical Branch, Galveston, 1996.
2. Casadevall, A., Climate change brings the specter of new infectious diseases. American Society for Clinical Investigation. *J. Clin. Invest.*, 130, 2, 553–555, 2020, https://doi.org/10.1172/JCI135003.
3. Hoek, L.V.D., Pyrc, K., Jebbink, M.F., Vermeulen-Oost, W., Berkhout, R.J.M., Wolthers, K.C., Wertheim-van Dillen, P.M.E., Kaandorp, J., Spaargaren, J., Berkhout, B., Identification of a new human coronavirus. *Nat. Med.*, 10, 4, 368–373, 2004, https://doi.org/10.1038/nm1024.
4. Song, F., Shi, N., Shan, F., Zhang, Z., Shen, J., Lu, H., Ling, Y., Jiang, Y., Shi, Y., Emerging 2019 Novel Coronavirus (2019-nCoV) Pneumonia. *Radiology*, 295, 1, 210–217, 2020, https://doi.org/10.1148/radiol.2020200274.
5. Zhu, N., Zhang, D., Wang, W., Li, X., Yang, B., Song, J., Zhao, X., Huang, B., Shi, W., Lu, R., Niu, P., A novel coronavirus from patients with pneumonia in China. *N. Engl. J. Med.*, 82, 8, 727–733, 2020, https://doi.org/10.1056/NEJMoa2001017.
6. Su, S., Wong, G., Shi, W., Liu, J., Lai, A.C., Zhou, J., Liu, W., Bi, Y., Gao, G.F., Epidemiology, Genetic Recombination, and Pathogenesis of Coronaviruses. *Trends. Microbiol.*, 24, 6, 490–502, 2016, https://doi.org/10.1016/j.tim.2016.03.003.
7. Cui, J., Li, F., Shi, Z.L., Origin and evolution of pathogenic coronaviruses. *Nat. Rev. Microbiol.*, 17, 3, 181–192, 2018, https://doi.org/10.1038/s41579-018-0118-9.
8. Zhong, N.S., Zheng, B.J., Li, Y.M., Poon, L.L.M., Xie, Z.H., Chan, K.H., Li, P.H., Tan, S.Y., Chang, Q., Xie, J.P., Liu, X.Q., Epidemiology and cause of severe acute respiratory syndrome (SARS) in Guangdong, People's Republic of China. *Lancet*, 362, 9393, 1353–1358, 2003, https://doi.org/10.1016/s0140-6736(03)14630-2.
9. Ksiazek, T.G., Erdman, D., Goldsmith, C.S., Zaki, S.R., Peret, T., Emery, S., Tong, S., Urbani, C., Comer, J.A., Lim, W., Rollin, P.E., A Novel Coronavirus

Associated with Severe Acute Respiratory Syndrome. *N. Engl. J. Med.*, 348, 20, 1953–1966, 2003, https://doi.org/10.1056/NEJMoa030781.
10. Drosten, C., Günther, S., Preiser, W., Van Der Werf, S., Brodt, H.R., Becker, S., Rabenau, H., Panning, M., Kolesnikova, L., Fouchier, R.A., Berger, A., Identification of a Novel Coronavirus in Patients with Severe Acute Respiratory Syndrome. *N. Engl. J. Med.*, 348, 20, 1967–1976, 2003, https://doi.org/10.1056/NEJMoa030747.
11. Zaki, A.M., Van Boheemen, S., Bestebroer, T.M., Osterhaus, A.D., Fouchier, R.A., Isolation of a novel coronavirus from a man with pneumonia in Saudi Arabia. *N. Engl. J. Med.*, 367, 19, 1814–1820, 2012, https://doi.org/10.1056/NEJMoa1211721.
12. Chen, N., Zhou, M., Dong, X., Qu, J., Gong, F., Han, Y., Qiu, Y., Wang, J., Liu, Y., Wei, Y., Yu, T., Epidemiological and clinical characteristics of 99 cases of 2019 novel coronavirus pneumonia in Wuhan, China: A descriptive study. *Lancet*, 395, 10223, 507–513, 2020, https://doi.org/10.1016/S0140-6736(20)30211-7.
13. Rothan, H.A. and Byrareddy, S.N., The epidemiology and pathogenesis of coronavirus disease (COVID-19) outbreak. *J. Autoimmun.*, 109, 102433, 2020, https://doi.org/10.1016/j.jaut.2020.102433.
14. Wuhan Municipal Health Commission, *Report of clustering pneumonia of unknown etiology in Wuhan City*, Wuhan Municipal Health Commission: Wuhan City health committee, WHO Headquarters in Geneva, Avenue Appia, Geneva, 2019.
15. Hui, D.S., Azhar, E.I., Madani, T.A., Ntoumi, F., Kock, R., Dar, O., Ippolito, G., Mchugh, T.D., Memish, Z.A., Drosten, C., Zumla, A., The continuing 2019-nCoV epidemic threat of novel coronaviruses to global health—The latest 2019 novel coronavirus outbreak in Wuhan, China. *Int. J. Infect. Dis.*, 91, 264–266, 2020, https://doi.org/10.1016/j.ijid.2020.01.009.
16. Hamzah, F.B., Lau, C., Nazri, H., Ligot, D.V., Lee, G., Tan, C.L., Shaib, M. K.B.M., Zaidon, U.H.B., Abdullah, A.B., Chung, M.H., CoronaTracker: worldwide COVID-19 outbreak data analysis and prediction. *Bull World Health Organ.*, 1, 32, 1–2, 2020.
17. Toit, A.D., Outbreak of a novel coronavirus. *Nat. Rev. Microbiol.*, 18, 3, 123–123, 2020, https://doi.org/10.1038/s41579-020-0332-0.
18. India Corona Dashboard, https://www.zoho.com/covid/india/
19. Ren, L.L., Wang, Y.M., Wu, Z.Q., Xiang, Z.C., Guo, L., Xu, T., Jiang, Y.Z., Xiong, Y., Li, Y.J., Li, X.W., Li, H., Identification of a novel coronavirus causing severe pneumonia in human. *Chin. Med. J.*, 133, 9, 1015–1024, 2020, https://doi.org/10.1097/CM9.0000000000000722.
20. Huang, C., Wang, Y., Li, X., Ren, L., Zhao, J., Hu, Y., Zhang, L., Fan, G., Xu, J., Gu, X., Cheng, Z., Clinical features of patients infected with 2019 novel coronavirus in Wuhan, China. *Lancet*, 395, 10223, 497–506, 2020, https://doi.org/10.1016/S0140-6736(20)30183-5.

21. Li, Q., Guan, X., Wu, P., Wang, X., Zhou, L., Tong, Y., Ren, R., Leung, K.S., Lau, E.H., Wong, J.Y., Xing, X., Early Transmission Dynamics in Wuhan, China, of Novel Coronavirus–Infected Pneumonia. *N. Engl. J. Med.*, 382, 13, 1199–1207, 2020, https://doi.org/10.1056/NEJMoa2001316.
22. Wang, Y., Wang, Y., Chen, Y., Qin, Q., Unique epidemiological and clinical features of the emerging 2019 novel coronavirus pneumonia (COVID-19) implicate special control measures, Unique epidemiological and clinical features of the emerging 2019 novel coronavirus pneumonia (COVID-19) implicate special control measures. *J. Med. Virol.*, 92, 6, 568–576, 2020, https://doi.org/10.1002/jmv.25748.
23. Assiri, A., Al-Tawfiq, J.A., Al-Rabeeah, A.A., Al-Rabiah, F.A., Al-Hajjar, S., Al-Barrak, A., Flemban, H., Al-Nassir, W.N., Balkhy, H.H., Al-Hakeem, R.F., Makhdoom, H.Q., Epidemiological, demographic, and clinical characteristics of 47 cases of Middle East respiratory syndrome coronavirus disease from Saudi Arabia: A descriptive study. *Lancet Infect. Dis.*, 13, 9, 752–761, 2013, https://doi.org/10.1016/S1473-3099(13)70204-4.
24. Lee, N., Hui, D., Wu, A., Chan, P., Cameron, P., Joynt, G.M., Ahuja, A., Yung, M.Y., Leung, C.B., To, K.F., Lui, S.F., A Major Outbreak of Severe Acute Respiratory Syndrome in Hong Kong. *N. Engl. J. Med.*, 348, 20, 1986–1994, 2003, https://doi.org/10.1056/NEJMoa030685.
25. Zhou, P., Yang, X.L., Wang, X.G., Hu, B., Zhang, L., Zhang, W., Si, H.R., Zhu, Y., Li, B., Huang, C.L., Chen, H.D., A pneumonia outbreak associated with a new coronavirus of probable bat origin. *Nature*, 579, 7798, 270–273, 2020, https://doi.org/10.1038/s41586-020-2012-7.
26. Lu, H., Drug treatment options for the 2019-new coronavirus (2019-nCoV). *Biosci. Trends*, 14, 1, 69–71, 2020, https://doi.org/10.5582/bst.2020.01020.
27. Wang, Y., Wang, Y., Chen, Y., Qin, Q., Unique epidemiological and clinical features of the emerging 2019 novel coronavirus pneumonia (COVID-19) implicate special control measures. *J. Med. Virol.*, 92, 6, 568–576, 2020, https://doi.org/10.1002/jmv.25748.
28. Toots, M., Yoon, J.J., Cox, R.M., Hart, M., Sticher, Z.M., Makhsous, N., Plesker, R., Barrena, A.H., Reddy, P.G., Mitchell, D.G., Shean, R.C., Characterization of orally efficacious influenza drug with high resistance barrier in ferrets and human airway epithelia. *Sci. Transl. Med.*, 11, 515, eaax5866, 2019, https://doi.org/10.1126/scitranslmed.aax5866.
29. Chen, L., Xiong, J., Bao, L., Shi, Y. Convalescent plasma as a potential therapy for COVID-19. *Lancet Infect. Dis.*, 20, 4, 398–400, 2020.
30. Wang, W., Tang, J., Wei, F., Updated understanding of the outbreak of 2019 novel coronavirus (2019-nCoV) in Wuhan, China. *J. Med. Virol.*, 92, 4, 441–447, 2020, https://doi.org/10.1002/jmv.25689.
31. Hua, J., and Shaw, R., Corona virus (COVID-19) "infodemic" and emerging issues through a data lens: The case of china. *Int. J. Env. Res. Pub. He.*, 17, 7, 2309, 2020.

32. Yang, Z., Zeng, Z., Wang, K., Wong, S.S., Liang, W., Zanin, M., Liu, P., Cao, X., Gao, Z., Mai, Z., Liang, J., Modified SEIR and AI prediction of the epidemics trend of COVID-19 in China under public health interventions. *J. Thorac. Dis.*, 12, 3, 165–174, 2020, https://doi.org/10.21037/jtd.2020.02.64.
33. Wu, J.T., Leung, K.K., Leung, G.M., Nowcasting and forecasting the potential domestic and international spread of the 2019-nCoV outbreak originating in Wuhan, China: A modelling study. *Lancet*, 395, 10225, 689–697, 2020, https://doi.org/10.1016/S0140-6736(20)30260-9.
34. Tang, B., Wang, X., Li, Q., Bragazzi, N.L., Tang, S., Xiao, Y., Wu, J., Estimation of the Transmission Risk of the 2019-nCoV and Its Implication for Public Health Interventions. *J. Clin. Med.*, 9, 2, 462, 2020, https://doi.org/10.3390/jcm9020462.
35. Roosa, K., Lee, Y., Luo, R., Kirpich, A., Rothenberg, R., Hyman, J.M., Yan, P., Chowell, G., Real-time forecasts of the COVID-19 epidemic in China from February 5th to February 24th, 2020. *Infect. Dis. Model.*, 5, 256–263, 2020, https://doi.org/10.1016/j.idm.2020.02.002.
36. Kucharski, A.J., Russell, T.W., Diamond, C., Liu, Y., Edmunds, J., Funk, S., Eggo, R.M., *et al.* Early dynamics of transmission and control of COVID-19: a mathematical modelling study. *Lancet Infect. Dis.*, 20, 5, 553–558, 2020.
37. Alluri, A. and Nazmi, S., *Coronavirus: Is India the next global hotspot?*, BBC News, Delhi, 9 July 2020, https://www.bbc.com/news/world-asia-india-53284144.
38. Jia, L., Li, K., Jiang, Y., Guo, X., Prediction and analysis of Coronavirus Disease. arXiv preprint arXiv:2003.05447, 2019.
39. Lin, Q., Zhao, S., Gao, D., Lou, Y., Yang, S., Musa, S., Wang, M.H., Cai, Y., Wang, W., Yang, L., He, D., A conceptual model for the coronavirus disease 2019 (COVID-19) outbreak in Wuhan, China with individual reaction and governmental action. *Int. J. Infect. Dis.*, 93, 211–216, 2020, https://doi.org/10.1016/j.ijid.2020.02.058.
40. Bauckhage, C., The Math of Epidemic Outbreaks and Spread (Part 2) Least Squares Parameter Estimation for Logistic Models-A Technical report and link https://www.researchgate.net/publication/340389204, 2020.
41. Cakir, Z. and Savas, H.B., A Mathematical Modelling Approach in the Spread of the Novel 2019 Coronavirus SARS-CoV-2 (COVID-19) Pandemic. *Electron. J. Gen. Med.*, 17, 4, em205. 5, 2020, https://doi.org/10.29333/ejgm/7861.
42. Nesteruk, I., Statistics-Based Predictions of Coronavirus Epidemic Spreading in Mainland China. *Innov. Biosyst. Bioeng.*, 4, 1, 13–18, 2020. https://doi.org/10.20535/ibb.2020.4.1.195074.
43. Kermack, W.O. and McKendrick, A.G., A contribution to the mathematical theory of epidemics, in: *Proceedings of the royal society of London. Series A, Containing papers of a mathematical and physical character*, vol. 115, pp. 700–721, 1927, https://doi.org/10.1098/rspa.1927.0118.

44. Kumar, V., Kumar, D., Pooja, S.I.R., Model of Swine Flu in Shimla, in: *Advanced Computing and Communication Technologies*, pp. 297–303, Springer, Singapore, 2016.
45. Lin, Q., Chiu, A.P., Zhao, S., He, D., Modeling the spread of Middle East respiratory syndrome coronavirus in Saudi Arabia. *Stat. Methods Med. Res.*, 27, 7, 1968–1978, 2018, https://doi.org/10.1177/0962280217746442.
46. Greenwood, P.E. and Gordillo, L.F., Stochastic epidemic modelling, in: *Mathematical and statistical estimation approaches in epidemiology*, pp. 31–52, Springer, Dordrecht, 2009.
47. Allen, L.J., A primer on stochastic epidemic models: Formulation, numerical simulation, and analysi. *Infect. Dis. Model.*, 2, 2, 128–142, 2017, https://doi.org/10.1016/j.idm.2017.03.001.
48. Nguyen, C. and Carlson, J.M., Optimizing real-time vaccine allocation in a stochastic SIR model. *PloS One*, 11, 4, e0152950, 2016, https://doi.org/10.1371/journal.pone.0152950.

15

Machine Learning: A Tool to Combat COVID-19

Shakti Arora[1*], Vijay Anant Athavale[1†] and Tanvi Singh[2‡]

[1]Department of Computer Science and Engineering, Panipat Institute of Engineering & Technology, Panipat, India
[2]Department of Civil Engineering, Panipat Institute of Engineering & Technology, Panipat, India

Abstract
COVID-19 has become a global challenge and is threatening mankind. The global economy is in crisis due to a long tranche of partial to complete lockdown. Forecasting the number of COVID-19 cases is a challenge as cases are both symptomatic as well as asymptomatic, recurrence after recovery is another challenge. Careful data analysis is required to predict and estimate the number of affected cases as well as death ratio. During this pandemic situation, forecasting uncertainty is of utmost importance in decision making. In this chapter, authors have developed a model to predict the COVID-19 confirmed cases. The prediction is based on the data collected in different phases of lockdown in India. In this study, a model is developed using machine learning approaches based on the analysis of data of two Indian states Delhi and Maharashtra where maximum infected cases are found. This study is an attempt to help the decision-makers in better planning and actions. In this study, Neural Network (NN) and M5P model trees are applied to forecast the number of infected cases with each progressive day. Results suggest that the performance of the neural network-based model is slightly better than the M5P model tree in forecasting COVID-19 cases.

***Keywords*:** COVID-19, machine learning, neural network, M5P model tree, Weka

**Corresponding author*: shakti.nagpal@gmail.com
†*Corresponding author*: vijay.athavale@gmail.com
‡*Corresponding author*: tanvisinghnitkkr@gmail.com

Abhinav Juneja, Vikram Bali, Sapna Juneja, Vishal Jain and Prashant Tyagi (eds.) Enabling Healthcare 4.0 for Pandemics: A Roadmap Using AI, Machine Learning, IoT and Cognitive Technologies, (299–316) © 2021 Scrivener Publishing LLC

15.1 Introduction

COVID-19 a global challenge has affected the world. It is a global health crisis. On 22nd March 2020 total cases in the world were 534 and new cases reported were only 142. As of 7th May 2020, approximately 3.72M people are affected and 0.2M deaths are confirmed, whereas 0.083M cases increased on that day [1]. As a precautionary measure government of different countries has announced lockdown of varying degrees from partial to total lockdown covering all schools, colleges, businesses, all social activities, and places of worship. Studies show that it is very difficult to detect the infection in affected persons in early stages so there is always uncertainty in forecasting the number of cases. Countries are having a limited number of test kits, so to test every person of any country or state is challenging. Further, the accuracy of the test kit result is also a challenge. Bird flu and other seasonal infection have similar symptoms making it even more challenging to identify COVID-19 patients, so infected casualties could be misreported. The present study is based on only confirmed cases, we have not considered the number of people whose reports are pending.

According to World Health Organization (WHO), COVID-19 takes approximately 67 days to infect the group of first 100,000 clusters of population, and in another two weeks, it can affect another cluster of 10M in the third stage which is the most dangerous stage takes almost another 4 days to infect another cluster of 100,000 [2]. By the last week of March 2020 approximately 300,000 cases were reported. As of May 7, 2020, the analysis of confirmed, recovered, and death cases of five different countries are shown in Table 15.1. The research paper is divided into 7 sections. Section 15.1 Introduction, Section 15.2 Recent Survey and analysis, Section 15.3 Contribution, Section 15.4 State-wise Analysis of COVID data, Section 15.5

Table 15.1 COVID-2019 data of five different countries on May 7, 2020 [1].

S. no.	Countries	Confirmed	Recovered
1	United States	1.26M	0.17M
2	Spain	0.22M	0.12M
3	Italy	0.21M	0.093M
4	UK	0.20M	0.30M
5	Germany	0.16M	0.013M

Results and Discussion, this section also compares the results of the two proposed approaches along with the linear regression machine learning approach, Section 15.6 Conclusion and Section 15.7 Future Scope.

15.1.1 Recent Survey and Analysis

In the last four months, approximately 124,000 articles have been published on and processed data is was collected from thousands of patients release, where the majority of the study done in these articles is based on the scientific methods still standard methods suffers from two important challenges, considered critical to the pandemic situation: 1) considerable expertise and human inputs 2) very limited hypotheses available at a time.

Ahmed *et al.* designed an artificial intelligence model to review the analysis of COVID-19 cases [26]. The big datasets of COVID-19 infected patients can be used and analyzed by applying advanced machine learning algorithms. It helps in good understanding the common patterns of viral infection spread. The people based upon genetic and physiological characteristics are identified which are more suspectible to infection patterns. In Table 15.2 a summary of different machine learning algorithms adopted by several researchers with the objective and optimal results given by each model is described.

Pinter *et al.* [4] applied the artificial neural network method to predict the total infected cases and mortality rate. Kumar *et al.* [5] used Decision

Table 15.2 Different machine learning algorithm adopted by different researchers [4–12].

References	Aim	Machine learning models	Outputs received from optimal output model
Pinter *et al.* [4]	Prediction of mortality and infected cases of COVID-19	Applied Hybrid method of ANN model	Infected cases count Root Mean Squared Error of MLP-ICA-167.88 Mortality rate RMSE of MLP-ICA: 8:32

(Continued)

Table 15.2 Different machine learning algorithm adopted by different researchers [4–12]. (*Continued*)

References	Aim	Machine learning models	Outputs received from optimal output model
Onovo *et al.* [5]	Correlation between different patterns of COVID-19	Lasoo Regression	Mean Squared Errors of adaptive lasso:2.72 * 10^{-28} R-Squad of adaptive Lasoo 1.0000
Balde [6]	Prediction of the evolution of COVID-19	SIR Model	No numerical outcomes mentioned
Kumar *et al.* [7]	To forecast the rise of COVID-19 infected cases by analyzing the daily data	Gaussian Process Regression Support Vector Machine algorithm	No numerical outcomes mentioned
Sattler *et al.* [8]	forcast cases of COVID-19 based on BLE signal strength measurement	Linear Regression	AUC:0.96
Tiwari *et al.* [9]	Assesing the number infected COVID-19 cases	Machine learning approaches but the model description is not mentioned	Numerical cases of confirmed, death and recovery cases
Margi *et al.* [10]	To provide a quantitative estimate about contact, recovery, and death	ODE solver and SRD Model	No numerical outcomes mentioned

(*Continued*)

Table 15.2 Different machine learning algorithm adopted by different researchers [4–12]. (*Continued*)

References	Aim	Machine learning models	Outputs received from optimal output model
Sujatha *et al.* [11]	To predict trends of spread of COVID-19 impact in India	Linear Regression MLP	No numerical outcomes mentioned
Jo *et al.* [12]	Find and analyze the novel COVID-19	Time-dependent parameters model of SIR	No numerical outcomes mentioned

tree, SVM and Gussain Process Regression methods but doesn't reach to any numerical computation.

15.2 Our Contribution

We aim to predict the count of COVID-19 infected cases in India, as well as based on the data from two states which are declared as hotspot areas having very heavy number COVID-19 cases reported and they were identified as a hotspot on the map. On 30th January 2020, the first COVID-19 case was detected in India. On 3rd February 2020, only 3 cases were reported. Till 10th of March 2 more cases were reported and total count increased to 50 but no deaths were reported till then. 17th March 2020 the number changed to 137, while 3 infected lost their lives due to COVID-19 and by 7th May 2020, a total of 0.052M infected cases were reported and 1,783 lost their lives. The reported infected cases increased to 10 times in two weeks between 10th-25th March 2020. As a precautionary measure, the Government of India announced a complete pandemic lockdown from 25th March–14th April 2020 and limited the movement of the entire 1.3 billion population. The first step was taken on 22nd March 2020 when Janta Curfew was imposed on 24th followed by the first phase of lockdown. This helps arrest the spread by reducing the doubling of cases from 6 to 8 days. On 14th April 2020 lockdown was extended till 3rd May 2020 with conditional relaxation in some of the states [3]. During the lockdown government aimed to make policies, plans and making some necessary arrangements to fight this uncertain pandemic situation. All the markets, offices, industries remained close during the lockdown. All social gatherings and activities are strictly prohibited. Gathering more than five people at a place was prohibited. Table 15.2 depicts the statistics of incidents found in different Indian states are depicted. These statistics are changing rapidly, data collected on 7th May 2020, a total of 0.52M cases were infected with COVID-19 infection, total deaths 1,783.

According to ICMR, a total number of 1,357,413 samples were tested as of 7th May 2020 and 0.52M cases have been confirmed positive [3].

The statistical report is presented for the lockdown period in India and every week's estimation report is designed. The data set is taken from Ministry health and family welfare from 2nd March 2020 (considering as Day 1 for analysis using machine learning) to 7th May 2020 (considering as Day 68). India declared the national lockdown on 23rd March 2020 to control the number of infected cases in India.

The data used for the first phase of the forecast was between 23rd March 2020 and 4th April 2020. The log series is taken for analysis for getting better predictions. The seven days ahead point-forecast of India along with the prediction interval were estimated and presented in Figure 15.1. Note the vertical axis in the figure represents the log series. The dark gray and light gray shaded region in the plot represents the 95% confidence level of prediction, respectively.

During the first lockdown the total number of cases reached more than 10,000 so the Indian Government decided to extend the lockdown to resist its spread. The government decided to extend the Lockdown period from 15th April–3rd May 2020. Figure 15.2 shows the number of infected cases during the First Lockdown.

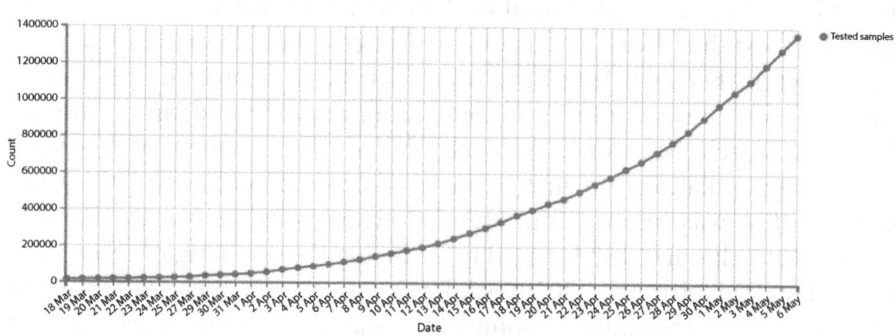

Figure 15.1 Test statistics of India till 6th May 2020 [3].

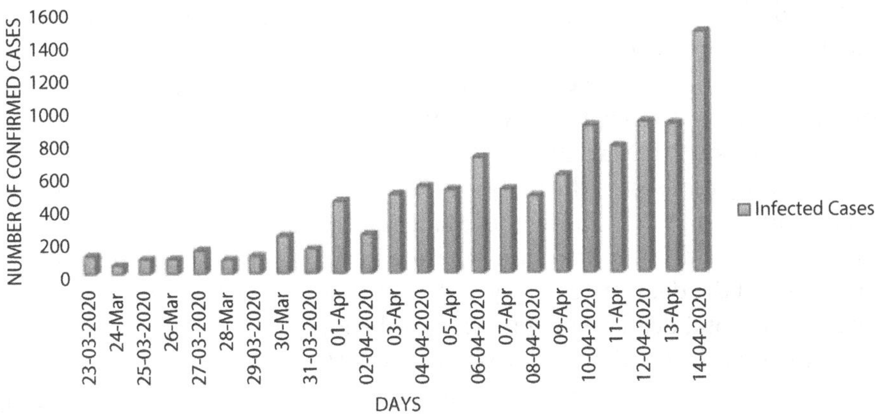

Figure 15.2 Lock down analysis phase-1 [4].

The data used for the second phase of the forecast was between 14th April and 4th May 2020, analysis is done with 95% confidence level of prediction.

In Lockdown phase-2 where people were strictly bound to stay at home, social distancing and all the hygiene protocols were properly followed still approximately 29,944 new infected cases were reported.

The cases increased rapidly and the government of India has decided to increase the lockdown from 4th May–17th May 2020. In Figure 15.3 the four days analysis of infected cases are given, the prediction analysis for

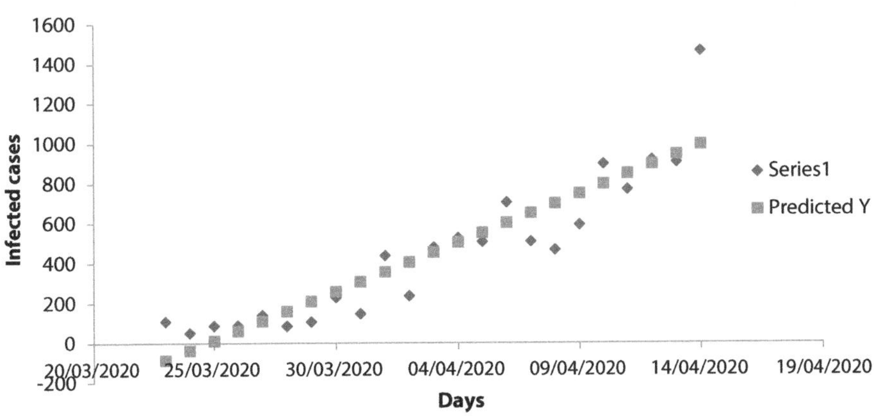

Figure 15.3 Regression analysis lockdown phase-1 [4].

the third phase is not done because of a smaller number of days are with us for the compilation.

The following mentioned states are highly affected and have a maximum of the people infected with COVID-19. The details are taken from the government site on 7th May 2020.

This study focuses on the daily statistics report of the cases found in two highly infected states: Delhi and Maharashtra. Maharashtra became the hotspot of COVID-19 infection where a large number of the people are affected and the death rate is very high. In India, 23% of total infected cases and 46% of total death belong to Maharashtra [4].

Delhi was declared as a hotspot of COVID-19, where second-largest infected cases of Indian union territory are found till 7th May 2020. On 2nd March 2022 first cases of COVID-19 were identified. On 18th April 2020, Delhi was having 29.8% of total infected cases in India [4]. In Figure 15.4

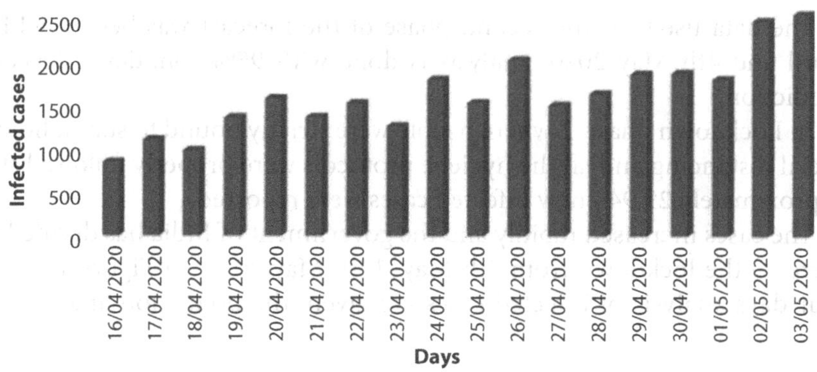

Figure 15.4 Lock down analysis phase-2 [14].

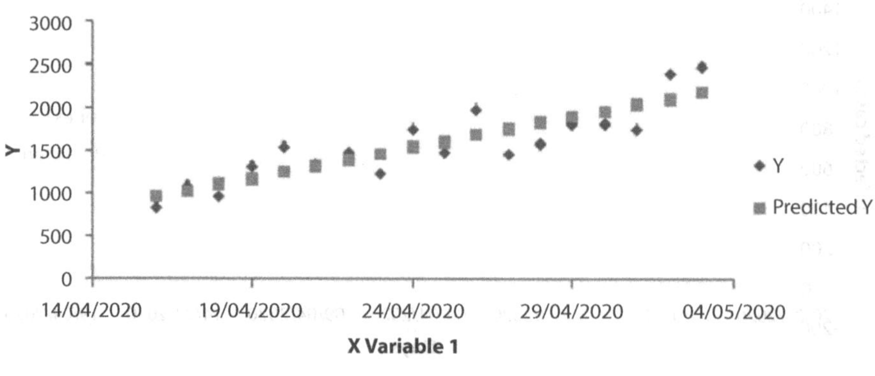

Figure 15.5 Regression analysis of lockdown phase-2 [14].

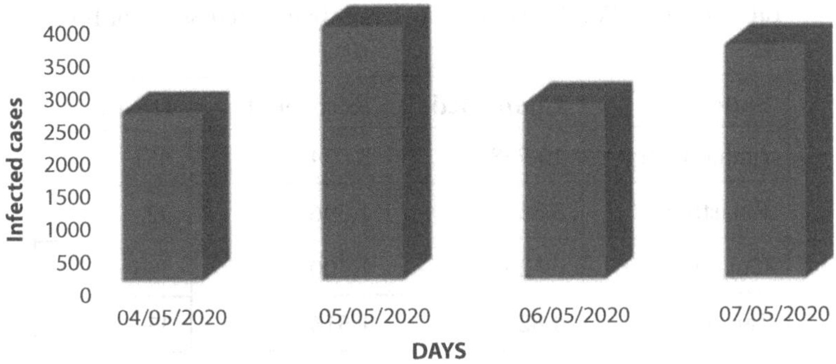

Figure 15.6 Lock down analysis phase-3 [15].

day wise analysis of infected cases is shown. Figure 15.5 depicts the prediction for the upcoming cases in future and Figure 15.6 day wise analysis of cases in Lock down 3 is shown.

In Figure 15.7 the analysis of 22nd April–7th May 2020 for the Maharashtra states is depicted, where the total number of active cases is 16,758 to date.

In Figure 15.8 the last 15 days analysis approximately from 23rd March - 7th May 2020, the analysis report is highlighting the number of infected cases in the Delhi region only.

15.3 State-Wise Data Set and Analysis

The dataset of Delhi and Maharashtra is collected from the Government official sites and machine learning models are applied to predict the futuristic analysis report for the decision-maker and authorities' agencies. This report will help the medical department as well as the health department to make a plan of action to handle the epidemic.

Data set reterived from the authentic website of Ministry of Government and family welfare [13–15, 18]. Out of the total data set (68 samples), two-third of randomly selected data was considered as training data set and the remaining one third data set was applied for testing of the model generated from the training data set. Machine learning models have been applied to the dataset retrieved from the sites to predict the infected cases of COVID-19 [19–23]. The input parameter was consisting of several days and output was the number of confirmed infected cases. For quantitative evaluation of the results, we applied two of the modeling approaches and performance

Table 15.3 COVID-19 data of five highly infected States of India [4].

State	Confirmed	Recovered	Death
Maharashtra	16,758	3,094	651
Rajasthan	3,317	1,596	92
Gujarat	6,625	1,500	395
Tamil Naidu	4,829	1,516	35
Delhi	5,532	1,542	65
Uttar Pradesh	2,998	1,130	60

evaluators obtained from them are used for testing and comparison. WEKA 3.8 was used to implement the two machine learning approaches viz Neural Network (NN) and M5P model tree (M5P). To obtain the best results from both modeling approach one need to tune several user-defined parameters. Various trials were made and performance evaluators are compared. Table 15.3 provides the optimal value of user-defined parameters which depicts the accuracy of the models used to predict the confirmed cases.

15.4 Neural Network

The Neural Network (NN) [27, 28] is extensively used to predict numerical values for different types of data sets. NN has layers for input, output, and one layer each for input and output as well as one or more hidden layers. Every single layer comprises several nodes. The weighted linkage between these layers represents the connection between these nodes. Input layer nodes which are equivalent to the number of input parameters allocate the data. Nodes do not help in processing. The final processing unit is the output layer. When NN is applied to the data, the input layer is implemented with the input value, which then travels through the interconnections between nodes, then these values are multiplied by the weights linked to them summation of which is equal to find the net output (O_b) to the unit:

$$O_b = \sum L_{iab} * x_i$$

Where L_{iab} is the weight of interconnection from Unit a to Unit b,
x_a = value of value at the input layer,
O_b = Output value.

15.4.1 M5P Model Tree

M5P model Tree [24–26] depicts a binary decision tree. For predicting continuous numerical attributes M5P model tree implement linear regression at the terminal node which is called a leaf. This process involves two stages for creating of model tree. In the first stage, a decision tree is developed by generating splitting criteria that depend upon treating the standard deviation of class value and this process causes a smaller amount of standard deviation in child node in comparison to parent node hence are purer. There are several possible splits while generating splitting criteria, and the criteria which reduces the error to the maximum is considered. The process of splitting the data likely to overgrow the tree and can cause overfitting. Here comes the second stage which removes the overfitting by a method called pruning method. This method prunes back overgrown trees by replacing the subtrees with linear regression. Parameter space is split into surfaces in this procedure of tree generation and constructing a linear regression model in each space.

The applied M5P [16, 17] model tree uses the standard deviation values to measure the error at nodes and calculates the expected reduction in error. Standard reduction formula (SDR) is given as [24]

$$SDR = sd(T) - \sum \frac{|T_I|}{|T|} sd(T_i)$$

Where
T—Set of examples that arrive at the node,
Ti—Outcome of a subset of examples of a potential set,
sd—Standard deviation.

15.5 Results and Discussion

The objective of the present study is to predict the confirmed cases obtained from coronavirus infection. The present section utilizes the potential of two machine learning algorithms viz Neural Network (NN) and M5P tree to generate the model for predicting coronavirus cases. Figures 15.7 and 15.8 show graphical representation of actual versus predicted confirmed cases of coronavirus obtained from NN and M5P [28–30]. From Figures 15.8 and 15.9 it can be observed that the predicted value is nearby of agreement line suggesting that predicted confirmed from both the modeling approach is close to actual confirmed cases. Table 15.4 gives the value of the performance evaluator parameter for training and testing data set from

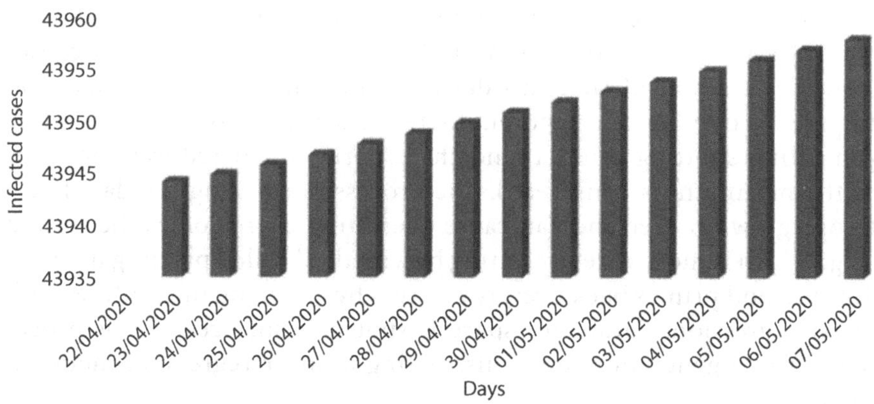

Figure 15.7 15-day analysis of COVID-19 cases in Maharashtra [14].

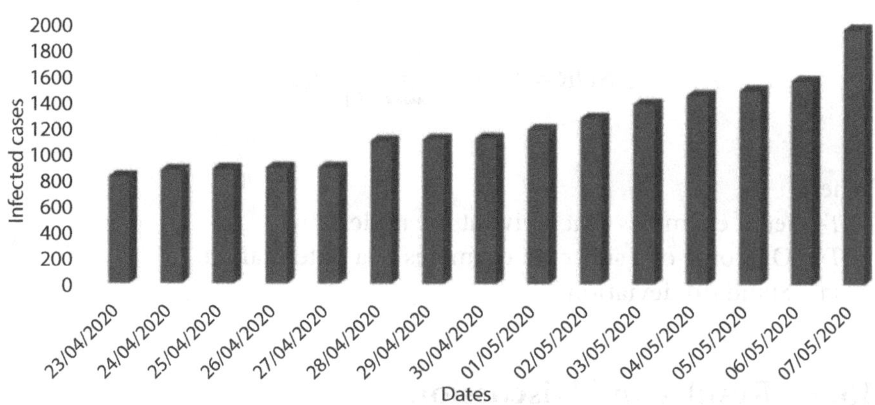

Figure 15.8 15-day analysis of COVID-19 cases in Delhi [15].

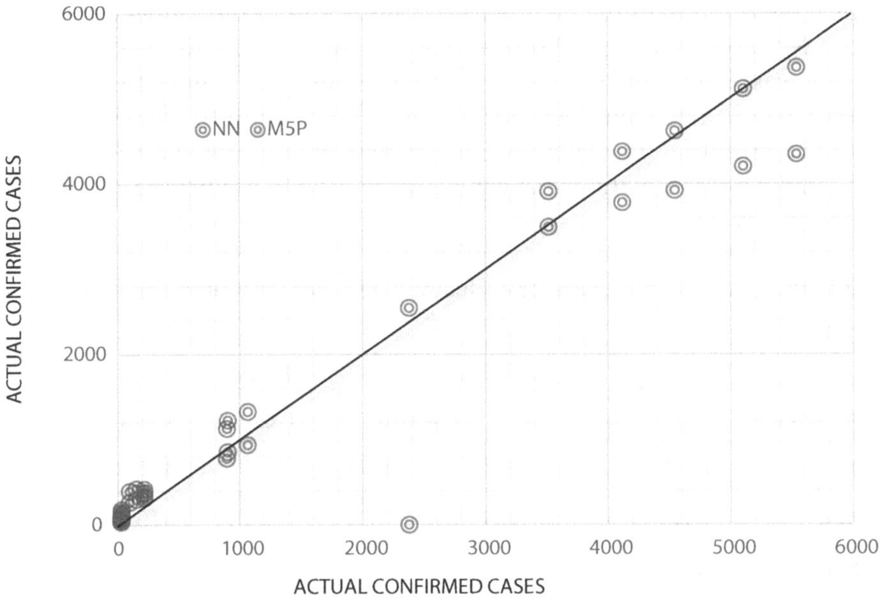

Figure 15.9 Actual vs predicted confirmed cases for Delhi.

Table 15.4 Value of performance evaluator parameter for training and testing data set.

		Training		Testing	
Approach	**State**	**CC**	**RMSE**	**CC**	**RMSE**
NN	Delhi	0.9943	157.3878	0.9976	136.4826
M5P	Delhi	0.9759	327.9551	0.9829	410.4817
NN	Maharashtra	0.9993	169.7154	0.9979	681.7666
M5P	Maharashtra	0.9802	887.0128	0.9757	1824.233

which we can obtain the quantitative comparison of the model generated from NN and M5P. It is observed from Table 15.5 that the performance of NN was slightly better than M5P for both the state. Figure 15.10 depict the rules obtained using M5P for the cases reported in the states of Delhi and Maharashtra. The benefit of using M5P is that it provides rules or can say simple linear equationsthat can be easily used to predict the confirmed cases on any day.

Table 15.5 Value of performance evaluator parameter for training and testing data.

		Training		Testing	
Approach	**State**	**CC**	**RMSE**	**CC**	**RMSE**
NN	Delhi	0.9943	157.3878	0.9976	136.4826
M5P	Delhi	0.9759	327.9551	0.9829	410.4817
NN	Maharastra	0.9993	169.7154	0.9979	681.7666
M5P	Maharastra	0.9802	887.0128	0.9757	1,824.233

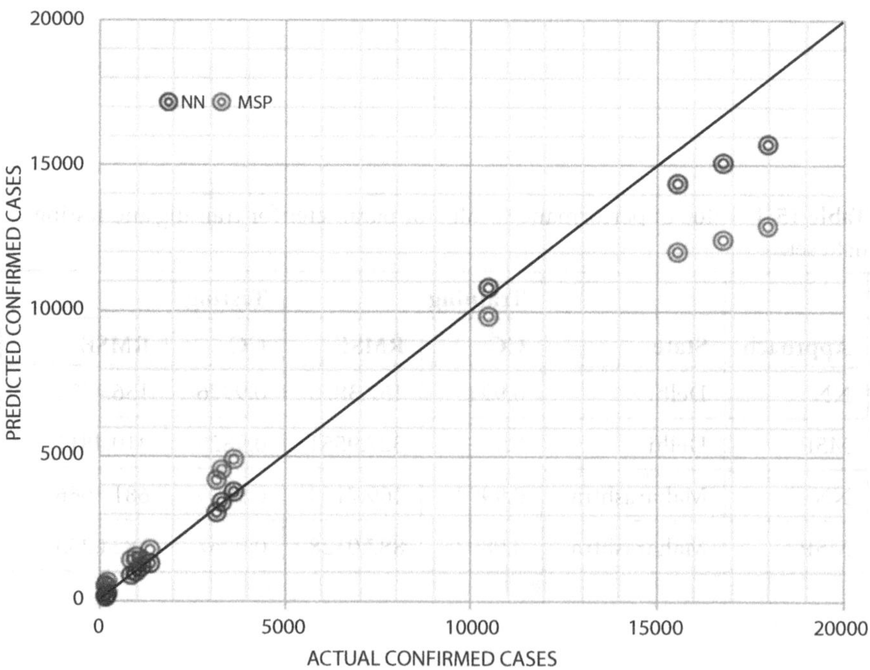

Figure 15.10 Actual vs predicted confirmed cases for Maharashtra.

Rules obtained from M5P Model Tree for Delhi

Day <= 31.5: LM1 (19/1.48%)

Day > 31.5:

| Day <= 54: LM2 (17/5.963%)

| Day > 54: LM3 (9/12.892%)

LM num: 1

Confirmed Cases = 30.2839 * Day - 513.7907

LM num: 2

Confirmed Cases = 101.0647 * Day - 2915.9157

LM num: 3

Confirmed Cases = 141.7789 * Day - 5155.0776

Number of Rules: 3

Rules obtained from M5P model tree for Maharashtra

Day < = 31.5: LM1 (20/4.634%)

Day > 31.5:

| Day < = 46.5:

| | Day < = 41: LM2 (6/1.191%)

| | Day > 41: LM3 (4/0.577%)

| Day > 46.5: LM4 (11/7.257%)

LM num: 1

Confirmed Cases = 95.5508 * Day - 1410.3348

LM num: 2

Confirmed Cases = 347.2962 * Day - 9652.7301

LM num: 3

Confirmed Cases = 358.5388 * Day - 10121.6165

LM num: 4

Confirmed Cases = 439.671 * Day - 13907.7941

15.6 Conclusion

In this paper an analytical report is prepared on different phases of lockdown in India, as well as date wise comparative analysis is also prepared to predict the infected cases of COVID-19. This analysis will further help the decision-makers to make a plan of action, as well it will provide the help to different researchers in the future to work on the problem areas identified during COVID-19 and can provide solutions for this type of pandemic situations. Two different machine learning techniques are applied to predict the infected cases on a daily basis. The comparative analysis of both techniques is also given in the results sections, whereas the Neural network model is providing optimal solutions.

15.7 Future Scope

The data analysis was done for two different states considered to be a hotspot region. The prediction model is applied to the limited data set approximately total 67 days sample is used for designing the predicted model further improvements in the prediction can be done by increasing the number of data samples as well as analysis of different states can make the comparative analysis more beneficial and accurate. Although as the accuracy of the data set is still not clearly stated by the government because testing process is time-consuming and all the symptoms of COVID-19 are very much similar to common flu or bird flu so it is difficult to predict the accuracy of infected cases until confirm test report is out.

References

1. Batselier, J. and Vanhoucke, M., Improving project forecast accuracy by integrating earned value management with exponential smoothing and reference class forecasting. *Int. J. Project Manage.*, 35, 1, 28–43, 2017.
2. BBC, *Coronavirus: Sharp increase in deaths and cases in Hubei*, 2020, https://www.bbc.co.uk/news/worldasia- china-51482994 accesses on April 5, 2020.
3. World meters, Countries in the World by population, 2020, https://www.worldometers.info/world-population/population-by-country.
4. CNN, The world's largest coronavirus lockdown is having a dramatic impact on pollution in India, 2020, https://edition.cnn.com/2020/03/31/asia/coronavirus-lockdown-impact-pollution-india-intl-hnk/index.html. Accessed on April 10, 2020.

5. Pinter, G., Felde, I., Mosavi, A., Ghamisi, P., Gloaguen, R., COVID-19 Pandemic Prediction for Hungary: A Hybrid Machine Learning Approach, Preprint Article, 2020, https://www.preprints.org/manuscript/202005.0031/v1
6. Onovo, A., Atobatele, A., Kalaiwo, A., Obanubi, C., James, E., Gado, P., Odezugo, G., Magaji, D., Ogundehin, D., Russell, M., Using Supervised Machine Learning and Empirical Bayesian Kriging to reveal Correlates and Patterns of COVID-19 Disease outbreak in sub-Saharan Africa: Exploratory Data Analysis, Preprint Article, 2020, https://doi.org/10.1101/2020.04.27.20082057.
7. Balde, M.A.M.T., Fitting the SIR model to COVID-19 pandemic data and comparative forecasting with machine learning, Preprint Article, 2020, https://doi.org/10.1101/2020.04.26.20081042.
8. Kumar, A., Khan, F.M., Gupta, R., Puppala, H., Preparedness and Mitigation by projecting the risk against COVID-19 transmission using Machine Learning Techniques, Preprint Article, 2020, https://www.medrxiv.org/content/10.1101/2020.04.26.20080655v1.
9. Wrapp, D., Wang, N., Corbett, K. S., Goldsmith, J. A., Hsieh, C.–L., Abiona, O., Graham, B. S., McLellan. J. S., Cryo-em structure of the 2019-ncov spike in the prefusion conformation. *Science*, 367, 6483, 1260–1263, 2020.
10. Tiwari, S., Kumar, S., Guleria, K., Outbreak Trends of Coronavirus Disease–2019 in India: A Prediction. *Disaster Med. Public Health Preparedness*, 14, 5, 33–38, 2020.
11. Magri, L. and Doan, N.A.K., First-principles machine learning modeling of COVID-19, Preprint Article, arXiv:2004.09478.
12. Sujatha, R., Chatterjee, J., Hassanien, A.E., A machine learning forecasting model for COVID-19 pandemic in India. *Stoch. Environ. Res. Risk Assess.*, 1–14, 30 May. 2020.
13. Jo, H., Son, H., Jung, S.Y., Hwang, H.J., Analysis of COVID-19 spreading in South Korea using the SIR model with time-dependent parameters and deep learning, Preprint Article, https://www.medrxiv.org/content/10.1101/2020.04.13.20063412v1.
14. Government of Maharashtra Public Health Department, 2020, https://arogya.maharashtra.gov.in/.
15. Health & Family Welfare Department Government of Delhi, 2020, https://stopcorona.delhi.gov.in.
16. Hyndman, R.J., Koehler, A.B., Snyder, R.D., Grose, S., A state-space framework for automatic forecasting using exponential smoothing methods. *Int. J. Forecasting*, 18, 3, 439–454, 2002.
17. Makridakis, S. and Hibon, M., The M3-Competition: Results, conclusions, and implications. *Int. J. Forecasting*, 16, 4, 451–476, 2000, https://doi.org/10.1016/S0169-2070(00)00057-1.
18. Ministry of Health and Welfare, 2020, https://www.mohfw.gov.in.

19. Petropoulos, F., Kourentzes, N., Nikolopoulos, K., Siemsen, E., Judgmental selection of forecasting models. *J. Oper. Manage.*, 60, 34–46, 2018.
20. Ahmad, A., Sachin, A., Ishan, M.X., Munroe, P.B., Artificial intelligence and machine learning to fight COVID-19. *Physiol. Genomics*, 52, 200–202, 2020.
21. Nguyen, T.T., Artificial intelligence in the battle against coronavirus (COVID-19): A survey and future research directions. Preprint Article, 2020.
22. Kumar, S., Jain, H., Arora, S., Soft Computing based two Novel Machine Learning Approaches. *Test Eng. Manage.*, 83, 14073–14079, 2020.
23. Katare, A. and Athavale, V.A., Behaviour Analysis of Different Decision Tree Algorithms. *Int. J. Comput. Technol. Electron. Eng. (IJCTEE)*, 1, 143–47, 2011.
24. Kumar, S.C., Chowdary, E.D., Venkatramaphanikumar, S., Kishore, K.V.K., M5P model tree in predicting student performance: A case study. *2016 IEEE International Conference on Recent Trends in Electronics, Information & Communication Technology (RTEICT)*, Bangalore, pp. 1103–1107, 2016.
25. Nguyen, T.T., Artificial intelligence in the battle against coronavirus (COVID-19): A survey and future research directions. Preprint Article, 2020, https://www.academia.edu/42616076.
26. Alimadadi, A., Aryal, S., Manandhar, I., Munroe, P.B., Joe, B., Cheng, X., Artificial intelligence and machine learning to fight COVID-19. *Physiol. Genomics*, 52, 4, 200–202, 2020 Apr 1.
27. Anthony, G., COVID-19 Open Research Dataset Challenge (CORD-19), distributed by Allen institute for AI, https://www.kaggle.com/allen-institute-for-ai/CORD-19-research challenge?select=cord_19_embeddings
28. Xie, X., Li, Y., Chwang, A.T., Ho, P.L., Seto, W.H., How far droplets can move in indoor environments–revisiting the wells evaporation falling curve. *Indoor Air*, 17, 3, 211–225, 2007.
29. Wanga, G., Ledwochb, A., Hasania, R.M., Grosua, R., Brintrup, A., A generative neural network model for the quality prediction of work in progress products. *Appl. Soft Comput.*, 85, 1–19, 105683, December 2019.
30. Petruseva, S., Neural Network Prediction Model for Construction Project Duration. *Int. J. Eng. Res. Technol.*, 1, 02, 2012.

Index

Printed in the USA/Agawam, MA
September 16, 2026

910661.013